The Language of Food in Japanese

Converging Evidence in Language and Communication Research (CELCR)

ISSN 1566-7774

Over the past decades, linguists have taken a broader view of language and are borrowing methods and findings from other disciplines such as cognition and computer sciences, neurology, biology, sociology, psychology, and anthropology. This development has enriched our knowledge of language and communication, but at the same time it has made it difficult for researchers in a particular field of language studies to be aware of how their findings might relate to those in other (sub-)disciplines.

CELCR seeks to address this problem by taking a cross-disciplinary approach to the study of language and communication. The books in the series focus on a specific linguistic topic and offer studies pertaining to this topic from different disciplinary angles, thus taking converging evidence in language and communication research as its basic methodology.

For an overview of all books published in this series, please see
benjamins.com/catalog/celcr

Volume 25

The Language of Food in Japanese. Cognitive perspectives and beyond
Edited by Kiyoko Toratani

The Language of Food in Japanese

Cognitive perspectives and beyond

Edited by

Kiyoko Toratani

York University

John Benjamins Publishing Company

Amsterdam / Philadelphia

The paper used in this publication meets the minimum requirements of the American National Standard for Information Sciences – Permanence of Paper for Printed Library Materials, ANSI Z39.48-1984.

DOI 10.1075/celcr.25

Cataloging-in-Publication Data available from Library of Congress: LCCN 2021052783

ISBN 978 90 272 1082 1 (HB)
ISBN 978 90 272 5799 4 (E-BOOK)

John Benjamins Publishing Company · https://benjamins.com

Table of contents

Abbreviations

ACC	accusative
ADV	adverb(ial)
CAUS	causative
CL	classifier
COMP	complementizer
COND	conditional
CONJ	conjunct
COP	copula
DAT	dative
FP	Final particle
GEN	genitive
HON	honorific
HUMB	humble
INST	Instrumental
LOC	locative
NEG	negation, negative
NMLZ	nominalizer/nominalization
NOM	nominative
OBJ	object
PASS	passive
POL	polite
POT	potential
PROG	progressive
PST	past
Q	question particle/marker
QUOT	quotative
RES	resultative
TOP	topic

Acknowledgements

I would like to express my gratitude to a number of people for their assistance in this book project. First and foremost, I would like to acknowledge three people for their intellectual inspiration and moral support. Dr. Natsuko Tsujimura introduced me to the topic of the language of food in 2015 and encouraged me to complete this project on a number of occasions with productive words. Italian Linguist Dr. Roberta Iannacito-Provenzano and late Historian Dr. Gabriele Scardellato, colleagues at the Department of Languages, Literatures, and Linguistics, encouraged me to participate in a stimulating conference they hosted at York University in 2017, "Italian Foodways Worldwide: A Conference on the Dispersal of Italian Cuisine(s)," and they inspired me to host a conference for linguistics in Japanese the following May.

This book features a collection of seven papers presented at the "Conference on the Language of Japanese Food," held May 4–5, 2018, at York University, Canada, along with four additional contributions solicited to strengthen the book's cognitive theme. The conference was partially funded by York University, Faculty of Liberal Arts & Professional Studies Research (Dean's Office), Department of Languages, Literatures, and Linguistics, York Centre for Asian Research, and Japan Foundation. I am extremely grateful for their support. My appreciation is also extended to the conference participants, especially the three keynote speakers, Dr. Masako Hiraga, Dr. Polly Szatrowski, and Dr. Natsuko Tsujimura, and conference co-organizer Dr. Mitsuaki Shimojo for their engaging discussions and insightful questions and comments, from which some of the contributors greatly benefited.

The book could not have been realized in its current format without the external and internal anonymous reviewers whose valuable insights and productive comments substantially improved the quality of the chapters. I also deeply appreciate the timely cooperation of all contributors to my numerous editorial requests and queries. I would like to thank Dr. Kimi Akita, Dr. Yoshihiko Ikegami and Dr. Kazuko Shinohara for their valuable guidance on logistics to compile the volume. I am also grateful to Dr. Elizabeth Thompson for her editorial assistance at different stages.

The global pandemic has posed an enormous challenge to all of us, but everyone involved in the project acted promptly and responsively to move things forward. Once again, I would like to extend my gratitude to the authors of the volume and the reviewers for their commitment to prioritize this project.

Finally, I would like to express my deepest gratitude to Ms. Esther Roth from John Benjamins for her timely and helpful support and to Dr. Ninke Stukker and Dr. Kris Heylen, the series editors of Converging Evidence in Language and Communication Research, for their productive and insightful comments on the project at different stages, and to Dr. Stukker for her tactful guidance when I was finalizing the manuscript.

Kiyoko Toratani
December, 2020

Introduction to the volume

Kiyoko Toratani
York University

1. Background

The term *food* is a simple word we encounter on a daily basis, but at the same time, it is a loaded word, tied to myriad activities and concepts fundamental to culture and society. Despite the importance of food, its linguistic study remained out of the spotlight for a long time. Around 2000, this started to change, and the language of food emerged as a topic worthy of linguistic consideration. The past decade has observed a dramatic upsurge in publications, ranging from edited volumes (Balirano & Guzzo, 2019; Goded Rambaud & Poves Luelmo, 2010; Hosking, 2010; Gerhardt, Frobenius, & Ley, 2013b; Szatrowski, 2014; Temmerman & Dubois, 2017), to single- and co-authored books (Bagli, 2020; Caballero, Suárez-Toste & Paradis, 2019; Diederich, 2015; Jurafsky, 2014; Lehrer, 2009; Matwick & Matwick, 2019; Tominc, 2017), and a plethora of independent articles (Caballero, 2019; Lehrer & Lehrer, 2016; Levin, Glass & Jurafsky, 2019; Nakagawa, 2012; Pérez-Hernández, 2019; Schultz, 2016; Smith, Barratt & Zlatev, 2014; Wertz, 2013; Wiegand & Klakow, 2015, to name just a few). Building on a series of pioneering studies (Lehrer, 1978; Levi-Strauss, 1966; McCawley, 1984; Norrick, 1983; Zwicky & Zwicky, 1980, among others), this more recent work sheds light on how language interacts with food.

Two tendencies are noticeable in the research on the language of food to date, at least in the publications in English. One is that more work deals with Indo-European languages, notably English, characterizing food from the West. For instance, studies on wine vocabularies and wine discourse primarily deal with English (e.g., Caballero, 2007; Croijmans, Hendrickx, Lefever, Majid, & Van Den Bosch, 2020; Gluck, 2003; Hirokawa, Flanagan, Suzuki, & Yin, 2014; Lehrer, 1975, 2009; Paradis, 2009; Paradis & Eeg-Olofsson, 2013) and Spanish (e.g., Breit, 2014; Caballero, 2017; Caballero, Suárez-Toste, & Paradis, 2019; López-Arroyo & Roberts, 2014, 2016), while work on recipes seems to cover mostly English expressions (e.g., Carroll, 1999; Cotter, 1997; Culy, 1996; Diemer, 2013; Fisher, 1983, Chapter 1; Lakoff, 2006; Norrick, 1983, 2011; Schultze, 2008; Westney, 2007; Wharton, 2010). The other is that discourse analysis (in the sense of an analysis beyond the sentence unit) seems

https://doi.org/10.1075/celcr.25.int

to have increased more rapidly than other analytical approaches (e.g., Achiba, 2012; Ariyasriwatana & Quiroga, 2016; Choe, 2019; Cook, Reed & Twiner, 2009; Diemer, Brunner, & Schmidt, 2014; Gerhardt, Frobenius & Ley, 2013a; Hoffman & Kytö, 2017; Hsiao, 2019; Matwick & Matwick, 2019, 2020; Tominc, 2014; Szatrowski, 2014). In the past, study areas of the language of food were dispersed over a range of linguistic subfields, without one particular area or approach dominating. These include lexicography (e.g., Cassidy, 1995; Atkins, Kegl, & Levin, 1988), dialectology (e.g., Zwicky & Zwicky, 1980), sociolinguistics (e.g., Culy, 1996), gender studies (e.g., Hines, 1999), psycholinguistics (e.g., Staats & Hammond, 1972), syntax (e.g., Massam & Roberge, 1989), and lexical semantics (e.g., Backhouse, 1994; Lehrer, 1969, 1972). At times, the work has appeared in cross-disciplinary or other disciplinary fields, such as homemaking (Cotter, 1997), psychology (Myers, 1904), and anthropology (Ochs, Pontecorvo, & Fasulo, 1996).

Albeit less prominent, two newer trends are evident as well. The first is that work on non-Indo-European languages, especially East Asian languages, is on the rise. For instance, Rhee and Koo (2017) probe the lexicalization system of Korean taste terms; Choe (2019) analyzes computer-mediated food discourse in Korean, drawing on insights from interactional sociolinguistics and conversation analysis; Hsiao (2019) offers a discourse analysis of writer-reader interactions observed in Mandarin Chinese food blogs featuring recipes; Yao and Su (2019) provide an exploratory study of Chinese food terms, suggesting implications for future research directions; and Tsujimura (2018) offers a lexical semantic account of the patterns of change in recipe names in Japanese cookbooks over the past 87 years. The second observation is that some researchers have begun to adopt Cognitive Linguistics to gain deeper insights into the characteristics of the language of food (Croft, 2009; Caballero, Suárez-Toste, & Paradis, 2019; Diederich, 2015; Hiraga, 2009; Pérez-Hernández, 2013, 2019; Smith, Barratt, & Zlatev, 2014; Yamaguchi, 2009). Although pioneering work in Cognitive Linguistics began to appear in the late 1970s, the approach has only recently gained critical prominence in research of the language of food.

This volume joins the latter thrust of the research, but with the following innovative intersections. First, it examines the use of the Japanese language as a native language spoken in Japan or as the donor language in cases of borrowing. Second, it focuses on a non-discursive unit (sound, word, phrase, clause, sentence). Third, it adopts Cognitive Linguistics as a main framework.

With its ensemble of fresh intersections, the book sheds new light on research on the language of food in Japanese. First, concentration on Japanese makes it possible to offer a consolidated view of the characteristic features of the language of food in Japanese. Second, by focusing on a non-discursive unit, the volume is able to cover research topics distinct from those commonly taken up by the steadily increasing studies of discourse analysis, especially in Japanese (Kroo & Matsumoto, 2018; Kuroshima, 2010; Mayes, 1999; Szatrowski, 2014; Sasamoto, 2019, Chapter 5; Shimojo, 2019; Strauss, Chang, & Matsumoto, 2018, among others). Third, the topics discussed in the traditional Japanese literature on the language of food, such as taste terms (cf. Tsujimura, this volume), tend to be descriptive, and the adoption of a cognitive perspective enables us to look at things in a new light. Sakaguchi (this volume) is a good illustration of this point, as he is able to efficiently account for the polysemous senses of taste terms, such as *amai* 'sweet', by using the system developed in FrameNet. Fourth, the volume adds insights gleaned from the analysis of Japanese data to the topic of Cognitive Linguistics, hitherto discussed only in the context of Indo-European languages. Yoshinari's chapter is an application and re-evaluation of Caballero's (2007) work on English manner-of-motion verbs in wine tasting notes. It applies Talmy's (1985, 2000) two-way typology of spatial motion events to non-spatial motion events realized in wine tasting descriptions. Fifth, for topics discussed in Cognitive Linguistics but not specifically dealing with the language of food, the volume offers a model from Japanese on which researchers of other languages can draw. Abe's chapter is illustrative. The idea of force dynamics (Talmy, 1988) is often employed to elaborate on a grammatical notion, such as causation and modality (e.g., Sweetser, 1990), but the examples are usually not taken from a particular genre. Focusing on taste descriptions, Abe shows force dynamics can be used to analyze a diverse range of force interactions among event participants on the food tasting scene (e.g., Food as a seducer, such as chocolate, lures Taster into a trap of eating), potentially realizable in any language. Last but by no means least, the volume should inspire comparative studies of Japanese and other languages with similar characteristics. An example of this is the ideophone, alternatively known as a mimetic or expressive, defined as "a member of an open lexical class of marked words that depict sensory imagery" (Dingemanse, 2019, p. 16). Many languages are richly endowed with ideophones (Voeltz & Kilian-Hatz, 2001). Japanese alone has several hundred core lexical items (cf. Akita & Pardeshi, 2019). Ideophones are especially interesting for their ability to depict organoleptic sensations (Tsujimura, this volume), for instance, a sizzling sound (*jūjū*), the smooth sensation of food moving into the gullet (*tsururi*), the fluffy sensation of food felt on the tongue (*fuwafuwa*), or the manner of a freshly baked food's smell floating into the nostrils (*pūn*). The volume includes two studies that foreground the use of ideophones: the chapter by Uno, Kobayashi, Shinohara, and Odake is concerned with the texture of rice crackers, and the chapter by Akita and Murasugi examines the organizational structure of innovative compounds, including a combination of two ideophones (e.g., *fuwa-toro* 'fluffy and creamy'). These initial explorations can be extended to include ideophones in other languages, in food descriptions and beyond. Needless to say, the work presented here is in line with the current robust thinking on ideophones, positioning them as an integral part of a linguistic system and emancipated from their century-old (but still recurring) marginalization by Ferdinand de Saussure (1916/2011, p. 69).

2. Goal

The volume offers a deeper understanding of the characteristics of the language of food in Japanese by exploring the motivations underlying the instantiation of a particular form given a meaning, within the framework of Cognitive Linguistics. Its foundational ideas, outlined hereinafter, can help illuminate different aspects of the language of food.

2.1 The embodied cognition thesis

One of the most pertinent contributions of Cognitive Linguistics to the study of the language of food in Japanese is the idea of embodied cognition (Johnson, 1987; Lakoff, 1987; Talmy, 1983, 1988), or the "embodied cognition thesis" (Evans & Green, 2006, Chapter 2). In essence, the embodied cognition thesis suggests meaning is embodied, and the study of language cannot be divorced from human cognition, perceptions, and embodiment,[1] because "as animals we have bodies connected to the natural world, such that our consciousness and rationality are tied to our bodily orientations and interactions in and with our environment" (Johnson, 1987, p. xxxviii). In contrast, an objectivist's view of language posits meaning as "an abstract relation between symbolic representations (either words or mental representations) and objective (i.e., mind independent) reality" (Johnson, 1987, p. xxii). The relevance of the language of food to the embodied cognition thesis is immediately apparent, as the most common food-related activity is eating, a bodily interaction in and with the environment. Above all, eating is intricately tied to multimodal perception. Consider, for example, language on food ingestion compared to language on a non-food topic, such as clothing. It is evident that the former is more vitally tied to multimodal-based perceptual experiences than the latter, as language on clothing presumably relies more on vision- and tactility- centered experiences.

To elaborate, language on food ingestion deals with how we take food from the environment into the digestive system, embracing various perceptive activities, multimodally detected – when a food appears right before our eyes, we perceive its

1. For different senses of embodiment, see Rohrer (2010).

color (visual), while sniffing it (olfactory);[2] once the food is inside the mouth, we taste it (gustatory); we feel the texture while it is on the tongue, as we bite into it, or as the food goes down our throat (tactile); during the entire process, our audition remains active (auditory) to detect any sounds emitted.

These sensory experiences can be the target of verbalization, although how precisely or granularly they can be expressed must be studied for each language (e.g., O'Meara & Majid, 2016; Winter, 2019).[3] Notably, some expressions are directly related to how our bodily features obtain. Take taste terms, as an example. Our specific tasting experiences are determined by the physical characteristics of our oral apparatus, such as having a human-specific number of taste buds. The corollary of this is the development of specific terms for a taste concept within a given linguistic community. English has four basic terms, *sweet, sour, salty*, and *bitter* (cf. McBurney & Gent, 1979), while Japanese has four equivalents, *amami* 'sweetness', *sanmi* 'sourness', *kanmi* 'saltiness', and *nigami* 'bitterness', and a fifth term, *umami*, "[t]he characteristic taste of monosodium glutamate and 5'-ribonucleotides" (Yamaguchi, 1979, p. 33; cf. O'Mahony & Ishii, 1986, p. 162), derived from particular food stuff (e.g., the broth made from *kombu* (seaweed)), deeply rooted in the Japanese food culture.[4]

Importantly, some sensory expressions are experientially grounded. Shimoda, Sasaki, Doi, Kameda, and Osajima (1989), who examined how subjects described an odor of food, found 44 odor-descriptive terms can be grouped into two basic categories: (i) those appealing to an abstract concept, such as *hōkōsei* 'aromaticity', and (ii) those comparing a smell with a concrete item in the environment, as in *ki no nioi* 'smell of a tree', *ninniku-yoo* 'garlic-like', or *kinzoku-shū* 'smell of metal'. As for the latter group, the subjects, or the cognizers, presumably recalled their past experiences of interacting with the substance in their environment, such as 'garlic' or 'tree', and searched for the smell they were asked to identify during the experiment; without these past experiences, an expression like *ki no nioi* 'smell of a tree'

2. As explained in Section 5 of the present introduction, this sense corresponds to orthonasal olfaction (Barwich, 2020).

3. There is a growing interest in investigating to what extent the perceptual information gathered by a specific modality is linguistically codable (e.g., Jędrzejowski & Staniewski, 2021; Winter, 2019). For instance, the lexicon of olfaction has traditionally been considered more limited than other modalities such as vision but recent studies show some languages have a richer olfactory vocabulary than traditionally thought (see, e.g., Burenhult & Majid, 2011; Majid & Burenhult, 2014; Wnuk & Majid, 2014). Another example is Auvray and Spence (2008, p. 1026), who argue that flavor can be considered "a perceptual modality that is unified by the act of eating."

4. See Tsujimura, this volume, for other ways to express taste.

would not have surfaced.[5] A glance at 445 texture terms compiled in Hayakawa et al. (2005) raises a similar point. To focus on hardness, even though the list contains an adjective *katai* 'hard', it is common to use an expression that refers to a concrete item (including its shape), as in *sunap-poi* 'sand-like', *kyūjō* 'lump-like', and *gotsugotsu* 'rough' – the last of which does not mention a specific item but is an ideophone expressing a rough sensation obtained when we touch an object like a rock. These terms must have entered the list of texture terms because of the participants' previous experiences in the environment.[6]

Needless to say, sensory expressions are not realized just as a single word. Allied with our broader perceptual or cognitive abilities, tasting or flavoring experiences can be, for instance, conceptualized as motion events, arriving at an expression such as *Amami ga kuchi ippai ni hirogaru* 'Sweetness spreads throughout my mouth' (Yoshinari, this volume). It is notable that the use of *hirogar-* 'spread' is drawn from our spatial cognition whereby an entity is cognized as gradually emanating in front of us, covering a wide area; without embodied cognition, this kind of expression would not have come to be used.

The chapters in Sections II–V deal with language use based on our bodily or perceptual interactions in or with the environment, including moving, acting on an object as in manipulating Japanese food-related items, eating, and flavoring, which can further serve as a basis for constructing a more abstract meaning, for instance, by way of conceptual metaphor; these various analyses all lend themselves to Cognitive Linguistics.

2.2 Non-single-doctrine based

As Geeraerts (2008) summarizes, Cognitive Linguistics is "a conglomerate of more or less extensive, more or less active centers of linguistic research that are closely knit together by a shared perspective," with "no single, uniform theoretical doctrine according to which these research topics belong together" (p. 2). As it is more flexible than a theory with a rigid doctrine that operates only within a particular module such as syntax, Cognitive Linguistics is better able to develop cordial relations with

5. Most terms in the first category are adjectival and often come from other modalities. For instance, *odayaka na* 'calm' comes from vison, *kawaita* 'dried' primarily from tactility, and *suppai* 'sour' from gustation.

6. These examples suggest hardness is dominantly perceived as a tactile interaction with physical objects.

other scholarly fields (Ruiz de Mendoza & Peña Cervel, 2005, p. 11).[7] The language of food presents intricate connections with human perceptions (Section 2.1), thus offering itself to rich interdisciplinary research with fields, such as cognitive psychology, cognitive neuroscience, sensory science, food science, and business dealing with the commodification of food products and their marketing. This line of research has already been undertaken by scholars such as Diederich (2015), Winter (2019), Larsson and Swahn (2011), and Majid and her colleagues (e.g., Croijmans & Majid, 2016; Croijmans, et al., 2020; O'Meara, Kung, & Majid, 2019; Majid & Burenhult, 2014), to name a few. This volume adds to the research in a chapter using Japanese data (Uno et al.'s chapter).

2.3 Commitment to usage

Studies in Cognitive Linguistics commonly adopt a usage-based perspective (Bybee & Hopper, 2001; Croft & Cruse, 2004; Kemmer & Barlow, 2000; Langacker, 1990; Tomasello, 2000, among others). Despite differences in research focus across studies, the usage-based model prioritizes language use, embracing the idea that our knowledge of language is constructed from our observation of how we use language in a given context and milieu, and this, in turn, is applied to construct or interpret usage.

How is a framework that places importance on usage suited to an analysis of the language of food? For one thing, the language of food in Japanese is constantly changing, mirroring the appearance of new food products, recipes, food reviews, and so forth. To stay on top of these changes, we need a framework that values usage. For another, the language of food often appears in genre-specific media, with some usage being particular to the medium (Tsujimura, this volume). For instance, English recipes are known to include particular structures, such as the imperative with *take*, as in "*Take a pound of shrimps*" (Fisher, 1983, p. 21), or recommendations in English wine tasting notes containing the middle construction: "*This beauty should drink well for 10–12 years*" (Paradis, 2009, p. 53). These characteristics would not have come to light if we had not observed the actual use of language in a specific medium. Cognitive Linguistics seriously attends to this type of data, making it an appropriate framework to analyze the language of food.

All chapters of this volume use naturally occurring data, either directly or indirectly. Two adopt an experiential method, using pseudo snack names (Kumagai

7. Although cognitive linguists may use such terms as phonology and morphology (as we do here), it is for a practical reason, simply referring to the traditionally recognized content areas of linguistics.

et al.) and imagined texture descriptions (Uno et al.). Although the test materials used for their various experiments are constructed, both sets of authors create them in consultation with the currently available names and texture terms; moreover, if realized, they could appear on packages or in advertisements. Thus, the authors indirectly use naturally occurring data. All other chapters directly draw on naturally occurring instances appearing in different media or corpora, including: the Balanced Corpus of Contemporary Written Japanese (Nonaka; Sakaguchi), menus (Toratani), newspapers and/or blogs (Akita & Murasugi; Yamaguchi), online food columns (Abe), *sake* books and magazines (Fukushima), and wine magazines (Yoshinari).

2.4 Language use in context

Related closely to the point addressed in Section 2.3, an examination of the language of food cannot be detached from the linguistic context or socio-cultural milieu, and this makes Cognitive Linguistics well-suited for critical use.

A simple example is a polysemous word, whose meaning can be properly understood only when it is situated in a context. Take *madeleine* as an example, a loanword from French in English. According to the Oxford English Dictionary (OED), its primary meaning is a small cake, but it has another sense, "something that strongly evokes memories or nostalgia" à la Marcel Proust ("Madeleine," n.d.).[8] So if someone says *It is my madeleine*, in one context, *madeleine* may refer to a small cake, but in another, it can be a memory-evoking food, and this could be any food item, as in the following usage: "'I think cucumber salad is my madeleine,' I remarked to my husband last week. […] It brings me back to my childhood, sitting at a dining room table with my family, listening to stories and laughing together" (Paar, 2020).

Japanese also borrowed this term from French, pronounced as *madorēnu* 'madeleine', but it only has the cake sense. Accordingly, the translation equivalent of the above is nonsensical (*Kyūri sarada wa watashi no madorēnu da to omou.* 'I think cucumber salad is my madeleine.'), albeit grammatical. This instance shows that the meaning of a word is context-dependent in the sense of (i) where the word appears in the textual context (sense1 vs. sense2) and (ii) who interprets it (English vs. Japanese) within a socio-cultural milieu.

The book's chapters consider the meaning of a form in a situated context, with some addressing the issue more directly than others. For instance, Yamaguchi's chapter considers the semantic and formal changes in Japanese eating verbs (*taberu*

8. According to the OED, the second sense comes from a scene from Marcel Proust's 1922 writing (Proust & Carter, 2013).

'eat', *kuu* 'eat') with reference to a historical context, exploring how their changes interrelate with the social structure of Japan and the Japanese psyche. Uno et al. report the result of an experimental study on the hardness of Japanese rice crackers, comparing two contexts: "real" and "imagined." Sakaguchi adopts frame semantics (Fillmore, 1982) as a way to define the context and account for semantic extensions of taste terms, such as *amai* 'sweet' and *shibui* 'astringent'.

2.5 An encyclopaedic view of word meaning

A standpoint on our knowledge of word meanings are often divided into two categories: definitional (or dictionary) and encyclopaedic. The definitional view of word meaning corresponds to our knowledge of "the *essential* properties of the entities and categories that the words designate" (Lakoff, 1987, p. 172), just like what we see in a physical dictionary, with an entry containing a few self-contained definitions. This standpoint is often aligned with an objectivist's view of word meanings, which takes these definitions as deterministic. In contrast, the encyclopaedic view corresponds to our knowledge of "the *contingent* properties of the entities and properties that the words designate" (Lakoff, 1987, p. 172). It is more holistic than the former, covering various facets of our knowledge that center on the word, and more dynamic in that the information about the word becomes updated as we gain more experience about the properties and concepts the word expresses. Studies in Cognitive Linguistics consider this encyclopaedic aspect critical to fully account for word meaning (Fillmore, 1982; Haiman, 1980; Lakoff, 1987; Langacker, 1987; Taylor, 2003, among others).

The importance of the encyclopaedic view of word meaning for an analysis of the language of food is highlighted in the chapters examining word meaning. To cite one example, Fukushima's chapter directly addresses the dynamic aspect of word meaning, demonstrating how the meanings of words that describe the taste of *sake* differ from those appearing in a dictionary. For example, the dictionary meaning of *tōmei* can be 'clear' or 'transparent', but in the context of defining the taste of *sake, tōmei* can be used to express "the lightness of *sake*'s body, clean sweetness, or a quick-fading of the aftertaste." Fukushima explains how the meanings of *sake* taste terms come to be realized by examining the co-occurrence patterns with other words in the domain of *sake* tasting. It is unclear how such domain-specific meanings of the taste term can be captured in a dictionary view, as pre-defined meanings are stored in the lexicon.

To sum up, the volume makes a concerted effort to analyze the language of food in Japanese, using Cognitive Linguistics as a main framework. In addition to the above-mentioned views, some chapters adopt more specific notions or theories, including: active zone (Langacker, 1987), categorization and prototype (Lakoff, 1987; Tayler, 1989), conceptual blending (Fauconnier & Turner, 1998), conceptual metaphor and metonymy (Lakoff & Johnson, 1980), Construction Morphology (Booij, 2010), force dynamics (Talmy, 1988), frame semantics (Fillmore, 1982), frame-shifting (Coulson, 2001), iconicity (Haiman, 1983), the idealized cognitive model (Lakoff, 1987), and motion events (Talmy, 1985, 2000).

3. Organization of the volume

The book consists of five sections. The first section, "Overview," contains a special contribution by Natsuko Tsujimura, "The language of food in Japanese through a linguistic lens." The chapter reviews past research on the language of food, with a focus on the Japanese language, including major work that non-Japanese communities will have difficulty accessing. As such, the chapter plays a valuable role by introducing representative work on the language of food, helping readers, especially those new to the topic, to gain foundational knowledge about general research trends. The chapter explains that the language of food richly interacts with cognition, culture, and society, reflected in language variations specific to a social group or in various linguistic practices, including the adaptation of loanwords and coinage of new dish names – some of which are fascinatingly witty and creative. Tsujimura's chapter also serves as a helpful prelude to Sections II–V, as it contains topics treated later in the volume, including sound-symbolism, neologisms, and taste descriptions in Japanese. The chapter sets up the volume as exemplary of the interactions between linguistics and the language of food in Japanese, hinting at the development of deeper insights into how we use language and possibilities for new research.

Section II, "Mimetics and sound-symbolism in food names and food descriptions," contains three chapters. The first two are experimental studies. In Chapter 2, "Analysis of the use of Japanese mimetics in the eating and imagined eating of rice crackers," Ryoko Uno, Fumiyuki Kobayashi, Kazuko Shinohara, and Sachiko Odake, two cognitive linguists and two food engineering specialists, collaborate to investigate how the use of mimetics differs when the participants actually eat (situation 1) or just imagine eating (situation 2) rice crackers of different degrees of hardness, where hardness is measured by the "breaking load." They report different usage of mimetics in the two situations and use iconicity to explain their finding.

In Chapter 3, "The sound-symbolic effects of consonants on food texture: An experimental study of snack names in Japanese," Gakuji Kumagai, Ryoko Uno, and Kazuko Shinohara investigate to what extent sound-symbolic associations obtain for obstruents and images of hardness of food. They find that both voicing and place of articulation affect the image of the hardness of snacks. They argue articulatory or acoustic accounts of sound symbolism can be offered within the scope of Cognitive Linguistics, given its embodied cognition thesis.

The third chapter in the section (Chapter 4) is by Kimi Akita and Keiko Murasugi, "Innovative binomial adjectives in Japanese food descriptions and beyond." Building on ideas from phonology, morphology, semantics, anthropological linguistics, and applying Cognitive Linguistics, the authors probe the patterns of combinations of two words to create innovative binomial adjectives [IBAs], such as *fuwa-toro* 'fluffy and creamy' and *saku-uma* 'crunchy and yummy', that enable speakers to convey delicate shades of meaning of taste and texture, among others. They identify six types of semantic relations (synonymy, antonymy, sequence, causation, degree, argument-predicate) and argue they are subject to four constraints (obstruency, right-headedness, iconicity on linearity, and a structural character). They show the productivity and creativity of each type of IBA are captured by the hierarchical view of the lexicon offered by Construction Morphology (Booij, 2010), and they detail which part of the morphological network is affected by the four constraints.

Section III, "Change in the language of food," comprises two chapters. Chapter 5, a study by Toshiko Yamaguchi, "Verbs of eating: From active zones, cultures, metonymy, and metaphor to withdrawal," represents a relatively new attempt to bring together historical linguistics and Cognitive Linguistics. It investigates semantic changes in two Japanese verbs of eating, *kuu* and *taberu*, citing evidence from as early as the Old Japanese period (710–800). The chapter corroborates a point made by Geeraerts (2008, p. 5), namely that "languages may embody the historical and cultural experience of groups of speakers," by cogently analyzing how the literal and figurative senses of the two verbs relate to each other based on cognitive notions, including "active zone" (e.g., Langacker, 1987), metaphor, and metonymy (cf. Allan, 2010).

Chapter 6 is by Kiyoko Toratani, "Naturalization of the Japanese loanword *sushi* in English: A cognitive account." In her chapter, Toratani brings the discussion back to the present-day language of food but moves it to usage outside Japan, applying a cognitive perspective to loanword research. This in-depth study of the term *sushi* considers how both meaning and usage change when the word is borrowed into the target language, English. It offers a counter-argument to Doi's (2014) model, which views naturalization as a rigidly staged and sequenced process, by drawing on insights from Construction Morphology (Booij, 2010). The chapter argues that the concepts of entrenchment and the encyclopaedic view of word meaning shed useful light on the extent to which the loanword is assimilated into English.

Section IV, "Taste terms," contains two chapters. In Chapter 7, "Clear is sweet: Defining aesthetic *sake* taste terms with a usage-based approach," Hiroki

Fukushima offers a usage-based analysis of the meanings of *sake* taste terms, focusing on adjectival elements such as *tōmei* 'clear'. He compiles his own *sake* tasting comment corpus, including data elicited by an intriguingly novel method that brings in insights from phenomenology and a theory of aesthetics. Then, he examines the concordanced output for token and type frequency of the words that co-occur with the target taste term. For instance, a target term like *futoi* '(lit.) fat' is shown to frequently co-occur with words expressing taste (*sanmi* 'acidity'), parts of the mouth (*kōchū* 'in the mouth'), organoleptic feel (*nobiyaka* 'smooth'), movement (*nagare* 'flow'), and structure (*rinkaku* 'frame'). Although this may initially seem a collage of un-consorted words, the list tells us a "story of the taste," giving a glimpse into how different tasters privately experience *sake*. Fukushima argues meanings of *sake* taste terms are complex, dynamic, and experientially constructed, a position in harmony with the encyclopaedic view of word meaning embraced by Cognitive Linguistics.

In Chapter 8, "A frame-semantic approach to Japanese taste terms," Kei Sakaguchi integrates the idea of frames into Conceptual Metaphor Theory (Lakoff & Johnson, 1980), following Sullivan (2013), to explore the extended senses of taste terms. He examines combinations such as *nigai keiken* 'bitter experience', arguing that both the literal and the extended senses of the taste terms are associated with (un)desirability. Sakaguchi considers why a particular combination is rendered (in) felicitous, detailing the definitions of a given frame, using FrameNet annotations.

The last section, Section V, "Motion and force in the language of food," is an assemblage of three chapters. In Chapter 9, "Verbs of seasoning in Japanese, with special reference to the locative alternation in English," Daisuke Nonaka discusses how movements of seasonings (e.g., salt) onto the main ingredient (e.g., meat) are realized in Japanese, reporting the results of a corpus study inspecting characteristics of verbs of seasoning in Japanese. According to Nonaka, some verbs of seasoning in English participate in the locative alternation (e.g., *Sprinkle salt over the meat.* vs. *Sprinkle the meat with salt*), whereas corresponding verbs of seasoning in Japanese hardly ever do so (e.g., *shio o furikakeru* 'sprinkle salt' vs. *shio de ajitsuke suru* 'season (something) with salt'). This difference between English and Japanese is explained by the comparative weakness of the result-orientation of Japanese verbs (cf. Ikegami, 1985).

Chapter 10 by Yuko Yoshinari, "Motion expressions in Japanese wine-tasting descriptions," is a pioneering attempt to examine how Japanese wine tasting notes realize expressions of motion events, applying Talmy's (1985, 2000) two-way typology – a typology which has been hotly debated because of its analysis of literal spatial descriptions of motion events: specifically, how verb-framed languages (e.g., Japanese) differ from satellite-framed languages (e.g., English) in mapping motion event concepts onto linguistic forms. Yoshinari's investigation confirms that Japanese wine tasting notes show the verb-framed language patterns and are analogous to the literal spatial expressions.

Sayaka Abe's contribution in Chapter 11, "Applying force dynamics to analyze taste descriptions in Japanese online columns," closes Section V and the book. It offers an interesting attempt to analyze taste descriptions by applying a Talmyan cognitive semantics notion, force dynamics. It identifies the patterns where Food opposes Food/Taster. For instance, in the Food-enhances-Food pattern, realized in an expression such as *niku no umami o saidaigen ni hikidasu tate-yakusha* 'the leading actor [i.e., salt], which maximally draws out the *umami* of the meat', the weaker (i.e., the agonist, the meat's *umami*) is conceptualized as being drawn out by the stronger (i.e., the antagonist, salt). In Abe's view, Talmy's (1988) image-schematic system of the force dynamics patterns can illuminate the intricate interactional patterns among the event participants on the food tasting scene.

4. Concluding remarks

The chapters in this volume collectively analyze the language of food in Japanese through the critical prism of Cognitive Linguistics, foregrounding the following characteristic features.

First, they show the prominence of ideophones in food descriptions. The chapters by Uno et al., Fukushima, and Yoshinari reinforce Tsujimura's point (this volume) that ideophones play an important role in food naming and descriptions as sound-symbolism-embodied sensory words that can directly but subtly and sometimes synaesthetically depict our perceptive experiences upon ingesting food and drinks. Akita and Murasugi's chapter reveals a new aspect of ideophones: they can dynamically participate in word-formation as they can be combined with words from any lexical stratum (native, Sino-Japanese, ideophonic, foreign) to convey nuanced multimodal-based subjective meanings, thus implying their vast contribution to neologization in Japanese. Meanwhile, Ibarretxe-Antuñano (2021) argues ideophones can function as sensory words and supports this with a sample set from crosslinguistic data. It is left for other researchers to determine whether other languages, especially ideophone-rich languages, such as Basque, Korean, Siwu, and Pastaza Quechua, can deploy ideophones as sensory expressions and lexical items that can participate in neologization to the same extent as Japanese.

Second, the language of food includes expressions that evoke a sense of directness in terms of imagic iconicity (i.e., a sign that "resembles its referent with respect to some … characteristic" (Haiman, 1980, p. 515)) and diagrammatic iconicity (i.e., "a systematic arrangement of signs, … whose relationships to each other mirror the relationships of their referents" (Haiman, 1980, p. 515). Imagic iconicity is illustrated in Kumagai et al.'s chapter, where a sound is argued to be iconically mapped onto a meaning. For instance, voiced obstruents are perceived as directly evoking an image of hardness in rice crackers more strongly than their voiceless counterparts (See also Uno et al's chaper). Diagrammatic iconicity is illustrated in two completely different chapters (Akita & Murasugi's chapter and Sakaguchi's chapter), which consider the sequence of two adjectival elements (in compounds and complex predicates in the two chapters, respectively), where the state of the first element is argued to be sensed first, and that of the second element to be sensed second. Future work will determine what other forms in food descriptions can be accounted for by the idea of iconicity.

Third, the language of food contains words that clearly encode culture- and society-specific constructs. Yamaguchi's chapter offers a diachronic account of how the Japanese 'eat'-verbs extend meanings to reflect the hierarchical social structure of Japan and the Japanese psyche (adversity). Toratani's chapter implies the culturally significant aspect of the meaning of *sushi* is lost when it becomes a loanword in English. Sakaguchi's chapter discusses the polysemy of taste terms, including how the usage of *amai* 'sweet' reflects the Japanese psyche (*amae* 'dependence' (Doi, 1973)).

Fourth, creative and unique expressions are common in Japanese food naming and descriptions. As Fukushima's chapter shows, the meanings of sensory terms that describe *sake* taste are unique, as they are specific to the *sake* community. Akita and Murasugi's chapter introduces various creative compounds (e.g., *mazu-uma* 'bad-tasting but yummy'). Yoshinari's and Abe's chapters point to the use of transitive verbs in flavoring descriptions, despite a common observation that the grammatical subject of a transitive verb in Japanese is commonly animate (cf. Mayes, 1999). For instance, in a sentence like *san ga ekitai ni eregansu o atae* 'The acidity gives elegance to wine', an inanimate such as *san* 'acidity' occurs as the subject of the transitive verb, *atae-* 'give' (Yoshinari, this volume). While it is reasonable that an inanimate can be the subject of a transitive verb, as tasting and flavoring take place inside our body, this kind of characteristic is conceived as unique. At the same time, it encourages us to continuously attend to usage, a theme echoed in numerous cognitive linguistic studies, so that we can more aptly elucidate how we conceptualize the experience of food ingestion and flavoring and how we linguistically recast the experience. Another relevant point is that conceptual metaphors drive the meaning extension and imaginative conveyance of sensory experiences. For example, Sakaguchi's and Yamaguchi's chapters map elements from the food domain to the non-food domain, while Fukushima goes in the opposite direction. Yoshinari's and Abe's chapters use the term "metaphor" to describe the imaginative motion and force relations of food flavor and ingredients but neither characterizes the phenomena specifically as conceptual metaphors. The precise relation between conceptual metaphor and motion event or force dynamics in taste descriptions remains to be determined. Nor do we know which metaphors underlie the Japanese expressions, if any. We encourage others to pursue this line of inquiry.

By intersecting the language of food and Cognitive Linguistics, we have also shown how the incorporation of insights from other disciplinary fields can lead to the establishment of a new research method and thence to new findings. Uno et al.'s chapter, the joint work of linguists and food scientists, presents a new experimental method, exploring the relations between the scientifically measured hardness of rice crackers, the participants' perception of hardness, and their use of linguistic expressions to characterize the hardness and finds that the three types of hardness do not necessarily coincide. Fukushima proposes an innovative method to elicit *sake* tasting terms, combining insights from a theory of phenomenology of communication and a theory of aesthetics. He shows that the lexicon of *sake* taste terms is intricate and subjective, and their word network cannot be satisfactorily explained simply by the idea of lexical relations such as antonyms and synonyms (cf. Lehrer, 2009). Together, these chapters imply the examination of the language of food using a cognitive perspective can be expanded to strong collaborative work or unique (sub-)disciplinary work, which can be applied to other languages.

While the volume makes an important first step towards a better understanding of the characteristics of the language of food in Japanese, many more topics deserve attention. One is typological study of constructions, seeking to explain differences between Japanese and other languages: in other words, to ask how Japanese provides a conventionalized means to express a given concept in food descriptions when other languages have already been shown to use a given construction. For instance, in English, a recommendation in wine reviews is conveyed using the middle construction (Paradis, 2009). But how is a recommendation conveyed in Japanese? Another topic to consider is the multimodal aspect of sensory expressions. This is particularly relevant to Japanese because many ideophones convey a multimodally gleaned sense (e.g., *gorigori* 'grating sound'/'coarse tactile sensation'). Previous investigation of Japanese ideophones has focused on kinetic aspects of multimodality, such as gesture (Kita, 1997) or gaze (Akita, 2019). We need empirical work that centers on the sensory use of ideophones, exploring such questions as the extent to which the one-to-one correspondence between an ideophone and a modality is maintained or refuted. A final topic to consider is the language of smell, which relates to the second point, as the senses of smell are related to taste (Spence, Smith, & Auvray, 2015; Winter, 2019). In *Smellosophy: What the nose tells the mind*, Barwich (2020, p. 86) asks readers "why coffee smells excellent but tastes disappointing" or "why people eat stinky French cheese despite its, well, awful stink," thus explaining two senses of odor: what we experience orthonasally and retronasally.[9] The former is the sense when we initially sniff, for instance, as we welcome an enticing smell of coffee, whereas the latter is the aroma created when we chew a food such as cheese. In this case, food odorants travel up the pathway linking the oral cavity, back of the throat, and nasal cavity (Barwich, 2020, pp. 84–85). To the best of my knowledge, no work has examined the language use for the two senses of smell in Japanese and how it covaries with the food stuff, implying the language of olfaction can be a topic of future interdisciplinary consideration.[10]

In an interview with the *New York Times*, Dan Jurafsky commented: "The language of food is this secret hidden in plain sight. [...] We have all this amazing data all around us. How can we not use it?" (cited in Schuessler, 2014). This book responds to Jurafsky's call, with a special focus on Japanese. We hope the ideas and methods presented herein stimulate a broader discussion, leading to exciting new possibilities for future studies, going beyond (sub-)disciplinary boundaries, to gain better understanding of how language interacts with foods situated in a culture and a society.

References

Achiba, M. (2012). Development of interactional competence: Changes in participation over cooking sessions. *Pragmatics and Society*, *3*(1), 1–30. https://doi.org/10.1075/ps.3.1.01ach

Akita, K. (2019). Mimetics, gaze, and facial expressions in a multimodal corpus of Japanese. In K. Akita & P. Pardeshi, *Ideophones, mimetics and expressives* (pp. 229–247). Amsterdam/Philadelphia: John Benjamins. https://doi.org/10.1075/ill.16.10aki

Akita, K., & Pardeshi, P. (2019). Introduction: Ideophones, mimetics, and expressives: Theoretical and typological perspectives. In K. Akita & P. Pardeshi, *Ideophones, mimetics and expressives* (pp. 1–9). Amsterdam/Philadelphia: John Benjamins. https://doi.org/10.1075/ill.16.01aki

Allan, K. (2010). Tracing metonymic polysemy through time: MATERIAL FOR OBJECT mappings in the OED. In M. E. Winters, H. Tissari, & K. Allan (Eds.), *Historical cognitive linguistics* (pp. 163–196). Berlin/NY: De Gruyter Mouton. https://doi.org/10.1515/9783110226447.163

Ariyasriwatana, W., & Quiroga, L. M. (2016). A thousand ways to say 'Delicious!' -- Categorizing expressions of deliciousness from restaurant reviews on the social network site Yelp. *Appetite*, *104*, 18–32. https://doi.org/10.1016/j.appet.2016.01.002

Atkins, B. T., Kegl, J., & Levin, B. (1988). Anatomy of a verb entry: From linguistic theory to lexicographic practice. *International Journal of Lexicography*, *1*(2), 84–126. https://doi.org/10.1093/ijl/1.2.84

Auvray, M., & Spence, C. (2008). The multisensory perception of flavor. *Consciousness and Cognition*, *17*, 1016–1031. https://doi.org/10.1016/j.concog.2007.06.005

9. I thank Hiroki Fukushima for referring me to the work by Barwich (2020).

10. Fukushima (this volume, p. 211) briefly touches on the topic.

Backhouse, A. E. (1994). *The lexical field of taste: A semantic study of Japanese taste terms*. Cambridge: Cambridge University Press. https://doi.org/10.1017/CBO9780511554322

Bagli, M. (2020). *Tastes we live by: The linguistic conceptualization of taste in English*. Berlin/NY: De Gruyter Mouton.

Balirano, G., & Guzzo, S. (Eds.). (2019). *Food across cultures: Linguistic insights in transcultural tastes*. Switzerland: Springer. https://doi.org/10.1007/978-3-030-11153-3

Barwich, A. S. (2020). *Smellosophy: What the nose tells the mind*. Cambridge, Massachusetts: Harvard University Press. https://doi.org/10.4159/9780674245426

Booij, G. (2010). *Construction Morphology*. Oxford: Oxford University Press.

Breit, W. B. (2014). Appraisal theory applied to the wine tasting sheet in English and Spanish. *Iberica, 27*, 97–120. Retrieved from http://www.aelfe.org/?s=revista&veure=27

Burenhult, N., & Majid, A. (2011). Olfaction in Asian ideology and language. *Senses and Society, 6*(1), 19–29. https://doi.org/10.2752/174589311X12893982233597

Bybee, J., & Hopper, J. (2001). Introduction. In B. Joan & P. Hopper (Eds.), *Frequency and the emergence of linguistic structure* (pp. 1–24) Amsterdam/Philadelphia: John Benjamins. https://doi.org/10.1075/tsl.45.01byb

Caballero, R. (2007). Manner-of-motion verbs in wine description. *Journal of Pragmatics, 39*, 2095–2114. https://doi.org/10.1016/j.pragma.2007.07.005

Caballero, R. (2017). From the glass through the nose and the mouth: Motion in the description of sensory data about wine in English and Spanish. *Terminology, 23*(1), 66–88. https://doi.org/10.1075/term.23.1.03cab

Caballero, R. (2019). Sensory experiences, meaning and metaphor: The case of wine. In L. J. Speed, C. O'Meara, L. S. Roque, & A. Majid (Eds.), *Perception metaphors* (pp. 127–143). Amsterdam/Philadelphia: John Benjamins. https://doi.org/10.1075/celcr.19.07cab

Caballero, R., Suárez-Toste, E., & Paradis, C. (2019). *Representing wine- sensory perceptions, communication and cultures*. Amsterdam/Philadelphia: John Benjamins. https://doi.org/10.1075/celcr.21

Carroll, R. (1999). The middle English recipe as a text-type. *Neuphilologische Mitteilungen, 100*(1), 27–42.

Cassidy, F. G. (1995). The etymology of moxie. *Dictionaries, 16*, 208–211. https://doi.org/10.1353/dic.1995.0007

Choe, H. (2019). Eating together multimodally: Collaborative eating in mukbang, a Korean livestream of eating. *Language in Society, 48*(2), 171–208. https://doi.org/10.1017/S0047404518001355

Cook, G., Reed, M. & Twiner, A. (2009). "But it's all true!": commercialism and commitment in the discourse of organic food promotion. *Text & Talk – An Interdisciplinary Journal of Language, Discourse Communication Studies, 29*(2), 151–173. https://doi.org/10.1515/TEXT.2009.007

Cotter, C. (1997). Claiming a piece of the pie: How the language of recipes defines community. In A. L. Bower (Ed.), *Recipes for reading: community cookbooks, stories, histories* (pp. 51–72). Amherst, MA: University of Massachusetts Press.

Coulson, S. (2001). *Semantic leaps: Frame-shifting and conceptual blending in meaning construction*. Cambridge: Cambridge University Press. https://doi.org/10.1017/CBO9780511551352

Croft, W. (2009). Connecting frames and constructions: A case study of eat and feed. *Constructions and Frames, 1*(1), 7–28. https://doi.org/10.1075/cf.1.1.02cro

Croft, W., & Cruse, D. A. (2004). *Cognitive Linguistics*. Cambridge: Cambridge University Press. https://doi.org/10.1017/CBO9780511803864

Croijmans, I., & Majid, A. (2016). Not all flavor expertise is equal: The language of wine and coffee experts. *PLoS ONE*, *11*(6), e0155845. https://doi.org/10.1371/journal.pone.0155845
Croijmans, I., Hendrickx, I., Lefever, E., Majid, A., & Van Den Bosch, A. (2020). Uncovering the language of wine experts. *Natural Language Engineering*, *26*(5), 1–20. https://doi.org/10.1017/S1351324919000500
Culy, C. (1996). Null objects in English recipes. *Language Variation and Change*, *8*(1), 91–124. https://doi.org/10.1017/S0954394500001083
de Saussure, F. (2011). *Course in general linguistics*. (R. Harris, Trans., P. Meisel & H. Saussy, Eds.). New York: Columbia University Press. (Original work published 1916).
Diederich, C. (2015). *Sensory adjectives in the discourse of food: A frame-semantic approach to language and perception*. Amsterdam/Philadelphia: John Benjamins. https://doi.org/10.1075/celcr.16
Diemer, S. (2013). Recipes and food discourse in English – a historical menu. In C. Gerhardt, M. Frobenius, & S. Ley (Eds.), *Culinary linguistics: The chef's special* (pp. 139–156). Amsterdam/Philadelphia: John Benjamins. https://doi.org/10.1075/clu.10.06die
Diemer, S., Brunner, M-L., & Schmidt, S. (2014). "Like, pasta, pizza and stuff" – new trends in online food discourse. *Speaking in the Food Voice*, *5*(2). Retrieved from https://www.erudit.org/en/journals/cuizine/2014-v5-n2-cuizine01533/1026769ar/
Dingemanse, M. (2019). 'Ideophone' as a comparative concept. In K. Akita & P. Pardeshi, *Ideophones, mimetics and expressives* (pp. 13–33). Amsterdam/Philadelphia: John Benjamins. https://doi.org/10.1075/ill.16.02din
Doi, S. (2014). The naturalisation process of the Japanese loanwords found in the Oxford English Dictionary. *English Studies*, *95*(6), 674–699. https://doi.org/10.1080/0013838X.2014.942100
Doi, T. (1973). *The anatomy of dependence*. Tokyo: Kodansha International.
Evans, V., & Green, M. (2006). *Cognitive linguistics: An introduction*. Edinburgh: Edinburgh University Press Ltd.
Fauconnier, G., & Turner, M. (1998). Conceptual integration networks. *Cognitive Science*, *22*, 133–187. https://doi.org/10.1207/s15516709cog2202_1
Fillmore, C. (1982). Frame semantics. In Linguistic Society of Korea (Ed.), *Linguistics in the morning calm* (pp. 111–37). Seoul: Hanshin Publishing.
Fisher, M. F. K. (1983). *With bold knife and fork*. London: Chatto & Windus.
Geeraerts, D. (2008). Introduction: A rough guide to Cognitive Linguistics. In D. Geeraerts (Ed.), *Cognitive linguistics: Basic readings* (pp. 1–28). Berlin/NY: De Gruyter Mouton.
Gerhardt, C., Frobenius, M., & Ley, S. (2013a). Men eat for muscle, women eat for weight loss: Discourses about food and gender in men's health and women's health magazines. In C. Gerhardt, M. Frobenius & S. Ley (Eds.), *Culinary Linguistics: The chef's special* (pp. 261–279). Amsterdam/Philadelphia: John Benjamins. https://doi.org/10.1075/clu.10
Gerhardt, C., Frobenius, M., & Ley, S. (Eds.). (2013b). *Culinary Linguistics: The chef's special*. Amsterdam/Philadelphia: John Benjamins. https://doi.org/10.1075/clu.10
Gluck, M. (2003). Useful language: Useful idiom or idiot speak? In J. Aitchison & D. Lewis (Eds.), *New Media Language* (1st ed.) (pp. 107–115). New York: Routledge.
Goded Rambaud, M., & Poves Luelmo, A. (Eds.). (2010). *Proceedings of the first international workshop on linguistic approaches to food and wine description*. Madrid: UNED.
Haiman, J. (1980). The iconicity of grammar: Isomorphism and motivation. *Language*, *56*(3), 515–540. https://doi.org/10.2307/414448
Haiman, J. (1983). Iconic and economic motivation. *Language*, *59*(4), 781–819. https://doi.org/10.2307/413373

Hayakawa, F., Ioku, K., Akuzawa, S., Saito, M., Nishinari, K., Yamano, Y., & Kohyama, K. (2005). Collection of Japanese texture terms. (Studies on Japanese texture terms Part 1) [In Japanese]. *Nippon Shokuhin Kagaku Kogaku Kaishi. 52*(8), 337–346. https://doi.org/10.3136/nskkk.52.337

Hines, C. (1999). Rebaking the Pie: The WOMAN AS DESSERT Metaphor. In M. Bucholtz, A. C. Liang, & L. A. Sutton, *Reinventing identities: The gendered self in discourse* (pp. 145–162). Oxford: Oxford University Press.

Hiraga, M. (2009). Food for thought: CONDUIT VS. FOOD metaphors for communication. In K. Turner (Ed.), *Language in life, and a life in language: Jacob Mey, a Festschrift* (pp. 165–171). Bingley, UK: Emerald.

Hirokawa, S., Flanagan, B., Suzuki, T., & Yin, C. (2014). Learning winespeak from mind map of wine blogs. In S. Yamamoto (Eds.), *Human interface and the management of information. Information and knowledge in applications and services. HIMI 2014. Lecture Notes in Computer Science, 8522*, 383–393. https://doi.org/10.1007/978-3-319-07863-2_37

Hoffman, A., & Kytö, M. (2017). The linguistic landscapes of Swedish heritage cookbooks in the American Midwest, 1895–2005. *Studia Neophilologica, 89*(2), 261–286. https://doi.org/10.1080/00393274.2017.1301783

Hosking, R. (2010). *Food and language: Proceedings of the Oxford symposium on food and cookery, 2009*. Totnes: Prospect Books.

Hsiao, C. (2019). Linguistic strategies prompting interactions in recipes from Mandarin Chinese food blogs. *Text & Talk, 39*(4), 489–510. https://doi.org/10.1515/text-2019-2037

Ibarretxe-Antuñano, I. (2021). The domain of olfaction in Basque. In Ł. Jędrzejowski & P. Staniewski (Eds.), *The Linguistics of olfaction*. Amsterdam/Philadelphia: John Benjamins. https://doi.org/10.1075/tsl.131.03iba

Ikegami, Y. (1985). Activity-accomplishment-achievement-A language that can't say *I burned it but it did not burn* and one that can. In A. Makkai & A. K. Melby (Eds.), *Linguistics and philosophy: Essays in honor of Rulon S. Wells* (pp. 265–304). Amsterdam/Philadelphia: John Benjamins. https://doi.org/10.1075/cilt.42.21ike

Jędrzejowski, Ł., & Staniewski, P. (Eds.). (2021). *The Linguistics of olfaction*. Amsterdam/Philadelphia: John Benjamins. https://doi.org/10.1075/tsl.131

Johnson, M. (1987). *The body in the mind : The bodily basis of meaning, imagination, and reason*. Chicago: University of Chicago Press. https://doi.org/10.7208/chicago/9780226177847.001.0001

Jurafsky, D. (2014). *The language of food: A linguist reads the menu*. New York: W.W. Norton.

Kemmer, S., & Barlow, M. (2000). Introduction: A usage-based conception of language. In M. Barlow & S. Kemmer (Eds.), *Usage-based models of language* (pp. vii–xxviii). Stanford, California: CSLI publications.

Kita, S. (1997). Two-dimensional semantic analysis of Japanese mimetics. *Linguistics, 35*, 79–415. https://doi.org/10.1515/ling.1997.35.2.379

Kroo, J., & Matsumoto, Y. (2018). The case of Japanese *otona* 'adult': Mediatized gender as a marketing device. *Discourse & Communication, 12*(4), 401–423. https://doi.org/10.1177/1750481318757776

Kuroshima, S. (2010). Another look at the service encounter: Progressivity, intersubjectivity, and trust in a Japanese sushi restaurant. *Journal of Pragmatics, 42*(3), 856–869. https://doi.org/10.1016/j.pragma.2009.08.009

Lakoff, G. (1987). *Women, fire, and dangerous things*. Chicago: The University of Chicago Press. https://doi.org/10.7208/chicago/9780226471013.001.0001

Lakoff, G., & Johnson, M. (1980). *Metaphors we live by*. Chicago: University of Chicago Press.
Lakoff, R. (2006). Identity a la carte; or, you are what you eat. In A. D. Fina, D. Schiffrin, & M. Bamberg, *Discourse and identity (Studies in interactional sociolinguistics)* (pp. 147–165). Cambridge: Cambridge University Press. https://doi.org/10.1017/CBO9780511584459.008
Langacker, R. W. (1987). *Foundations of cognitive grammar: Theoretical prerequisites*. Stanford, CA: Stanford University Press.
Langacker, R. W. (1990). *Concept, image, and symbol: The cognitive basis of grammar*. Berlin: Mouton de Gruyter.
Larsson, U., & Swahn, J. (2011). Green frames: A semantic study in the lexicon of babyleaf salad. *Studia Neophilologica*, *83*, 149–168. https://doi.org/10.1080/00393274.2011.603905
Lehrer, A. (1969). Semantic cuisine. *Journal of Linguistics*, *5*(1), 39–55. https://doi.org/10.1017/S0022226700002048
Lehrer, A. (1972). Cooking vocabularies and the Culinary Triangle of Lévi-Strauss. *Anthropological Linguistics*, *14*(5), 155–171.
Lehrer, A. (1975). Talking about wine. *Language*, *51*(4), 901–923. https://doi.org/10.2307/412700
Lehrer, A. (1978). We drank wine, we talked, and a good time was had by all. *Semiotica*, *23*(3/4), 243–278. https://doi.org/10.1515/semi.1978.23.3-4.243
Lehrer, A. (2009). *Wine and conversation*. Oxford/New York: Oxford University Press. https://doi.org/10.1093/acprof:oso/9780195307931.001.0001
Lehrer, K., & Lehrer, A. (2016). The language of taste. *Inquiry*, *59*(6), 752–765. https://doi.org/10.1080/0020174X.2016.1208925
Levin, B., Glass, L., & Jurafsky, D. (2019). Systematicity in the semantics of noun compounds: The role of artifacts vs. natural kinds. *Linguistics*, *57*(3), 429–471. https://doi.org/10.1515/ling-2019-0013
Levi-Strauss, C. (1966). The culinary triangle. *Partisan Review*, *33*, 586–595.
López-Arroyo, B., & Roberts, R. P. (2014). English and Spanish descriptors in wine tasting terminology. *Terminology*, *20*(1), 25–49. https://doi.org/10.1075/term.20.1.02lop
López-Arroyo, B., & Roberts, R. P. (2016). Differences in wine tasting notes in English and Spanish. *Babel*, *62*(3), 370–401. https://doi.org/10.1075/babel.62.3.02lop
Madeleine. (n.d.). In *OED Online*. Oxford University Press, December 2020. Web.
Majid, A., & Burenhult, N. (2014). Odors are expressible in language, as long as you speak the right language. *Cognition*, *130*(2), 266–270. https://doi.org/10.1016/j.cognition.2013.11.004
Massam, D., & Roberge, Y. (1989). Recipe context null objects in English. *Linguistic Inquiry*, *20*(1), 134–139.
Matwick, K., & Matwick, K. (2019). *Food discourse of celebrity chefs of food network*. Cham: Palgrave Macmillan. https://doi.org/10.1007/978-3-030-31430-9
Matwick, K., & Matwick, K. (2020). Bloopers and backstage talk on TV cooking shows. *Text & Talk*, *40*(1), 49–74. https://doi.org/10.1515/text-2019-2052
Mayes, P. D. (1999). Linguistic reflections of social structure and culture: A comparison of Japanese and American cooking class genres. (Doctoral dissertation). Available from ProQuest Dissertations and Theses database. (UMI NO. 9961503)
McBurney, D. H., & Gent, J. F. (1979). On the nature of taste qualities. *Psychological Bulletin*, *86*(1), 151–167. https://doi.org/10.1037/0033-2909.86.1.151
McCawley, J. (1984). *The eater's guide to Chinese characters*. Chicago, IL: University of Chicago Press.
Myers, C. S. (1904). The taste-names of primitive peoples. *British Journal of Psychology*, *1*(2), 117–126.

Nakagawa, H. (2012). The importance of TASTE verbs in some Khoe languages. *Linguistics, 50*(3), 395–420. https://doi.org/10.1515/ling-2012-0014

Norrick, N. R. (1983). Recipes as texts: Technical language in the kitchen. In R. Jongen, S. D. Knop, P. H. Nelde, & M-P. Quix (Eds.), *Sprache, Diskurs und Text, Akten des 17. Linguistischen Kolloquiums, Brussel, 1982* (pp. 173–182). Tubingen: Niemeyer. https://doi.org/10.1515/9783111351254.173

Norrick, N. R. (2011). Conversational recipe telling. *Journal of Pragmatics, 43*, 2740–2761. https://doi.org/10.1016/j.pragma.2011.04.010

O'Mahony, M., & Ishii, R. (1986). A comparison of English and Japanese taste languages: Taste descriptive methodology, codability and the *umami* taste. *British Journal of Psychology, 77*, 161–174. https://doi.org/10.1111/j.2044-8295.1986.tb01991.x

O'Meara, C., & Majid, A. (2016). How changing lifestyles impact Seri smellscapes and smell language. *Anthropological Linguistics, 58*(2), 107–131. https://doi.org/10.1353/anl.2016.0024

O'Meara, C., Kung, S. S., & Majid, A. (2019). The challenge of olfactory ideophones: Reconsidering ineffability from the Totonac-Tepehua perspective. *International Journal of American Linguistics, 85*, 173–212. https://doi.org/10.1086/701801

Ochs, E., Pontecorvo, C., Fasulo, A. (1996). Socializing taste. *Ethnos, 61*(1–2), 7–46. https://doi.org/10.1080/00141844.1996.9981526

Paar, M. (2020, July 18). There is a season: Cuke salad's a cool summer treat. *Daily Hampshire Gazette*. Retrieved from https://www.gazettenet.com/Cuke-salad-s-a-cool-summer-treat-35252027

Paradis, C. (2009). "This beauty should drink well for 10–12 years": A note on recommendations as semantic middles. *Text & Talk, 29*(1), 53–73. https://doi.org/10.1515/TEXT.2009.003

Paradis, C., & Eeg-Olofsson, M. (2013). Describing sensory experience: The genre of wine reviews. *Metaphor and Symbol, 28*(1), 22–40. https://doi.org/10.1080/10926488.2013.742838

Pérez-Hernández, L. (2013). A pragmatic-cognitive approach to brand names: A case study of Rioja wine brands. *Names: A Journal of Onomastics, 61*(1), 33–46. https://doi.org/10.1179/0027773812Z.00000000038

Pérez-Hernández, L. (2019). XL burgers, shiny pizzas, and ascending drinks: Primary metaphors and conceptual interaction in fast food printed advertising. *Cognitive Linguistics, 30*(3), 531–570. https://doi.org/10.1515/cog-2018-0014

Proust, M., & Carter, W. C. (2013). *In search of lost time. Volume 1, Swann's way*. New Haven: Yale University Press.

Rhee, S., & Koo, H. J. (2017). Multifaceted gustation: Systematicity and productivity of taste terms in Korean. *Terminology, 23*(1), 38–65. https://doi.org/10.1075/term.23.1.02rhe

Rohrer, R. (2010). Embodiment and experientialism. In D. Geeraerts & H. Cuyckens (Eds.), *The Oxford handbook of cognitive linguistics* (pp. 25–47). Oxford: Oxford University Press.

Ruiz de Mendoza Ibáñez, F. J., and Peña Cervel, S. M. (2005). Introduction. In F. J. Ruiz de Mendoza Ibáñez & S. M. Peña Cervel (Eds.) *Cognitive linguistics: Internal dynamics and interdisciplinary interaction* (pp. 1–15). Berlin: Mouton de Gruyter.

Sasamoto, R. (2019). *Onomatopoeia and relevance: Communication of impressions via sound*. London: Palgrave Macmillan. https://doi.org/10.1007/978-3-030-26318-8

Schuessler, J. (2014, September 15). Deciphering the menu. Retrieved from https://www.nytimes.com/2014/09/17/dining/dan-jurafsky-a-linguist-decodes-restaurant-menus.html

Schultz, J. (2016). The semantic development of nineteenth-century French cookery terms in English: Tendencies of borrowings relating to dishes, desserts and confectionary. *Journal of Language Contact, 9*, 477–512. https://doi.org/10.1163/19552629-00903003

Schultze, D. (2008). Hippocras bag, oil of Exeter and Manus Christi: Recipes in BL Harley 1706. *Anglia - Zeitschrift Für Englische Philologie, 126*(3), 429–460. https://doi.org/10.1515/angl.2008.063

Shimoda, M., Sasaki, H., Doi, Y., Kameda, W., & Osajima, Y. (1989). Characterization of concrete terms for odor-description of food products [in Japanese]. *Nippon Shokuhin Kogyo Gakkaishi, 36*(1), 17–25. https://doi.org/10.3136/nskkk1962.36.17

Shimojo, M. (2019). Topicalization in Japanese cooking discourse. *Open Linguistics, 5*, 511–531. https://doi.org/10.1515/opli-2019-0028

Smith, V., Barratt, D. Y., & Zlatev, J. (2014). Unpacking noun-noun compounds: Interpreting novel and conventional food names in isolation and on food labels. *Cognitive Linguistics, 25*(1), 99–147. https://doi.org/10.1515/cog-2013-0032

Spence, C., Smith, B., & Auvray, M. (2015). Confusing tastes and flavours. In D. Stokes, M. Matthen, & S. Biggs (Eds.), *Perception and its modalities* (pp. 247–274). Oxford: Oxford University Press.

Staats, A. W., & Hammond, O. W. (1972). Natural words as physiological conditioned stimuli: Food-word-elicited salivation and deprivation effects. *Journal of Experimental Psychology, 96*(1), 206–208. https://doi.org/10.1037/h0033508

Strauss, S. G., Chang, H., & Matsumoto, Y. (2018). Genre and the cultural realms of taste in Japanese, Korean, and U.S. online recipes. In M. E. Hudson, Y. Matsumoto, J. Mori, & M. Shibatani. *Pragmatics of Japanese: Perspectives on grammar, interaction and culture* (pp. 219–244). Amsterdam/Philadelphia: John Benjamins. https://doi.org/10.1075/pbns.285.09str

Sullivan, K. (2013). *Frames and constructions in metaphoric language*. Amsterdam/Philadelphia: John Benjamins. https://doi.org/10.1075/cal.14

Sweetser, E. (1990). *From etymology to pragmatics: Metaphorical and cultural aspects of semantic structure*. Cambridge: Cambridge University Press. https://doi.org/10.1017/CBO9780511620904

Szatrowski, P. E. (Ed.). (2014). *Language and food: Verbal and nonverbal experiences*. Amsterdam/Philadelphia: John Benjamins. https://doi.org/10.1075/pbns.238

Talmy, L. (1983). How language structures space. In H. L. Pick, Jr. & L. P. Acredolo (Eds.), *Spatial orientation: Theory, research, and application* (pp. 225–282). New York: Plenum Press. https://doi.org/10.1007/978-1-4615-9325-6_11

Talmy, L. (1985). Lexicalization patterns: Semantic structure in lexical forms. In T. Shopen (Ed.), *Language typology and syntactic description 3: Grammatical categories and the lexicon* (pp. 57–149). Cambridge: Cambridge University Press.

Talmy, L. (1988). Force dynamics in language and cognition. *Cognitive Science, 12*, 49–100. https://doi.org/10.1207/s15516709cog1201_2

Talmy, L. (2000). *Toward a cognitive semantics, Volume I: Concept structuring systems*. Cambridge, MA: MIT Press.

Tayler, J. (1989). *Linguistic categorization*. Oxford: Oxford University Press.

Taylor, J. (2003). Meaning and context. In H. Cuyckens, T. Berg, R. Dirven, & K. Panther (Eds.), *Motivation in language: Studies in honor of Günter Radden* (pp. 28–48). Amsterdam/Philadelphia: John Benjamins. https://doi.org/10.1075/cilt.243.06tay

Temmerman, D., & Dubois, R. (Eds.) (2017). Food and terminology: Expressing sensory experience in several languages. Special issue of *Terminology 23*(1).

Tomasello, M. (2000). First steps toward a usage-based theory of language acquisition. *Cognitive Linguistics, 11*(12), 61–82.

Tominc, A. (2014). Tolstoy in a recipe: Globalisation and cookbook discourse in postmodernity. *Nutrition & Food Science*, *44*(4), 310–323. https://doi.org/10.1108/NFS-01-2014-0009

Tominc, A. (2017). *The discursive construction of class and lifestyle celebrity chef cookbooks in post-socialist Slovenia*. Amsterdam/Philadelphia: John Benjamins. https://doi.org/10.1075/dapsac.75

Tsujimura, N. (2018). Recipe names in Japanese cookbooks as a gateway to interpersonal communication. *Names: A Journal of Onomastics*, *66*(2), 1–13. https://doi.org/10.1080/00277738.2018.1452941

Voeltz, F. K. E., & Kilian-Hatz, C. (Eds.) (2001). *Ideophones*. Amsterdam/Philadelphia: John Benjamins. https://doi.org/10.1075/tsl.44

Wertz, S. K. (2013). The elements of taste: How many are there? *Journal of Aesthetic Education*, *47*(1), 46–57. https://doi.org/10.5406/jaesteduc.47.1.0046

Westney, L. (2007). From courtesans to queens: Recipes named for women. *Names*, *55*(3), 277–285. https://doi.org/10.1179/nam.2007.55.3.277

Wharton, T. (2010). Recipes: Beyond the words. *Gastronomica*, *10*(4), 67–73. https://doi.org/10.1525/gfc.2010.10.4.67

Wiegand, M., & Klakow, D. (2015). Detecting conditional healthiness of food items from natural language text. *Language Resources and Evaluation*, *49*(4), 777–830. https://doi.org/10.1007/s10579-015-9314-7

Winter, B. (2019). *Sensory linguistics: Language, perception and metaphor*. Amsterdam/Philadelphia: John Benjamins. https://doi.org/10.1075/celcr.20

Wnuk, E., & Majid, A. (2014). Revisiting the limits of language: The odor lexicon of Maniq. *Cognition*, *131*(1), 125–138. https://doi.org/10.1016/j.cognition.2013.12.008

Yamaguchi, S. (1979). The umami taste. In J. C. Boudreau (Ed.), *Food taste chemistry* (pp. 33–51). Washington, D.C.: American Chemical Society. https://doi.org/10.1021/bk-1979-0115.ch002

Yamaguchi, T. (2009). Literal and figurative uses of Japanese 'eat' and 'drink'. In J. Newman (Ed.), *The linguistics of eating and drinking* (pp. 173–193). Amsterdam/Philadelphia: John Benjamins. https://doi.org/10.1075/tsl.84.09yam

Yao, Y., & Su, Q. (2019). Chinese, food and menus. In C-R. Huang, Z. Jing-Schmidt, & B. Meisterernst (Eds.), *The Routledge handbook of Chinese applied linguistics* (pp. 81–91). New York: Routledge. https://doi.org/10.4324/9781315625157-6

Zwicky, A., & Zwicky, A. (1980). America's national dish: The style of restaurant menus. *American Speech*, *55*(83), 87–92. https://doi.org/10.2307/3050498

SECTION I

Overview

CHAPTER 1

The language of food in Japanese through a linguistic lens

Natsuko Tsujimura
Indiana University

Communication by language and nourishment by food are among the few things that indispensably shape our daily life. These two critical elements of human life may not appear to hold reciprocal relationships, but language indeed plays a vital role in our food culture in ways that are not always obvious. In rich and creative descriptions of our food experiences, for instance, how, where, and by whom taste expressions are used can reflect upon issues of linguistic analysis. This chapter overviews the ways in which investigations of the language of food, when viewed through a linguistic lens, can make a significant contribution towards a better understanding of Japanese language, culture, and society.

Keywords: communication, culture, identity, perception, society

1. Introduction

The 21st century has witnessed an enormous wealth of food both in quantity and in variety, so much so that those who are fortunate enough to experience the richness frequently forget there are serious problems with hunger in the world in which we live. The food we consume for nutrition and (at least from time to time) for pleasure is undeniably tied to culture. As the world becomes increasingly globalized, so too are more food choices made available to us. When we appreciate the richness and uniqueness of food that specific cultures bring to the world, we are reminded that food shares and interacts greatly with language in intriguing ways. At the same time, we realize that food, culture, and language form an inseparable and integral part of our lives.

Let me give a few anecdotal examples for illustration. In an area of Toronto established by immigrants from Asian countries, there was a Chinese restaurant that specialized in congee. Not having heard of the term "congee," nor knowing exactly what I ordered, I salivated with excitement for my "fish ball congee" to arrive. At a

https://doi.org/10.1075/celcr.25.01tsu

first glance I was disappointed because what I saw in front of me looked like *okayu* (Japanese term for porridge), which I unpleasantly associated with being ill from my childhood memory. The only consolation was a few succulent-looking fish balls that floated in a pool of porridge. Instantly, though, the hearty mixture of ginger and sesame oil travelled through my nostrils making me immensely ashamed of my initial reaction. My congee experience at the Chinese restaurant made me realize that there is a wide variety of food items that are similar in concept but are referred to by language-specific labels. For example, the same or similar dish has been called *juk* in Korea, *canja* in Portugal, *lugaw* in the Philippines, and *bubur* in Malay, just to name a few. Interestingly, the Japanese term *okayu* could bring back an unpleasant memory whereas what is represented by the name "congee" gave me a new sense of appreciation of virtually the same food item. Not only do names for dishes serve as linguistic labels but they often embed indelible memories and undeniable sentiment.

In another restaurant in Toronto that served Caribbean-inspired food, I had "dhalpiri roti," which epitomizes globalization and glocalization in the culinary world. Roti, generally known as flatbread like naan, originated in India, but is adopted and adapted not only in south Asian countries but in Africa and the Caribbean. The Trinidadian-Guyanese adaptation that I ordered is a soft, crepe-like dough that wraps a succulent filling. The dhalpuri roti is an example of localizing Indian flatbread into a Caribbean inspired food item. This path is akin to the adoption-and-adaptation process of loanwords: words in one language are adopted by another language and are subsequently adapted to match the linguistic system of the borrowing language. In both cases of food and word borrowing, we could end up with creating something unauthentic or uninterpretable in their original sources, such as *chop suey* for food, and *dokutā-sutoppu* [doctor-stop] 'doctor's order (to not do/eat something)' and *pēpā-doraibā* [paper-driver] 'a person who has a driver's license but does not drive'.[1] Food and language are each essential in our daily life, in the form of eating and speaking for communication. So, food and language (communication) reflect cultural constructs in a significant way although we may not realize it. And, when they are put together, food and language can exert a surprising amount of power in how we think about food in a specific culture.

1. Irwin (2011) calls "assembled compounds" and "semantically remodeled compounds" those compounds whose meanings diverge from their potential meanings (as compounds) in the donor language. In many cases of assembled or semantically remodeled compounds in Japanese, compound members individually exist in the donor language but they have been "assembled" once they are borrowed into Japanese, resulting in compounds that do not exist in the donor language.

A strong association between food and language in a larger social context is more directly illustrated in food writing such as cookbooks and recipes, especially when we focus on language as a communication tool. Anybody who cooks or likes to cook for personal or professional reasons knows that recipes are about food, and that their essential purpose is to give instructions on how to prepare dishes. But, the medium of language is an integral part of recipes far beyond a series of instructions in prose style. Language used in recipes, depending on how we use it, can influence the degree to which a given recipe appeals to the reader. Furthermore, at a conceptual level, the language of recipes can tell us much about how we think about food as well as how we view people and culture in the local and global setting. As many scholars have demonstrated, recipes and cookbooks provide an intriguing window through which the social and historical situation and local atmosphere at a given time can be ascertained.

The important role that language plays in our food culture is not limited just to individual examples like those given above but extends far more widely to the language of food as it is more broadly conceived. While achieving the communicative goal of expressing one's experience of food, it reflects on cultural beliefs and social constructs. The extent to which the language of food contributes to inter- and multi-disciplinary issues revolving around foodways can be better understood when we investigate a variety of ways in which linguistic concepts and analytical tools are applied. The current chapter is intended to complement the Introduction of this volume by Toratani, which overviews the ways in which Cognitive Linguistics provides the conceptual groundwork in dealing with the language of food. The primary goal of this chapter, instead, is to peruse the extent to which concepts and analytical tools in linguistics can contribute to a better understanding of a broad range of phenomena observed in the language of food with specific reference to Japanese. Micro- and macro-level examination of the phenomena through a linguistic lens ultimately provides a coherent way of illuminating the nature of the Japanese sociocultural construct to which the language of food alludes.

2. Linguistic concepts and mechanisms in the language of food

This section reviews some research programs in linguistics and cognitive science that have been conducted in recent years and can be applied to the language of food. Micro-level examinations of these studies highlight the ways in which linguistic theories and approaches can motivate scholarly investigations into human cognition and thought while in turn offering an analytical apparatus that can help systematically explain a range of phenomena that would otherwise remain arbitrary.

2.1 Sound-symbolism and mimetics

Sound-symbolism in a variety of languages has a long research history in linguistics and related disciplinary areas. In Japanese the topic has been extensively pursued under the term mimetics (e.g., Kita, 1997; Hamano, 1998; Tamori & Schourup, 1999; Akita, 2009). As some of the chapters in this volume discuss (e.g., Uno, Kobayashi, Shinohara & Odake; Kumagai, Uno & Shinohara), mimetics are ubiquitous in the language of food, particularly in the vocabulary that is used to describe the texture of food.[2] As the packaging of food products clearly displays, mimetics serve as a shorthand of product names: not only do they make lengthy verbal descriptions unnecessary but they can highlight the products' selling points far more vividly. For instance, on a commercial package for green tea candies, pictures of two kinds of candies are shown along with *sakusaku-maccha* 'sakusaku-green tea' and *torori-maccha* 'torori-green tea'. The first members of these compounds are mimetics: *sakusaku* refers to light, crunchy texture, while *toror*i suggests smooth and creamy filling. Another food package for cooked rice with barley says *puripuri-no shokkan-ga oishii!* 'puripuri mouth-feel is delicious!'. In this phrase, *puripuri* characterizes the rice to be plump and bouncy when it is heated in a microwave. The use of mimetics for food advertisements is effective due to their direct appeal to our five senses.

In more general terms, much research on sound symbolism in the world's languages has shown that the association between sound with meaning is not arbitrary (Hinton, Nichols, & Ohala, 1994). Under this premise, stops are associated with "abrupt sounds and acts," continuants with "continuing sounds and acts," fricatives with "quick audible motion of an object through air," and nasals with "ringing, reverberating sounds" (pp. 9–10). The last consonants of English words, *bunt, punt, crack, thunk, pop,* and *thump* can be associated with the abruptness of the sounds or acts that these verbs infer based on the non-arbitrary sound-meaning association. In a similar vein, Ohala's (1994) Frequency Code claims that high frequency sounds (front vowels such as /i/) are associated with small, thin, and light things, while low frequency sounds (back vowels like /u/) are associated with the opposite meanings. In English, for example, the smallness associated with the front vowel /i/ is reflected by the hypocoristic forms ending with [i], such as *Jenny, Billy,* and *Stephie*. Hypocoristic forms do not necessarily refer to physical size, but as terms of endearment, there is sense of smallness underlying them.

2. Hayakawa's series of work (e.g., Hayakawa, 2003a, 2003b, 2004a, 2004b, 2006; Hayakawa, Hatae, & Shimada, 2000) give extensive examinations of mimetics that are used to describe food. Although the orientation of her work is not linguistics, she makes a number of interesting observations that have significant implications to linguistic research and that, in turn, seem to benefit from applying linguistic principles. Also, see Muto (2003).

The generalizations over sound symbolism have been drawn from mimetics in Japanese as well with varying theoretical implications. Hamano (1998) demonstrates that the voicing of the initial consonants of mimetic expressions correlates with a semantic contrast. More specifically, voiced vs. voiceless initial obstruents in minimal pairs like *gotogoto* vs. *kotokoto* [cluttering noise of a heavy/light object], *zarazara* vs. *sarasara* [course/fine texture], and *botabota* vs. *potapota* [drop of thick/thin liquid] correspond to the "heavy/large/course/thick" meaning for mimetics with voiced obstruents while the opposite meaning holds for mimetics with voiceless counterparts. Minimal pairs consistent with this generalization among mimetics of food texture include *garigari* vs. *karikari, dorori* vs. *torori*, and *bariQ* vs. *pariQ*. Another generalization has to do with the sound symbolism regarding palatalization, as is discussed by Mester and Ito (1989) and Hamano (1998). Hamano (1998) describes that palatalization of consonants adds the meaning that ranges over "childishness, immaturity, instability, unreliability, uncoordinated movement, diversity, excessive energy, noisiness, lack of elegance, and cheapness," based on samples like *korokoro* "rolling on" vs. *kyorokyoro* "looking around inquisitively" and *pokopoko* "making holes here and there" vs. *pyokopyoko* "hopping around; in a childish, bobbing motion" (p. 184). Other sound-meaning correspondences that have been discussed in the linguistic literature on Japanese mimetics include the roles played by coda nasal, geminate consonants, vowel lengthening, and the word-final *-ri*, as well as reduplication.[3]

The non-arbitrary nature of sound symbolism including the claim of the Frequency Code has been tested not just in linguistics. Psychologists and marketing researchers have also demonstrated the so-called "power of language" over consumers, and this line of research includes examinations of the language of food. In particular, there have been a number of investigations regarding the ways in which sound symbolism in brand names influences people's perceptions of products, as is reported in, for examples, Klink (2000, 2001), Yorkston and Menon (2004); Ngo, Misra, & Spence (2011); Jurafsky (2014), and many more. This line of investigation extends to the language of food from a variety of angles. Based on the Frequency Code, Yorkston and Menon (2004) report on experiments to test sound symbolic effects on people. Two groups of participants were told that a new ice cream product is being introduced under the brand name *Frish* for one group and under *Frosh* for the other group. It follows from the Frequency Code that a back vowel symbolizes bigger, heavier, slower, and duller objects, and accordingly it was hypothesized that a name of an ice cream with a back vowel (Frosh) would be perceived as smoother, creamier, and richer than a name with a front vowel (Frish). The participants were

3. See Chapter 4 of Hamano (1998) for detailed discussion of the semantic roles that these elements play.

asked to read a prepared press release of the ice cream and to evaluate the product for its smoothness, creaminess, and richness. The results were borne out, confirming that sound symbolism influences potential consumer's judgments.

Similar experiments have been carried out concerning the effects of symbolism associated with consonants. Ngo et al. (2011) examined crossmodal relationships among taste, shape (vision), and words that reflect a sound symbolic contrast. Based again on the generalizations on sound symbolism that stops are associated with abrupt sounds or acts while continuants are associated with continuing sounds or acts, they tested how the nonsense words, *takete* and *maluma*, correspond with the taste and visual perceptions. Focusing on the consonantal contrast between /k/ in *takete* and /l/ in *maluma*, they predicted that the former corresponds with a bitter chocolate taste and an angular shape, while the latter with a creamier taste and a round shape. The results positively confirm the prediction, adding further credence to the effects of sound symbolism on our perceptions. A number of studies preceding and following these investigations all point to the psychological reality of the strong tie between sound and meaning and its non-arbitrary nature.[4]

The slew of research I have summarized above has been taken up for its application and extention to Japanese mimetics, as Uno et al.'s and Kumagai et al.'s chapters in this volume and studies preceding them show. These investigations commonly use nonsense words in their attempt successfully to verify how strongly sound symbolism underlies our evaluation of tastes and beyond. In relation to this but based on existing Japanese vocabulary, Ohashi (2015) compiles results from multi-year surveys that examine which word people connect to "delicious" tastes. A questionnaire was conducted in each of the three years, 2003, 2009, and 2015. Participants were asked whether selected words appeal to them as expressions that evoke a sense of deliciousness. The total of 305 questionnaire words, both mimetic and non-mimetic words, consist of three categories: (i) 90 items that refer to taste and smell (e.g., *amai* 'sweet', *kōmi* 'aromatic', *kotteri* 'rich' [mimetic]), (ii) 102 items that describe texture and sound (e.g., *katai* 'hard', *hagotae-no aru* 'chewy', *korikori* 'crunchy' [mimetic], and (iii) 113 items that are intended to give background information about food, including season, cooking method, and health-related information (e.g., *shun* 'seasonal', *agetate* 'just (deep-)fried', *non-oiru* 'oil-free'). It is reported that over the span of 12 years, mimetics ranked high in the total word list as well as within the category of texture and sound (pp. 18–19). The four mimetics in (1)–(4) are particularly highlighted in the report along with the word's ranking for each of the three years.

4. The references cited here and other investigations by Maurer, Pathman, and Mondloch (2006) and Jurafsky (2014), for example, indicate that the same range of perceptual effects of sound symbolism has been tested positively with names of crackers as well as still vs. carbonated water.

(1) mochimochi (e.g., for chewy texture of bread)
#8 (2003) → #2 (2009) → #1 (2015)

(2) mocchiri (e.g., for chewy texture of bread)
#11 (2003) → #3 (2009) → #3 (2015)

(3) torōri (e.g., for creaminess of custard)
#23 (2003) → #7 (2019) → #7 (2015)

(4) fuwafuwa (e.g., for fluffiness of a sponge cake)
#38 (2003) → #12 (2009) → #11 (2015)

In contrast, some mimetics, listed in (5) ranked low in invoking a sense of deliciousness (p. 27).

(5) gotsugotsu, dorodoro, zarazara, jarijari, dorori, garigari

The commentary in Ohashi's report states that the (initial) voiced consonants of these mimetics are attributed to the unfavorable impression as "delicious words," and explains that voiced consonants of these words signifies an unpleasant sense of strong friction that one might feel in the mouth (p. 26). The feeling of strong friction that is connected to voiced consonants is not elaborated on in the report, leaving this account somewhat subjective. On the one hand, Ohashi's (2015) survey report is not strictly founded on scholarly methods and argumentation, which may be attributed to its more general readership as a target audience. On the other hand, I wish to stress that the results indeed have benefited from the research in linguistics and related fields discussed above. That is, Hamano's (1998) examinations of sound-meaning relationships pertinent to voiced vs. voiceless obstruents exactly hit the nail on the head: voiced obstruents have a significant association with the "heavy/large/coarse/thick" meaning for mimetics when minimal pairs with voiceless counterparts exist. While she does not claim that the "heavy/large/coarse/thick" sense that the initial voiced obstruents of mimetics bear is always negatively interpreted, voiced alternants in contrastive situations are prone to garner unfavorable judgments, including unpleasantness (e.g., *shitoshito* vs. *jitojito* for rain), coarseness as opposed to refinedness (e.g., *sarasara* vs. *zarazara* for salt), and incompleteness (e.g., *satto* vs. *zatto* for boiling ingredients) (Hamano, 1998, p. 85, p. 129). So, the generalizations of sound symbolism that have been made for Japanese mimetics have a direct contribution in explicating the findings of the survey, while at the same time substantiating the line of linguistic research involving sound symbolism in general.

Interestingly, the survey also shows that some results deviate from the sound symbolic generalizations. Within female speakers, the age group distribution of mimetic words that belong to the texture and sounds category is highlighted in (6), following Ohashi (2015, p. 21). The female participants chose these mimetics as descriptive words that evoke deliciousness.

(6) a. 15–19: pururun, purupuru, funwari, sakuhuwa, **zakutto**, **zakuzaku**
b. 20–29: torōri, mochitto, mochimochi, fuwafuwa, **juwā**, **juwatto**, karikari
c. 30–39: mocchiri, karitto, tsurutto, puripuri, puritto, nebaneba
d. 40–49: fuwatoro, torotto, sakusaku, karatto
e. 50–59: hokkuri, hokkori, tsurutsuru
f. 60–60: shittori

The bold-faced mimetic expressions in (6a) and (6b) have voiced initial obstruents. Despite the unpleasantness expected by the sound symbolic association, speakers younger than 30 years old selected them as "delicious" expressions, while none of these mimetics were favorably viewed by the participants of the older generations. While (6a) and (6b) may appear to be outliers of the generalizations that explained (5), they can actually be given an account that is consistent with what has been discussed, especially in light of the fact that the deviation is specific to the younger age groups among the age stratification. It should be remembered that Hamano (1998) characterizes the voiced initial obstruents of mimetics to relate to the sense of "heavy/large/coarse/thick." One of the notions that fall under the rubric is "force" (Hamano, 1998, p. 129), which can be construed with a positive nuance in trying to ascertain possible reasons for the unexpected inclusions in (6a) and (6b). That is, the "force" associated with voiced obstruents may mirror exertion of youthful energy. Especially in this category of texture or mouth-feel, the solid bite of a hard-baked rice cracker or any other crunchy food item is perhaps more welcomed to the youth than to aging populations who are likely to favor food with a tender feel that is particularly easy on the teeth, for example. So, the meaning symbolized by a particular sound can often be subjectively and flexibly construed according to individuals and circumstances. On the other hand, once younger age groups get older and likely change their food (especially texture) preferences, their perceptions of which words describe tastiness would evolve. That is, changes in physical conditions and capacities related to aging may well alter our sense-based reactions and subsequently the verbal expressions describing our sensual experiences.

2.2 Morphological regularities and innovations

One of the great abilities that language users have is to manipulate existing words or create new words to form original catch phrases and brand names. This is particularly helpful and necessary for successful marketing and advertising purposes, as it is attested in the food domain and beyond (see Akita & Murasugi's and Toratani's chapters in this volume). Effective and ingenious names and phrases are often built upon various types of word formation including affixation, compounding, clipping, abbreviation and acronym, blending, and borrowing (loanwords).

To illustrate, examples of blends in English are ubiquitously found: *cronut* (croissant + donut), *Tofurky* (turkey substitute made of tofu), *Subtember* (a Subway sandwich featured in September), *waffalicious* (descriptor used on an IHOP menu), and *Kebabalicious* (the name of a food truck in Austin, Texas). We also find creative phrases that use sound-based or word-based language play, deriving eye-catching names like *Expresso Yourself* as an ice cream flavor, and *Ale Asylum Hopalicious* and *New Belgium Citradelic IPA* for beer names. Likewise, in Japanese, there are numerous attention-grabbing product names and recipe names that combine lexical items from the four strata (i.e., Native, Sino-Japanese, Mimetic, and Loanword) by way of different word formation tools. For instance, the recipe name *ebi-mayo* 'shrimp-mayonnaise' is a compound consisting of a native word *ebi* 'shrimp' and a clipped loanword *mayo* (< *mayonēzu*) 'mayonnaise'; and another one, *shaki-puchi-sarada* 'crisp-bubbly salad' is a three-member compound, where the first two are mimetics (based on *shakiQ* or *shakishaki*; *puchiQ* or *puchipuchi*) while the last is an English loanword *sarada* 'salad'. Compounding and clipping, individually as well as in combination, are word formation types extensively utilized in Japanese, perfectly following general patterns of the morphological regularity of the language. Furthermore, the regularity allows for a straightforward substitution as a means to increase the variety of creative names. For example, Mr. Donut in Japan sells a donut called *pon-de-ringu*, which is named after a *Pão de queijo* (Brazilian cheese bread) in Portuguese and the last part *-ringu* 'ring' is added to describe the round shape of the adapted Japanese donut product. Based on the plain-flavored *pon-de-ringu* donut, the company advertises other varieties with brown sugar and strawberry glaze, each of which is marketed under *pon-de-kokutō* (*kokutō* 'brown sugar') and *pon-de-sutoroberī* (*sutoroberī* 'strawberry'). These word derivations are entirely intuitive and consistent with general patterns while giving enough leeway for the borrowing of foreign names, their linguistic adaptation, and creativity.

Drawing special attention of consumers is frequently at the heart of marketing strategies, and humor greatly contributes to that end. As briefly mentioned above, an assortment of word play such as puns and double meanings serves the purpose (Tsujimura, 2018a). The recipe names, *ton-ton karē* 'pork-pork curry' and *kan-kan raisu* 'can-can rice', present pertinent examples. The first part of *ton-ton karē, ton-ton,* is a reduplicated form of the base *ton*, which stands for pork, as in *tonkatsu* 'pork cutlet' and *tonjiru* 'pork soup', but the reduplicated form *ton-ton* iconically corresponds to two pork parts, spare rib and loin, as the primary ingredients of the curry dish. Upon looking at and sounding out *kan-kan raisu*, we might associate *kan-kan* with an onomatopoeic sound effect; or related to that, it may even evoke an image of rhythmic and energetic *kan-kan dansu* 'can-can dance' in Showa-ites' minds. The caption that appears in the recipe page says *kanzume-de kantan* 'easily prepared by using canned food'. The recipe calls for canned mushrooms, scallops, clams, and corn. So, the recipe name cleverly uses puns based on the ingredients (*kan* as in *kanzume* 'canned food') and the adjective describing the simplicity of the cooking process, *kantan* 'easy'. The possible rhythmic effect coming from *kan-kan* makes it easier to register in the reader's mind. The effectiveness of these names for piquing people's curiosity is achieved by the skillful way of using morphological mechanisms that are prevalent in the language as well as employing a phonetic impact.

We have thus far demonstrated how an interesting range of food-related names are productively created by deploying various morphological mechanisms. While relevant linguistic tools involved have centered on derivational morphology, inflectional morphology, although at a lesser degree, also participates in generating novel words in the language of food. A case in point is shown in *onigirazu* – an increasingly wide-spread food label especially in social media. The better known, or more common, name *onigiri* 'rice ball' is a house-hold term in Japanese food scenes. The word *onigiri* comes from the verb *nigir-u* 'grip', which describes the general process of squeezing cooked rice into a round or triangular shape by two hands. The verb enters into the standard inflectional paradigm, including the negative form *nigir-a-zu* 'not grip'. The rice dish termed *onigirazu* is made without molding rice into a ball but instead by stacking rice and other ingredients as layers just like a sandwich. That is, the absence of the nigiru-process gives rise to the name *onigirazu*, making good use of the inflectional morpheme of negation.

In addition to clipping, abbreviation is also extensively employed. However, original words and phrases that are abbreviated often show a mishmash of lexical and orthographical sources. Consider the two examples in (7).

(7) a. GBS poteto [GBS=garlic, butter, shōyu 'soy sauce']
    b. TKG [=tamago kake gohan 'rice with a raw egg poured over it']

According to a cookbook, GBS of *GBS poteto* 'GBS potato' in (7a) stands for "g" as in *garlic* in English and "b" as in *butter* in English, but "s" as in *shōyu* 'soy sauce' in Japanese rather than "s" as in *soy sauce* in English. That is, the last abbreviation comes from the English alphabet used in the Romanized version of a Japanese word. The abbreviation TKG in (7b) stands for *tamago-kake gohan* [egg-pouring rice]. Here, too, the abbreviation is based on *tamago-kake gohan* in Romanization, rather than in the hiragana or katakana syllabary. It should be noted that the abbreviation based on the Japanese syllabary would be *takago* (たかご), taking each mora of the three-word compound in Japanese as opposed to the abbreviation consisting of an initial consonantal phoneme in the Romanization. The pattern of abbreviation based on English letter names or the Romanized orthography seems outside the regularity of the language, but it may be attributed to media influences particularly on younger people as a recent socio-cultural trend. On the other hand, we actually see several old and new precedents for this, including NHK for *Nippon Hōsō Kyōkai* 'Japan Broadcasting Corporation', JK for *joshi kōsei* 'female student', and KY for *kūki yomenai* 'can't read the room'. Either way, the abbreviated expressions in (7) and other instances similar to them in the language of food would not surface without a recognized degree of entrenchment and familiarity of the corresponding unabbreviated counterparts, which is a prerequisite for the process of abbreviation.

Finally, loanword is an inevitable word formation process as the world of cuisine becomes more and more global. There are multiple reasons or motivations for lexical borrowing, but chief among them and relevant to the language of food are necessity and prestige (Haspelmath, 2009; Irwin, 2011). When food items and cooking techniques are new to a borrowing culture, it is unavoidable to borrow the original terms that refer to the new objects and concepts. Examples of necessity-based loanwords include *sushi, sashimi, sukiyaki*, and *umami*, which have already been immersed in the US food culture; and *furaido poteto* 'French fries', *namuru* 'namul (Korean)', *marine* 'marinade (French *mariné*)' commonly appear in Japanese menus and recipes. Loanwords motivated by prestige are a reflection of an attitudinal aspect of borrowing cultural objects and concepts but also mirrors one's level of sophistication or socio-economic class. A native speaker of English using *maguro* 'tuna' rather than *tuna* at a sushi-bar in the US or a Japanese native describing a texture of pasta as *arudente* 'al dente' instead of *hagotaeno-aru* 'chewy' is likely to show a higher level of cultural and linguistic knowledge.

There are several consequences following from lexical borrowing and its linguistic adaptation. The most notable one is phonetic because differences in the sound inventory and the phonological system between the donor language and the recipient language often need to be negotiated. For the rest of this subsection, though, I will focus more on morphosemantic aspects that are sometimes discussed under topics like doubling, coexistence, and (semantic) narrowing and broadening in the loanword literature (Smith, 2006; Haspelmath, 2009; Irwin, 2011). As Smith (2006) discusses, there are instances where a word in the donor language has ended up with two different pronunciations in the process of phonetic and phonological adjustments. Smith calls these pairings "loanword doublets"; those in (8) are examples of food-related loanword doublets, based on Smith (2006, p. 68).

(8) a. lemonade → [ramune], [remone:do]
b. pudding → [purin], [pudiŋgu]
c. roast → [ro:su], [ro:suto]

The variation in pronunciation is intriguing in its own right, but of further interest is the difference in meaning between the variants. The second pronunciations in (8a)–(8c) maintain the meanings of the source English words, but in contast, the first pronunciations refer to a carbonated beverage (like 7-Up) in (8a), custard pudding in (8b), and sirloin in (8c). So, the first of these pairings represents somewhat more specific or restricted meaning of what the original donor word denotes. A single form, thus, may be branched into more than one lexical item with unidentical phonetic and semantic properties as part of the process of lexical borrowing.[5] Semantic narrowing does not need to cooccur with phonetic adjustments of the sort observed in (8). Irwin (2011) explains, for example, that *ikura* 'salmon row' was borrowed from the Russian word that has the broader meaning of fish roe. Another example *jūsu* in Japanese means only fruit juice to drink, and unlike the original English, it cannot be used to refer to lemon juice, for example, as an ingredient for cooking.

An additional example of narrowing that Irwin (2011) includes *raisu* 'rice', but this example is further helpful in illustrating the coexistence phenomenon, i.e., the word "coexist[ing] with a native word with the same meaning" (Haspelmath, 2009, p. 49). A staple of daily food consumption in Japan, rice is not an object or concept that needed a new label since there are already *gohan* 'cooked rice' and *kome* 'rice (the grain form)' in the native vocabulary. The word *raisu* as a loanword has received a narrowed meaning while coexisting with the two native words. Irwin explains that *raisu* "refers specifically to boiled polished rice served on a plate (not in the usual bowl) and typically eaten with a spoon or a fork (not chopsticks)" (p. 154). Although strictly speaking, what *raisu* and *gohan* denote are the same, i.e., cooked rice, their purposes and serving styles diverge. The extension of the conceptual difference of western- vs. Japanese-style meals underlying this word choice is observed with compounds based on *raisu*, including *omu-raisu* 'omelette filled with stir-fried rice', *karē raisu* 'curry and rice', *raisu pirafu* 'rice pilaf', *chikin raisu* 'stir-fried rice with chicken', and *batā raisu* 'rice stir-fried in butter'. The dichotomy between *raisu* and *gohan* as well as the existence of yet another individual word *kome* seem to represent the situation in which what may be considered as unique as rice has undergone different cultural conceptualizations with their corresponding linguistic manifestations.

2.3 Lexicalization and metaphors

2.3.1 *Semantic dissection and lexicalization*

Food and cuisine in our daily life are deeply rooted in individual cultures. While certain dishes may share underlying concepts across cultures, as is the case with congee mentioned in the introduction, a variety of factors like geography and

5. An additional example is [kokoa] and [kakao] for *cocoa*, where the first pronunciation refers to the same as in English, i.e., hot chocolate, while the second means cacao trees. In this case, however, the term "semantic narrowing" may not be appropriate in characterizing the meaning split.

climate have restricted what is available both in food items as ingredients and in styles of cooking throughout the human history. In the midst of culinary globalization, we face the risk of taking "translation equivalents" at face value for convenience and overlooking the prospect that the "equivalents" are quite stretched in actual referents. Investigations into what comprises lexical meaning provide beneficial ways not only to ascertain the nature of such potential gaps but to understand the relationship that conceptualization patterns exhibit with the meaning of the vocabulary in the language of food.

Cooking terms present an interesting case for illustration (Lehrer, 1969, 1972; Tsujimura, 2018b, forthcoming). For instance, *wakasu* in Japanese and *boil* in English have very similar dictionary definitions, but what can be heated by these cooking processes differs and the distinction further leads to linguistic consequences and implications. The clearest difference between the two verbs is that *wakasu* describes only the process of boiling water whereas *boil* in English can refer to a wider range of boiling processes as long as what is heated has liquid. The two verbs share the features corresponding to the presence of liquid ([+liquid]) and vigorous cooking ([+vigorous cooking]) as semantic components that are built into their overall meanings. But they diverge in narrower semantic restriction on *wakasu*, which requires only the presence of water.[6] Furthermore, not only is the specification of water incorporated semantically, but the verb has to be stipulated for an object as its syntactic collocation. The stipulation must also require that the object of *wakasu* be *(o-)yu* 'hot water' instead of *mizu* '(cold) water', as in *(o-)yu-o wakasu* 'boil (hot) water' but not **mizu-o wakasu* 'boil (cold) water'. An implication to the lexical organization based on fine-grained lexical semantic properties (e.g., Levin, 1993) is that Japanese *wakasu* and English *boil* belong to distinct verb classes: the former is a creation verb while the latter is a change-of-state verb.[7] Thus, when linguistic analysis is applied to dissect what constitutes verb meaning, the fundamental differences of "translation equivalents," as is demonstrated by *wakasu* and *boil*, reside in the non-uniform ways in which the process of heating with liquid is conceptualized; and those conceptual differences are reflected by the semantic and syntactic properties of the language.

6. In Tsujimura (2018b, forthcoming), cooking verbs in Japanese are given componential analyses following Lehrer's (1969, 1972) earlier work.

7. Additional examples of creation verbs in Japanese include *amu* 'knit' as in *sētā-o amu* 'knit a sweather' and *horu* 'dig' as in *ana-o horu* 'dig a hole', where the objects refer to artifacts resulting from the processes denoted by the verbs. In contrast, with change-of-state verbs like *niru* as in *imo-o niru* 'cook potatoes' and *yaku* as in *sakana-o yaku* 'grill/bake fish', the objects refer to the items whose state is expected to change (i.e., from raw to cooked) through the cooking processes denoted by the verbs.

Another example can be drawn from *taku*, the verb that describes cooking rice. Lehrer (1969) analyzes the verb as a dual-process, consisting of what are referred to as boiling (*niru*) and steaming (*musu*).[8] It may be noted that this characterization of *taku* seems to be connected to the term "steamed rice" on Japanese and other Asian restaurant menus in the US. The general verb for steaming is *musu*, which crucially contrasts with *niru* in avoiding liquid submersion of ingredients. In this light, the steaming portion of the rice-cooking process is more accurately described by another verb *murasu* – the term that is almost exclusively used for rice-cooking. In cooking rice, the grain version of it, *kome*, is submerged in water, and then the mixture is boiled in a covered pot. When all the water is absorbed, the heat is turned off, but the cooked rice continues to absorb the residual heat, steam, and moisture in the pot. This last stage, which might resemble what "let sit" means in English, is critical to produce the desired fluffy and chewy texture, and is very important to the rice-eating culture. So, *murasu* is a type of *musu* but is virtually reserved for rice-cooking as a unique and indispensable aspect of the process. Interestingly, what the verb *taku* refers to includes the process described by *murasu*, the meaning of the latter being inclusive of that of the former. Furthermore, *taku* is a creation verb, just like *wakasu* mentioned earlier, and collocates with a product of the cooking process, *gohan* 'cooked rice', rather than ingredients to be cooked, *kome* 'rice (grain)'. This is attested by the grammatical sequence *gohan-o taku* vs. the anomalous **kome-o taku*. We may reasonably infer that the culinary terms reserved for cooking rice (*taku* and *murasu*) and the two narrowly defined nouns to refer to rice (*gohan* and *kome*) cannot be fully understood without considering cultural concepts that underlie them and their embodiments which may trigger specific patterns of lexicalization within the linguistic system.

2.3.2 *Taste descriptions by metaphors*

In describing the tastes of food, be it positive or negative, language users are able to detail the experiences so richly even though there are only five basic taste adjectives: *amai* 'sweet', *suppai* 'sour', *nigai* 'bitter', *shoppai* 'salty', and *karai* 'spicy'. To this, general terms like *oishii* 'delicious', *umai* 'delicious', and *mazui* 'not tasty' as well as the somewhat specific *shibui* 'astringent' can be added, but this vocabulary list is still very short. Of diverse ways of ameliorating this limitation, people rely on non-literal speech by using a variety of forms of metaphor (see Sakaguchi, this volume). For instance, the basic word *aji* 'taste' can expand its descriptive scope by a large number of adjectivals whose literal senses belong to non-food domains:

8. The verb *niru*, in capturing the meaning of *taku*, has been analyzed as a process requiring the presence of liquid and submersion of ingredients. See Tsujimura (forthcoming) for details.

jōhin-na aji 'elegant taste', *marui aji* 'round taste', *akarui aji* 'bright taste', *shizuka-na aji* 'quiet taste', *shitsukoi aji* 'persistent taste', *yasashii aji* 'kind taste', *fukai aji* 'deep taste', *kōkyū-na aji* 'high-class taste', and *shiawase-na aji* 'happy taste'. These are just a few starters, and abundant samples are ubiquitously found regardless of rhetorical styles of communication, as attested by the wide range of examples discussed in Seto (2003b) and Seto et al. (2005). Linguistic discussions in these resources and elsewhere (e.g., Tsujimura, 2018b) also include extensive illustrations of taste and cooking terms as metaphors for areas other than food and cooking.

Among general discussions of metaphor in the language of food, synesthetic metaphor is particularly interesting, not only to detect the breadth and depth of the role that metaphor plays to enrich our food-related expressions, but to provide a testing ground for generalizations over our cognitive system. The term synesthesia has been discussed in medical, psychological, and neuroscience research, but Lehrer's (1978, p. 116) definition of the term is sufficient for its application to our discussion of metaphor: "using a word from one sensory domain to describe sensations in another." Expressions like *akarui koe* 'bright voice' (vision → sound), *atatakai iro* 'warm color' (touch → vision), and *amai nioi* 'sweet smell' (taste → smell) exemplify metaphorical transfers from one sense to another. Based on English adjectives, Williams (1976, p. 463) claims that metaphorical transfers are uni-directional, as is schematized in (9).

(9)

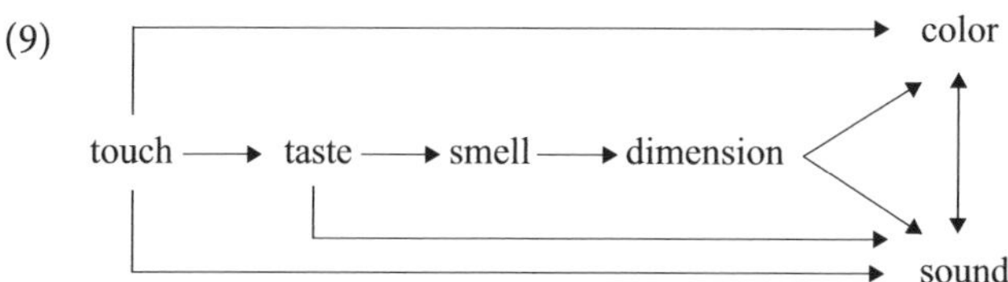

While Williams's generalization on the directionality of metaphorical transfers has several implications relevant to linguistic universality (especially of the regularity in semantic change), Japanese data provide a slew of counterexamples to Williams' claim, as shown by Seto's (2003a) compilation of samples that point to reverse directions. Limiting to cases that involve the taste sense, transfer types of sound → taste, vision (color & dimension) → taste, and smell → taste are exemplified in (10), taken from Seto's (2003a) list (p. 71).

(10) a. sound → taste
urusai/shizukana aji 'noisy/quiet taste', (kokoro-ni) hibiku aji 'taste that resonates the heart', aji-onchi 'taste-(tone)deafness', aji-no hāmonī 'taste harmony', aji-no sasayaki 'whispering of taste'

b. vision (color & dimension) → taste[9]
ō-aji [lit. large-taste] 'bland taste', bonyari-to shita aji 'vague taste', komayaka-na ajiwai 'delicate taste', aji-no rinkaku 'outline of taste', aji-no hirogari 'taste expanse', aji-no sō 'layer of tastes'

c. smell → taste
kōbashī amami 'aromatic sweetness', kusai aji 'smelly taste', tsun-to kuru aji 'pungent taste', namagusai aji 'fishy taste'

These extensive data suggest that synesthetic metaphors are widespread even in the narrow area of taste descriptions, and confirms that language users face no problems with the dearth of (direct) verbal expressions. At the same time, they make a significant contribution to ongoing research by presenting relevant resources to modify or sharpen the linguistic generalizations under debate.

2.4 Sociolinguistic context

2.4.1 *Regional variation*

Language variation has been examined through a number of sociolinguistic factors including region, gender, age, religion, social and economic class, and ethnicity. Each and together, these factors inform us greatly of the ways in which language can vary, and sometimes indirectly or implicitly of the nature of the society because how we speak and how we live are closely tied together. We think of regional dialects, for instance, as the most straightforward case of language variation, but behind several different pronunciations for the same word or distinct lexical froms to name the same thing, people have perceptions about "others" whose pronunciation and vocabulary selection are not the same as their own. For instance, it has been widely

9. For examples of the color → taste transfer, Komori (2003) lists phrases with *aji* 'taste' modified by color terms (e.g., white, red, yellow, and blue). The items in (i) are taken from his list (pp. 110–111).

(i) shiroi aji-no gohan 'white-tasting (cooked) rice', akai tōfu-wa akai aji-ga shita 'red tofu tasted red', tamago-no kusatta-yō-na kīroi aji 'yellow taste like spoiled egg', soramame-mitai-na aoi aji 'blue (green) taste like broad beans'

Additional examples like those in (ii)and (iii) are discussed by Yamaguchi (2003, pp.147–148).

(ii) ファーストフラッシュを好むのは日本人とドイツ人で若い、青い味はヨーロッパの人には好まれない。
"Only Germans and Japanese like 'first flush', and Europeans don't like blue taste."

(iii) 最近辛いラーメンに凝っているんで激辛ラーメンを頼む。真っ赤なラーメンだった。味の方は…やっぱり赤い味だった。
"I've been hooked to spicy ramen, so I ordered super-hot ramen. It was crimson red. The taste was, well, it tasted red as I had thought."

discussed that those who speak with the so-called "southern accent" or "southern drawl" in the US are stereotypically perceived as uneducated, poor, and politically conservative, but at the same time they are also perceived as friendly, polite, and welcoming.

One of the geographical boundaries for regional variation in Japanese is that of west vs. east. Shioda (2003) and Satake (2007) observe that the two regions have different names for the identical food items. Some of the contrasting expressions are presented in (11).

(11)	East	West	
a.	kake-udon	su-udon	'udon in broth (no topping)'
	pour-udon	bare/naked-udon	
b.	age-tama	ten-kasu	'bits of fried tempura batter'
	fried-ball	tem(pura)-dregs	
c.	niku-man	buta-man	'meat bun'
	meat-bun	pig-bun	

The udon dish named by the terms in (11a) is a bowl of udon noodles in a broth without any topping like tempura and *abura-age* 'deep-fried tofu'. The term *kake-udon* highlights the aspect of a broth poured over the noodles while *su-udon* focuses more on the simplicity of no additional ingredients. The prefix *su-* reminds us of the bareness that is imagined by other words with it like *su-ashi* 'bare foot' and *su-gao* 'face without make-up'. What is referred to by the names in (11b) is residual bits that have fallen apart from tempura batter, and are used as topping for soba and udon noodles (as *tanuki soba/udon*) or condiments of *yakisoba* 'stir-fried noodles' and other dishes. The eastern term *age-tama* is based on the shape of the bits looking like small balls, while the western *ten-kasu* more literally describes them as tempura residues that has no significant use. As for (11c) the meat filling in steamed buns is (ground) pork, *buta-niku* [pig-meat]. Either name obviously reflects the major ingredient, but the sole occurrence of *buta* without *niku* makes for a more direct connection to the animal source, pig, rather than the type of meat. The contrast in naming food items like those in (11) has led Satake (2007) to remark that the difference reveals that the western speakers use straightforward naming, virtually true to the fact, whereas the easterners rely more on euphemism, avoiding direct references.[10] Whether Satake's observation is widely shared or not,

10. Besides the paired examples in (11), Shioda (2003) gives additional contrasts between the two regions, E(ast)-W(est): *tonjiru* (E) vs. *butajiru* (W) 'pork soup' and *chāhan* (E) vs. *yakimeshi* 'fried rice'. Furthermore, *niru* (E) vs. *taku* (W) for 'cook (by boiling)' is a well-known regional difference, although they do not seem to have the kind of perceptual salience suggested for the words like (11).

perceptions about speakers based on the choice of the vocabulary like those in (11) seem to provide an insightful glimpse at people's attutide toward "others" and ultimately toward life in general.

2.4.2 *Language of social groups*

How people use language in a society can be seen as fitting the purpose of communication according to time and space. Socially defined subgroups within a society may develop and display specific covert ways of communicating, which can be referred to as "secret language." The main motivation for this is to devise a communication mode that can be shared exclusively by in-group members while keeping it unintelligible to out-group people; and it sometimes increases its effectiveness by using playfulness and humor. Its underlying sense of purpose is to build camaraderie into one form of social identity. A secret language may be formed by manipulating phonetic and phonological characteristics of words and phrases into a sequence of sounds and words that would not be recognizable by speakers of the language. Examples include the babibu language game and the jazz musician's language for Japanese, and the Pig Latin and the abi-dabi language game for English (Tsujimura, 2014). Secret languages can also be developed by resorting to semantic mechanisms like metaphor and euphemism. It has been reported that the language of food indeed shows several samples of this type of secret language.

The youth are remarkably ingenious coiners, as Yonekawa's (1998) numerous examples attest to. According to his survey, during the 1970s and 1980s, so-called *yasai-go* or *yasai-kotoba* 'vegetable words/language' was made fashionable by young people, many of whom seem to be college students. Vegetable names are used metaphorically, primarily based on their appearances, to describe the manner or content of (college) lectures as well as communication-related characteristics. For example, *hanashi-ga pīman* 'the content is green pepper' means that a lecture does not have much content, analogizing the hollow center of a green pepper to lack of important message in the lecture. Similarly, *kyūri* 'cucumber' is for "long" as in a lengthy lecture, *kyabetsu* 'cabbage' for "complicated," *chāhan* 'fried rice' for "messy," and *tomato* 'tomato' for "a lie." The last example, *tomato* for a lie, is based on the expression, *makka-na uso* [lit: crimson lie] 'downright lie', whereby redness intensifies the severeness of a lie. The *yasai-go* is not necessarily negative in meaning. Positive ones include *hanashi-ga serori* 'the lecture is celery' and *hanashi-ga paseri* 'the lecture is parsley', where there is a word play on *suji* 'stringiness' of celery based on the expression *suji-ga tooru* [lit: the strings go through] 'coherent'; and parsley is viewed as a delicate and stylish vegetable. It is readily imaginable that college students talk about class lectures, and especially when the nature of the discussion is negative, the use of playful and humorous language is tactful and offers an effective way of commiserating with fellow students. Furthermore, reference to every-day food items like those mentioned above seems to help maintain an equal level of social class. Although the neologism built around vegetable names did not survive for a long time, it is indicative that the language of food was immediately accessible to the generation of young college students to serve their specific purpose for communication. Note, too, that in constructing the communication medium, the members of the social group relied not only on visual metaphors but on some existing idioms like *suji-ga tooru* 'coherent, make sense' and *makka-na uso* 'downright lie', skillfully manipulating both literal and non-literal speech to arrive at the comical rhetoric.[11]

Members of particular professions are known to use a separate set of vocabulary (jargon) that is not familiar to lay people. The terminology at sushi restaurants is an example that is so well-known that the use of some vocabulary items is now extended beyond those in the profession. Terms like *shari* 'sushi rice', *agari* 'green tea', *gari* 'pickled ginger slices', and *hikari-mono* 'fish with silver-blue sheen' have frequently been mentioned by patrons at sushi restaurants in Japan. Other professions that make use of secret language discussed by Yonekawa (2007) include coffee shops, western-style restaurants, and vegetable stores. Behind these instances of naming often lies intriguing cultural history. Yonekawa's (2007) illustration of a secret language devised by Buddhist priests is especially telling. Yonekawa explains that Buddhist priests are disallowed to eat meat and fish and drink alcoholic beverages, but there were some who disobeyed the code. In their attempt to speak of the forbidden food and drink items, a special jargon was crafted. The jargon included *hannya-yu* [female.demon-hot.water] for sake, *awa-hannya* [bubbles-female.demon] for beer, *tōmegane* [eye glasses] for eggs, *maki-gami* [rolled-paper] for bonito flakes, and *kanagutsu* [horseshoe] for horse meat, to name a few. It is detected that semantic concepts of metaphor, euphemism, and metonym underlie many instances of the Buddhist priests' secret language, but at the same time, it seems undeniable that the association of alcohol with (the mask of) the female demon, while presumably humorous, reflects a culturally rooted view toward women.

3. Identity construct and sociocultural perception

Food is considered to have a strong association with our identity, as is suggested by the common cliché, "We are what we eat." Indeed, the relationship between food and identity construct has directly and indirectly appeared in a variety of scholarly

11. A secret language phenomenon motivated by solidarity and humor is further mentioned by Yonekawa (2007), who gives examples of jargons shared by prison inmates: *aka-renga* 'red brick' for salmon, *shiro-renga* 'white brick' for tofu, and *kasutera* 'sponge cake' for baked tofu. Visual metaphor and euphemism are linguistic concepts underlying the understanding of these words.

works across disciplinary fields (e.g., Bourdieu, 1984; Fischler, 1988; Lakoff, 2006; German, 2011). As we have discussed previously from the sociolinguistic perspective, the language of food can tell us much about how we think about food as well as how we view people and culture in the local and global setting. As many scholars have demonstrated, food writing like menus, recipes, and cookbooks is one of the many resources that provide an intriguing window through which the social and historical situation and local atmosphere at a given time can be ascertained. Cotter (1997), Lakoff (2006), and Higashiyotsuyanagi (2010), for instance, illustrate that menus and cooking instructions present informative portrayals of economic situations and women's roles that have transitioned from one time period to another across the continents.

Focusing on the relationship between food, language, and identity, Lakoff (2006) discusses that knowledge of food in different contexts of communication, both speaking and writing, can be regarded as markers of identity since "culinary preferences and sophistication contribute significantly to our sense of ourselves" (p. 165). For example, the extent to which foreign languages are used in menus, recipes, restaurant reviews, or even our daily conversation on food and cooking, consciously or unconsciously, serves as signs of specialized knowledge, educational background, or socio-economic class. Among Japanese restaurant menus in the US, those that list *toro* 'fatty tuna' (or even *chūtoro* 'medium fatty tuna' and *ōtoro* 'extra fatty tuna') are more likely to identify themselves with culinarily (and perhaps culturally) sophisticated clientele and probably belonging to a higher socio-economic class. If the English gloss is not added to these menu items, trained servers are expected to give patrons sufficient information verbally in lay terms. So, either through the written or spoken medium, restaurants create a full discourse of communication which becomes one aspect of a pleasurable experience that the proprieters intend to offer. As Lakoff (2006, p. 149) aptly states: "So we no longer go to restaurants just to eat – we go to *interact* with, to engage in *discourse* with, our food" [emphasis original]. The other side of the coin, however, is captured by the "continentalization" of food and culinary terms, filled with macaronic names (Zwicky & Zwicky, 1980). The afore-mentioned *pon-de-kokutō* and *pon-de-sutoroberī* (in Section 2.2), *aisu-yuzu-shitorasu-tī* [ice-yuzu-citrus-tea] and *kōhī-zerī-furapachīno* [coffee-jelly-frappuccino] at Starbucks Japan, and *teriyaki-chikin-fireo* [teriyaki-chicken-fillet-O] and *guran-kurabu-hausu* [grand-club-house] at McDonald's Japan probably demonstrate a murky line between loanwords and macaronic marketing strategies.

Gender is an important identity construct rigorously examined in a wide spectrum of fields. It constitutes a critical concept that opens an avenue to multiple topics that help reveal the nature of our society and culture. Language can index gender, as it has been well studied for languages including Japanese, but so, too, can specific food items. In much of the literature on gender and food, it has been discussed that the association of steak and beer with men, while salad and chocolate with women, instantiates stereotypical indexing of a given food item with a specific gender (e.g., Counihan, 2012; Cowan, 1991; Holtzman, 2018; Lupton, 1996; Sobal, 2005; Wilk & Hintulian, 2005). Similarly in cooking methods, preparing raw food or with direct heat like grilling is viewed as men's liking while women prefer to have food thoroughly cooked, like well-done steak. In advertising, gender indexing is effectively used as a practical strategy that target consumers' perceptions of genderized artifacts with a strong sense of femininity or masculinity. This is widely attested in advertisements including the Weight Watchers' advertisement introducing a diet program for men (such as a small piece of steak) with the caption, "Eat like a man. Not like a rabbit," and Arby's TV commercials where "We have the meats" is consistently announced by a man in a deep voice. These divisions have been interpreted to originate from gender roles and ideological expectations in the society. The dichotomy of men's role as bread winners and women's role as home makers, for instance, underlies and corelates with many genderized patterns in foodways across cultures.

There are ample examples of genderization of food in Japan. As is with the western culture, gendering meat with men and vegetables with women is not uncommon, as suggested by the coinage of *niku-shoku joshi* (肉食女子) 'meat-eating females' and *sōshoku-danshi* (草食男子) 'grass-eating (or herbivore) males' to cynically refer to males and females who break gender norms. However, the association of sweets with females seems to be more prevalent and deep-rooted in the Japanese culture. As Holtzman (2018) discusses, gender identity with sweets finds its deep roots in the cultural stereotypical belief in Japan that sweets are only for women and children while alcoholic beverages are for men; and preferences for (and tolerance to) sweets and alcohol are characterized respectively as *amatō* [lit. sweet-party] and *karatō* [lit. spicy-party], each of which is linked to femininity and masculinity. In Meiji Seika's advertisements for chocolate in Japan during the 1960s-1970s, sweetness and creaminess characterize female liking, whereas a bitter and stimulating taste with pure ingredients typifies male preferences. Some of the representative advertising catch phrases are contrastively given in (12)–(13).

(12) chocolate ads catering toward women
  a. redī-no chokorēto
     'chocolate for ladies'
  b. miruku-ga tappuri
     'lots of milk [=cream]'
  c. onnanoko-dake-no chokorēto
     'chocolate only for girls'

(13) chocolate ads catering toward men
  a. Nigamibashitta atarashii aji-desu.
     'It's a new manly taste.'
  b. junsui-no choko
     'pure chocolate'
  c. dansēmuki-no ii chocorēto
     'good chocolate for men'
  d. kuro isshoku-de tsutsumikonda chokorēto
     'chocolate wrapped only in black'
  e. amasa-o koroshita otoko-no chokorēto
     'chocolate for men with killed [=reduced, less] sweetness'

The language used in these advertising phrases clearly embodies the underlying concepts surrounding gendered food and taste. It makes sense to observe that the apparent feminine-masculine dichotomy is further enhanced by the red-or-black color coding of the wrapping, another form of gender indexing. Accompanying the products marketed under (12) is red wrapping while black packaging is used with the phrases in (13).

As the different verbal strategies in (12)–(13) and many more examples like them suggest, the language in advertising is intended to influence the consumers by the images that it projects about products. Conversely, the patterns of the language used to that end have much to inform us of cultural concepts and social norms by which we live in a community of speakers. In regard to alcoholic beverages gendered with males in many cultures including Japan, we may expect that gender identity and masculinity are well represented by the names of alcoholic drinks. Cherici and Tsujimura (2019) compared the names of craft beers produced in Italy, Japan, and California to investigate the link. In all regions, beer names consistently and most frequently include relevant information about the beer itself, such as the type (e.g., ale, porter, stout), color, taste, and ingredients. On the other hand, language-specific and culture-specific naming patterns are notable to make distinctions among the three regions. In Italian, beer names often refer to (female) gender and sex: typical names include female proper names and titles (e.g., *Nora*, *Contessa* 'countess') and descriptors for women (e.g., *Bastarda* 'bitch'). It is of note that *birra* 'beer' is a grammatically feminine noun, and the frequent mentioning of female gender and sexuality may be attributed to it. In stark contrast, Japanese beer names refer to nature: *Shizuku* 'dew', *Ryūsui* 'stream', *Shinsetsu* 'deep snow', and *Buna-no mori* 'beech forest'. Naming beers after the existence in nature is in fact consistent with Hiraga's (2018) study on sake names. Finally, California beer names frequently use word play, resulting in numerous comical and creative labels (e.g., *Dark of the Covenant, Land Hopportunity, For the Helles of it, Californipa*).

These names are characterized as "dudeification" presenting the image that the brewers and their clientele form an in-group of "dudes."[12] Cherici and Tsujimura's study suggests that while beer is typicaly gendered with males and masculinity is an associated image, its commercial naming is not uniform across cultures but instead embodys culture-specific conceptualizations of beer and beer-drinking that reflect cultural attitudes in garnering attention of potential clientele.

4. Conclusion

This chapter has demonstrated the extent to which cognitive, social, and cultural information is imbued in the language of food as it is manifested in a variety of media (e.g., recipes, advertisements, food names) and more broadly in communication about foodways. The language of food can benefit from linguistic analysis for a deeper understanding of how people think of food and how they verbally express their experience with food. In turn, the language of food provides abundant data resources as testing grounds for a wide gamut of research investigations that extend over various disciplinary and interdisciplinary areas. In these avenues of research exploration, both micro- and macro-level examinations, individually and collectively, lead us to updated information about how food and language have revolved around history, culture, and society. Research results have plentifully revealed that the language of food is as powerful as food itself. It is hoped that linguistic concepts and analytical tools continue to be instrumental and methodological guides for broader and deeper explorations of how language, food, and culture interact and feed each other.

Acknowledgements

The materials presented and discussed in this chapter resulted from research and teaching on the language of food in which I have been engaged for the past decade. The courses that I offered on the topic have particularly been a strong driving force for a broad range of inquiry. In this context, I am indebted to the undergraduate students who took the E350 and E320 courses and whose demonstrated curiousity furthered my research. I thank Professor Kiyoko Toratani for her tireless efforts in making this volume into a very valuable and fine scholarly contribution.

12. Cherici and Tsujimura (2019) use the terms "sexualization" and "beautification" to characterize the naming patterns of Italian and Japanese, respectively.

References

Akita, K. (2009). A grammar of sound-symbolic words in Japanese: Theoretical approaches to iconic and lexical properties of mimetics. (Unpublished doctoral dissertation). Kobe University, Kobe, Japan.

Bourdieu, P. (1984). *Distinction: A social critique of the judgment of taste*. Translated by R. Nice. Cambridge, MA: Harvard University Press.

Cherici, A. & Tsujimura, N. (January, 2019). Genderization, beautification, or dudeification? Different approaches to beer naming. Paper presened at the Annual Conference of the American Name Society, New York City, New York.

Cotter, C. (1977). Claiming a piece of the pie: How the language of recipes defines community. In A. L. Bower (Ed.), *Recipes for reading: Community cookbooks, stories histories* (pp. 51–71). Amherst: University of Massachusetts Press.

Counihan, C. (2012). Gendering food. In J. M. Pilcher (Ed.), *The Oxford handbook of food history* (pp. 99–116). Oxford: Oxford University Press.

Cowan, J. (1991). Going out for coffee? Contesting the grounds of gendered pleasures in everyday sociality. In P. Loizos & E. Papastaksiarchis (Eds.), *Contested identities: Gender and kinship in modern Greece* (pp. 180–202). Princeton: Princeton University Press. https://doi.org/10.1515/9781400884384-010

Fischler, C. (1988). Food, self and identity. *Social Science Information*, *27*(2), 275–292. https://doi.org/10.1177/053901888027002005

German, K. (2011). Memory, identity, and resistance: Recipes from the women in Theresienstadt. In J. M. Cramer, C. P. Greene, & L. M. Walters (Eds.), *Food as communication: Communication as food* (pp. 137–154). New York: Peter Lang.

Hamano, S. (1998). *The sound-symbolic system of Japanese*. Tokyo: Kurosio/CSLI.

Haspelmath, M. (2009). Lexical borrowing: Concepts and issues. In M. Haspelmath & U. Tadmor (Eds.), *Loanwords in the world's languages: A comparative handbook* (pp. 35–54). Berlin: Mouton de Gruyter. https://doi.org/10.1515/9783110218442.35

Hayakawa, F. (2003a). Tabemono no tekusuchā to gengohyōgen 1 [Food texture and language expression 1]. *Shokuseikatsu*, *97*(9), 40–45.

Hayakawa, F. (2003b). Tabemono no tekusuchā to gengohyōgen 2 [Food texture and language expression 2]. *Shokuseikatsu*, *97*(10), 38–42.

Hayakawa, F. (2004a). *Shokugo no hitotoki* [A restful moment after meal]. Tokyo: Mainichi Shinbunsha.

Hayakawa, F. (2004b). Shokukankaku no giongo/gitaigo [Mimetics of food texture]. *Ashita no Shokuhin Sangyō*, *9*, 9–13.

Hayakawa, F. (2006). *Taberu nihongo* [Japanese for eating].

Hayakawa, F., Hatae, K., & Shimada, J. (2000). Shokukankaku no giongo/gitaigo no tokuchōzuke [Characterization of mimetics for food texture]. *Nihon Shokuhin Kagaku Kōgaku Kaishi*, *47*, 197–207. https://doi.org/10.3136/nskkk.47.197

Higashiyotsuyanagi, S. (2010). The history of domestic cookbooks in modern Japan. In E. C. Rath, & S. Assmann, (Eds.), *Japanese foodways, past and present* (pp. 129–144). Champaign: University of Illinois Press.

Hinton, L., Nichols, J., & Ohala, J. (1994). Introduction: Sound-symbolic processes. In L. Hinton, J. Nichols, & J. Ohola (Eds.), *Sound Symbolism* (pp. 1–12). Cambridge: Cambridge University Press.

Hiraga, M. (May, 2018). What's in a name?: The case of Japanese *sake*. Paper presented at the Conference on the Language of Japanese Food, York University, Toronto, Canada.
Holtzman, J. (2018). The weakness of sweetness: Masculinity and confectionary in Japan. *Food, Culture & Society*, *21*(3), 280–295. https://doi.org/10.1080/15528014.2018.1451037
Irwin, M. (2011). *Loanwords in Japanese*. Amsterdam: John Benjamins. https://doi.org/10.1075/slcs.125
Jurafsky, D. (2014). *The language of food: A linguist reads the menu*. New York: W. W. Norton & Company.
Kita, S. (1997). Two-dimensional semantic analysis of Japanese mimetics. *Linguistics*, *35*, 379–415. https://doi.org/10.1515/ling.1997.35.2.379
Klink, R. R. (2000). Creating brand names with meaning: The use of sound symbolism. *Marketing Letters*, *11*(1), 5–20. https://doi.org/10.1023/A:1008184423824
Klink, R. R. (2001). Creating meaningful new brand names: A study of semantics and sound symbolism. *Journal of Marketing: Theory and Practice*, *9*, 27–34.
Komori, M. (2003). Motto gokan-de ajiwau [Savor with five senses]. In K. Seto (Ed.), *Kotoba-wa aji-o koeru* [Words exceed taste] (pp. 79–119). Tokyo: Kaimeisha.
Lakoff, R. (2006). Identity a la carte: You are what you eat. In A. de Fina, D. Schiffrin, & M. Bamberg (Eds.), *Discourse and identity* (pp. 142–165). Cambridge: Cambridge University Press. https://doi.org/10.1017/CBO9780511584459.008
Lehrer, A. (1969). Semantic cuisine. *Journal of Linguistics*, *5*, 39–56. https://doi.org/10.1017/S0022226700002048
Lehrer, A. (1972). Cooking vocabularies and the culinary triangle of Lévi-Strauss. *Anthropological Linguistics*, 155–71.
Lehrer, A. (1978). Structures of the lexicon and transfer of meaning. *Lingua*, *45*, 95–123. https://doi.org/10.1016/0024-3841(78)90001-3
Levin, B. (1993). *English verb classes and alternations: A preliminary investigation*. Chicago: The University of Chicago Press.
Lupton, D. (1996). *Food, the body and the self*. London: Sage Publications.
Maurer, D., Pathman, T., & Mondloch, C. J. (2006). The shape of boubas: Sound–shape correspondences in toddlers and adults. *Developmental Science*, *9*, 316–322. https://doi.org/10.1111/j.1467-7687.2006.00495.x
Mester, R. A., & Ito, J. (1989). Feature predictability and underspecification: Palatal prosody in Japanese mimetics. *Language*, *65*, 258–293. https://doi.org/10.2307/415333
Muto, A. (2003). Aji-kotoba-no giongo, gitaigo – Shoku-no onomatope [Taste-describing phonomimes and phenomimes – Mimetics on food]. In K. Seto, (Ed.), *Kotoba-wa aji-o koeru* [Words exceed taste] (pp. 241–300). Tokyo: Kaimeisha.
Ngo, M. K., Misra, R., & Spence, C. (2011). Assessing the shapes and speech sounds that people associate with chocolate samples varying in cocoa content. *Food Quality and Preference*, *22*, 567–572. https://doi.org/10.1016/j.foodqual.2011.03.009
Ohala, J. (1994). An ethological perspective on common cross-language utilization of F_0 of voice. *Phonetica*, *41*, 1–16. https://doi.org/10.1159/000261706
Ohashi, M. (2015). *Sizzle word: Shizuru wādo no genzai* [Sizzle word today]. Tokyo: B.M.F.T.
Satake, H. (2007). "Taku" to "niru" – Ikinokoru shoku-no hyōgen ["Taku" and "niru" – Surviving food expression]. *Vesta*, *65*, 16–19.
Seto, K. (2003a). Gokan-de ajiwau [Tasting with five senses]. In K. Seto (Ed.), *Kotoba-wa aji-o koeru* [Words exceed taste] (pp. 62–78). Tokyo: Kaimeisha.
Seto, K. (Ed.). (2003b). *Kotoba-wa aji-o koeru* [Words exceed taste]. Tokyo: Kaimeisha.

Seto, K., Yamamoto, T., Kusumi, T., Sawai, S., Tsujimoto, T., Yamaguchi, H., & Koyama, S. (2005). *Ajikotoba-no sekai* [The world of taste vocabulary]. Tokyo: Kaimeisha.

Shioda, T. (2003). Shoku-kanren-yōgo-o meguru goiteki-na "yure" [Variation in the food-related vocabulary]. *Hōsō Kenkyū to Chōsa, 10*, 32–53.

Smith, J. (2006). Loan phonology is not all perception: Evidence from Japanese loan doublets. *Japanese/Korean Linguistics, 14*, 63–74.

Sobal, J. (2005). Men, meat, and marriage: Models of masculinity. *Food and Foodways, 13*(1), 135–158. https://doi.org/10.1080/07409710590915409

Tamori, I., & Scourup, L. (1999). *Onomatope: Keitai to imi* [Onomatopoeia: Morphology and semantics]. Tokyo: Kurosio.

Tsujimura, N. (2014). *An introduction to Japanese linguistics*, 3rd edition. Oxford: Wiley Blackwell.

Tsujimura, N. (2018a). Recipe names in Japanese cookbooks as a gateway to interpersonal communication. *Names: A Journal of Onomastics, 66*(4), 233–245. https://doi.org/10.1080/00277738.2018.1452941

Tsujimura, N. (2018b). From tasty adjective to succulent metaphor: What the language of food reveals. *Japanese/Korean Linguistics, 25*, 309–326.

Tsujimura, N. (forthcoming). Cooking verbs and the cultural conceptualization of cooking processes in Japanese. In M. Reif and F. Polzenhagen (Eds.), *Cultural linguistics, ideologies and critical discourse studies*. Amsterdam: John Benjamins.

Wilk, R., & Hintulian, P. (2005). Cooking on their own: Cuisines of manly men. *Food and Foodways, 13*(1), 159–168. https://doi.org/10.1080/07409710590915418

Williams, J. (1976). Synaesthetic adjectives: A possible law of semantic change. *Language, 52*, 461–478. https://doi.org/10.2307/412571

Yamaguchi, H. (2003). Sarani gokan-de ajiwau [Savor with five senses]. In K. Seto (Ed.), *Kotoba-wa aji-o koeru* [Words exceed taste] (pp. 120–153). Tokyo: Kaimeisha.

Yonekawa, A. (1998). *Wakamonogo-o kagaku-suru* [A scientific study of youth language]. Tokyo: Meiji Shoin.

Yonekawa, A. (2007). Zokugo, ingo-wa naze umaretaka [Why was slang/secret language created]. *Vesta, 65*, 25–27.

Yorkson, E., & Menon, G. (2004). A sound idea: Phonetic effects of brand names on consumer judgments. *Journal of Consumer Research, 31*, 43–51. https://doi.org/10.1086/383422

Zwicky, A., & Zwicky, A. (1980). America's national dish: The style of restaurant menus. *American Speech, 55*, 87–92. https://doi.org/10.2307/3050498

SECTION II

Mimetics and sound-symbolism in food names and food descriptions

CHAPTER 2

Analysis of the use of Japanese mimetics in the eating and imagined eating of rice crackers

Ryoko Uno[1], Fumiyuki Kobayashi[2], Kazuko Shinohara[1] and Sachiko Odake[2]
[1]Tokyo University of Agriculture and Technology / [2]Nippon Veterinary and Life Science University

This chapter explores how Japanese mimetics are used to verbally express the texture of rice crackers in real and imagined cases. Two experiments were conducted to test whether the use of mimetics varies when eating rice crackers as opposed to merely imagining eating rice crackers. The analysis of the mimetics used to express the physically perceived texture and the imagined texture of the rice crackers shows that these two situations may have different prototypes of rice crackers. This study suggests that the degree of iconicity of the same mimetics can vary according to the contexts in which they are used.

Keywords: cognitive linguistics, iconicity, prototype, food texture, cultural knowledge

1. Introduction

Food is essential for human beings not only for taking in nutrition but also for having pleasure and feeling a sense of well-being. However, the importance of food is not limited to our health and well-being: how we express our experience of eating food provides insights for the study of language. This chapter deals with the experience of eating food and its relationship to some important aspects of language.

This study investigates how Japanese sound-symbolic words are used to express the experience of eating rice crackers (*senbei* in Japanese), a traditional and very popular Japanese snack. We focus on the texture of rice crackers to investigate the sound-symbolic words used for different textures of hardness. The Japanese language has a large inventory of sound-symbolic words called "mimetics," also known as "ideophones" or "expressives" (Childs, 1994; Dingemanse, 2011, 2012;

https://doi.org/10.1075/celcr.25.02uno

Kakei, Tamori & Schourup, 1996; Hamano, 1998; Akita, 2009, 2010, 2012, 2013; Tsujimura, this volume). The contexts in which mimetic words are used range from everyday conversations among family or friends to more serious and formal situations such as heated debates in the Diet (Hirata, Nakamura, Komatsu & Akita, 2015). In this study, we explore the relationship between Japanese mimetic words and various food textures, especially the hardness, of rice crackers. Which mimetic word tends to be used for harder rice crackers? What is the relationship between specific mimetic words and the hardness of the prototypical rice crackers? We aim to answer these questions and explore the functions of mimetic words in communication and introspection.

In this chapter, we report two experiments that compare two different situations: one wherein people are actually eating a piece of rice cracker and another wherein they are imagining eating a piece of rice cracker. We aim to demonstrate that these two situations influence the kinds of mimetic words people choose for expressing the textures of different rice crackers. Our results show that the mimetic words referring to the prototypical rice crackers vary across the two situations.

This chapter is structured as follows: Section 2 provides background information on Japanese rice crackers and mimetics, relevant previous studies, and our hypothesis to be tested. Section 3, the main part of the current chapter, presents our two experiments. Finally, Section 4 provides the general discussions and concluding remarks with suggestions for future studies.

2. Background

2.1 Japanese rice crackers

Japanese rice crackers enjoy a special status among Japanese snacks not only because they have a long history that may go back several hundred years (Soka City Website, 2014) but also because they are still loved by many Japanese people, from children to the elderly (Shokuhin Ryūtsū Jōhō Center, 2000; Takahashi et al., 2006). They are made from rice powder, which is kneaded into dough, shaped, and roasted until it is hard. Many different kinds of rice crackers are produced and sold in Japan, and they vary in taste, texture, size, shape, and flavor. Typical rice crackers have a salty, soy sauce flavor and are very crispy. Some are much harder and make a crunching sound when you bite into them. Rice crackers come in various shapes, but typical ones are flat and round and usually about five to ten centimeters in diameter (see Figure 1).

Figure 1. Typical Japanese rice crackers[1]

2.2 Mimetics and Iconicity

This study explores the relationship between a Japanese word class called "mimetics" and different textures of rice crackers. Mimetics constitute a lexical class of words that mimic sounds, voices, or other perceptual properties. They are thus considered to reflect iconicity – that is, a relationship of resemblance or similarity between the two aspects of a sign: its form and its meaning (Haiman, 1983, 1985a, 1985b). In many languages, mimetics form only a peripheral lexical group. However, this is not the case in Japanese, which has a large inventory of mimetic words relative to other languages. The largest mimetic dictionary published in Japanese has 4,500 entries (Ono, 2007). Because mimetics can vividly express different kinds of perceptual properties, Japanese people often use them for describing the texture of food (Takahashi et al., 2006; Takahashi, Itou, Yamamura, Arai & Yamada, 2009). This is advantageous for exploring the relationship between food texture and language, as we can obtain many different linguistic expressions for describing the texture of rice crackers.

Mimetic words often appear on the packages of snacks and crackers sold in Japan.[2] Our previous study (Funakubo, Kobayashi, Uno, Shinohara, & Odake, 2016) demonstrated that mimetic words printed on the packages of snacks influence people's perceptions of food texture. We contrasted two conditions: seeing the mimetic word before eating the sample snack and seeing the mimetic word

1. This image is being reproduced with the permission of the copyright holder: https://www.photo-ac.com/.

2. Our previous study revealed that many mimetic words, such as *karit-to* and *sakut-to*, are printed on the packages of snacks. See also Kumagai et al. (this volume).

after eating the sample snack. We found that people's judgements of the texture of a snack were more strongly influenced when they saw a mimetic word before eating the snack. That is, the influence of the mimetic word was stronger when it was presented before eating the snack than when it was presented after eating the snack. This shows that mimetic words influence people's judgements of the texture of snacks. It further shows that Japanese speakers are sensitive to sound-symbolic words to the extent that their judgments of the texture of foods can be influenced by such words. From this finding, we inferred that Japanese speakers may provide us with fine-grained data about mimetics. This is another advantage of focusing on mimetics in this study.

Japanese mimetics are usually classified into three main subtypes: phonomimes, phenomimes, and psychomimes (Akita, 2010, 2013). Phonomimes imitate voices or sounds by means of linguistic sounds, phenomimes synesthetically imitate visual, textural, or other non-auditory perceptions,[3] and psychomimes imitate bodily or emotional feelings that come from inside the body or mind rather than from the external world. For example, "cock-a-doodle-do" in English and *gachagacha* (clatter) in Japanese are phonomimes (they imitate a voice or sound), "zigzag" in English and *fuwafuwa* (airy and soft) in Japanese are phenomimes (they make synesthetic associations), and the Japanese word *kuyokuyo* (worrying and regretting) is a psychomime (it imitates an internal mental state).

Mimetic words for food textures are phenomimes because textures do not provide any auditory stimuli but simply give us a tactile sensation. In some cases, textures can also be expressed by mimetic words that typically belong to the subtype of phonomimes because eating food can sometimes simultaneously cause a sound and a perception of texture. For example, a rice cracker may feel *paripari*, in which case the word *paripari* could be interpreted as a phonomime because eating a rice cracker produces a sound; however, at the same time, the word *paripari* could also be interpreted as a phenomime, as it could refer to the texture of the rice cracker. In such a case, it may be possible that the same mimetic word is used as a phonomime and a phenomime at the same time, and the perception of sound and the perception of texture occur inseparably. In this study, we do not look at the auditory aspects of such mimetic words but treat them as phenomimes that express food texture.

Researchers agree that some mimetics may be more iconic than others. Akita (2013) predicted that there may be a correlation between the degree of lexical

3. Synesthetic association is a kind of cross-modal mapping. It links one perceptual modality, such as audition, with another modality, such as vision. Synesthetic association has been studied in linguistics (Shinohara & Nakayama, 2011; Williams, 1976; Yu, 2003) and in cognitive science and neuroscience (Ramachandran & Hubbard, 2001; Sakamoto & Watanabe, 2016; Simne, Cuskley & Kirby, 2010; Spence, 2015; Zampini & Spence, 2004).

iconicity and the degree of grammaticalization of lexical items. Among the three subtypes of mimetics mentioned above, phonomimes are considered to be the most iconic, whereas psychomimes are considered to be the least iconic (Akita, 2009, 2013); phenomimes come in the middle. This hypothesis is called the lexical iconicity hierarchy (Akita, 2009, 2013). Animal-voice mimetics and innovative (ad hoc) mimetics may be even higher in iconicity than voice phonomimes and noise phonomimes (Akita, 2013). Building upon this lexical iconicity hierarchy hypothesis, the present study demonstrates that the same mimetic word can reveal different degrees of iconicity without changing its form. This is observed in two different situations – eating rice crackers and merely imagining eating rice crackers – in our experiments.

2.3 Previous research on food and language

A substantial body of previous research on the relationship between linguistic expressions and the perception of food textures can be found in fields other than linguistics, such as cognitive science, psychology, and food science (Favalli, Skov, Spence & Byrne, 2013; Funakubo et al., 2016; Hayakawa et al., 2013; Sakamoto & Watanabe, 2016). However, quantitative linguistic studies dealing with food textures are less abundant. This tendency seems even clearer concerning experimental research in which human participants are asked to actually eat sample food.[4] Thus, most previous studies on this topic, especially those using real food with a certain degree of hardness, have been conducted in disciplines outside of linguistics (with a notable exception of Majid et al., (2018)).

Gallace, Boschin, and Spence (2011) presented an interesting study on this topic. They explore the relationship between 12 different kinds of food and the nonce words *takete*/*malma* and *bouba*/*kiki*. They report that potato chips and cranberry sauce are more like *takete* than brie cheese. Mint chocolate was rated as more like *kiki* than regular chocolate.

Similar studies focusing on Japanese mimetic words have also been conducted by scholars outside of linguistics. For example, Sakamoto and Watanabe (2016) used common drinks, such as Coca-Cola and milk, and uncommon drinks, such as mixtures of common drinks and soy sauce or water, to observe the way people coin new mimetics to express taste and texture. Another relevant study was conducted by Ishibashi, Fukazawa, and Miyata (2015), who examined sizzle words including mimetics to express the texture of rice crackers from the perspective of marketing. The linguistic implications of these studies will not be discussed here because their goals differ from the goal of our current study.

4. One possible reason for this scarcity may be ethical restrictions because asking to eat hard food could impose some physical risks on participants.

Most linguists cannot perform such experiments unless they have appropriate equipment in their laboratories and access to participants. For most linguists to perform such experiments, collaboration is usually needed with researchers in other fields, such as food engineering. For this reason, two cognitive linguists and two food engineers came together to collaborate on this study. This collaboration makes this study original, as it may be a rare case in which the expertise of food engineering specialists and the insights of cognitive linguists are combined into a single investigation.

2.4 Hypothesis and goals of the study

Actually eating something and merely imagining eating something are very different kinds of experiences. For example, when we actually eat rice crackers and try to describe their texture, we focus on our perceptual experiences using introspection. However, when we merely imagine eating rice crackers, we may not explore our perceptual experiences in our imagination so attentively, as we are not experiencing an actual perception and have no concrete target of perceptual exploration. Therefore, we hypothesize that in such cases, people resort to using conventionalized expressions that safely fit their pre-established concepts of eating rice crackers. Our prediction is that these two cases – that is, when people are actually eating rice crackers and when they are merely imagining eating rice crackers – will lead to different uses of mimetics.

To test this hypothesis, we conducted two experiments designed to distinguish between the uses of mimetics for (1) physical experiences of eating rice crackers and (2) merely imagining eating rice crackers. Although some previous studies have dealt with Japanese mimetic words used for textures (Hayakawa et al., 2013), no study has been conducted on mimetic words used in these two different situations: in which people are actually eating a food as opposed to merely imagining eating a food. To the best of our knowledge, this study is the first to test such a case.

3. Experiments

To test our hypothesis, we conducted two experiments, both of which test how people would describe their perceptions of the texture of rice crackers. To this end, Experiment 1 asked participants to taste some samples of rice crackers and verbally describe their texture, whereas Experiment 2 asked participants to imagine tasting a rice cracker and verbally describe the texture they imagine it to have. In addition to these two experiments, a preliminary survey was conducted to assess the familiarity of the participants with several different types of rice crackers. The preliminary survey will be reported in Section 3.1, the two experiments will be presented in Sections 3.2 and 3.3, respectively, and a summary discussion will be given in Section 3.4.

3.1 Preliminary survey: Familiarity with different types of rice crackers

3.1.1 *Method*

Many types of rice crackers are sold and consumed in Japan. Among them, seven popular brands were selected for the present study. A preliminary survey was conducted to check the familiarity of the participants with the different brands because it was important to determine which type of rice cracker was the prototypical one (familiarity is regarded as one of the main criteria of prototypicality). Twenty native Japanese speakers living in Tokyo (20–22 years old) participated in the preliminary survey. They were presented with photographs of seven types of rice crackers and photographs of their packages with brand names on them (see Figure 2).

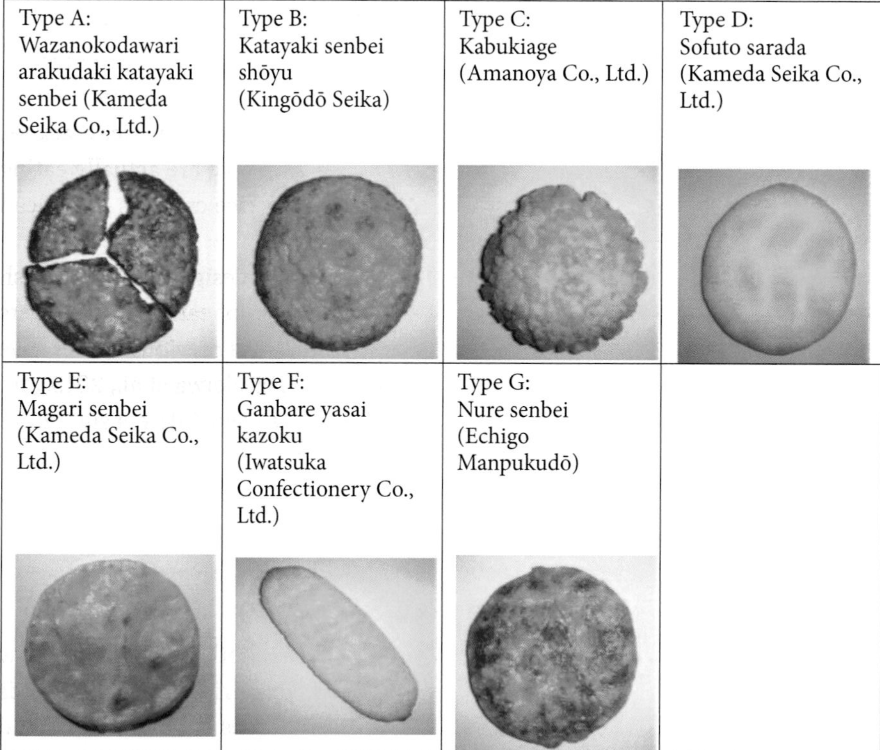

Type A:
Wazanokodawari arakudaki katayaki senbei (Kameda Seika Co., Ltd.)
Type B:
Katayaki senbei shōyu (Kingōdō Seika)
Type C:
Kabukiage (Amanoya Co., Ltd.)
Type D:
Sofuto sarada (Kameda Seika Co., Ltd.)
Type E:
Magari senbei (Kameda Seika Co., Ltd.)
Type F:
Ganbare yasai kazoku (Iwatsuka Confectionery Co., Ltd.)
Type G:
Nure senbei (Echigo Manpukudō)

Figure 2. The seven types of rice crackers used in this study (The phrases under the types are the brand names; parentheses indicate the names of the food companies.)[5]

5. All photos are taken by the fourth author of this chapter.

The participants performed two tasks on a written questionnaire. The first task was to describe how well they know each brand of rice cracker by choosing one of four options: "know very well," "know," "don't know well," or "don't know at all." The second task was to describe how frequently they eat each brand of rice cracker by choosing one of four options: "very often," "often," "not often," or "never."

3.1.2 *Results*

The results for the first task are shown in Table 1. The first and second rows present positive responses ("know very well" and "know"), whereas the third and fourth rows show negative responses ("don't know well" and "don't know at all"). Boldface indicates relatively high percentages for the positive responses. As Table 1 clearly shows, Types C and D had remarkably high percentages for the response indicating the highest familiarity (85%). Type E also had relatively high percentages for the highest (45%) and second highest familiarity (40%). For Type E, the positive responses accounted for 80%. Conversely, Types C, D, and E had very low percentages for the negative responses (0%–10%).

Table 1. Familiarity (percentage)

Cracker types	A	B	C	D	E	F	G
Know very well	20.0	15.0	**85.0**	**85.0**	**45.0**	5.0	30.0
Know	15.0	15.0	5.0	15.0	**40.0**	35.0	25.0
Don't know well	35.0	30.0	5.0	0.0	5.0	10.0	10.0
Don't know at all	30.0	40.0	5.0	0.0	10.0	50.0	35.0

The tendency becomes clear when the two positive responses ("know very well" and "know") and the two negative responses ("don't know well" and "don't know at all") are combined (see Figure 3). The levels of familiarity significantly varied among the seven types of rice crackers (χ^2 (6) = 42.871, $p < 0.01$, Cramer's $V = 0.553$). A residual analysis showed that Types C, D, and E were significantly more familiar to the participants, whereas Types A, B, and F were significantly less familiar.

In the second task, we asked participants about their frequency of eating each type of rice cracker. Table 2 shows the results. The first and second rows show positive responses ("very often" and "often"), whereas the third and fourth rows show negative responses ("not often" and "never"). Boldface indicates relatively high percentages for the positive responses. The results showed that Types C, D, and E had high percentages for the positive responses compared with the other types of rice crackers.

The tendency, again, becomes clear when the two positive responses ("very often" and "often") and two negative responses ("not often" and "never") are combined

Table 2. Frequency of eating (percentage)

Cracker types	A	B	C	D	E	F	G
Very Often	15.0	0.0	**30.0**	25.0	10.0	0.0	0.0
Often	0.0	0.0	**30.0**	**45.0**	**35.0**	0.0	10.0
Not often	15.0	30.0	15.0	20.0	30.0	0.0	10.0
Never	70.0	70.0	25.0	10.0	25.0	100.0	80.0

(see Figure 4). The frequency of eating varied among the seven types of rice crackers (χ^2 (6) = 50.330, $p < 0.01$, Cramer's V = 0.600). A residual analysis showed that Types C and D were eaten significantly more frequently, whereas Types B, F, and G were eaten significantly less frequently.

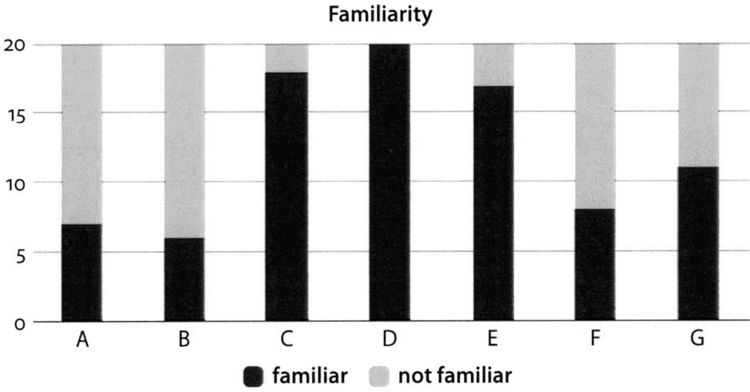

Figure 3. Familiarity of the rice crackers (The vertical axis shows the number of participants for each response.)

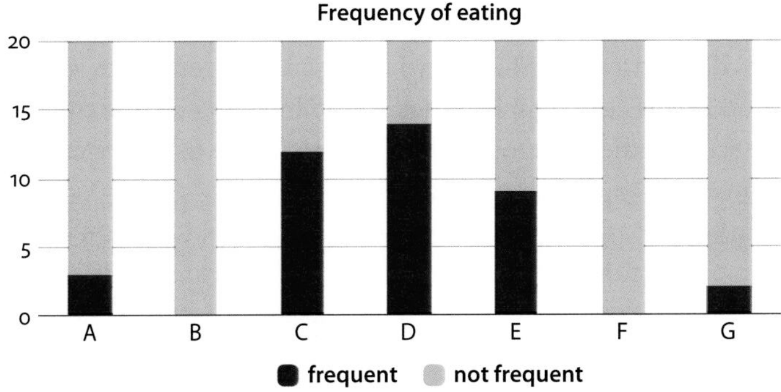

Figure 4. Frequency of eating each type of rice cracker (The vertical axis shows the number of participants for each response.)

Overall, our preliminary survey showed that the seven types of rice crackers can be divided into three classes based on familiarity and frequency of eating. Types C, D, and E form a class that includes familiar and frequently eaten rice crackers. Types A and B form a class that includes not-so-familiar and not-so-frequently eaten rice crackers. Types F and G form a class that includes not-familiar and not-frequently eaten rice crackers.

An important note concerning the preliminary survey is in order. Applying the notion of a "prototype," which means a typical, central, and representative exemplar of a category (Lakoff, 1987; Tayler, 1989), we can consider Types C, D, and E as prototypical rice crackers for Japanese speakers, especially among young people. Prototypicality has been one of the most frequently argued concepts in Cognitive Linguistics since its early history. In our two experiments, we will compare different types of rice crackers and their prototypicality using the mimetic expressions obtained from Japanese speakers.

3.2 Experiment 1: Mimetics for actually eating rice crackers

3.2.1 *Materials*

In Experiment 1, we used the same seven types of rice crackers as in the preliminary survey (Figure 2). We first obtained data concerning the physical hardness of the types of rice crackers. To objectively define the hardness of the rice crackers, we followed the convention used in the field of food engineering of determining its "breaking load," which is the amount of force required to break the food item. Thus, in this study, the hardness of the rice crackers was defined by their breaking loads.

To measure the breaking loads of the rice crackers, we used a rigidly controlled food analyzer, Rheoner RE-3305S (YAMADEN Co., Ltd.), which is a commonly used device in food engineering (the device is installed in the laboratory of the last author). This device works in the following way. A plunger moves with the velocity of 1mm/s and presses the sample under it. The breaking load of the sample is defined by the score at the peak top of the strain ratio (%) in the force (N) chart. The higher the breaking load, the harder the sample.

Using this device, we obtained the hardness of six out of the seven types of the rice crackers. Unfortunately, the sample of Type G (*Nuresenbei*) was so soft and flexible that its chart had no peak. Therefore, its hardness could not be defined by the breaking load. Instead, we used the compression line of Type G to obtain its compression force – that is, the force required to compress the cracker to 20% of its original thickness.

Table 3 shows the objective hardness of the seven types of rice crackers measured in terms of their breaking loads (N) (except for Type G, which is measured

Table 3. Objective hardness of the rice crackers

Cracker types	A	B	C	D	E	F	G
Breaking Load (N)	83.5	72.9	49.3	21.5	20.6	17.5	0.8

in terms of compression force). The types of crackers are ordered from hardest to softest: Type A is the hardest, whereas Type G is the softest.

Among the seven types of rice crackers, Types D and E had only slightly different breaking loads: 21.5 and 20.6 N, respectively (a difference of only 0.9 N). The breaking loads of the other types differed by more than three points: 10.6 N between Types A and B, 23.6 N between Types B and C, 27.8 N between Types C and D, 3.1 N between Types E and F, and 16.7 N between Types F and G. Types A, B, C, and D differed by more than 10 N. Thus, the difference between Types D and E was extremely small compared with the others.

3.2.2 *Method*

Eighty-five native Japanese speakers (18–22 years old) participated in Experiment 1. The stimuli were the seven types of rice crackers described in the previous section. One sample piece from each type of rice cracker was used; this means each participant was presented with seven sample pieces in total. The sample pieces were placed on a table in random order for each participant.

Each participant was asked to taste the seven samples one by one in random order. The participants were instructed to concentrate on the feeling of the rice cracker's texture while biting into it before it became soft from mixing with their saliva. Each participant then performed two tasks. In the first task, the participants rated the hardness of each sample cracker on a 10-point scale, the endpoints of which were "hard" and "soft." According to this rating system, 1 was the softest measurement whereas 10 was the hardest. In the second task, the participants described the texture of each sample in Japanese by writing down the expressions that came to their minds. They were allowed to use any expressions in Japanese, ranging from mimetics and figurative expressions, such as similes and metaphors, to more general expressions, such as adjectives, verbs, and nouns. The answer sheet provided space for only several words, so the participants could not explain the texture using long sentences.

3.2.3 *Results*

The average scores of the results from the first task are shown in Table 4. The hardness ratings in this table are subjective judgements made by the participants. Comparing these ratings with the objective hardness ratings of the rice crackers in Table 3, note that the hardness ratings of Types D and E were rated differently by the participants. That is, the participants rated Type E as harder than Type D on average, although the hardness of Types D and E as shown in Table 3 differed only slightly compared with that of the other types. The difference in the average hardness scores of Types D and E was only 0.9 N, although most of the other types had greater differences; for example, the difference between Types E and F was 2.9 N, between Types B and C was 2.4 N, between Types C and D was 2.2 N, and between Types A and B was 1.4 N.

Except for this slight inversion of the ratings between Types D and E, the hardness of all the other types of rice crackers was rated in the same order as the objectively measured hardness presented above. From these results, we can infer that the participants judged the hardness of the samples with a high degree of accuracy.

Table 4. Subjective hardness of crackers (On the soft–hard scale, 1 = softest, 10 = hardest)

Cracker types	A	B	C	D	E	F	G
Subjective hardness	10.0	8.6	6.2	4.0	5.1	2.2	1.4

For the second task, we obtained 2,644 responses in total from 85 participants. Among these responses, 1,579 tokens were mimetic words, which had 317 types. The other 1,065 responses were non-mimetic words, including figurative expressions and other words such as adjectives. This means that approximately 60% of the answers were mimetics. For each type of cracker, more than 50% of the expressions obtained were mimetics, as shown in Table 5 (for all the types of crackers, the percentages of mimetics were over 50%). These mimetics were included in our data set, whereas the other non-mimetic expressions (which accounted for about 40% of all the 2,644 responses) were excluded from our data set, as this study deals only with mimetics.

Table 5. Percentages of mimetics in participant responses

Cracker types	A	B	C	D	E	F	G
Mimetics (%)	55.6	60.4	65.9	60.2	60.9	53.2	62.0

The mimetic words we obtained included conventional and novel ones (for the creative use of mimetics, see Akita & Murasugi (this volume)). Among the 317 types of mimetics, we considered those which accounted for the top 10% of the mimetic words describing each type of cracker. That is, we extracted the most frequently used mimetics for each type of cracker. Because these mimetics are the ones most frequently used for each type of rice cracker, it can be assumed that they are characteristic or typical of the particular type.

Table 6 shows the results of this selection. In each "Mimetics" cell, the most frequently used mimetic word(s) that fell within the range of the top 10% are listed. Type A had *baribari* and *garigari* as the top 10% mimetics; Type B had only *baribari*; Type C had *sakusaku*; Types D and E had *sakusaku* and *paripari*; Type F had only *sakusaku*; and Type G had *funyafunya* and *mochimochi*.

Table 6. Characteristic mimetics

Cracker types	A	B	C	D	E	F	G
Mimetics	*bari-bari* (9); *gari-gari* (9)	*bari-bari* (22)	*saku-saku* (12)	*saku-saku* (24); *pari-pari* (13)	*saku-saku* (22); *pari-pari* (10)	*saku-saku* (15)	*funya-funya* (11) *mochi-mochi* (8)

Note: More than 10% in the first answers; numbers in the parentheses show the total numbers.

By selecting the most frequently used mimetics for each type of cracker, we observe a certain tendency in the overall distribution of mimetic words. As Table 6 shows, Types A and B had *baribari* as the most typical mimetic word; Types C, D, E, and F had *sakusaku* as the most typical; Types D and E had *paripari* as the most typical; Type G, in contrast to all the others, had completely different mimetic words, *funyafunya* and *mochimochi*, as the most typical.

These results allow us to categorize the seven types of rice crackers into three groups based on the typically used mimetic words. The first group comprises Types A and B, represented by the mimetic word *baribari*, which is usually used for something very hard. Types A and B have breaking loads of 72.9 and 83.5 N, respectively. The second group includes Types C, D, E, and F, represented by the mimetics *sakusaku*, which means crashing something very lightly or something slightly crispy, and *paripari*, which refers to something hard but less hard than *baribari*. These four types represent rice crackers that have breaking loads ranging from 17.5 to 49.3 N. The last group includes Type G, represented by the mimetics *funyafunya* (very soft and flexible) and *mochimochi* (soft and sticky). Type G seems to be exceptionally soft among the seven types of rice crackers. (See Tsujimura (this volume) for studies including some of these mimetics.)

Interestingly, the above distribution of mimetics is very similar to the distribution of the familiarity ratings presented in Section 3.1. As pointed out in Section 3.1, we can consider Types C and D as prototypical rice crackers for young Japanese people based on the familiarity ratings. In Experiment 1, we found a similar distribution based on the types of mimetic words assigned for each type of rice cracker. The mimetic words for the prototypical rice crackers were *sakusaku* and *paripari*.

Type E behaved like Types C and D – that is, the same mimetics, *sakusaku* and *paripari*, were assigned to Type E as well.

Types A and B were non-prototypical rice crackers from the perspective of familiarity. These were harder and less familiar than the prototypical rice crackers. In Experiment 1, they were described by the mimetics *baribari* and *garigari*.

This uneven distribution of mimetics was observed when each participant verbally described the textures of the rice crackers after actually eating them and feeling their textures. In this study, we aim to examine whether the same or a similar distribution of mimetics can be found when people are not actually eating rice crackers but are merely imagining eating them. Thus, we also conducted Experiment 2, in which participants were asked to come up with words to describe the textures of imagined rice crackers without actually eating them.

3.3 Experiment 2: Mimetics for imagined rice crackers

3.3.1 *Materials*

In Experiment 2, no real rice crackers were used. Participants only imagined a rice cracker in their mind.

3.3.2 *Method*

Fifty-two native Japanese speakers (18–22 years old) participated in Experiment 2. These participants did not participate in Experiment 1. They were asked to perform three tasks written on a questionnaire. In the first task, the participants were asked to imagine a rice cracker and then imagine biting into it. No specific instruction was given concerning the type of rice cracker to be imagined; that is, the participants could imagine any rice cracker. They were then asked to describe the texture of the imagined rice cracker using mimetic words and were allowed to write as many mimetic words as they liked.

In the second task, the participants were presented with five Japanese mimetic words. Four of them were *baribari, paripari, sakusaku,* and *funyafunya*. These were taken from the mimetic words obtained in Experiment 1, characterizing the three groups: *baribari* from the hardest group, *paripari* and *sakusaku* from the middle group, and *funyafunya* from the softest group. As the fifth mimetic word, we added *fuwafuwa* (meaning airy and soft), which represents a mimetic that is rarely used to describe rice crackers. The participants read the five mimetic words and were asked to list on the answer sheet several kinds of foods they believed fit with each word. They could write the names of as many foods as they liked.

In the third task, the participants rated the same five mimetic words based on how appropriate each of them was to describe the texture of rice crackers. Each word was rated on a three-point scale, with "1" representing "inappropriate" and "3" representing "appropriate." For example, if they thought *baribari* was an appropriate mimetic word for the texture of a rice cracker (in general), they checked "3" on the answer sheet.

3.3.3 *Results*

In total, 145 responses were obtained for the first task. Fifty-two participants wrote 145 mimetic words that they thought were appropriate to describe the texture of the rice cracker they imagined. The most frequent word among them was *baribari*, which accounted for 35.9% of all the answers. Among the 52 first-given answers, there were 16 tokens of *baribari*, which accounted for 80% of the total answers. Thus, *baribari* was the most popular mimetic word to describe the texture of an imagined rice cracker.

In the second task, the participants listed the foods that they believed best fit with each of the five mimetic words. Table 7 shows the results. The participants' most frequent answers for *baribari, paripari, sakusaku, funyafunya*, and *fuwafuwa* were "rice crackers," "potato chips," "cookies," "gummy candy," and "cotton candy," respectively.

Table 7. Typical foods for five mimetic words

Mimetics	*bari-bari*	*pari-pari*	*saku-saku*	*funya-funya*	*fuwa-fuwa*
Foods	Rice crackers	Potato chips	Cookies	Gummy candy	Cotton candy

In the third task, the same five mimetic words were used again. The participants rated each mimetic word based on their judgment as to whether it was appropriate to describe the texture of rice crackers. Table 8 shows the results. *Baribari* obtained the highest average rating.

Table 8. Appropriateness for describing rice crackers (1 = inappropriate, 3 = appropriate)

Mimetics	*bari-bari*	*pari-pari*	*saku-saku*	*funya-funya*	*fuwa-fuwa*
Appropriateness rating	2.8	2.5	1.9	1.7	1.0

Combining the results of the three tasks in Experiment 2, we can conclude that the mimetic word *baribari* was judged by the participants to be the best suited to describe the texture of imagined rice crackers.

3.4 Comparing the results

From Experiments 1 and 2, we obtained some conflicting results. In Experiment 1, *sakusaku* was assigned to the texture of the most prototypical type of rice crackers: Types C, D, and E. However, in Experiment 2, *baribari* was judged to be the best suited mimetic word to describe the texture of imagined rice crackers. Why did such a discrepancy arise? It could be attributable to the different natures of both experiments – that is, the difference between actually eating a rice cracker and merely imagining eating a rice cracker. The actual perception of eating a food and the imagined perception of eating a food may lead to different uses of mimetic words. We will discuss this issue in detail in the next section.

4. Discussion and conclusion

As described in the previous section, our two experiments tested two different situations regarding the eating of rice crackers. In one situation, participants were asked to eat some pieces of rice crackers and describe their texture in Japanese. Among the expressions they used, we extracted top 10% of mimetics for analysis. In the other situation, participants were asked to imagine eating a rice cracker and describe its imagined texture using Japanese mimetic words. The results of the two experiments showed that there was a gap between the mimetics used to describe the textures of typical rice crackers and typical imagined rice crackers. In Experiment 2, *baribari* was rated as the most suitable mimetic word to describe the texture of an imagined rice cracker. However, this did not correspond with the familiarity ratings revealed in our preliminary survey. The mimetic words assigned to the most familiar type of rice cracker in Experiment 1 were *sakusaku* and *paripari*. The word *baribari* was significantly more frequently assigned to the hardest rice crackers, which were not the prototypical ones. This gap requires explanation.

In this section, we discuss this gap together with some suggestions for future study. In what follows, we first present a tentative explanation of the above-mentioned gap using the concept of degrees of iconicity. Then, we discuss its implications for linguistics studies. Finally, we suggest broader issues for future study.

4.1 Degrees of iconicity

The above-mentioned gap may be attributable to the different degrees of iconicity in the mimetics used in the two situations. In Experiment 1, when the participants were asked to describe the textures of the rice crackers they ate using mimetic words, they needed to pay attention to the perceived texture of the rice crackers and the sound-symbolic aspects of each mimetic word and compare these two on-the-spot. In this kind of situation, the mimetics must be high in iconicity because the setting requires participants' direct reflection on their feelings toward their selection of words.

In contrast, in Experiment 2, when the participants were asked to describe the textures of the imagined rice crackers, they did not have an actual experience of eating the rice cracker. This means that they could not attend to their real-time, or simultaneous, perceptions when describing the texture. This lack of a real perception of the object of reference may have led the participants to simply recall linguistic knowledge about eating a rice cracker when describing its texture. They could only refer to their mental lexicon with contextual information and extract the mimetic words typically used to describe the texture of rice crackers. This situation is very different from that of Experiment 1, in which the participants were required to pay attention to the real-time perceptions of what was going on in their mouths when describing the texture of the rice crackers. The circumstances of Experiment 2 led to a less iconic use of mimetics.

Thus, we argue that the two situations, one involving real eating and the other involving imagined eating, are associated with different degrees of iconicity: the situation involving real eating led to a more iconic use of mimetic words, whereas the situation involving imagined eating led to a less iconic use of mimetic words.[6] In the next section, we discuss what this iconicity means for linguistics studies by referring to studies by Akita (2009, 2013) and the lexical iconicity hierarchy introduced in Section 2.2.

4.2 Implications for linguistics studies

The notion of different degrees of iconicity for mimetics has at least two implications for linguistics. First, although there have been arguments that different subtypes of mimetics (i.e., phonomimes, phenomimes, and psychomimes) have different degrees of iconicity, the idea that one and the same mimetic word can reveal different degrees of iconicity without changing its form has not been previously pointed out. As we saw in Section 2.2, Akita (2009, 2013) has argued that different types of mimetics, such as phonomimes, phenomimes, and psychomimes, have different degrees of iconicity according to their hierarchical order of iconicity. That is, phonomimes, which describe voices or sounds in terms of linguistic sounds, are more iconic than phenomimes, which describe the properties of other modalities of

6. An anonymous reviewer suggests that the discrepancy between the results of Experiments 1 and 2 could be explained in terms of frame semantics (cf. Sakaguchi, this volume). This possibility may be worth pursuing, which we will mention in Section 4.3.

perception using linguistic sounds; psychomimes, which describe emotions, pain, and other proprioceptive perceptions with linguistic sounds, are the least iconic among the three types of mimetics. However, in addition to the hierarchical order of iconicity among these lexical groups, our results indicate that the same mimetic words – that is, lexical items that belong to the same group of mimetics – can vary in their degrees of iconicity. For example, *baribari, sakusaku*, and *paripari*, all of which are meant to be phenomimes because they express the texture of rice crackers, have different degrees of iconicity in different situations: they had different degrees of iconicity when participants described the texture of rice crackers versus the texture of merely imagined rice crackers.

Another implication is related to the nature of the data used in linguistics. In Experiment 1 of this study, participants were instructed to concentrate on what they were feeling regarding the food in their mouths. The need to express the feeling in words may reinforce the intense attention toward one's own perceptions.[7] In contrast, in conversation or in writing, such intense attention is rarely paid to our perceptions, except in artistic contexts such as poetry. Language is used as an objective means to convey a message, at least in ordinary situations. Language tends to be used to convey speakers' ideas using combinations of shared or common meanings to other speakers in the language community. This situation is very different from that in which language users have to pay intense attention to their on-the-spot perceptions or, in other words, have to explore their own inner experiences. This difference may affect the nature of data in linguistics.

In most linguistics studies, the main data are usually taken from expressions made up by the researchers or found in corpora. Neither case involves real-time, on-the-spot perceptions of, for instance, eating rice crackers by the author of the expression. We need to carefully distinguish these two cases when dealing with linguistic data: data produced by focusing on one's own on-the-spot perceptions of eating a food and data taken from the ordinary use of language without such real-time perceptual experience accompanying the verbal act.

If the notion of different degrees of iconicity is unignorable, a question arises: what exactly is being described using mimetics when we imagine eating rice crackers if our real-time experience is not reflected? Our assumption is that when we are imagining eating rice crackers, we are more influenced by the cultural knowledge of rice crackers that we have gained from common resources, such as novels, comics, and advertisements. For example, one of the most authoritative Japanese dictionaries, *Kōjien*, describes the mimetic word *baribari* as that used to describe a

7. Fukushima (this volume) also uses real-time data based on the actual perception of tasting *sake*.

manner of eating rice crackers, as shown below in (1), whereas the entries in *Kōjien* for *paripari* and *sakusaku* do not include examples involving rice crackers.

(1) *senbei* *o* *baribari* *taberu*
rice.cracker ACC mimetic eat
"Eat rice crackers in a *baribari* manner."

To the extent that authoritative dictionaries represent the common knowledge of a word shared by the members of a language community, it is safe to say that our common knowledge of mimetic words expressing textures of food may, over the course of time, diverge from highly iconic uses such as on-the-spot ones and consequently may produce a gap. After such shifts, our common knowledge of the word may eventually override our real experience of eating.[8]

The above argument is based on our speculation. Currently, we do not have direct evidence demonstrating that linguistic input can shape our experiences, such as our perception of food textures. However, as we noted in Section 2.2, our previous study (Funakubo et al., 2016) showed that in a situation involving actually eating snacks, people tended to be affected by the mimetic words printed on the package. Such a finding suggests that linguistic descriptions of food can influence people's perceptions to some extent. In such situations, people will pay less attention to their real-time perceptions because they are led to notice the meaning of the word they see. Consequently, people's uses of mimetics may become less iconic: they may tend to choose conventional usage established in language over phono/morpho-semantic similarities based on personal sensations.

4.3 Suggestions for future studies

Three issues remain to be addressed in future studies: cross-linguistic exploration, consideration of frame-semantic views, and implications for functions of language. First, it may be interesting to examine whether the same results that we obtained can also be obtained in other languages. Through similar experiments in other languages, we may be able to determine whether the phenomenon we found in Japanese mimetics is cross-linguistically attested or a language-specific phenomenon. Although many studies have already been conducted on the relationship between food texture and English sound-symbolic words such as "crispy" and "crunchy" (Diederich, 2015; Dijksterhuis, Luyten, Wijk, & Mojet, 2007; Tunick

8. We thank an anonymous reviewer for suggesting an explanation based on frame semantics, such as evoking the Sound_symbolic frame vs. the Rice-cracker frame, or a cognitive frame vs. a linguistic frame. This possibility will be an intriguing topic for future study.

et al., 2013), a comparison of their uses in the contexts of real versus imagined eating has not been performed. We would like to investigate this topic in the future.

Second, as an anonymous reviewer has suggested, the two different situations in which we have obtained different results – the real-rice-cracker situation and the imagined-rice-cracker situation – might correspond to two different frames. Although this possibility has not been fully discussed in the present study, it may be of interest to see how frame semantics (Fillmore, 1982) can account for the introspective exploration of one's own sensation or perception of experiencing food texture.

Finally, we suggest a perspective for longer-term future studies on the functions of language. The present findings suggest a certain understudied function of language, that is, the function for the introspective exploration of one's own sensation or perception, which may be an important future topic. As Clark (1997) has argued, the roles for communication have been emphasized to such an extent that other important roles of language seem to have been overlooked.[9] These functions include the use of language as a tool by which we can extend our cognitive capacities. Such function of language, namely the cognitive extension function, can be categorized as a non-communicative role of language (Dennett, 1995; Jackendoff, 1996; Vygotsky, 1986). For example, taking notes that can expand our memory capacities, diagrams that help us calculate, and signs that navigate us in space fall into this category. This function of language directs inside oneself rather than directing outside for communication with others. In Experiment 1 of the present study, language was used for exploring the perception of food texture, which may be included in this category of language use. We would call this the function of "exploration of perception" within the category of cognitive extension.

To examine the adequacy of our proposal, further experiments on various types of texture exploration will be effective. We have started such exploration in our recent studies, aiming to expand this direction. For example, Uno, Ogai, Hirata-Mogi, and Hayashi (2017) have observed how people use mimetics to express the tactile sensation of non-familiar textures with various physical properties including mass, elasticity, and viscosity. Ongoing investigation examines the differences in the ways people express their perceptions of textures in a monologue situation and in a communicative situation (Preliminary results have been presented in Uno, Ogai,

9. Dingemanse (2011) pointed out that the poetic function of language proposed by Jakobson (1960) can be used to explain the "fun" nature of the use of mimetics. Jakobson's categorization of the functions of language, including the poetic one, however, emphasizes the communicative aspect of language, which concerns the use of language among people – that is, the social use of language rather than the introspective use of language inside the self.

Hirata-Mogi, Hayashi & Shinohara (2019).). Other perceptual modalities such as visual, auditory, or olfactory remain to be investigated.

In sum, in the present study, we have examined how people differently describe the texture of rice crackers after eating them as opposed to merely imagining eating them. We have argued that the mimetics used for typical crackers are different in these two cases. We have also suggested that this difference is attributable to the different degrees of iconicity of the mimetics used in the two cases. Because food has such extensive cultural significance, dealing with food in the study of language reminds us of the claim of Cognitive Linguistics that encyclopedic knowledge is inseparable from the semantics of words.

References

Akita, K. (2009). A grammar of sound-symbolic words in Japanese: Theoretical approaches to iconic and lexical properties of Japanese mimetics (Unpublished doctoral dissertation). Kobe University, Japan.

Akita, K. (2010). An embodied semantic analysis of psychological mimetics in Japanese. *Linguistics, 48*, 1195–1220. https://doi.org/10.1515/ling.2010.039

Akita, K. (2012). Toward a frame-semantic definition of sound-symbolic words. *Cognitive Linguistics, 23*, 67–90. https://doi.org/10.1515/cog-2012-0003

Akita, K. (2013). The lexical iconicity hierarchy and its grammatical correlates. In L. Elleström, O. Fischer, & C. Ljungberg (Eds.), *Iconic investigations* (pp. 331–349). Amsterdam/Philadelphia: John Benjamins. https://doi.org/10.1075/ill.12.24aki

Childs, G. T. (1994). African ideophones. In L. Hinton, J. Nichols, & J. J. Ohala (Eds.), *Sound symbolism* (pp. 178–204). Cambridge: Cambridge University Press.

Clark, A. (1997). *Being there: Putting brain, body and mind together*. Cambridge: MIT Press.

Dennett, D. (1995). *Darwin's dangerous idea: Evolution and the meanings of life*. New York: Simon and Schuster.

Diederich, C. (2015). *Sensory adjectives in the discourse of food*. Amsterdam/Philadelphia: John Benjamins. https://doi.org/10.1075/celcr.16

Dijksterhuis, G., Luyten, H., de Wijk, R. A. & Mojet, J. (2007). A new sensory vocabulary for crisp and crunchy dry model foods. *Food Quality and Preference, 18*, 37–50. https://doi.org/10.1016/j.foodqual.2005.07.012

Dingemanse, M. (2011). Ideophones and the aesthetics of everyday language in a West-African society. *The Senses & Society, 6*(1), 77–85. https://doi.org/10.2752/174589311X12893982233830

Dingemanse, M. (2012). Advances in the cross-linguistic study of ideophones. *Language and Linguistics Compass, 6*, 654–672. https://doi.org/10.1002/lnc3.361

Favalli, S., Skov, T., Spence, C. & Byrne, D. V. (2013). Do you say it like you eat it? The sound symbolism of food names and its role in the multisensory product experience. *Food Research International, 54*(1), 760–771. https://doi.org/10.1016/j.foodres.2013.08.022

Fillmore, C. (1982). Frame semantics. In Linguistic Society of Korea (Ed.), *Linguistics in the morning calm* (pp. 111–37). Seoul: Hanshin Publishing.

Funakubo, K., Kobayashi, F., Uno, R., Shinohara, K., & Odake, S. (2016, October). How the expression *karit* on the package changes our description of the food texture (In Japanese). Paper presented at *The 2016 Annual Meeting of the Kanto Branch of Japan Society for Bioscience, Biotechnology and Agrochemistry*, Tokyo, Japan.

Gallace, A., Boschin, E. & Spence, C. (2011). On the taste of "Bouba" and "Kiki": An exploration of word-food associations in neurologically normal participants. *Cognitive Neuroscience*, *2*(1), 34–46. https://doi.org/10.1080/17588928.2010.516820

Haiman, J. (1983). Iconic and economic motivation. *Language*, *59*, 781–819. https://doi.org/10.2307/413373

Haiman, J. (1985a). *Natural syntax*. Cambridge: Cambridge University Press.

Haiman, J. (Ed.). (1985b). *Iconicity in syntax*. Amsterdam: John Benjamins. https://doi.org/10.1075/tsl.6

Hamano, S. (1998). *The sound-symbolic system of Japanese*. Stanford: CSLI Publications.

Hayakawa, F., Kazami, Y., Nishinari, K., Ioku, K., Akuzawa, S., Yamano, Y., Baba, Y. & Kohyama, K. (2013). Classification of Japanese texture terms. *Journal of Texture Studies*, *44*, 140–159. https://doi.org/10.1111/jtxs.12006

Hirata, S., Nakamura, S., Komatsu, T., & Akita, K. (2015). Cross-regional comparison of mimetic word uses based on the minutes of the Diet of Japan (In Japanese). *Journal of the Japanese Society for Artificial Intelligence*, *30*(1), 274–281.

Ishibashi, K., Fukataki, S. & Miyata, K. (2015). Evaluation of human impressions regarding sizzle words for rice crackers (In Japanese). *Transactions of the Japanese Society for Artificial Intelligence*, *3*(1), 229–236. https://doi.org/10.1527/tjsai.30.229

Jackendoff, R. (1996). How language helps us think. *Pragmatics and Cognition*, *4*(1), 1–34. https://doi.org/10.1075/pc.4.1.03jac

Jakobson, R. (1960). Closing statement: Linguistics and poetics. In T. A. Sebeok (Ed.), *Style in language* (pp.350–77). Cambridge, MA: MIT Press.

Kakei, H., Tamori, I., & Schourup, L. (1996). *Dictionary of iconic expressions in Japanese*. Berlin: Muton de Gruyter. https://doi.org/10.1515/9783110809046

Lakoff, G. (1987). *Women, fire, and dangerous things*. Chicago: The University of Chicago Press. https://doi.org/10.7208/chicago/9780226471013.001.0001

Majid, A., Roberts, S. G., Cilissen, L., Emmorey, K., Nicodemus, B., O'Grady, L., Woll, B., LeLan, B., De Sousa, H., Cansler, B. L., Shayan, S., De Vos, C., Senft, G., Enfield, N. J., Razak, R. A., Fedden, S., Tufvesson, S., Dingemanse, M., Ozturk, O., Brown, P., Hill, C., Le Guen, O., Hirtzel, V., Van Gijn, R., Sicoli, M. A., & Levinson, S. C. (2018). Differential coding of perception in the world's languages. *Proceedings of the National Academy of Sciences*, *115*(45), 11369–11376. https://doi.org/10.1073/pnas.1720419115

Ono, M. (Ed.). (2007). *Dictionary of mimetics in Japanese* (In Japanese). Tokyo: Sougakukan.

Ramachandran, V. S., & Hubbard, E. M. (2001). Synaesthesia – A window into perception, thought and language. *Journal of Consciousness Studies*, *8*(12), 3–34.

Sakamoto, M. & Watanabe, J. (2016). Cross-modal associations between sounds and drink tastes/textures: A study with spontaneous production of sound-symbolic words. *Chemical Senses*, *41*(3), 197–203. https://doi.org/10.1093/chemse/bjv078

Shinohara, K., & Nakayama, A. (2011). Modalities and directions in synaesthetic metaphors in Japanese. *Cognitive Studies*, *18*(3), 491–507.

Shokuhin Ryūtsū Jōhō Center [Food Distribution Information Center]. (Ed.). (2000). *Shokuseikatsu dēta sōgō tōkei nenpō* [General Statistics of Dietary Habit Data] (p. 451). Tokyo: Koyosha.

Simner, J., Cuskley, C. & Kirby, S. (2010). What sound does that taste? Cross-modal mappings across gustation and audition. *Perception*, *39*, 553–569. https://doi.org/10.1068/p6591

Soka City Website. (2014). "Soka senbei-no rekishi-to genzai [The history and the present state of Soka rice crackers]." Retrieved July 12, 2019, from http://www.city.soka.saitama.jp/cont/s1403/010/010/020/01.html

Spence, C. (2015). Eating with our ears: Assessing the importance of the sounds of consumption on our perception and enjoyment of multisensory flavour experiences. *Flavor*, *4*(3). https://doi.org/10.1186/2044-7248-4-3

Takahashi, H., Itou, A., Egawa, H., Watanabe, T., Inoue, M., Arai, E. & Yamada, Y. (2006). Development of rice cracker for aged people (In Japanese). *Journal of Japanese Society for Masticatory Science and Health Promotion*, *16*(3), 70–82.

Takahashi, H., Itou, A., Yamamura, K., Arai, E., & Yamada, Y. (2009). Classification of rice crackers based on hardness (In Japanese). *Journal of Japanese Society for Masticatory Science and Health Promotion*, *19*(1), 29–38.

Tayler, J. (1989). *Linguistic categorization*. Oxford: Oxford University Press.

Tunick, M. H., Onwulata, C. I., Thomas, A. E., Phillips, J. G., Mukhopadhyay, S., Sheen, S., Liu, C., Latona, N., Pimentel, M. R., & Cooke, P. H. (2013). Critical evaluation of crispy and crunchy textures: A review. *International Journal of Food Properties*, *16*(5), 949–963. https://doi.org/10.1080/10942912.2011.573116

Uno, R., Ogai, Y., Mogi-Hirata, S., & Hayashi, Y. (2017). Confidence in expressing novel textures: An analysis of Japanese ideophones that describe visually-induced textures. *Proceedings of IEEE 3rd International Conference on Cybernetics*. https://doi.org/10.1109/CYBConf.2017.7985768

Uno, R., Ogai, Y., Mogi-Hirata, S., Hayashi, Y., & Shinohara, K. (2019). How communication affects the use of ideophones describing virtual textures (in Japanese). *Handbook of the 36th Annual Meeting of Japanese Cognitive Science Society*, 662–665.

Vygotsky, L. S. (1986). *Thought and language* (translation of 1962 edition). MA: MIT Press.

Williams, J. (1976). Synaesthetic adjective: A possible law of semantic change. *Language*, *52*, 461–478. https://doi.org/10.2307/412571

Yu, N. (2003). Synesthetic metaphor: A cognitive perspective. *Journal of Literary Semantics*, *32*(1), 19–34. https://doi.org/10.1515/jlse.2003.001

Zampini, M. & Spence, C. (2004). The role of auditory cues in modulating the perceived crispness and staleness of potato chips. *Journal of Sensory Studies*, *19*, 347–363. https://doi.org/10.1111/j.1745-459X.2004.080403.x

CHAPTER 3

The sound-symbolic effects of consonants on food texture

An experimental study of snack names in Japanese

Gakuji Kumagai[1], Ryoko Uno[2] and Kazuko Shinohara[2]
[1]Kansai University / [2]Tokyo University of Agriculture and Technology

This study explores the sound-symbolic effects of Japanese consonants on image of food textures. Our experiment tested whether voiced vs. voiceless plosives, at various places of articulation, could affect participants' image of the hardness of a snack. The results revealed that both voicing and place of articulation had effects and that voicing had a stronger effect. Our results support the explanation of sound symbolism based on embodied motivation, as discussed in Cognitive Linguistics. Regarding the voicing of obstruents, the acoustic account cannot explain our results, while the articulatory and the lexical accounts are compatible with them. Regarding the place of articulation, all three accounts can explain our results. These findings can provide insights for food product marketing and related fields.

Keywords: voicing in plosives, obstruents, place of articulation, hardness, experimental approach, phonetics, embodiment

1. Introduction: Sound-symbolic phenomena in the language of Japanese food

1.1 Background and research focus

Food and language are related. Linguistic expressions about food can affect our experience of eating, and vice versa. One of the most important effects of language on our experience of eating is found in a phenomenon called "sound symbolism" (named by Jespersen, 1922), which can be summarized as the inherent connections between sounds and meanings and a kind of iconicity in language (Haiman, 1983, 1985a, 1985b). Sound symbolism has long been investigated in linguistics and related fields, such as cognitive science, psychology, neuroscience, computer science,

https://doi.org/10.1075/celcr.25.03kum

robotics, artificial intelligence, sports science, food science, literature, and marketing (Akita, 2009; Dingemanse, Blasi, Lupyan, Christianson, & Monaghan, 2015; Hinton, Nichols, & Ohala 1994/2006; Jespersen, 1922/1933; Kawahara, Shinohara, & Uchimoto, 2008; Kumagai & Kawahara, 2017, 2019, 2020; Köhler, 1929/1947; Parise & Spence, 2012; Perniss, Thompson, & Vigliocco, 2010; Perniss & Vigliocco, 2014; Ramachandran & Hubbard, 2001; Sapir, 1929; Shinohara & Kawahara, 2016; Shinohara, Yamauchi, Kawahara, & Tanaka, 2016, among others).[1]

Sound symbolism connects sounds in the form of linguistic signs (or words) and our perceptual images in a motivated way. Contrary to de Saussure's (1916) claim that "there is no inherent connection between meanings and sounds,"[2] many researchers have claimed that certain linguistic sounds can evoke certain perceptual images. These include images of an object's size (Jespersen, 1922/1933; Sapir, 1929; Shinohara & Kawahara, 2016, among others), shape (Ahlner & Zlatev, 2010; Berlin, 2006; Irwin & Newland, 1940; Kawahara & Shinohara, 2012; Köhler, 1929/1947; Parise & Spence, 2012; Ramachandran & Hubbard, 2001; Uemura, 1965, among others), weight (Yoshida & Shinohara, 2009), brightness (Reilly, Biun, Cowles, & Peelle, 2008; Sato, 2011), and dirtiness (Kawahara, Shinohara, & Uchimoto, 2008; Shinohara & Kawahara, 2009). In addition, sound-symbolic associations may permeate even non-perceptual or more subjective images, such as personality traits (Kawahara, Shinohara, & Grady, 2015; Shinohara & Kawahara, 2013) and emotions (Kawahara & Shinohara, 2012; Kawahara, Shinohara, & Grady, 2015). Thus, it has become evident that sounds, in human language, are not totally neutral or meaningless, as de Saussure asserted, but rather can induce symbolic effects on our perceptions and feelings. Moreover, these sound-symbolic associations are considered to have some sort of embodied motivation, one rooted in our physical experiences (Shinohara & Kawahara, 2016).

If sound symbolism has such influence on our perceptual images, it should not come as a surprise that linguistic sounds may, in some way, affect our perceptual experiences related to food.[3] Indeed, there has been a substantial body of research that demonstrates sound-symbolic effects on images of food. For example, Klink's (2000) experimental study examined the sound-symbolic effects of vowels

1. The phenomenon is also referred to as "phonetic symbolism" (Sapir, 1929), "phonosymbolism" (Malkiel, 1990), or "phonaesthesia" (Levin, Liberman, Blonk, & La Barbara, 2003). The systematicities in combinations of sequences of sounds and meanings seen in some English words are often referred to as "phonesthemes" (Bergen, 2004; Firth, 1930).

2. Hockett (1963) also argued the same idea, but the arbitrariness thesis is usually attributed to de Saussure.

3. It is also reported that physical, non-linguistic sounds can also affect the perception of eating food (Spence, 2015).

in names of food products such as ketchup and beer, demonstrating that back vowels are more likely to be associated with thickness and darkness than front vowels. Yorkston and Menon (2004) studied the relationship between vowels and ice cream flavors, suggesting that back vowels tend to evoke smoothness and creaminess in the perceptions of English speakers. Jurafsky (2014) showed that the names of ice cream flavors tend to contain more back vowels than front vowels (e.g., "coconut," "rocky road," and "chocolate"), while the product names of light foods such as crackers tend to contain more front vowels than back vowels (e.g., "Ritz"). In short, the relationship between linguistic sounds, such as vowels, and certain features of food has been well established in the study of language (see Tsujimura, this volume, for an overview of research on sound symbolism).

Building on this background, we explore food-related sound-symbolic phenomena induced by consonants, specifically investigating snack names in Japanese. The rationale for this topic will be discussed in detail in Section 1.3.

1.2 Research history of sound symbolism

Before discussing the reason for the choice of our topic (i.e., snack names in Japanese), a brief survey of the history of the investigation of sound symbolism is in order. As mentioned above, de Saussure (1916) explicitly claimed that the primary principle of human language is the "arbitrariness" of linguistic signs or words. This means that the arrangement of phonemes in any word in human language is not motivated in any way but chosen and established only by the conventionalized habits of the community in which the language is spoken. Ever since de Saussure's thoughts on language were published by his students, researchers have attempted to present counterexamples to the arbitrariness thesis. One of the most frequently cited works is Sapir's (1929) empirical study. It was inspired by Jespersen's (1922/1933) suggestion that the vowel [i] tends to be linked with small things. Sapir examined various vowels using a forced-choice method and showed that most of the English-speaking participants reacted in the same way. When presented with a pair of nonce words such as *mal* and *mil* and a pair of tables, one of which was big and the other small, and asked to match the members of these two pairs, they tended to match *mal* with the big table and *mil* with the small one. Because *mal* and *mil* are a minimal pair that differ only in the vowels [a] and [i], the difference in the image of the objects' sizes can be attributed to these two vowels: [a] is felt as "bigger" than [i]. Subsequent corpus and experimental studies (e.g., Berlin, 2006; Shinohara & Kawahara, 2016; Ultan, 1978) have also revealed that low or back vowels such as [a] are associated with an image of "largeness" and high or front vowels such as [i] with that of "smallness."

Sound-symbolic associations are not limited to the size of objects. Köhler (1947), a representative gestalt psychologist, carried out a well-known experiment on sound symbolism related to perception of two-dimensional shapes. As shown in Figure 1, Köhler used a roundish shape and an angular, spiky shape, asking his participants to match the figures with the nonce words *maluma* and *takete*. The results indicated that people tended to match the roundish shape with the word *maluma* and the angular shape with the word *takete*.

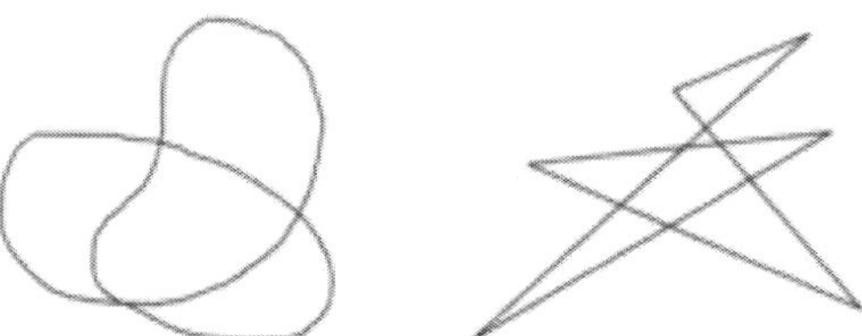

Figure 1. Köhler's shapes

This synaesthetic tendency became well-known as an example of sound-shape symbolism. Subsequent studies confirmed Köhler's discovery of the stochastic tendency for sonorants, such as /m, n, r, l, w, j/, to be associated with round shapes and obstruents, especially plosives such as /p, t, k, b, d, g/, to be associated with angular, straight, or spiky shapes. Thus, although de Saussure's principle of arbitrariness was a mainstream belief in linguistics in the twentieth century, the study of sound symbolism involving certain perceptual images, such as size and shape, developed and became influential, not only in linguistics but also in psychology and other related fields, by the end of that same century.[4]

Around the turn of the twenty-first century, an influential work by Ramachandran and Hubbard (2001) appeared, which has made sound symbolism an important issue in science. Their neurological research on synaesthesia, which describes certain linkages between different perceptual modalities, such as the visual, auditory, tactile, olfactory, and gustatory, has demonstrated that although synesthesia itself is a phenomenon that occurs only in certain individuals, called "synesthetes," the same kind of tendency, though with much less intensity, can also be seen in ordinary people.[5] They found a stochastic trend among ordinary people

4. Other studies that appeared in the Twentieth Century include works by Bolinger (1946) and Jakobson (1978).

5. Ramachandran and Hubbard (2001, p. 4) define synaesthesia as "a curious condition in which an otherwise normal person experiences sensations in one modality when a second modality is stimulated."

(non-synesthetes) to associate the nonce word *bouba* with a roundish shape and the nonce word *kiki* with an angular, spiky shape. While these findings are similar to those of Köhler, the term "*bouba-kiki* effect" has come to be broadly used in cognitive science and many related disciplines. After Ramachandran and Hubbard's influential work, studies on sound symbolism soared in number and quality, spurring more interdisciplinary research.

Thus, over the past two decades, sound symbolism has become a flourishing research field (see, e.g., Blasi, Wichmann, Hammarström, Stadler, & Christianson, 2016; Dingemanse, Blasi, Lupyan, Christianson, & Monaghan, 2015; Hinton, Nichols, & Ohala 1994/2006; Kawahara, 2017, 2020; Lockwood & Dingemanse, 2015; Nuckolls, 1999; Sidhu & Pexman, 2018, for recent surveys and overviews; for a more general overview of cross-modal correspondences, see Spence, 2011). This is especially true in the study of the Japanese language because Japanese has a rich inventory of sound-symbolic words, called "mimetics" or "ideophones" (Akita, 2009, 2015; Hamano, 1998; Uno, Kobayashi, Shinohara, & Odake, this volume). Particularly intriguing is the fact that the Japanese system of mimetics includes not only "phonomimes" (mimetic words referring to sounds) but also "phenomimes" (mimetic words referring to perceptual properties other than sounds, such as visual, tactile, olfactory, and gustatory impressions) and "psychomimes" (those referring to internal subjective experiences, such as emotions or types of pain). Due to their systematicity and richness, Japanese mimetic words can express wide varieties of visual, tactile, and other perceptual impressions (for innovative aspects of morphological variation of Japanese mimetics, see Akita and Murasugi, this volume). This makes the Japanese language a useful and rich source for the study of sound symbolism, including mimetics and other word types. In fact, research on sound symbolism using the Japanese language has contributed a great deal to the development of this field of study (Akita, 2009, 2015; Hamano, 1998; Kawahara & Shinohara, 2008; Kumagai & Kawahara, 2019; Shinohara & Kawahara, 2016, among others).

The study we present in this chapter builds on these trends, exploring how research on sound symbolism can connect the two main topics of this volume: the study of Japanese food and the study of the Japanese language. The present study adopts the framework of Cognitive Linguistics (Lakoff, 1987; Lakoff & Johnson, 1980, 1999; Langacker, 1987), as other chapters in this volume do, accepting the assumption that human language is not an autonomous system of arbitrary signs but a motivated system of symbols. We employ a quantitative method, which has been a trend in this discipline since the so-called "quantitative turn," reported to have occurred around 2008 (Janda, 2013).

1.3 Sound symbolism in snack names

As mentioned in the previous sections, sound symbolism is a flourishing topic in linguistic and psychological investigation. The present study aims to pursue this topic further, building on the large body of research examining sound-symbolic patterns in proper names. The general thesis behind this trend is that names are not chosen randomly. Rather, types of sound with particular phonological or phonetic properties may be chosen to capture aspects of the named object or person. Previous studies suggest that male names and female names are characterized by different phonological features in English (Brown & Ford, 1961; Cassidy, Kelly, & Sharoni, 1999; Cutler, McQueen, & Robinson, 1990; Slater & Feinman, 1985; Tessier, 2010; Whissell, 2001; Wright & Hay, 2002; Wright, Hay, & Tessa, 2005). For instance, male names are more likely to contain obstruents (oral stops, fricatives, and affricates) than female names, while female names are more likely to contain sonorants (nasals, liquids, and glides) than male names. These generalizations hold in Japanese as well (Kawahara, Shinohara, & Grady, 2015; Shinohara & Kawahara, 2013; Uemura, 1965). It is also known that in many languages, including Japanese, less sonorous consonants are more likely to appear in initial positions in words for "father" than for "mother" (e.g., [papa] vs. [mama], or [dæd] vs. [mɑm]) (Lewis, 1934; Murdock, 1959), which accords with the tendency seen in male and female names.

These generalizations are rooted in a sound-symbolic relationship in which obstruents are associated with "angularity," "inaccessibility," and/or "unfriendliness," while sonorants are associated with "roundness," "accessibility," and/or "friendliness" (Kawahara, Shinohara, & Grady, 2015; Köhler, 1947; Lindauer, 1990; Shinohara & Kawahara, 2013; Uemura, 1965). Some studies also argue that these kinds of sound-symbolic relationships may derive from abrupt modulations of amplitude in the bursts and frication characteristic of obstruents, which involve waveforms that look spiky and angular (Jurafsky, 2014; Kawahara & Shinohara, 2012). It can be argued that auditory representations of these sounds, when shaped by listening to their acoustic characteristics, may affect speakers' linguistic knowledge, yielding sound-symbolic meanings (Perniss & Vigliocco, 2014).

More recently, studies have shown that the names of characters in Pokémon (a popular computer game produced in Japan and now sold all over the world) exhibit certain symbolic patterns (Kawahara, Godoy, & Kumagai, 2020; Kawahara, Isobe, Kobayashi, Monou, & Okabe, 2018; Kawahara & Kumagai, 2019a, 2019b; Kawahara, Noto, & Kumagai, 2018; Kumagai & Kawahara, 2019; Shih, Ackerman, Hermalin, Inkelas, & Kavitskaya, 2018). Each of the more than 800 characters in Pokémon possesses particular attributes of weight, size, and strength. These attributes, when statistically analyzed in relation to the sounds in the characters' names, reveal some systematic patterns. For instance, voiced obstruents ([b], [d], [ɡ], [z]) tended to be associated with characters that are larger, heavier, and stronger (Kawahara, Noto, & Kumagai, 2018). In addition, experimental studies using newly created names for Pokémon-like characters have shown that this sound-symbolic association is productive in Japanese (Kawahara et al., 2018; Kawahara & Kumagai, 2019a; Kumagai & Kawahara, 2019). Other studies on Japanese Pokémon names have also shown that bilabial consonants are associated with smaller characters (Shih, Ackerman, Hermalin, Inkelas, & Kavitskaya, 2018).[6]

In summary, it is evident that the names of people and imaginary characters have been found to reflect certain sound-symbolic tendencies. This indicates that names can carry some meanings or images inherent to the person or character. Moreover, such sound-symbolic phenomena are not limited to personal names. The names of non-human or non-living objects, including commercial products such as foods, also contain sound-symbolic associations. As mentioned above, previous studies have examined the relationships between the sounds in the names of food products and the properties of the food (Jurafsky, 2014; Klink, 2000; Yorkston & Menon, 2004). These relationships are arguably based on certain sound-symbolic associations. Just as people's names and imaginary characters' names can convey sound-symbolic images, it is expected that food product names will also participate in such sound-symbolic phenomena. Hence, we chose this topic as the focus of our study.

We have another reason for selecting the sound symbolism of food in Japanese as our topic. It concerns the lexical structure and linguistic customs of Japanese. As mentioned above, the Japanese language has a large inventory of mimetic words, including phenomimes expressing various kinds of texture. Japanese people frequently express food texture using these mimetics in daily life. These mimetic words are encountered not only in conversation but also often on packages of snacks and crackers sold in Japan. In fact, our pilot study revealed that there are many mimetic words, such as *karit-to, sakut-to,* and so on, printed on snack packages.

Some previous studies empirically tested the effect of mimetic words on packages of snacks. Funakubo, Kobayashi, Uno, Shinohara, and Odake (2016) examined whether mimetic words printed on packages of snacks had an influence on perceptions of food texture. They asked their participants to eat a snack and judge the extent to which the mimetic word used for the snack fitted the food texture. When the mimetic word was presented before eating the snack, the participants tended to report that the mimetic word was appropriate for the texture of the snack. When the mimetic word was presented after eating the snack, however, such a strong tendency was not found. Their findings reveal that Japanese speakers are sensitive

6. For example, the five smallest Pokémons are *Bachuru, Furabebe, Aburii, Kyuwawaa,* and *Kosumoumu,* all of which contain bilabial consonants.

to sound-symbolic words to the extent that their experience of eating a food is influenced by the mimetic words they see in relation to that food. This suggests that Japanese speakers may provide us with useful data on sound-symbolic intuition if we conduct a properly designed experiment. This is the second reason for our choice of the topic, namely the sound-symbolic associations between the texture of snacks and linguistic sounds in Japanese.

The insights discussed above lead us to the following question: what kinds of linguistic sounds evoke what kinds of images of food texture? The current study explores this question. Because it is not feasible to treat all the phonetic features in the Japanese language and all the perceptual features of food texture at the same time, we limit our study to a small number of consonant features and one food texture: voicing and place of articulation as the phonetic features and the image of hardness as the food texture.

2. Experiment

2.1 Hypotheses tested

The current study explores the question mentioned in Section 1.3. That is, what kinds of linguistic sounds would evoke what kinds of images of food texture. To answer this question, we test two hypotheses concerning the sound-symbolic associations between obstruents and images of the hardness of food. One is that voicing in obstruents affects the images of hardness. Specifically, voiced plosives [b, d, g] are more likely to be associated with the images of hardness than voiceless plosives [p, t, k]. The second is that the places of articulation of obstruents affect the images of hardness. Specifically, velar plosives [g] or [k] can evoke the hardest image, alveolar plosives [d] or [t] come next, and bilabial plosives [b] or [p] evoke the least hard image. These hypotheses will be represented in this chapter as follows:

(1) Voiceless < Voiced

(2) Bilabial < Alveolar < Velar

Hypothesis (1) has been derived from the findings of studies on mimetics. For instance, Uno, Kobayashi, Shinohara, and Odake (this volume) demonstrate that Japanese mimetic words that have a voiced obstruent in the initial position are likely to be associated with harder image than those that have a voiceless obstruent in the initial position. It remains to be seen, however, whether this tendency applies only to the particular lexical class of mimetics or there is a general sound-symbolic tendency that voiced obstruents carry harder images than voiceless obstruents. Hence, we explore this second possibility and hypothesize that in general, voiced obstruents can carry harder images than voiceless obstruents.

Sound-symbolic associations have been found in words other than mimetics. A substantial body of previous research has demonstrated, using nonce words that are not mimetics, that this is the case (Sapir, 1929; Köhler, 1929/1947; Ramachandran & Hubbard, 2001; Blasi, Wichmann, Hammarström, Stadler, & Christianson, 2016, among others). This is also the case with Japanese. Several experimental studies have shown that at least some perceptual properties, such as size and shape, take part in sound-symbolic associations (Shinohara & Kawahara, 2016; Uemura, 1965). The hardness of food, however, remains understudied. Therefore, in the current study, we use nonce words to investigate whether voiced obstruents are associated with images of hardness of food.

Hypothesis (2) is derived primarily from an inference concerning the phonetic characteristics of plosives, i.e., the strength of burst. Plosives, or oral stops, are produced when articulators form a complete closure in the vocal tract. For example, the sound [p], the voiceless bilabial plosive, is produced with the two lips closed; the sound [t], the voiceless alveolar plosive, is produced when the blade of the tongue touches the alveolar ridge firmly enough to form a closure; and the sound [k], the voiceless velar plosive, is produced when the back of the tongue contacts the soft palate and forms a closure. When voiceless plosives [p, t, k] are articulated with release, a burst occurs due to differences between the intra-oral pressure and the atmospheric pressure. The strength of the burst varies according to the size of the space between the position of the closure and the glottis: the narrower the space is, the stronger the burst becomes. Therefore, the air pressure of the burst that accompanies the articulation of [k] is the strongest, while the air pressure of the burst that accompanies the articulation of [p] is the weakest. Thus, we have good phonetic and aerodynamic reasons to expect that velar plosives are more likely to evoke stronger images than alveolar and bilabial plosives and that alveolar plosives are more likely to evoke stronger images than bilabial plosives. In full, the order of the image of strength should be "bilabial < alveolar < velar."

From this hypothetical scale of the image of strength, we have derived our second hypothesis to be tested in the current study, the hypothesis regarding the image of hardness. As stated in (2), we hypothesize that the scale of the image of hardness can be represented as the formula "bilabial < alveolar < velar." This scale means that velar plosives are likely to evoke the hardest image among the three places of articulation, alveolar plosives may come in the middle, and bilabial plosives may be the least likely to evoke an image of hardness.[7]

7. Here, the image of strength is replaced by the image of hardness. This reasoning is metaphoric in a Cognitive Linguistic sense (STRENGTH IS HARDNESS). Also, as an anonymous reviewer suggests, hardness and strength may be metonymically linked: hard objects generally tend to be stronger and more durable than soft objects. However, we do not have enough space to develop this argument.

There are at least two other ideas forming the grounds for our hypothesis (2). One is related to the sound-symbolic images of bilabials in the names of products such as baby diapers; the other is related to sounds that appear in existing mimetic words in Japanese. Regarding the former, Kumagai and Kawahara (2017, 2020) demonstrate that in Japanese, bilabial consonants (i.e., [p, b, m, ɸ, w]) are associated with the image of diapers for babies. They conducted three kinds of studies: first, a survey of existing names of diaper brands sold in Japan; second, a psycholinguistic experiment using nonce words to detect differences in the effects of places of articulation, especially those of bilabials vs. other places; and third, an elicitation task involving the generation of names for a new diaper product and a new cosmetic product. In all three studies, they found that bilabial consonants tended to be associated with baby diapers. Thus, it is inferred that bilabials may induce baby-like images, which should be soft rather than hard, because babies have round and soft bodies.[8] Other places of articulation, such as alveolar and velar, are not sound-symbolically associated with the image of babies. Thus, the findings by Kumagai and Kawahara provide us with a good reason to predict that bilabials will be the least likely to evoke the image of hardness among the three places of articulation in Hypothesis (2).[9]

The other grounds for the hardness scale mentioned in Hypothesis (2) come from the study of mimetic words in Japanese. Sounds that appear in existing mimetic words in Japanese show that velar plosives tend to carry an image of hardness. For example, Japanese mimetic words that contain /k, g/ tend to describe situations in which something hits a surface that is hard (e.g., *kaan, kin,* and *goon*) (Hamano, 1998, 2014). Although the relationship between sounds in mimetic words and the psychological phenomenon of sound symbolism have not been completely clarified, we can predict that velar plosives may be associated with very hard images as compared with plosives at other places of articulation.

Hypothesis (2), "bilabial < alveolar < velar" as a hardness scale, has been drawn from these perceptual, psycholinguistic, and lexical considerations. First,

8. An anonymous reviewer suggests another possible motivation: it may be because we are supposed to be gentle and "soft" when we take care of babies.

9. The findings by Kumagai and Kawahara (2017, 2020) also induced other sound-symbolic studies. For example, Hosokawa, Atsumi, Uno, and Shinohara (2018) and Uno, Shinohara, Hosokawa, Atsumi, Kumagai, and Kawahara (2020) demonstrate that bilabial consonants are associated with "innocence" and are, thus, less likely to appear in villains' names when analyzing Disney characters in English and Japanese Pokémon characters. Shih, Ackerman, Hermalin, Inkelas, and Kavitskaya (2018) demonstrated that the names of "small" characters in Japanese Pokémon tend to contain bilabial consonants. Kumagai (2019, 2020) demonstrated that bilabials carry the image of "cuteness" by empirically testing nicknames.

the characteristics of kinesthetic perception we experience while articulating bilabial, alveolar, and velar plosives predict that velars may be the hardest, alveolar may come next, and bilabial may be the least hard. Second, previous studies by the first author of the present chapter, including a corpus study, psycholinguistic judgment tasks, and elicitation tasks, have revealed that bilabials tend to evoke the image of babies, leading to the inference that these sounds may be associated with softness. Third, the consideration of existing mimetic words in Japanese points to the tendency of velar plosives to be linked with an image of hardness. In sum, we can infer that velar plosives may be felt hardest, alveolar plosives may come next, and bilabial plosives will be the lowest on the hardness scale.

As specified in our hypotheses, the present study only tests the sound-symbolic effects of plosives. We exclude fricatives /s, z, ɕ, ɸ/ and affricates /t͡ɕ, d͡z, t͡s/, though Japanese has these obstruent consonants. Firstly, the reason for excluding fricatives is to make Hypothesis (2) statistically testable. Because the fricatives /s/ and /z/ are alveolar, they overlap with /t/ and /d/ regarding the place of articulation. On the other hand, Japanese lacks the voiced bilabial fricative, voiced velar fricative, and voiceless velar fricative. Thus, we cannot balance the number of voiced-voiceless pairs for each place of articulation if we include fricatives. This makes statistical analysis difficult. Instead, it is necessary to use the same number of pairs for all the three places of articulation. Therefore, we exclude fricatives. Second, affricates are also excluded because in Japanese, palatalized consonants are known to carry strong sound-symbolic images of "cuteness" or "smallness." Because the affricates /t͡ɕ, d͡ʑ/ are palatals, these sounds can have a particular influence on the images of words, which could distort our results. For this reason, affricates are excluded. Thus, the present study limits the obstruents to be tested to plosives alone, i.e., bilabial plosives /p, b/, alveolar plosives /t, d/, and velar plosives /k, g/. Each of these three pairs contains a voiceless member (/p/, /t/, or /k/) and a voiced member (/b/, /d/, or /g/). Using these plosives, we can statistically test the hypotheses.

These are the rationales for Hypotheses (1) and (2). Before moving on to the next section, a short note is in order. The hypotheses can be interpreted in two ways regarding which scale has stronger effects on the images of hardness. One interpretation is that voicing would be stronger; the other is that places of articulation would be stronger. We expect that voicing will have a stronger impact on the images of hardness because previous studies suggest that voicing in obstruents has sound-symbolic effects (Kawahara & Shinohara, 2008; Kawahara, Shinohara, & Uchimoto, 2008; Shinohara & Kawahara, 2016), while the sound-symbolic effect of places of articulation is scarcely reported (D'Onofrio, 2014; Nobile, 2015). However, we do not have enough evidence to tease apart the strengths of these two scales. Therefore, in this study, we will explore which may be a dominant factor among these two, in addition to testing each hypothesis.

2.2 Method

2.2.1 *Materials*

The current experiment aims to test the two hypotheses concerning sound-symbolic associations between obstruents and images of the hardness of food. As explained in the previous section, the first hypothesis is that voicing in obstruents affects the images of hardness. Specifically, we predict that voiced plosives [b, d, g] are more likely to be associated with the images of hardness than voiceless plosives [p, t, k]. The second hypothesis is that the places of articulation of the obstruents affect the images of hardness. Specifically, we predict that velar plosives [g] and [k] will evoke the hardest image, alveolar plosives [d] and [t] will come next, and bilabial plosives [b] and [p] will evoke the least hard image.

In our experiment, these two hypotheses are tested by means of a forced-choice method, in which participants are asked to read visually presented nonce words and choose one of the responses provided as six alternatives, ranging between the two adjectival poles "very hard" to "very soft" (i.e., a method similar to the semantic differential technique developed by Osgood, Suci, and Tannenbaum (1957)). For this purpose, we created stimuli that contain all the items to be tested: voiced plosives [b, d, g] and voiceless plosives [p, t, k].

The materials used as stimuli in the current experiment were targeted at native speakers of Japanese because our goal was to test the intuition of Japanese speakers. The materials consisted of 36 nonce words (i.e., words that do not exist in Japanese). Because these words were meaningless for Japanese speakers, we could avoid inferences based on the meanings of existing vocabulary.

The 36 nonce words were created based on the following principles. First, as already stated, none of them were real words in Japanese; that is, they did not exist in the Japanese lexicon. Second, each of them consisted of phonemes existing in Japanese. This is because our participants were all speakers of Japanese. Phonemes that are not included in one's native language may be incorrectly perceived or improperly distinguished; therefore, in our experiment, phonemes from other languages were avoided. Third, the phonemes were arranged so that they were perceivable for Japanese speakers. Not only the phonemes themselves but also the arrangements of phonemes should follow the phonological rules of the language in order for native speakers to be able to read the words, even though they have no pre-established meaning. Concretely, the stimuli words consisted only of open syllables (or CV-light syllables). This is because the most frequent syllabic pattern in Japanese is the CV (one consonant plus one vowel) form.

In addition to these general principles, the materials were prepared based on the following specific rules. First, all the target plosives [p, t, k, b, d, g] were used only word-initially.[10] That is, each plosive appeared only once, in the initial position of each word. Second, only three vowels [a, e, o] were used in the first syllable, even though Japanese has five vowels [a, e, o, i, u]. Third, the rest of each word was either "*-heru*" or "*-hira*". In all, we used six consonants for the initial syllable, three vowels for the initial syllable, and two patterns as the remaining syllables, which gives us a total of 36 words (6*3*2 = 36). Table 1 shows these 36 stimuli.

Table 1. Stimuli

	Voiceless			Voiced		
	p	t	k	b	d	g
_a	paheru	taheru	kaheru	baheru	daheru	gaheru
	pahira	tahira	kahira	bahira	dahira	gahira
_e	peheru	teheru	keheru	beheru	deheru	geheru
	pehira	tehira	kehira	behira	dehira	gehira
_o	poheru	toheru	koheru	boheru	doheru	goheru
	pohira	tohira	kohira	bohira	dohira	gohira

Several points should be noted concerning the construction of the stimuli. First, the decision to limit the target consonants in the initial position was based on previous insights into psycholinguistic tendencies. In our experiment, the target consonants appeared only in the initial position of each stimulus word because the sounds in the word-initial position have stronger psychological effects than sounds in other positions. This effect has been demonstrated by a considerable body of literature (e.g., Freedman & Landauer, 1966; Nooteboom, 1981; see Hawkins & Cutler, 1988, for further examples). The same kind of positional effects have also been reported for sound symbolism: word-initial sounds tend to have stronger effects on sound-symbolic associations (Kawahara, Shinohara, & Uchimoto, 2008). Subsequent experimental studies on sound symbolism have adopted similar approaches, using the word-initial position for target sounds (e.g., Kawahara & Kumagai, 2019a; Kumagai, 2019). The present study considered this positional effect on sound symbolism. Thus, we used the target consonant only in the word-initial position.[11]

10. To indicate each sound, brackets [ ] are used here, though these sounds were presented to the participants as Japanese phonemes. We used [ ] instead of / / because we consider the phonetic properties of the sounds in our discussion.

11. Aside from sound-symbolic studies, Kawahara and Shinohara (2011) demonstrate positional effects on pun formation in Japanese. In their empirical study, the pun phrases with word-initial mismatches in sounds were judged to be less acceptable as puns (or less likely to be puns), while the pun phrases with word-initial sounds that completely matched were more acceptable as puns, indicating that word-initial positions are more prominent in pun formation.

Second, the reason why the vowels [i, u] were excluded from the first syllable in our stimuli stems from the fact that these high vowels change the alveolar plosives [t, d] phonetically. When followed by the vowel [i], the voiceless alveolar plosive [t] becomes [t͡ɕ], which is an affricate. Thus, the syllable becomes [t͡ɕi] instead of [ti]. The voiced alveolar plosive [d] becomes an affricate [d͡ʑ] before [i]. Thus, the syllable becomes [d͡ʑi] instead of [di]. In the same way, [t] becomes an affricate [t͡s] before [u], and [d] becomes an affricate [d͡z] before [u]. Thus, the high vowels [i] and [u] change the phonetic properties of the alveolar plosives [t] and [d] in Japanese. For this reason, we avoided using [i] and [u] in the first syllable in the stimuli. Thus, the first syllable in each of our stimuli contained one of the three vowels [a, e, o].

Lastly, the above 36 stimuli were converted to *katakana* characters, which are syllabic characters used in the writing system of Japanese.[12] For example, the syllable /pa/ is represented by one *katakana* character, パ; /ke/ is represented by another *katakana* character, ケ; and so on. By using *katakana* character, with which ordinary Japanese speakers are familiar, participants could read each stimulus word easily and with no mistakes. Because the Roman alphabet is less familiar to Japanese speakers, using alphabetically represented words in the experiment might induce mistakes in reading the stimuli, and participants might thus imagine the wrong sounds.

2.2.2 *Participants*

Twenty-eight native speakers of Japanese (26 females and 2 males, ranging in age from 18 to 30 years) participated in this experiment voluntarily, receiving no reward for their participation. The third author obtained IRB permission for this study from her university.

2.2.3 *Procedure*

The experiment was carried out online using the survey-building software SurveyMonkey (www.surveymonkey.com). On the first page of the survey, the informed consent form was provided. Participants read it and clicked the button to indicate their agreement to participate; otherwise, they could exit the survey immediately.

---

12. In the Japanese writing system, four sets of characters are used: (1) *kanji*, which are Chinese characters first borrowed into Japanese more than one thousand years ago; (2) *katakana*, a set of syllabic characters that can represent all the Japanese syllables and moras, mainly used for non-Chinese origin foreign or loan words; (3) *hiragana*, another set of syllabic characters, mainly used for the original lexical group in Japanese, called *yamato*, and most functional morphemes; and (4) the Roman alphabet, which is used for foreign words, especially for abbreviations such as "USB".

The main task assigned to participants was to judge their images of hardness or softness for nonce words given as snack names. After giving their consent, participants proceeded to the page explaining the setting and general instructions. The instructions were to (1) imagine that they were creating new snack products in Japanese, (2) read the imaginary snack names that appeared on the page one by one, and (3) judge how hard or soft the snack might be based on the impression made by the sound of the name. They were also told that they should indicate their judgments by giving each word a rating on a six-point scale (1 = very soft, 2 = soft, 3 = slightly soft; 4 = slightly hard, 5 = hard, 6 = very hard). After the instructions page, the respondents answered a practice question to confirm that they understood how to perform the task. When the participants were ready, they proceeded to the main task block, in which 36 stimuli were visually presented in *katakana*, one at a time, in random order. Each word was presented on a separate page so that the participants could not look at all the words at once and compare their responses. They were instructed to avoid going back to the previous page once they had made their choice and proceeded to the next question. After responding to all questions, they were asked to provide their personal information: whether they had ever participated in experiments on sound symbolism, whether they were native speakers of Japanese, their gender, and their age. None of the participants in the current experiment had previously participated in experiments on sound symbolism, and all 28 participants were native speakers of Japanese.

2.3 Results

Figure 2 shows the average rating for each target plosive: [p] = 2.43; [t] = 2.88; [k] = 3.07; [b] = 3.98; [d] = 4.02; [g] = 4.54. A linear mixed model showed that there was a significant difference in average score between the voiced plosives and the voiceless plosives (4.18 vs. 2.79; $t = 17.99$, $p < .001$). The highest of the three voiceless plosives was [k], whose average was 3.07, while the lowest of the three voiced plosives was [b], whose average was 3.98. The average rating for [b] was significantly higher than the average rating for [k] (3.07 vs. 3.98; $t = -7.25$, $p < .001$). Thus, the voiced plosives were more likely to evoke images of hardness than the voiceless plosives.

Figure 2 also shows that place of articulation influenced the image of hardness. The voiceless plosives [p, t, k] were arranged in this order from left to right. That is, [p] was at the softest position, [t] was next, and [k] was at the hardest position among the three. The voiced plosives [b, d, g] showed a similar tendency. Specifically, [b] appears to the right of [k] (i.e., at a harder position than [k]), but [b] was the softest of the three voiced plosives. Then, [d] came next, and [g] was at the hardest position. In summary, the bilabials [p] and [b] were each softest within

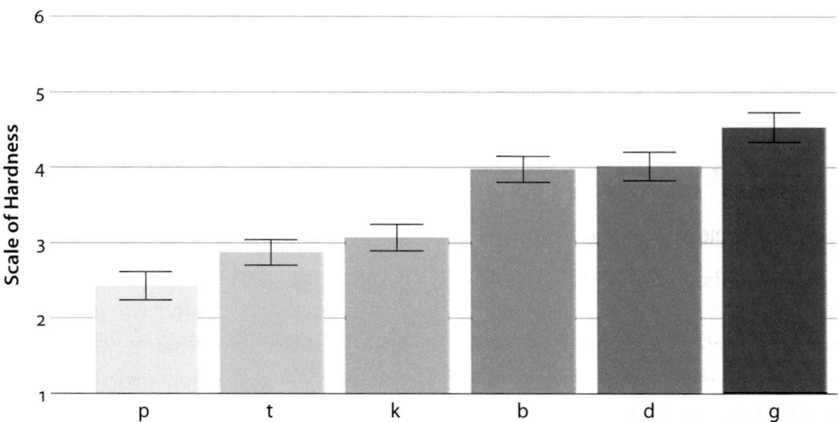

Figure 2. Average rating for each plosive

the voiceless group and voiced group respectively, the alveolars [t] and [d] were next in each group, and the velars [k] and [g] were hardest in each group. Thus, the place of articulation evoked an image of hardness in the order of "bilabials < alveolars < velars."

This overall tendency was supported by statistical analysis. Among the voiceless plosives, there were significant differences between [p] and [t] (2.43 vs. 2.88; $t = 3.47, p < .001$) and between [p] and [k] (2.43 vs. 3.07; $t = -5.04, p < .001$), though [t] and [k] showed no significant difference (2.88 vs. 3.07; $t = -1.54$, *ns*). Among the voiced plosives, there were significant differences between [b] and [g] (3.98 vs. 4.54; $t = 4.2, p < .001$) and between [d] and [g] (4.02 vs. 4.54: $t = 3.76, p < .001$), though [b] and [d] showed no significant difference (3.98 vs. 4.02; $t = -0.31$, *ns*). These statistical results show that place of articulation had overall effects in evoking sound-symbolic associations of hardness.[13,14]

13. In addition to the result concerning the hypothesis on places of articulation, it was also shown that among the six plosives in Japanese, [g] was perceived as hardest, while [p] was perceived as softest. This individual result has not been reported in the literature on sound symbolism; thus, it is a novel finding.

14. While the effects of consonants were clear, the effects of vowels were not significant. Among voiceless obstruents, the average scores for the three vowels were similar: /a/ = 2.85; /e/ = 2.71; /o/ = 2.82. Regression analyses showed no correlation between /a/ and /e/ ($t = -1.05$, *ns*), between /a/ and /o/ ($t = -0.18$, *ns*), or between /e/ and /o/ ($t = 0.86$, *ns*). Among voiced obstruents, again, the average scores for the three vowels were similar: /a/ = 4.22; /e/ = 4.01; /o/ = 4.3. Statistically, we found no correlation between /a/ and /e/ ($t = -1.54$, *ns*) or between /a/ and /o/ ($t = 0.57$, *ns*). A positive correlation between /e/ and /o/ was found ($t = 2.07, p < .05$). Because the sound-symbolic effects evoked by vowels are not included in our hypotheses, exploring the reason for this correlation will be left for future research.

3. Discussion

3.1 Comparison of the factors influencing the image of hardness of food

As shown in the previous section, both of our two hypotheses, (3) and (4), were supported. We will repeat them here.

(3) Voiceless < Voiced

(4) Bilabial < Alveolar < Velar

Hypothesis (3) holds that voicing in obstruents affects the images of hardness: voiced plosives [b, d, g] are more likely to be associated with hardness than voiceless plosives [p, t, k]. Hypothesis (4) holds that for obstruents, place of articulation affects the image of hardness: the velar plosives [g] or [k] may evoke the hardest image, the alveolar plosives [d] or [t] may come next, and the bilabial plosives [b] or [p] may evoke the least hard image. The results described in the previous section support both hypotheses.

Although we have discussed our two hypotheses separately, our findings suggest that we can explore the connections between them. From our results, we can attempt to determine which of the two factors, voicing in obstruents or place of articulation, is the stronger factor in determining sound-symbolic associations related to the hardness of food. By combining our results regarding the two hypotheses, the following one-dimensional hardness scale is obtained.

(5) voiceless labial [p] < voiceless alveolar [t] = voiceless velar [k] < voiced labial [b] = voiced alveolar [d] < voiced velar [g]

This scale indicates that voicing is the more dominant determining feature of the sound symbolism of the hardness of food, over place of articulation. As is clear from the scale represented in (5), all three voiced obstruents [b, d, g] evoke harder images than all the three voiceless obstruents [p, t, k]. If the place of articulation were the more dominant determining factor, we would have obtained the scale represented in (6), in which the two velar plosives [k] and [g] have the hardest positions, regardless of voicing.

(6) voiceless labial [p] < voiced labial [b] < voiceless alveolar [t] < voiced alveolar [d] < voiceless velar [k] < voiced velar [g]

In reality, (6) was not the case. Voiced plosives in all three places of articulation had significantly stronger effects on the image of hardness than either of the voiceless plosives. Therefore, we can argue that voicing may be the stronger source for the sound-symbolic image of the hardness of food as compared to the place of articulation for obstruents. We add this finding to the two hypotheses we supported in this study.

3.2 Motivations for sound-symbolic associations

As is well known, the Cognitive Linguistic view of language supports the idea that the structures of human language may be essentially embodied and motivated (Johnson, 1987; Lakoff, 1987; Lakoff & Johnson, 1980, 1999). Also, the idea that all linguistic units are symbols (Langacker, 1987) leads to the assumption that at each level of linguistic structures, the units are motivated by non-linguistic factors, such as other cognitive abilities or tendencies, physiological experiences, and the physical and cultural environment. It has been also argued that linguistic knowledge and intuition are acquired from our experiences of concrete usages, which are fed into our general cognitive ability to schematize (Tomasello, 2003). In short, Cognitive Linguistics regards language as a motivated, non-autonomous human ability, contrary to de Saussure's (1916) well-known thesis of arbitrariness.

Sound symbolism is a good example of a non-arbitrary, motivated linguistic phenomenon because the relationships between linguistic sounds and various images are motivated by non-autonomous and non-arbitrary associations. For this reason, a discussion of motivation is essential in the study of sound symbolism. In this section, therefore, we discuss motivations for the sound-symbolic associations that we have found in the present experiment.

More specifically, we will examine the three types of motivation for sound symbolism that have been most frequently discussed in previous studies: (1) acoustic, (2) articulatory, and (3) lexical motivations. In Section 3.2.1, we will provide an overview of these three types of motivation. Then, in Section 3.2.2 and 3.2.3, we will discuss how these three kinds of motivation can explain the results regarding Hypotheses (3) and (4). In 3.2.2, we will see whether acoustic, articulatory, and lexical motivations can explain the sound-symbolic associations between voiced/voiceless obstruents and the image of the hardness of food. In Section 3.2.3, we will examine whether the three types of motivation can explain the sound-symbolic associations between place of articulation and the image of the hardness of food.[15]

3.2.1 *Motivations for sound symbolism: Acoustic, articulatory, and lexical explanations*

In a large body of previous studies on sound symbolism, leading researchers have suggested several primary motivations for sound symbolism (Shinohara & Kawahara, 2016; Sidhu & Pexman, 2018). Among them, three types of explanation

15. It should be noted that discussions of motivation inevitably overlap, at least partly, with the logic of drawing hypotheses because evidence from previous studies is used in constructing hypotheses. In this section, we summarize the evidence at hand that can support our findings, with some overlap with the rationale for our hypotheses.

are often argued for. One is the acoustic explanation, based on the physical properties of sounds, such as frequencies. Another is the articulatory explanation, based on the movements or actions of our speech organs while pronouncing linguistic sounds. The third is the lexical explanation, which refers to the phonology and semantics of existing words in a particular language. In the present chapter, we examine all three types of motivation.

The major theory belonging to the first type (i.e., the acoustic explanation of sound symbolism) is represented by the Frequency Code Hypothesis, which was explicitly put forward by John Ohala (1984, 1994/2006). This hypothesis, referring to the acoustic properties of the linguistic sounds in question, suggests plausible motivations for sound-symbolic associations, especially those related to size. Ohala (1994/2006, p. 343) argues that a high F_0 (the fundamental frequency) signifies smallness, a non-threatening attitude, and a desire for the goodwill of the receiver, while a low F_0 conveys images of largeness, threat, self-confidence, and self-sufficiency. Thus, Ohala points to F_0 as the primary motivation for sound symbolism regarding size. The rationale is that F_0, all other things being equal, is inversely related to the mass of the vibrating membrane. This, in turn, is correlated with overall body mass (p. 333). This knowledge is instinctively utilized by animals: if an animal desires to threaten an antagonist, it is likely to produce sounds with a lower frequency by making the space in its speech organ expand. Because such instinctive knowledge is shared by many animals, there is no reason to deny that humans may also utilize this kind of acoustic mechanism, even unconsciously. In this way, the acoustic account has been particularly successful in explaining sound symbolism of size or magnitude. Hinton, Nichols, and Ohala (1994/2006, p. 10) provide an insightful suggestion concerning an acoustic account of sound symbolism in consonants, claiming that high-frequency consonants tend to be associated with images such as small size, sharpness, and rapid movement, while low-frequency consonants are associated with large size, softness, and heavy, slow movements. Thus, not only vowels but also consonants participate in sound symbolism motivated by the frequency code.

In addition to the acoustic account, an articulation-based account has been also discussed (Shinohara & Kawahara, 2016; Shinohara et al., 2016; Sidhu & Pexman, 2018). This account emphasizes iconic relationships between the movements of our articulatory organs and sound-symbolically conveyed images. For example, when articulating low vowels like [a], we open our mouth wide. In contrast, we make the oral cavity rather narrow by raising our lower jaw when we pronounce the high front vowel [i]. It is argued that we feel [a] to be bigger than [i] because these associations are motivated by the articulatory facts of the movements of our speech organs. The articulation-based explanation points to this kind of articulatory fact in explaining sound-symbolic associations (for an articulatory account of voiced obstruents associated with largeness, see Shinohara and Kawahara, 2016).

The third type of account (i.e., the lexical motivation) refers to the phonological and semantic properties of existing vocabulary in the language being studied. One such account is Firth's (1930) notion of *phonesthemes*. We can find many cases of (partially) systematic pairings of form and meaning in languages. For example, English words such as *glare, gleam, glimmer, glisten, glitter, gloss*, and *glow* all share the meaning of "light" or "vision" and share the sequence of phonemes *gl-*, so it can be inferred that *gl-* may be associated with the meaning of "light" or "vision". Speakers of English may extract this tendency from these existing words and develop the intuition that *gl-* may mean something like "light" or "vision". Other examples in English include *sn-*, which is related to the mouth or nose, as in *snack, snarl, snicker*, and *snout*, and *sl-*, which suggests frictionless, smooth motion, as in *slick, slide*, and *sled*. It should be noted, however, that for many cases of such phonesthemes, it is difficult to find direct motivations based on acoustic or articulatory facts. Thus, the motivation is lexical, rather than acoustic or articulatory.

Another case of lexical motivation can be seen in more randomly distributed phonemes in words that have similar meanings. For example, in Japanese, many words denoting sharp, angular shapes include obstruents rather than sonorants, such as *kado* 'edge', *toge* 'thorn', *tsuno* 'horn', and *saki* 'tip'. In contrast, words denoting a roundish shape or soft texture tend to have sonorants, such as *maru* 'circle', *nameraka* 'smooth', and *yawarakai* 'soft'. This uneven distribution of phonemes may develop, in Japanese speakers, a kind of intuition that obstruents fit sharp, angular shapes while sonorants fit round, smooth, soft objects or materials. Thus, lexical influences that stem from the uneven distribution of phonemes in existing words may be one of the motivations for sound symbolism. This kind of lexical motivation is not mutually exclusive with acoustic or articulatory motivations. The tendency of obstruents and sonorants to evoke angular and roundish shapes, respectively, is exactly what Köhler (1929/1947) demonstrated, and such sound-symbolic associations are considered to have physical motivations (Kawahara & Shinohara, 2012; Kawahara, Shinohara, & Grady, 2015; Shinohara & Kawahara, 2013; Shinohara et al., 2016).

These accounts of the motivation for sound-symbolic associations, especially the acoustic and the articulatory accounts, are sometimes treated as competing with one another. Researchers may ask which of the motivations is the strongest or which is the most agreed upon among researchers (Sidhu & Pexman, 2018). In reality, however, it may be inappropriate to seek only one type of motivation to apply to all sound-symbolic associations. Rather, more than one type of motivation may play a role in sound symbolism, and there may be combinatory effects. This is an open question. At the present stage of research, it is essential to accumulate empirical data to examine exactly what influences sound-symbolic associations. In this chapter, we will examine all three major motivations stated above to explain the sound symbolism of the hardness of food in terms of each of them. In what follows, we first examine Hypothesis (3) (the effect of voicing in obstruents), then Hypothesis (4) (the effect of the place of articulation). We will then point out that some motivations appear to explain our results, but others may not.

3.2.2 *Motivations for the sound-symbolic effect of voicing*

To investigate the role of the voiced/voiceless distinction in evoking sound-symbolic images of the hardness of food, we first examine the acoustic account, then the articulatory account, and finally, the lexical account. We will argue, first, that the acoustic account cannot explain our results and, second, that the articulatory and lexical accounts can explain them.

The acoustic account cannot explain our results for the following reasons. First, the most frequently discussed acoustic explanation for sound symbolism, i.e., the Frequency Code Hypothesis (Ohala, 1994/2006), is incompatible with our results regarding the effect of voicing in obstruents on the image of the hardness of food. This hypothesis predicts that consonants with lower frequencies should be associated with softness (Hinton, Nichols, & Ohala, 1994/2006, p. 10). Cross-linguistically, vowels have lower F_0 next to voiced obstruents than next to voiceless obstruents (Kingston & Diehl, 1994). Thus, voiced obstruents contribute to lower frequencies, suggesting that they may evoke softer images, according to the Frequency Code Hypothesis. In fact, however, our results demonstrate that consonants with lower frequencies, such as [b], tend to evoke harder images than consonants with higher frequencies, such as [p]. Therefore, the acoustic account based on the Frequency Code Hypothesis cannot explain our results.

Second, another acoustic factor, the intensity of burst in releasing plosives, also does not explain our results. Because voiceless plosives have a stronger burst than voiced plosives, an explanation based on the intensity of burst predicts that voiceless plosives will have a stronger association with hardness via the "strength is hardness" metaphor. However, as our results indicate, voiced plosives were more likely to be associated with hardness than voiceless plosives. Based on these two kinds of evidence, we conclude that the acoustic account cannot explain our results.

Meanwhile, the second of the three major accounts of sound symbolism, the articulatory account, can explain our results. The evidence comes from the physiological mechanism of the articulation of voiced obstruents. As Shinohara and Kawahara (2016) discuss in detail, the articulation of voiced obstruents involves an increase in air pressure in the sub-glottal cavity. This increase involves a hardening of the muscles in the vocal organs, and the proprioceptive perception of muscular hardness may lead to the sound-symbolic image of hardness. The mechanism operates as follows. When speakers pronounce voiced obstruents, they expand their oral cavities (Ohala, 1984). The entire oral cavity consists of two smaller spaces separated by the glottis: the oral cavity and the sub-glottal cavity. The air pressure in the oral cavity (intraoral air pressure) must be lower than the air pressure in the sub-glottal cavity (subglottal air pressure) in order for the air to flow across the glottis. However, the intraoral air pressure increases when the airway is significantly obstructed. This condition makes it difficult to pronounce voiced obstruents: speakers must execute muscular energy to keep the subglottal air pressure lower than the intraoral air pressure while articulating voiced obstruents. Indeed, in order to keep the intraoral air pressure sufficiently low, speakers expand their oral cavity in various ways: the larynx descends, the velum rises, and the cheeks expand (Ohala, 1984). In the course of this articulatory effort, speakers may feel muscular hardness because the muscles become harder when they expend energy. Thus, we can find a potential explanation for the sound-symbolic association between voiced obstruents and hardness in the articulatory account.

Finally, the lexical account for the sound symbolism of hardness can also explain our results. In general, lexical systems are language-specific; therefore, this explanation is essentially language-specific. It is well known that the Japanese language has a large inventory of mimetic words (see Tsujimura, this volume; Uno, Kobayashi, Shinohara, and Odake, this volume), and it has been demonstrated that voiced obstruents tend to occur in mimetic words that denote something hard, large, and heavy (Hamano, 1998). For example, *kotsun*, which has a voiceless obstruent [k] in its stem, imitates the sound of something hitting a hard surface. This mimetic word has a counterpart that has a voiced obstruent [g], i.e., *gotsun* which means something harder, bigger, or heavier hitting a hard surface. The mimetic *gotsun* makes us feel that the impact of the hitting is harder and more intense than *kotsun*.[16] Such contrast between voiced and voiceless obstruents in Japanese mimetics is highly systematic and pervasive: mimetic words that have voiced obstruents in the stem are associated with harder, larger, or heavier meanings than those with voiceless obstruents. It is, therefore, natural that voiced obstruents tend to evoke harder images in the intuition of Japanese speakers because they possess a lexical

16. An anonymous reviewer suspects that /g/-initial mimetics are felt "harder" than their /k/-initial counterparts not because they depict "harder" objects but because they primarily depict "larger" or "heavier" objects and these images may then be linked to the "harder" image by inference. However, *gotsun* is used to describe not a large but a soft object, such as a huge ball of wool, or a heavy but soft object, such as a rubber balloon filled with mercury or liquid concrete, hitting something. Hardness seems to be necessary for something to be depicted by *gotsun*. Likewise, it may be assumed that /g/-initial mimetics depict harder objects than their /k/-initial counterparts in general.

knowledge of mimetics. Based on this knowledge, Japanese speakers may associate voiced obstruents in general with the image of hardness.

In summary, while the acoustic account does not explain our results, the other two accounts, the articulatory and lexical accounts, are compatible with them. The articulatory account points to universal tendencies because the physiology of articulation may be common to all human beings. On the other hand, the lexical account depends on the lexical structure of each language and, in this sense, does not imply universality. Our results bridge these two accounts. Therefore, we cannot readily answer the question of the universality of the motivations for sound symbolism based on the present results.

3.2.3 *Motivations for the sound-symbolic effect of place of articulation*

To investigate the role of place of articulation in evoking sound-symbolic images of the hardness of food, we again examine the acoustic account, the articulatory account, and finally, the lexical account. All three types of accounts can explain our results, at least in part or indirectly. By combining them all, we can convincingly argue that the places of articulation of obstruents we investigated, i.e., bilabial, alveolar, and velar, evoke different images of hardness of food in motivated ways.

First, the acoustic account can partly explain our results regarding place of articulation for the following reasons. Previous studies have shown that bilabial consonants have relatively lower frequencies. For example, according to Stevens and Blumstein's (1978) theoretical calculation, the F_2 of [p] is estimated to distribute around 1,000 Hz, that of [k] around 1,500 Hz, and that of [t] around 2,000 Hz. This means that the bilabial plosive [p] has the lowest frequency, while the alveolar plosive [t] and velar plosive [k] have comparatively higher frequencies. In addition, bilabial consonants, including [p], influence the formants of the surrounding vowels so that the frequencies of the vowels become lower (Delattre, Liberman, & Cooper, 1955; Stevens & Blumstein, 1978). In short, bilabials are linked with lower frequencies. Again, according to the Frequency Code Hypothesis, lower frequencies evoke softer images. Therefore, the acoustic account can explain our results concerning the places of articulation of obstruents, at least for bilabials and alveolars/velars.[17]

Further evidence for the acoustic account appears the intensity of airflow in plosives at three places of articulation.[18] As Berlin (2006, p. 36) reports in his per-

17. Note that [t] has the highest frequency among the three plosives in Stevens and Blumstein's calculation. From this comparison, it is inferred that [t] may be the hardest of the three, which is not compatible with our results. It is for this reason we argue that the acoustic account can only partly explain our results.

18. The differences in the intensity of airflow may be felt by the articulatory organs. In this sense, this explanation could be also articulatory.

sonal communication with John Ohala, the voiceless stops [p], [t], and [k] are graded in terms of the intensity of the airflow (burst) in the order "[p] < [t] < [k]". This means that the plosive [k] has the strongest burst among the three, [t] the next, and [p] the weakest. We can infer that a stronger burst may be felt as harder than a weaker one because a burst is a kind of magnitude of energy. Thus, the above order may parallel the images of hardness: [k] evokes the hardest image, [t] the next, and [p] the least hard. Thus, we can find at least some acoustic explanations for the sound-symbolic images of hardness regarding the three places of articulation examined in this study.

We can also find articulatory accounts that explain our results. Bilabial consonants are produced by contact of the upper lip with the lower lip. This may be directly associated with the image of softness because lips are softer organs than the alveolar ridge or the velum. Tongues are harder than lips because they consist of muscles. In addition, when pronouncing alveolar plosives, the tip of the tongue touches the alveolar ridge, which is not as soft as the lips or the tongue. The velar plosives are articulated by touching the velum with the root of the tongue, and while performing this gesture, we cannot feel the softness of the root of the tongue or the velum. It is our physical experience of pronouncing bilabial, alveolar, and velar plosives that makes us feel that the bilabials are the softest of the three. Thus, the articulatory account can explain why bilabials occupy the softest position in our scale.

Finally, the lexical account can explain our results, at least in part. Kumagai and Kawahara (2017, 2020) have demonstrated that bilabial consonants tend to evoke the image of babies. They investigated diaper names in Japanese and English and argue that there is a strong tendency for diaper names to contain bilabial sounds, as in *Pampers, Moony, Merries*, and *Mamypoko*. The same tendency has been observed in their psycholinguistic experiments using nonce words for fictitious diaper brands. Kumagai (2019, 2020) also demonstrates that bilabials are associated with the image of cuteness. These previous studies suggest that bilabials may evoke small, cute, and soft beings like babies. From these findings, we can infer that bilabials may be felt as softer than alveolars or velars and that this tendency may be mediated by a lexical association with existing proper names. Of course, this tendency may also be the result of phonetically motivated sound-symbolic associations. Because the acoustic and articulatory accounts can independently explain why bilabials are perceived as softer, it can be argued that the three types of motivation may work together to produce an overall tendency on the part of places of articulation of plosives to contribute to different levels of association with hardness.

In conclusion, the acoustic, the articulatory, and the lexical accounts are all compatible with our results regarding place of articulation, though some explain our scale only partially. At the least, the three accounts explain very clearly why bilabials tend to evoke softer images than the other two places of articulation. The difference between alveolar and velar plosives in evoking images of hardness remains to be seen.[19]

4. Conclusions and implications

4.1 Conclusions

The findings of this study can be summarized as follows. First, our two hypotheses concerning the sound symbolism of the hardness of food were both supported by the results of our experiment. First, voiced obstruents are more likely to evoke the image of hardness of food than voiceless obstruents. Second, place of articulation affects how sound-symbolic images of hardness are evoked: velars are most likely to evoke hard images, alveolars next, and bilabials the least likely. In addition to the positive evaluation of the two hypotheses, our results also suggest that voicing is a stronger factor than place of articulation in evoking the image of the hardness of food.

We also discussed the motivations for these sound-symbolic associations. The acoustic, articulatory, and lexical accounts were examined. Regarding the voicing of obstruents, the acoustic account cannot explain our results, while the other two accounts, the articulatory and lexical accounts, are compatible with them. Regarding the place of articulation, all three accounts can explain our results, at least in part.

4.2 Implications for further studies

There are some remaining questions that have not been answered by the present study. First, we limited our target to the image of hardness in snacks; therefore, in order to investigate the sound symbolism of food texture in general, it will be appropriate to extend the target of study to other textures, such as viscosity and thickness. Second, though we restricted our study to Japanese, a cross-linguistic comparison of the sound symbolism of food texture may be fruitful, especially in determining whether this kind of sound symbolism is universal. Third, other research methods can also be attempted. For example, an extensive corpus study of existing names

19. As an anonymous reviewer suggests, Japanese mimetics have a certain number of velar-initial mimetics for hardness (e.g., *konkon, kachikachi, korikori*) and some alveolar-initial mimetics for softness (e.g., *torotoro, debudebu, darudaru*). However, because there are also velar-initial mimetics that express softness (e.g., *kunyakunya, kunekune, gunyogunyo*), it is difficult to explain the difference between alveolar and velar plosives in evoking the images of hardness in terms of existing mimetic words in Japanese.

for food products may be helpful in determining whether the present results are attested in real words. It may also be intriguing to investigate the relationship between adult intuition regarding sound-symbolic association and language acquisition by children (see Imai & Kita, 2014; Perry, Perlman, Winter, Massaro, & Lupyan, 2018). Of course, the topics for further studies are not limited to the above.

The present study also has broader implications for interdisciplinary research. For example, the details of sound-symbolic phenomena in language can be applied to marketing. In language-related studies, there have been many previous reports on how sound-symbolic effects are reflected in brand or product names, including those of foods (Bolts, Mangigian, & Allen, 2016; Jurafsky, 2014; Klink, 2000; Kumagai & Kawahara, 2017, 2020; Peterson & Ross, 1972; Yorkston & Menon, 2004, among others). The findings of such studies, in combination with experimental studies such as this one, may be useful for marketing because food product names can be selected for their sound-symbolic effectiveness.

Another possibility for interdisciplinary inquiry involves collaboration with food technology, an industry in which researchers are investigating the relationship between the properties of food and the perceptual reactions they evoke in consumers. These studies often use language-based data, such as words and phrases obtained from human participants (Funakubo et al., 2016). For example, many studies have been carried out using an elicitation method: i.e., asking participants to describe food characteristics, such as texture and taste, using language. To establish a solid foundation for such studies, it may be important to possess detailed information about language, including sound-symbolic associations between linguistic sounds and the properties of food. Thus, studying the language of food can contribute to advances in food technology.

In addition, studies of sound symbolism can, of course, be linked to the general field of cognitive science because sound symbolism is a type of cognitive phenomena rooted in the human mental structure. Since the publication of the seminal work by Ramachandran and Hubbard (2001), sound symbolism has been a hot topic in cognitive science, neuroscience, artificial intelligence, and many other modern disciplines. It should be possible for researchers investigating sound symbolism to fruitfully collaborate with researchers in these other fields.

Finally, studies of the sound symbolism of food texture can contribute to research into the food-related language used in the media. Although we did not use Japanese food-related media in a direct way, our method of experimentation, using pseudo-names for snacks, can provide a basis for research on the relationship between Japanese food and the Japanese language. As some studies have revealed, language use can affect our experience of eating (Funakubo et al., 2016). Therefore, it is important to look closely into the mechanism relating our perceptions of language and food. The present chapter provides an example of such an academic pursuit.

Acknowledgements

We express our thanks to the two anonymous reviewers for very useful comments. The usual disclaimer applies.

Funding

This chapter is based on a study supported by a Grant-in-Aid for Early-Career Scientists from JSPS (#19K13164), awarded to the first author, and a Grant-in-Aid for Challenging Exploratory Research from JSPS (#17K02679), awarded to the third author.

References

Ahlner, F., & Zlatev, J. (2010). Cross-modal iconicity: A cognitive semiotic approach to sound symbolism. *Sign Systems Studies*, *38*(1/4), 298–348. https://doi.org/10.12697/SSS.2010.38.1-4.11

Akita, K. (2009). A grammar of sound-symbolic words in Japanese: Theoretical approaches to iconic and lexical properties of mimetics (unpublished doctoral dissertation). Kobe University, Japan. Retrieved from http://www.lib.kobeu.ac.jp/infolib/meta_pub/G0000003kernel_D1004724

Akita, K. (2015). Sound symbolism. In J.-O. Östman & J. Verschueren (Eds.), *Handbook of pragmatics*. Amsterdam: John Benjamins. https://doi.org/10.1075/hop.19.sou1

Bergen, B. (2004). The psychological reality of phonaesthemes. *Language*, *80*(2), 290–311. https://doi.org/10.1353/lan.2004.0056

Berlin, B. (2006). The first congress of ethonozoological nomenclature. *Journal of Royal Anthropological Institution*, *12*, 23–44. https://doi.org/10.1111/j.1467-9655.2006.00271.x

Blasi, D. E., Wichmann, S., Hammarström, H., Stadler, P. F., & Christianson, M. H. (2016). Sound-meaning association biases evidenced across thousands of languages. *PNAS*, *113*(39), 10818–10823. https://doi.org/10.1073/pnas.1605782113

Bolinger, D. L. (1946). The sign is not arbitrary. *Thesaurus. Tomo V. Núms. 1, 2 y 3*, 52–62.

Bolts, M. G., Mangigian, G. M., & Allen, M. B. (2016). Phonetic symbolism and memory for advertisements. *Applied Cognitive Psychology*, *30*(6), 1088–1092. https://doi.org/10.1002/acp.3284

Brown, R., & Ford, M. (1961). Address in American English. *Journal of Abnormal and Social Psychology*, *62*, 375–385. https://doi.org/10.1037/h0042862

Cassidy, K. W., Kelly, M. H., & Sharoni, L. J. (1999). Inferring gender from name phonology. *Journal of Experimental Psychology: General*, *128*, 362–381. https://doi.org/10.1037/0096-3445.128.3.362

Cutler, A., McQueen, J., & Robinson, K. (1990). Elizabeth and John: Sound patterns of men's and women's names. *Journal of Linguistics*, *26*, 471–482. https://doi.org/10.1017/S0022226700014754

Delattre, P. C., Liberman, A. M., & Cooper, F. S. (1955). Acoustic loci and transitional cues for consonants. *Journal of the Acoustical Society of America*, *27*, 769–773. https://doi.org/10.1121/1.1908024

D'Onofrio, A. (2014). Phonetic detail and dimensionality in sound-shape correspondences: Refining the bouba-kiki paradigm. *Language and Speech*, *57*(3), 367–393. https://doi.org/10.1177/0023830913507694

de Saussure, F. (1916). *Course in general linguistics*. London: Peter Owen.

Dingemanse, M., Blasi, D. E., Lupyan, G., Christianson, M. H., & Monaghan, P. (2015). Arbitrariness, iconicity and systematicity in language. *Trends in Cognitive Sciences*, *19*(10), 603–615. https://doi.org/10.1016/j.tics.2015.07.013

Firth, J. R. (1930). *Speech*. London: Benn's Sixpenny Library.

Freedman, J. L., & Landauer, T. K. (1966). Retrieval of long-term memory: 'Tip-of-the-tongue' phenomenon. *Psychonomic Science*, *4*, 309–310. https://doi.org/10.3758/BF03342310

Funakubo, K., Kobayashi, F., Uno, R., Shinohara, K., & Odake, S. (2016). Gaisoo pakkeeji-ni okeru shokkan-hyoogen "karit"-to kisshokuji shokkan-hyoogen-no icchisei [Correspondence between texture expressions while eating food and the word *karit* on the package]. Paper presented at Kanto Branch, Japan Society for Bioscience, Biotechnology, and Agrochemistry, Tokyo: Nippon Veterinary and Life Science University.

Haiman, J. (1983). Iconic and economic motivation. *Language*, *59*, 781–819. https://doi.org/10.2307/413373

Haiman, J. (1985a). *Natural syntax*. Cambridge: Cambridge University Press.

Haiman, J. (Ed.) (1985b). *Iconicity in syntax*. Amsterdam: John Benjamins. https://doi.org/10.1075/tsl.6

Hamano, S. (1998). *The sound-symbolic system of Japanese*. Stanford: CSLI Publications.

Hamano, S. (2014). *Nihongo no onomatope: On'syootyoo to koozoo* [Onomatopoeia in Japanese: Sound symbolism and structure]. Tokyo: Kuroshio.

Hawkins, J. A., & Cutler, A. (1988). Psycholinguistic factors in morphological asymmetry. In J. A. Hawkins (Ed.), *Explaining language universals* (pp. 280–317). Oxford: Basil Blackwell.

Hinton, L., Nichols, J., & Ohala, J. (1994/2006). Introduction: sound-symbolic processes. In L. Hinton, J. Nichols, & J. Ohala (Eds.) *Sound symbolism* (pp. 1–12) Cambridge: Cambridge University Press.

Hockett, C. (1963). The problem of universals in language. In J. Greenberg (Ed.), *Universals of language* (pp. 1–22). Cambridge, MA: MIT Press.

Hosokawa, Y., Atsumi, N., Uno, R., & Shinohara, K. (2018). Evil or not? Sound symbolism in Pokémon and Disney character names. Poster session presented at the 1st Conference on Pokémonastics, Keio University, Japan.

Imai, M., & Kita, S. (2014). The sound symbolism bootstrapping hypothesis for language acquisition and language evolution. *Philosophical Transactions of the Royal Society B* 369, 20130298 https://doi.org/10.1098/rstb.2013.0298

Irwin, F. W., & Newland, E. (1940). A genetic study of the naming of visual figures. *Journal of Psychology*, *9*, 3–16. https://doi.org/10.1080/00223980.1940.9917674

Jakobson, R. (1978). *Six lectures on sound and meaning*. Cambridge, MA: Cambridge University Press.

Janda, L. A. (2013). Quantitative methods in Cognitive Linguistics: An introduction. In L. A. Janda (ed.), *Cognitive linguistics: The quantitative turn* (pp. 1–32). Berlin: De Gruyter Mouton. https://doi.org/10.1515/9783110335255.1

Jespersen, O. (1922/1933). Symbolic value of the vowel *i*. In *Phonologica. Selected papers in English, French and German* (Vol. 1) (pp. 283–303). Copenhagen: Levin and Munksgaard.

Johnson, M. (1987). *The body in the mind: The bodily basis of meaning, imagination, and reason*. Chicago: University of Chicago Press. https://doi.org/10.7208/chicago/9780226177847.001.0001

Jurafsky, D. (2014). *The language of food: A linguist reads the menu*. New York: W. W. Norton & Company.

Kawahara, S. (2017). *"A" ha "i" yori ookii? Onsyootyoo de manabu onseigaku nyuumon* [Introducing phonetics through sound symbolism]. Tokyo: Hituzi Shobo.

Kawahara, S. (2020). Sound symbolism and theoretical phonology. *Language and Linguistic Compass, 14*(8), e12372. https://doi.org/10.1111/lnc3.12372

Kawahara, S., Isobe, M., Kobayashi, Y., Monou, T., & Okabe, R. (2018). Acquisition of sound symbolic values of vowels and voiced obstruents by Japanese children: Using a Pokémonastics paradigm. *Journal of the Phonetic Society of Japan, 22*(2), 122–130.

Kawahara, S., Noto, A., & Kumagai, G. (2018). Sound symbolic patterns in Pokémon names. *Phonetica, 75*(3), 219–244. https://doi.org/10.1159/000484938

Kawahara, S., & Kumagai, G. (2019a). Expressing evolution in Pokémon names: Experimental explorations. *Journal of Japanese Linguistics, 35*(1), 3–38. https://doi.org/10.1515/jjl-2019-2002

Kawahara, S., & Kumagai, G. (2019b). Inferring Pokémon types using sound symbolism: The effects of voicing and labiality. *Onsei Kenkyu* [Journal of the Phonetic Society of Japan], *23*(2), 111–116.

Kawahara, S., Godoy, M. C., & Kumagai, G. (2020). Do sibilants fly? Evidence from the sound symbolic pattern in Pokémon names. *Open Linguistics, 6*(1), 386–400. https://doi.org/10.1515/opli-2020-0027

Kawahara, S., & Shinohara, K. (2008). A cross-linguistic study of sound symbolism: A case of voicing. Paper presented at International Conference on Language, Cognition, and Communication, Brighton University, UK.

Kawahara, S., & Shinohara, K. (2011). Phonetic and psycholinguistic prominences in pun formation: Experimental evidence for positional faithfulness. In M. den Dikken & W. McClure (Eds.), *Japanese/Korean Linguistics, 18* (pp. 177–188). Stanford: CSLI Publications.

Kawahara, S., & Shinohara, K. (2012). A tripartite trans-module relationship between sounds, shapes and emotions: A case of abrupt modulation. In N. Miyake, D. Peebles, & R. P., Cooper (Eds.), *Proceedings of the 34th Annual Meeting of the Cognitive Science Society* (pp. 569–574). Austin, TX: Cognitive Science Society.

Kawahara, S., Shinohara, K., & Grady, J. (2015). Iconic inferences about personality: From sounds and shapes. In M. Hiraga, W. Herlofsky, K. Shinohara, & K. Akita (Eds.), *Iconicity: East meets west* (pp. 57–69). Amsterdam: John Benjamins. https://doi.org/10.1075/ill.14.03kaw

Kawahara, S., Shinohara, K., & Uchimoto, Y. (2008). A positional effect in sound symbolism: An experimental study. *Proceedings of the 8th Meeting of Japan Cognitive Linguistics Association*, 417–427.

Kingston, J., & Diehl, R. (1994). Phonetic knowledge. *Language, 70*(3), 419–454. https://doi.org/10.1353/lan.1994.0023

Klink, R. R. (2000). Creating brand names with meaning: the use of sound symbolism. *Marketing Letters, 11*, 5–20. https://doi.org/10.1023/A:1008184423824

Köhler, W. (1929/1947). *Gestalt psychology: An introduction to new concepts in modern psychology*. New York: Liveright.

Kumagai, G. (2019). A sound-symbolic alternation to express cuteness and the orthographic Lyman's Law in Japanese. *Journal of Japanese Linguistics, 35*(1), 39–74. https://doi.org/10.1515/jjl-2019-2004

Kumagai, G. (2020). The pluripotentiality of bilabial consonants: The images of softness and cuteness in Japanese and English. *Open Linguistics, 6*, 693–707. https://doi.org/10.1515/opli-2020-0040

Kumagai, G., & Kawahara, S. (2017). Onsyootyoo no tyuusyoosei: Akatyan- yoo-omutu no neemingu ni okeru sin'on [How abstract is sound symbolism? Labiality in Japanese diaper names]. *Proceedings of the 31st Meeting of the Phonetic Society of Japan*, 49–54.

Kumagai, G., & Kawahara, S. (2019). Pokemon no naduke ni okeru boin to yuusei-sogaion no kooka: Jikken to riron kara no apurooti [Effects of vowels and voiced obstruents on Pokémon names: Experimental and theoretical approaches]. *Gengo Kenkyu* [Journal of the Linguistic Society of Japan], *155*, 65–99.

Kumagai, G., & Kawahara, S. (2020). On'insosee ni motoduku onsyootyoo: Akatyan- yoo-omutu no naduke ni okeru sin'on [Feature-based sound symbolism: Labiality and diaper names in Japanese]. *Gengo Kenkyu* [Journal of the Linguistic Society of Japan], *157*, 149–161.

Lakoff, G. (1987). *Women, Fire, and Dangerous Things: What Categories Reveal About the Mind.* University of Chicago Press. https://doi.org/10.7208/chicago/9780226471013.001.0001

Lakoff, G., & Johnson, M. (1980). *Metaphors we live by*. Chicago: Chicago University Press.

Lakoff, G., & Johnson, M. (1999). *Philosophy in the flesh*. New York: Basic Books.

Langacker, R. W. (1987). *Foundations of Cognitive Grammar: Volume I: Theoretical Prerequisites.* Stanford, CA: Stanford University Press.

Levin, G., Liberman, Z., Blonk, J., & La Barbara, J. (2003). *Messa di voce*: an audiovisual performance and installation for voice and interactive media. Retrieved from http://tmema.org/messa/messa.html#background

Lewis, M. M. (1934). *Infant speech: A study of the beginnings of language*. London: Routledge.

Lindauer, S. M. (1990). The meanings of the physiognomic stimuli *taketa* and *maluma*. *Bulletin of Psychonomic Society*, *28*(1), 47–50. https://doi.org/10.3758/BF03337645

Lockwood, G., & Dingemanse, M. (2015). Iconicity in the lab: A review of behavioral, developmental, and neuroimaging research into sound-symbolism. *Frontiers in Psychology*, *6*, 1–14.

Malkile, Y. (1990). Diachronic problems in phonosymbolism. Edita and Inedita, 1979–1980, Volume I. Amsterdam/Philadelphia: John Benjamins Publishing Company. https://doi.org/10.1075/z.eai1

Murdock, G. P. (1959). Cross-language parallels in parental kin terms. *Anthropological Linguistics*, *1*(9), 1–5.

Nobile, L. (2015). Phonemes as images: An experimental inquiry into shape-sound symbolism applied to the distinctive features of French. In M. K. Higara, W. J. Herlofsky, K. Shinohara, & K. Akita (Eds.), *Iconicity: East Meets West* (pp. 71–91). Amsterdam: John Benjamins. https://doi.org/10.1075/ill.14.04nob

Nooteboom, S. G. (1981). Lexical retrieval from fragments of spoken words: Beginnings vs. endings. *Journal of Phonetics*, *9*, 407–424. https://doi.org/10.1016/S0095-4470(19)31017-4

Nuckolls, J. B. (1999). The case for sound symbolism. *Annual Review of Anthropology*, *28*, 225–252. https://doi.org/10.1146/annurev.anthro.28.1.225

Ohala, J. (1984). An ethological perspective on common cross-language utilization of F0 of voice. *Phonetica*, *41*, 1–16. https://doi.org/10.1159/000261706

Ohala, J. (1994/2006). The frequency code underlies the sound symbolic use of voice pitch. In L. Hinton, J. Nichols, & J. Ohala (Eds.), *Sound symbolism* (pp. 325–347). Cambridge: Cambridge University Press.

Osgood, C. E., Suci, G., & Tannenbaum, P. (1957). *The measurement of meaning*. Urbana, Illinois: University of Illinois Press.

Parise, C. V. & Spence, C. (2012). Audiovisual crossmodal correspondences and sound symbolism: A study using the implicit association test. *Experimental Brain Research*, *220*(3–4), 319–333. https://doi.org/10.1007/s00221-012-3140-6

Perniss, P., Thompson, R. L., & Vigliocco, G. (2010). Iconicity as a general property of language: Evidence from spoken and signed languages. *Frontiers in Psychology*. Volume 1. Article 227. https://doi.org/10.3389/fpsyg.2010.00227

Perniss, P., & Vigliocco, G. (2014). The bridge of iconicity: from a world of experience to the experiment of language. *Philosophical Transactions of the Royal Society B* 369: 20130300. https://doi.org/10.1098/rstb.2014.0179

Perry, L. K., Perlman, M., Winter, B., Massaro, D. W., & Lupyan, G. (2018). Iconicity in the speech of children and adults. *Developmental Science, 21*(3), e12572. https://doi.org/10.1111/desc.12572

Peterson, R. A., & Ross, I. (1972). How to name new brand names. *Journal of Advertising Research, 12*(6), 29–34.

Ramachandran, V. S., & Hubbard, E. M. (2001). Synesthesia: A window into perception, thought, and language. *Journal of Consciousness Studies, 8*(12), 3–34.

Reilly, J., Biun, D., Cowles, W., & Peelle, J. (2008). Where did words come from? A linking theory of sound symbolism and natural language evolution. *Nature Proceedings*. https://doi.org/10.1038/npre.2008.2369.1

Sapir, E. (1929). A study in phonetic symbolism. *Journal of Experimental Psychology, 12*, 225–239. https://doi.org/10.1037/h0070931

Sato, Y. (2011). Shikisai-meido-to shiin-no yuuseisei-ni mirareru onshouchouteki kankei [Sound symbolic relation in brightness in color and voicing in consonants] (unpublished master's thesis). Tokyo University of Agriculture and Technology, Japan.

Shih, S. S., Ackerman, J., Hermalin, N., Inkelas, S., & Kavitskaya, D. (2018). Pokémonikers: A study of sound symbolism and Pokémon names. *Proceedings of Linguistic Society of America 2018, 3*(42), 1–6. https://doi.org/10.3765/plsa.v3i1.4335

Shinohara, K., & Kawahara, S. (2009). Onshoutyou-no gengokan hikaku: yuuseisei-no imeeji-ni kansuru jikken kenkyuu [A cross-linguistic study of sound symbolism: images evoked by voicing]. Paper presented at the 26th Meeting of Japanese Cognitive Science Society. Keio University, Japan.

Shinohara, K., & Kawahara, S. (2013). The sound symbolic nature of Japanese maid names. *Proceedings of the 13th Annual Meeting of the Japanese Cognitive Linguistics Association, 13*, 183–193.

Shinohara, K., & Kawahara, S. (2016). A cross-linguistic study of sound symbolism: The images of size. *Proceedings of the 36th Annual Meeting of the Berkeley Linguistics Society*, 396–410.

Shinohara, K., Yamauchi, N., Kawahara, S., & Tanaka, H. (2016). *Takete* and *maluma* in action: A cross-modal relationship between gestures and sounds. *PLoS ONE, 11*(9), e0163525. https://doi.org/10.1371/journal.pone.0163525

Sidhu, D. D., & Pexman, P. M. (2018). Five mechanisms of sound symbolic association. *Psychonomic Bulletin & Review, 25*(5), 1619–1643. https://doi.org/10.3758/s13423-017-1361-1

Slater, A. S., & Feinman, S. (1985). Gender and the phonology of North American first names. *Sex Roles, 13*, 429–440. https://doi.org/10.1007/BF00287953

Spence, C. (2011). Crossmodal correspondences: A tutorial review. *Attention, Perception, & Psychophysics, 73*, 971–995. https://doi.org/10.3758/s13414-010-0073-7

Spence, C. (2015). Eating with our ears: Assessing the importance of the sounds of consumption on out perception and enjoyment of multisensory flavor experiences. *Flavor, 4*(3). https://doi.org/10.1186/2044-7248-4-3

Stevens, K., & Blumstein, S. (1978). Invariant cues for place of articulation in stop consonants. *Journal of the Acoustical Society of America, 64*, 1358–1368. https://doi.org/10.1121/1.382102

Tessier, A.-M. (2010). Short, but not sweet: Markedness preferences and reversals in English hypocoristics. Paper presented at the Annual Conference of the Canadian Linguistic Association, Montreal, Concordia University.

Tomasello, M. (2003). *Constructing a language: A usage-based theory of language acquisition*. Cambridge, MA: Harvard University Press.

Uemura, Y. (1965). Onsei-no hyoushousei-ni tsuite [On the symbolic aspects of sounds]. *Gengo seikatsu* (171), 66–70. Tokyo: Chikumashobo.

Ultan, R. (1978). Size-sound symbolism. In J. Greenberg (Ed.), *Universals of human language II: Phonology* (pp. 525–568). Stanford: Stanford University Press.

Uno, R., Shinohara, K., Hosokawa, Y., Atsumi, N., Kumagai, G., & Kawahara, S. (2020). What's in a villain's name? Sound symbolic values of voiced obstruents and bilabial consonants. *Review of Cognitive Linguistics*, *18*(2), 428–457. https://doi.org/10.1075/rcl.00066.uno

Whissell, C. (2001). Cues to referent gender in randomly constructed names. *Perceptual and Motor Skills*, *93*, 856–858. https://doi.org/10.2466/pms.2001.93.3.856

Wright, S., & Hay, J. (2002). Fred and Trema: A phonological conspiracy. In S. Benor, M. Rose, D. Sharma, J. Sweetland, & Q. Zhang (Eds.), *Gendered practices in language* (pp. 175–191). Stanford: CSLI Publications.

Wright, S., Hay, J., & Tessa, B. (2005). Ladies first? Phonology, frequency, and the naming conspiracy. *Linguistics*, *43*(3), 531–561. https://doi.org/10.1515/ling.2005.43.3.531

Yorkston, E., & Menon, G. (2004). A sound idea: phonetic effects of brand names on consumer judgments. *Journal of Consumer Research*, *31*, 43–51. https://doi.org/10.1086/383422

Yoshida, W., & Shinohara, K. (2009). Onsee-sosee ni yoru imeeji kanki [Evoking of images by phonetic features]. Paper presented at the 26th Japanese Cognitive Science Conference, Kanagawa: Keio University, SFC.

CHAPTER 4

Innovative binomial adjectives in Japanese food descriptions and beyond

Kimi Akita and Keiko Murasugi
Nagoya University / Nanzan University

Over the past two decades, the casual register of Japanese has developed a new class of binomial adjectives, such as *fuwa-toro* 'fluffy and creamy' and *gū-kawa* 'overwhelmingly cute'. These terms are particularly common in creative, nuanced descriptions of food, fashion, and personality. This paper identifies four general constraints on the element ordering of these binomial adjectives that apply to different parts of the morphological network. Similar to mimetic (ideophonic) words, these adjectives are immediate to specific situations or sensory experiences and help us to express subjective, multimodal impressions that are otherwise inexpressible.

Keywords: Construction Morphology, hierarchical lexicon, iconicity, ideophones, immediacy, irreversibility, linguistic freezes, mimetics, morphology, neologisms

1. Introduction

The creativity of language allows us to describe our subjective, multimodal experience in eating food. The present study focuses on a new set of colloquial adjectives in Japanese termed "innovative binomial adjectives" (henceforth IBAs) that typically describe nuanced multimodal food experiences or people's conspicuous appearances and personalities that may otherwise be inexpressible (e.g., *saku-uma* 'crispy and yummy', *yuru-fuwa* 'loose and fluffy') (for multimodal food perception, see Bult, de Wijk, & Hummel, 2007; Verhagen, 2007). These terms are binomial freezes (Cooper & Ross, 1975; Landsberg, 1995), which consist of two constituents and exhibit different degrees of irreversibility (e.g., **uma-saku* 'yummy and crispy', ??*fuwa-yuru* 'fluffy and loose'). They are especially common in blogs, magazines, product names, and young people's conversation, both face-to-face and online.

To our knowledge, the current project is the first to investigate IBAs with a large dataset. The main purpose of this paper is to classify 115 IBAs collected from

https://doi.org/10.1075/celcr.25.04aki

university students and the internet into six semantic types and identify four general constraints that contribute to their more or less fixed element order. We argue that the hierarchical view of the lexicon in Construction Morphology (Booij, 2010) appropriately captures the productivity and creativity of each type of IBA and explains how the four constraints are applied to different parts of the morphological network.

The organization of this paper is as follows. In Section 2, we summarize previous findings about the phonological and semantic constraints on the element ordering of binomial expressions. In Section 3, we introduce basic properties of IBAs that make them similar to mimetics (ideophones), imitative lexemes such as onomatopoeia. In Section 4, we propose a six-way semantic classification of IBAs, and in Section 5, we identify four ordering constraints on them. In Section 6, we delve into the culture-specific aspect of IBAs as subjective, multimodal expressions that are immediate to specific situations or sensory experiences. In Section 7, we conclude this paper.

2. Previous studies on binomial freezes

Since the seminal work by Cooper and Ross (1975), numerous linguists and psycholinguists have investigated the semantic and phonological constraints on the conjunct ordering of binomial expressions in English (e.g., *here and there, walkie-talkie, this and that*) (Benor & Levy, 2006; Cutler & Cooper, 1978; Jespersen, 1942; Kopaczyk & Sauer, 2017; Landsberg, 1995; Malkiel, 1959; Mollin, 2014; Pinker & Birdsong, 1979; Tachihara & Goldberg, 2020) and other languages (Oakeshott-Taylor, 1984; Sánchez, 2013). In this section, we briefly introduce a semantic principle (the Me First principle) and two phonological hierarchies (a consonantal hierarchy and a vocalic hierarchy) that are known to give rise to linguistic freezes.

Cooper and Ross's (1975) "Me First" principle is one of the most general semantic constraints, which says, "First conjuncts refer to those factors which describe the prototypical speaker (whom we will sometimes refer to as 'Me')" (p. 67). This constraint accounts for a number of linguistic freezes, such as *here and there, now and then, people and things, friend and foe,* and *land and sea*. The first elements in these freezes (e.g., *here, now, people, friend, land*) are literally or metaphorically closer to the speaker than the second elements (e.g., *there, then, things, foe, sea*). Assuming that the speaker (or the first person) has primary status in linguistic communication, the Me First principle can be considered an iconic principle (for iconicity in language, see Haiman, 1985; Meir & Tkachman, 2014, among others).

Many binomials also follow phonological constraints (Cooper & Ross, 1975; Pinker & Birdsong, 1979), two of which pertain to the present study. One is a consonantal constraint that prefers greater obstruency in the initial segment of the second element than in that of the first element. This constraint is based on the hierarchy of obstruency in (1).

(1) stops > fricatives > nasals > liquids > glides (> vowels) (decreasing obstruency)[1]
(adapted from Cooper & Ross, 1975, p. 72)

The frozen order of English rhyming reduplication, such as *walkie-talkie, razzle-dazzle, roly-poly, razzamatazz, namby-pamby, mumbo-jumbo, willy-nilly,* and *super-duper,* is attributed to this constraint on initial consonants.

The other phonological constraint says that if all else is equal, then the second element contains a vowel with a lower second formant (F_2) frequency than the first element. The vocalic hierarchy underlying this generalization is cited in (2).

(2) i > ɪ > ɛ > æ > a > ɔ > o > u (decreasing F_2) (Cooper & Ross, 1975, p. 73)

English examples that illustrate the vocalic constraint include *this and that* and *cats and dogs.*

Similar phonological constraints have also been attested in Japanese, the language we focus on in the current study. Kwon and Masuda (2019) replicate the consonantal and vocalic generalizations in their study on conventional mimetic binomials and dvandva compounds in Japanese (and Korean) (see also Kumagai & Kawahara, 2017; Labrune, 2006; Murata, 1984). Some mimetic(-like) binomials that illustrate the phonological generalizations are given in (3) and (4). The vocalic constraint is based on the hierarchy given in (5).

(3) *yabure-kabure* 'desperate', *norari-kurari* 'idle', *mecha-kucha* 'messed up', *suta-kora* 'scurrying', *ata-futa* 'haste'

(4) *gasa-goso* 'rustling', *chira-hora* 'scattered here and there', *etchira-otchira* 'dragging one's feet', *suta-kora* 'scurrying', *ata-futa* 'haste'

(5) i > e > u > a > o[2] (Kwon & Masuda, 2019, p. 40)

The present study investigates innovative binomial adjectives in colloquial Japanese as another set of binomial freezes. We demonstrate that the irreversibility of IBAs is a complex phenomenon, attributed to different principles and constraints

1. "Vowels" (or the absence of an initial consonant) is our addition based on examples such as *easy-peasy, itty-bitty,* and *orgy-porgy.*

2. Murata (1984) employs a slightly different vocalic hierarchy (i > u > e > a > o) in his analysis of novel mimetic binomials in Japanese, although neither this nor (5) perfectly reflects the F_2 frequency of the Japanese vowels ([i] > [e] > [a] > [u] > [o]) (Nishi, Strange, Akahane-Yamada, Kubo, & Trent-Brown, 2008).

that work at different levels of the morphological network. In the next two sections, we describe the formal and functional properties of IBAs in preparation for the discussion on their irreversibility in Section 5.

3. Mimetic-like properties of IBAs

We collected 115 IBAs in our informal classroom discussions with over 500 undergraduate and graduate students in the Nagoya and Kobe areas and in our random internet search (see Appendix for a full list with annotations). In the informal discussions, we first familiarized the students with IBAs by giving some examples and then asked the students to list as many IBAs as possible. The students were allowed to talk with one another during the sessions. When the students gave new IBAs, we asked them to make example sentences with the IBAs. In this section, based on the word list, we describe the basic properties of IBAs, which lead us to conclude that IBAs are closely related to and partly motivated by the mimetic (ideophonic) lexicon.

IBAs arguably constitute a subclass of (nominal) adjectives in the casual register of present-day Japanese. As illustrated in (6), which includes examples taken from the internet, IBAs are followed by a copula, used as a predicate without an inflectional element, or compounded with a noun.

(6) a. Kanari **fuwa-toro** no omuraisu, taihen oishiku
rather fluffy-creamy COP omelet.rice very delicious
itadaki mashi-ta.
get.HON HON-PST
'[I] had a rather fluffy and creamy omuraisu, which was very delicious.' (Utsunomiya, 2005)

b. Shikkari to ushi no umami ga kanji-rare-te **yaba-uma** na
well QUOT beef GEN flavor NOM feel-POT-GER risky-yummy COP
ip-pin deshi-ta.
1-CL COP.HON-PST
'[It] was a surprisingly yummy dish from which we could taste the flavor of beef well.' (Shōki, 2016)

c. Watashi orību daisuki! **Mazu-uma** da yo ne.
1SG olive love bad.tasting-yummy COP FP FP
'I love olives! They taste bad but yummy, don't they?' (Onēko, 2012)

d. Henteko ken **gū-kawa**
odd dog ugh-cute
'[This] odd dog is overwhelmingly cute.' (Hitodasuke, 2016)

e. **Yuru-fuwa** sukāto wa sonzaikan ga aru bannō aitemu.
loose-fluffy skirt TOP presence NOM be all.purpose item
'A loose and fluffy skirt is an all-purpose item that has a strong presence.'
(Hair, 2017)

IBAs are gradable predicates as suggested by their compatibility with the degree adverb *kanari* 'rather' in (6a) and the copula *na* in (6b). Note that Japanese has two copulas for noun modification (i.e., *na* and *no*), and *na* is strongly associated with gradable semantics (Oshima, Akita, & Sano, 2019; Uehara, 1998).

Morpho-phonologically, IBAs are four moras long and do not involve an abrupt pitch fall that marks an accent nucleus (for similar phonological phenomena, see Kubozono, 2019). As shown in Table 1, they consist of two elements that are typically mimetic or adjectival roots (e.g., *fuwa-fuwa* 'fluffy' [mimetic] + *toro-toro* 'creamy' [mimetic] → *fuwa-toro*; *yuru(-i)* 'loose' [adjective] + *fuwa-fuwa* 'fluffy' [mimetic] → *yuru-fuwa*) (Akita, 2014).

Table 1. Categories of the first (X) and second (Y) elements of IBAs

		Y					
		Mimetic	**Adjective**	**Verb**	**Noun**	**Prefix**	**Total**
X	Mimetic	31	13	4	0	0	48
	Adjective	1	21	2	0	0	24
	Verb	1	2	0	0	0	3
	Noun	1	7	2	0	0	10
	Prefix	0	23	7	0	0	30
	Total	**34**	**66**	**15**	**0**	**0**	**115**

These functional and formal properties make IBAs similar to reduplicated mimetics. Mimetic words prototypically have marked forms (e.g., exceptional phonotactics, reduplication, prominent prosody) that imitatively depict various sensory experiences (Dingemanse, 2011). Similar to IBAs, reduplicated mimetics are common in Japanese food descriptions as illustrated in (7) (see Tsujimura, this volume; Uno, Kobayashi, Shinohara, & Odake, this volume). Crucially, these reduplicated mimetics are four moras long, unaccented, usable in the grammatical constructions illustrated in (6), and gradable (see Sells, 2017; Toratani, 2013).

(7) a. Tori-dango wa kanari **fuwa-fuwa** no shokkan nanode …
chicken-dumpling TOP rather MIM COP mouthfeel because
'As the chicken dumpling has a rather fluffy mouthfeel …'
(Kusunoki, 2017)

b. Soshite, yawarakaku **toro-toro** na tamanegi
and soft MIM COP onion
'And [I enjoyed] the soft pulpy onion' (Anchan, 2015)

c. San-sō no ritchi na shokkan ni **mero-mero** deshi-ta!
3-layer GEN rich COP mouthfeel DAT MIM COP.HON-PST
'[I] was madly in love with the rich mouthfeel of the three-layered [cheese cake]!' (Cheesecake, n.d.)

d. Usugiri niku de kantan ni tsukur-e-te, shikamo
thin.slice meat with easy COP make-POT-GER moreover
chō **saku-saku**!!
super crispy
'[This deep-fried pork cutlet] is easy to cook with thinly sliced meat and, moreover, super-crispy!!' (Usugiri, 2019)

e. O-tōfu **mochi-mochi** pan
HON-tofu MIM bread
'Chewy tofu bread' (O-tōfu, 2007)

This parallelism suggests that IBAs are a lexical class that is based on reduplicated mimetic adjectives. Put differently, the creative system of Japanese mimetics is an essential source of IBAs, while IBAs contribute back to the expansion of the mimetic lexicon. The mimetic basis of IBAs is further suggested in Table 1, in which 51 out of 115 items (44.35%) contain mimetic elements (see Toratani, 2019 for another word formation process involving mimetics).[3]

4. Semantic classification of IBAs

In this section, we propose a six-way semantic classification of IBAs that helps us to identify four distinct constraints on their element order in Section 5. The classification is based on how the two constituents of IBAs are related to each other as shown in (8).

(8) a. Synonymy (30 types):
mochi-fuwa 'chewy and fluffy', *yuru-fuwa* 'loose and fluffy', *mote-kawa* 'popular and cute', *uru-tsuya* 'moist and glossy', *gosu-rori* 'Gothic and Lolita'

3. It is worth noting that mimetics as well as mimetic-based IBAs used in Japanese food descriptions represent mouthfeels or eating sounds that evoke particular mouthfeels (Uno et al., this volume). Highly private sensory perceptions, such as taste and smell, are known to be relatively difficult for mimetics (sound-based icons) to imitate across languages (Akita, 2009; Dingemanse, 2011; McLean, 2021; see also Winter, Perlman, Perry, & Lupyan, 2017).

b. Antonymy (18 types):
kimo-kawa 'disgusting but cute', *uza-kawa* 'annoying but cute', *dasa-ike* 'unfashionable but cool', *mazu-uma* 'bad-tasting but yummy'
c. Sequence (15 types):
fuwa-toro 'first fluffy, then creamy (of an omelet)', *saku-toro* 'first crispy, then creamy', *tsun-dere* 'first aloof but later kind-hearted'
d. Causation (6 types):
saku-uma 'crispy and therefore yummy', *horo-uma* 'crumbling and therefore yummy', *waku-teka* 'looking forward to something and therefore shining (with excitement)'
e. Degree (40 types):
mecha-kawa 'absolutely cute', *yaba-uma* 'terrifically yummy', *choi-waru* 'a little bit like a playboy', *maji-oko* 'really angry', *oni-yaba* 'extremely risky'
f. Argument-predicate (6 types):
dare-toku (who-benefit) 'pointless', *fuk-karu* 'light-footed', *meshi-uma* (rice-yummy) 'pleasantly pitiful'

Many IBAs are classified into the Synonymy type. Synonymy-type IBAs consist of two similar elements that are semantically coordinated by AND, such as *mochi(-mochi)* 'chewy' and *fuwa(-fuwa)* 'fluffy' in *mochi-fuwa* 'chewy and fluffy'. On the other hand, the Antonymy type involves opposite elements that are semantically coordinated by BUT, such as *kimo(-i)* 'disgusting' and *kawa(i-i)* 'cute' in *kimo-kawa* 'disgusting but cute'. As with expressions such as *open secret* and *alone together*, Antonymy-type IBAs are oxymorons that encode seemingly contradictory properties.[4]

Sequence-type IBAs consist of two elements that represent temporally sequential events or properties. For example, in *fuwa-toro* 'first fluffy, then creamy', the first element *fuwa(-fuwa)* 'fluffy (of the surface of an omelet)' and the second element *toro(-toro)* 'creamy (of the inside of an omelet)' represent the sequential appearances or mouthfeels of food one perceives first and second, respectively. The Causation type is similar to the Sequence type but involves a causal relation. For example, when one eats a croquette that is described by *saku-uma* 'crispy and therefore yummy', its crispiness contributes to one's perception of deliciousness, and not vice versa.[5]

4. As an anonymous reviewer pointed out, so-called coordinated compounds, such as dvandvas, may also be classified into synonymic and antonymic types (Bauer, 2008). We leave it open for future research how IBAs are related to coordinated compounds (for a related observation, see Akita & Murasugi, 2019).

5. The Synonymy, Antonymy, Sequence, and Causation types may be grouped together as "coordination" (see Akita & Murasugi, 2019). Under this coarse-grained classification, the four specific relations would be attributed to the semantics of the two constituents.

The Degree type is the most productive. Most IBAs in this category involve intensification, as in *mecha-kawa* 'absolutely cute' and *yaba-uma* 'terrifically yummy'. The first element of Degree-type IBAs is either an "affixoid" (e.g., *yaba-* 'terrifically (< risky)', *oni-* 'extremely (< ogre)'), whose bleached meaning is more or less unique to IBAs (Booij, 2010), or a fully productive affix (e.g., *mecha-* 'absolutely', *choi-* 'a little bit').

Argument-predicate-type IBAs are limited in number and consist of a predicate and its theme argument. For example, in *dare-toku* 'pointless', *dare* 'who' is an argument of the verb *toku (suru)* 'benefit'. Similarly, in *fuk-karu* 'light-footed', *fut(to)* 'foot' is an argument of the adjective *karu(-i)* 'light'.

Thus, IBAs can represent a wide variety of semantic relations.[6] This semantic diversity appears to be attributed to the phrasal nature of the input of IBAs. As we discussed in Akita and Murasugi (2019), some IBAs can be analyzed as truncated phrases. For example, *gū-kawa* 'overwhelmingly cute' is obviously derived from the idiomatic phrase *gū no ne mo denai hodo kawaii* 'as cute as one cannot even growl'. This type of phrasal semantics is more or less shared by most IBAs as suggested by their translations in (8) and contributes to their creative, nuanced descriptions of food, appearances, and personality.

In the next section, we show that all six types of IBAs are irreversible but to different degrees. We argue that four distinct constraints that are associated with the proposed semantic classification of IBAs give rise to the freezing effects.

5. IBAs as linguistic freezes

In this section, we focus on the freezing effects of IBAs. In Section 5.1, we analyze internet data to examine the reversibility of each semantic type of IBA. In Section 5.2, we identify four constraints on the element ordering in IBAs. In Section 5.3, we propose a morphological network that captures our findings and clarifies the uniformity and diversity of IBAs.

5.1 Irreversibility of IBAs

Table 2 presents the mean rates of reversed binomials for the six types of IBAs (hits of YX divided by hits of XY) on *Yahoo! Japan* (https://www.yahoo.co.jp; 29 April 2019). Each item was searched in its most common orthography. It should be noted

6. We currently do not know which of the six types represents the "central" meaning from which the other types are derived. A diachronic investigation to answer this question is beyond the scope of this paper.

Table 2. Rates of reversed binomials on the internet

	YX/XY	Example of YX
Synonymy	0.13	*fuwa-mochi* (fluffy-chewy)
Antonymy	0.14	*kawa-kimo* (cute-disgusting)
Sequence	0.18	*toro-fuwa* (creamy-fluffy)
Causation	0.02	*uma-saku* (yummy-crispy)
Degree	0.05	*kawa-mecha* (cute-absolutely)
Argument-predicate	0.28	*toku-dare* (benefit-who)
Mean	**0.13**	

that the data contain considerable noise due to technical limitations. For example, what appears to be an instance of YX might in fact be part of a repeated occurrence of XY (e.g., *fuwa-***toro** ***fuwa***-*toro*).

Despite their limited reliability, the present results clearly show that the element order of IBAs is highly fixed across the board and the Causation and Degree types are the least flexible. Using the lm function in R (R Core Team, 2018), we conducted a linear model analysis with the semantic type (Causation and Degree vs. the rest) as a fixed effect and the reversibility score (YX/XY) as a response variable, and it revealed a significant effect of the semantic type ($F(1, 113) = 8.91, p < .01$). See Figure 1 for the mean log-transformed reversibility scores for the six semantic types of IBAs.

The low reversibility of the Causation and Degree types is attributed to the clearly asymmetrical relationship (or "right-headedness") they involve. The high reversibility of the Synonymy type, on the other hand, comes from the semantic equilibrium of its components (or "double-headedness"). The Antonymy and Sequence types also look relatively flexible, but when they are reversed, their meanings are also reversed, as illustrated by *kimo-kawa* 'disgusting but cute' vs. *kawa-kimo* 'cute

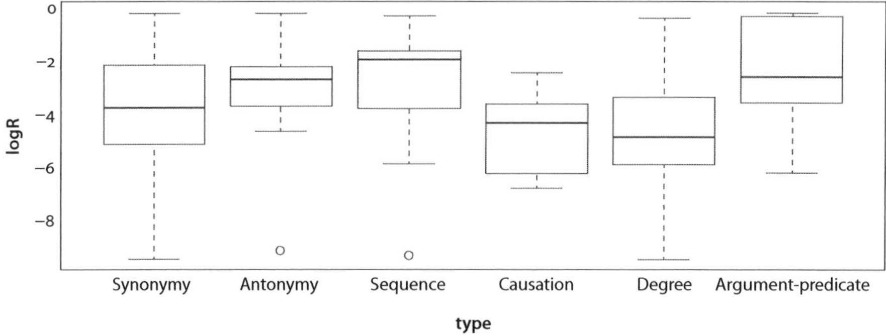

Figure 1. Reversibility (log-transformed reversibility scores) of the six types of IBAs

but disgusting' and *fuwa-toro* 'first fluffy, then creamy' vs. *toro-fuwa* 'first creamy, then fluffy'. Therefore, the reversibility of these two types of IBAs crucially depends on how likely the reversed events or properties are in the real world.

5.2 Constraints on the element order of IBAs

In this section, we identify four general constraints on IBAs that concern their phonology, semantics/semiotics, and syntax. We demonstrate how these constraints account for the varying degrees of reversibility of IBAs.

The first constraint is the obstruency constraint, which we introduced in Section 2. This weak constraint is applied exclusively to the Synonymy type as illustrated by *mochi-fuwa* 'chewy and fluffy', *yuru-fuwa* 'loose and fluffy', and *mote-kawa* 'popular and cute'. Table 3 numerically shows this local application of the constraint. "N/A" stands for IBAs whose first and second elements do not contrast in initial obstruency (e.g., *kari-toro* (both stops) 'first crunchy, then creamy'). Fisher's exact test revealed that the Synonymy type is more likely than the other five types to follow the constraint ($p < .05$).[7] The localization of the obstruency effect is ascribed to the fact that the Synonymy type is double-headed, whereas the other five types are right-headed (see Kwon & Masuda, 2019 for a related discussion).

Table 3. Number of IBAs that (do not) follow the obstruency constraint

	Yes	No	N/A
Synonymy	16	6	8
Antonymy	6	2	10
Sequence	6	3	6
Causation	1	5	0
Degree	6	21	13
Argument-predicate	4	1	1
Total	**39**	**38**	**38**

As for the vocalic hierarchy that was also introduced in Section 2, the present data are not incompatible with the previous findings but are less evident as shown in Table 4. Fisher's exact test revealed no significant difference between the Synonymy type and the rest ($p = .81$). Synonymy-type IBAs that follow the vocalic hierarchy include *gachi-muchi* 'sturdy and plump' and *neba-toro* 'sticky and creamy'.

7. An experimental approach using novel word stimuli will be needed for more extensive quantification (cf. Murata, 1984).

Table 4. Number of IBAs that (do not) follow the vocalic constraint

	Yes	No	N/A
Synonymy	13	9	8
Antonymy	9	6	3
Sequence	7	4	4
Causation	0	5	1
Degree	19	16	5
Argument-predicate	4	0	2
Total	**52**	**40**	**23**

The second constraint (or rule) concerns five types of IBAs. As we mentioned above, non-Synonymy-type IBAs are all right-headed, and this consistency is attributed to the Righthand Head Rule (henceforth RHR) (Williams, 1981). The RHR says that the righthand element determines the word class and essential semantic information of the entire morphological structure.[8] For example, the Japanese nominal compounds *choko banana* (chocolate banana) and *banana choko* (banana chocolate) denote a kind of banana ('chocolate-coated banana') and a kind of chocolate ('banana-flavored chocolate'), respectively. This general rule accounts for the irreversibility of the Antonymy and Degree types. As mentioned in Section 5.1, the antonymic IBA *kimo-kawa* (disgusting-cute), whose head is *kawa*, means 'disgusting but cute', and the reversed form *kawa-kimo* (cute-disgusting), whose head is *kimo*, would mean 'cute but disgusting'. On the other hand, Degree-type IBAs involve degree morphemes, which are realized as non-head, prefixal elements, such as *mecha-* of *mecha-kawa* 'absolutely cute' and *choi-* of *choi-waru* 'a little bit like a playboy'. The RHR also works in the Sequence and Causation types and in the Argument-predicate type, although in combination with the third and fourth constraints, respectively.

The third constraint is iconicity of linearity (Haiman, 1985; among others). The Sequence and Causation types involve an asymmetrical semantic structure in which two eventualities are temporally and causally related, respectively. For example, when we eat bread described as *kari-mofu* (crunchy-fluffy), we feel crispness first and fluffiness next. Similarly, a *saku-uma* (crispy-yummy) croquette has a crispy texture, which may cause our perception of yumminess. These IBAs

8. As an anonymous reviewer pointed out, the truncated nature of some IBAs (see Section 4) might be incompatible with the RHR, which primarily applies to compounding, derivational morphology, and inflectional morphology. An alternative account would be that those right-headed IBAs are products of the head-final syntax of Japanese. For example, *gū-kawa* 'overwhelmingly cute' is headed by *kawa(i-i)* 'cute', which also heads the original, untruncated phrase *gū no ne mo denai hodo kawaii* 'as cute as one cannot even growl'.

iconically reflect the order of experiences. It is worth noting that the iconicity principle is widely attested in serial verb constructions. For example, many verb-verb compounds in Japanese encode manner and result in this order (e.g., *oshi-akeru* (push-open) 'push open', *naguri-korosu* (punch-kill) 'punch to death') because the manner causes the result and not vice versa (Kageyama, 1993, p. 139; see also Haspelmath, 2016; Li, 1991).

The fourth and final constraint is the First Sister Principle (henceforth FSP), which says that "All verbal compounds are formed by incorporation of a word in first sister position of the verb" (Roeper & Siegel, 1978, p. 208). This structural principle accounts for various compounding phenomena, including the well-formedness of *taxi-driver* and *night-driving* and the ill-formedness of **man-driving*. Argument-predicate-type IBAs also involve argument incorporation, in which a predicate realized as a righthand, head element (e.g., *karu(-i)* 'light') incorporates its first sister realized as a left-hand element (e.g., *fut(to)* 'foot'). As the FSP predicts, the incorporation of non-first sister elements results in unnatural tones as illustrated by **oji-karu* (old.man-light) 'an old man being light-footed' (intended).

In this subsection, we have shown that four distinct constraints – the obstruency constraint, the RHR, the iconicity-of-linearity principle, and the FSP – give rise to the varying degrees of freezing phenomena in IBAs. It should be noted that none of these constraints is unique to IBAs. This fact supports the general view that neologisms share essential grammatical systems with conventional linguistic expressions (Kubozono, 2002; Nasu, 2007; Pitzl, 2013). IBAs are not complete strangers and thus expand the Japanese lexicon in creative but conventional ways (see Section 3).

5.3 Morphological network of IBAs

Thus far, we have observed that the four constraints apply to different subsets of IBAs. The obstruency constraint only works in the Synonymy type (i.e., double-headed IBAs), which is free from the other three constraints. The RHR constrains the other five types (i.e., right-headed IBAs). Iconicity of linearity is unique to the Sequence and Causation types. The FSP is concerned with the Argument-predicate type, which is a syntactically defined category. Figure 2 visualizes these findings in the form of a "hierarchical lexicon" (Booij, 2010), which allows for formal and functional generalizations at different levels of schematization.

This diagrammatic summary clearly represents the uniformity and diversity of the form and meaning of IBAs. Despite their morpho-phonological uniformity, IBAs are divided into two major groups based on headedness, and the right-headed group is further divided into five groups. The four constraints are applied to four different parts/levels of the network.

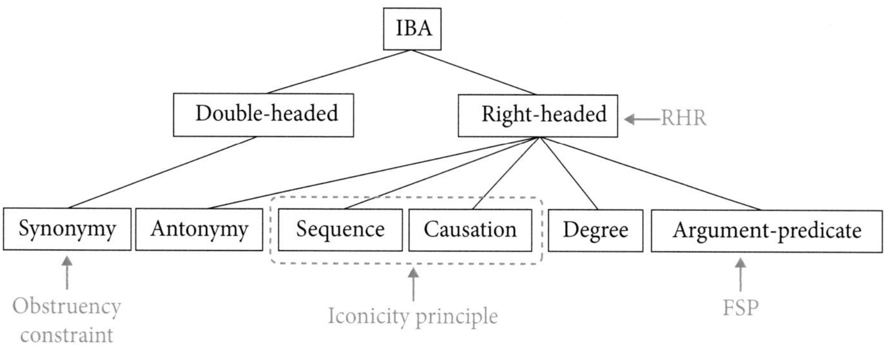

Figure 2. Simplified morphological network of IBAs

These characteristics of the morphological network of IBAs are consistent with what has been documented in the recent explorations in Construction Morphology. Construction Morphology is a (Cognitive) Construction Grammar approach to words and word-like units (Booij, 2010; for Construction Grammar, see Hoffmann & Trousdale, 2013). Centering on the hierarchical view of the lexicon, this approach takes an output-oriented perspective on word formation. For example, Chen and Matsumoto (2018) revisit the uniformity and diversity of verb-verb compounds in Japanese from a constructional point of view. The two component verbs of verbal compounds have to have the same subject, while they may have various semantic relations to each other: for example, cause-effect (e.g., *uki-agar(-u)* (float-rise) 'float up'), manner-result (e.g., *mai-ochi(-ru)* (dance-fall) 'flutter down'), and concomitance (e.g., *sagashi-mawar(-u)* (search-go.around) 'look around for'). Chen and Matsumoto (2018) capture these features by positing a general principle of subject sharing for the whole set of verb-verb compounds (i.e., the top node of the morphological network) and various subschemas for the semantic subtypes. In just the same way, the current analysis of IBAs provides another piece of evidence for the hierarchical structure of the lexicon.

6. Immediate semantics of IBAs

IBAs allow Japanese speakers to mix otherwise separate perceptions and express minute, multimodal feelings about food, fashion, and personality. Here, envisaging a possible connection between theoretical linguistics and anthropological linguistics, we make a few additional notes on the cultural implications that IBAs and related linguistic phenomena may have.

One of the key extralinguistic notions that may explain the established word formation system of IBAs is "immediacy." Immediacy refers to our subjective sensory perception that is tied to a specific place and time and is sometimes used to describe the special semantic characteristic of mimetic and other performative expressions (Dingemanse, 2011; Lahti, Barrett, & Webster, 2014). It is generally true that mimetics depict the speaker's highly specific perceptions that are immediate to his/her subjective experiences (Akita, 2012; Dingemanse, 2011; Nuckolls, 2019). As we discussed in Section 3, IBAs are formally and functionally parallel to mimetic adjectives, and many of them have their origin in the mimetic lexicon.

The immediate semantics of IBAs is particularly evident in the Antonymy type, which mixes seemingly contradictory perceptions that would normally be expressed by phrases (e.g., *kimo-kawa* 'disgusting but cute', *mazu-uma* 'bad-tasting but yummy') (Akita & Murasugi, 2019). These nuanced expressions are interpretable only in relation to specific experiences, such as an elusive taste or feeling the speaker experiences for the first time. This semantic characteristic is clearly illustrated by the actual use of *mazu-uma* 'bad-tasting but yummy' in (9), in which the blogger tries to describe the not-too-bad taste of "B-ranked" food that would otherwise be inexpressible. B-ranked food is cheap eats that may be less delicious than high-class cuisines but are attracting increasing gourmet attention, often as symbols of specific regions of Japan.

(9) Tebanashide oishiiii! bimi degozaimas-uu! to wa i-e-nai
unreservedly tasty.NPST delicious COP.HON-NPST QUOT TOP say-POT-NEG
keredo nanka suki mitai na "**mazu-uma**" na mono …
but somehow fond like COP bad.tasting-yummy COP thing
'Something untasty but yummy that [I] somehow like though [I] can't describe it as "tasty!" or "delicious!" [attracts me].' (Bī-kyū, 2006)

In branding, the immediacy of IBAs is often used creatively. For example, (10) is the name of an egg-shaped cake that contains custard mousse and cream and is coated with white chocolate.

(10) **Fuwa-puru** tamago-chan
fluffy-jiggly egg-DIM
'Fluffy-jiggly eggie' (Yamazaki Baking Co., 2011)

This innovative name projects a vivid image of an egg product that feels like cotton candy (a typical referent of *fuwa-fuwa* 'fluffy') and jello (a typical referent of *puru-puru* 'jiggly') at the same time, which makes consumers want to try the new product.

Similarly, (11) is the heading of an online recipe.

(11) **Saku-shuwa**♪ Merenge kukkii
crisp-fizzy meringue cookie
'Crisp and fizzy♪ Meringue cookies' (Miura, 2018)

The innovative combination of *saku(-saku)* 'crisp' and *shuwa(-shuwa)* 'fizzy' motivates us to bake the cookies and experience the new mouthfeel. Thus, helping us to share our subjective experiences, the situation-specific, multimodal semantics of IBAs appears to represent the immediate aspect of the Japanese language.

The immediacy of the Japanese language might have a cultural basis. The current Japanese culture and subculture appreciate some types of "childishness" and "immaturity" as attractive features. For example, both children and adults in Japan love anime. Japanese social media have been full of emoji and emoticons since their early days. Personified animals, plants, vehicles, and even buildings are very common not only in children's books and old stories of supernatural monsters called *yōkai* but also in adult-targeted products and advertisements (Allison, 2006; McVeigh, 2000). Many young adult women use their first names as first person nouns (e.g., *Miyu mo sore suki* 'I like it, too (lit. Miyu likes it, too)'). Even some adults may be evaluated as *kawaii* 'cute' when they look and act cute. It might even be that humilifics as part of the honorification system of Japanese (Hasegawa, 2015, pp. 264–266), which linguistically depreciate the speaker (e.g., *gu-soku* 'my stupid son'), are also based on the idea that being humble and immature is of great virtue.

This cultural trait may account partly for the abundance of immediate expressions such as mimetics and IBAs in Japanese discourse. Immediate expressions allow us to express our subjective feelings with minimum abstraction. Recall that many IBAs have a complex, phrase-like semantic structure that involves an antonymic relation or temporal sequence. We speculate that the absence of higher-level abstraction is a product of the Japanese culture's high receptivity to childishness and immaturity.

Last but not least, we do not intend to argue that culture explains everything about the rich inventory of immediate expressions in Japanese. It may be true that the Japanese honorification system is closely related to the Japanese culture. However, this does not entail that this linguistic system is solely attributed to the cultural background. Likewise, as we showed in Section 5, IBAs are highly systematic and subject to general linguistic constraints. The same has long been noted for mimetics (Hamano, 1998). Even if linguistic and cultural explanations overlap with each other, they will have to be distinguished as clearly as possible. Further research is needed to clarify specifically what gave rise to the immediacy of the Japanese language.

7. Conclusions

In this paper, we identified six semantic types of IBAs in Japanese and four general constraints on their constituent ordering. A hierarchical view of the lexicon in Construction Morphology allowed us to clarify how the four constraints contribute to the different degrees of irreversibility in IBAs. We have also shown that creative food descriptions in recipes, blogs, and brand names, among others, are rich resources for linguistic investigations of immediate sensory expressions. Fine-grained linguistic expressions, such as IBAs and mimetics, are coupled with highly specific experiences or situations that may be culture-specific. We hope that future research will investigate how these expressions help Japanese speakers to communicate their subjective feelings in these media as well as in actual conversation (cf. Szatrowski, 2018).

Acknowledgements

An earlier version of this paper was presented at the Conference on the Language of Japanese Food held at York University, Toronto in May 2018. We thank Kiyoko Toratani for organizing the conference and editing this fantastic volume and Sachiko Saito for her active contribution to the current project as a representative young Japanese speaker. Our sincere gratitude also goes to the two anonymous reviewers, whose comments led to some significant improvements. Any remaining inadequacies are our own.

Funding

This study was partly supported by JSPS Grants-in-Aid to KA (no. 15K16741) and KM (no. 17K02752) and by Pache Research Subsidy I-A-2 for the 2018–2020 academic years to KM.

Abbreviations

A	adjective	SG	singular
DIM	diminutive	V	verb
GER	gerundive	X	first element
M/MIM	mimetic	Y	second element
N	noun	1	first person
P	prefix		

References

Akita, K. (2009). A grammar of sound-symbolic words in Japanese: Theoretical approaches to iconic and lexical properties of mimetics (Unpublished doctoral dissertation). Kobe University, Hyogo.

Akita, K. (2012). Toward a frame-semantic definition of sound-symbolic words: A collocational analysis of Japanese mimetics. *Cognitive Linguistics*, *23*(1), 67–90. https://doi.org/10.1515/cog-2012-0003

Akita, K. (2014). Register-specific morphophonological constructions in Japanese. *Berkeley Linguistics Society, 38*, 3–18. https://doi.org/10.3765/bls.v38i0.3267

Akita, K., & Murasugi, K. (2019). Innovative bipartite adjectives in Japanese: A preliminary semantic description. *Nanzan Linguistics, 14*, 1–7.

Allison, A. (2006). Cuteness as Japan's millennial product. In J. Tobin (Ed.), *Pikachu's global adventure: The rise and fall of Pokémon* (pp. 34–49). Durham, NC: Duke University Press.

Anchan. (2015, November 19). [Blog post]. Retrieved from https://tabelog.com/matome/3718/

Bauer, L. (2008). Dvandva. *Word Structure, 1*(1), 1–20. https://doi.org/10.3366/E1750124508000044

Benor, S. B., & Levy, R. (2006). The chicken or the egg? A probabilistic analysis of English binomials. *Language, 82*(2), 233–274. https://doi.org/10.1353/lan.2006.0077

Bī-kyū. (2006, March 7). [Blog post]. Retrieved from https://yatsudokiya.at.webry.info/200603/article_6.html

Booij, G. (2010). *Construction Morphology*. Oxford: Oxford University Press.

Bult, J. H. F., de Wijk, R. A., & Hummel, T. (2007). Investigations on multimodal sensory integration: Texture, taste, and ortho- and retronasal olfactory stimuli in concert. *Neuroscience Letters, 411*, 6–10. https://doi.org/10.1016/j.neulet.2006.09.036

Cheesecake. (n.d.). [Blog post]. Retrieved from https://chakublog.com/vtuber-sejoishiicheesecake

Chen, Y., & Matsumoto, Y. (2018). *Nihongo goiteki fukugōgo no imi to keitai: Konsutorakushon keitairon to furēmu imiron* [The semantics and organization of Japanese lexical compound verbs: Construction Morphology and Frame Semantics]. Tokyo: Hituzi Syobo.

Cooper, W. E., & Ross, J. R. (1975). World order. *Chicago Linguistic Society, 11*(2), 63–111.

Cutler, A., & Cooper, W. E. (1978). Phoneme-monitoring in the context of different phonetic sequences. *Journal of Phonetics, 6*, 221–225. https://doi.org/10.1016/S0095-4470(19)31154-4

Dingemanse, M. (2011). The meaning and use of ideophones in Siwu (Unpublished doctoral dissertation). Max Planck Institute for Psycholinguistics/Radboud University, Nijmegen.

Haiman, J. (Ed.). (1985). *Iconicity in syntax: Proceedings of a symposium on iconicity in syntax, Stanford, June 24–26, 1983*. Amsterdam: John Benjamins. https://doi.org/10.1075/tsl.6

Hair. (2017, August 27). [Blog post]. Retrieved from https://hair.cm/article-35215/

Hamano, S. (1998). *The sound-symbolic system of Japanese*. Stanford: CSLI Publications.

Hasegawa, Y. (2015). *Japanese: A linguistic introduction*. Cambridge: Cambridge University Press. https://doi.org/10.1017/CBO9781139507127

Haspelmath, M. (2016). The serial verb construction: Comparative concept and cross-linguistic generalizations. *Language and Linguistics, 17*(3), 291–319.

Hitodasuke. (2016, December 23). [Blog post]. Retrieved from http://otumamiokashi.com/post-7486/

Hoffmann, T., & Trousdale, G. (Eds.). (2013). *The Oxford handbook of Construction Grammar*. Oxford: Oxford University Press. https://doi.org/10.1093/oxfordhb/9780195396683.001.0001

Jespersen, O. (1942). *A modern English grammar, Part VI, morphology*. Copenhagen: Ejnar Munksgaard.

Kageyama, T. (1993). *Bunpō to gokeisei* [Grammar and word formation]. Tokyo: Hituzi Syobo.

Kopaczyk, J., & Sauer, H. (Eds.). (2017). *Binomials in the history of English: Fixed and flexible*. Cambridge: Cambridge University Press. https://doi.org/10.1017/9781316339770

Kubozono, H. (2002). *Shingo wa kōshite tsukurareru* [How are new words coined?]. Tokyo: Iwanami.

Kubozono, H. (2019). Gokeisei to akusento [Word formation and accent]. In H. Kishimoto (Ed.), *Rekishikon no gendai riron to sono ōyō* [Modern theories of lexicon and their applications] (pp. 49–71). Tokyo: Kurosio.

Kumagai, G., & Kawahara, S. (2017). Stochastic phonological knowledge and word formation in Japanese. *Gengo Kenkyu: Journal of the Linguistic Society of Japan, 153*, 57–83.

Kusunoki, M. (2017, September 9). [Blog post]. Retrieved from https://oceans-nadia.com/user/10254/recipe/190659

Kwon, N., & Masuda, K. (2019). On the ordering of elements in ideophonic echo-words versus prosaic dvandva compounds, with special reference to Korean and Japanese. *Journal of East Asian Linguistics, 28*(1), 29–53. https://doi.org/10.1007/s10831-019-09189-1

Labrune, L. (2006). Patterns of phonemic preferences in Japanese non-headed binary compounds: What *waa-puro, are-kore* and *mecha-kucha* have in common. *Gengo Kenkyu: Journal of the Linguistic Society of Japan, 129*, 3–41.

Lahti, K., Barrett, R., & Webster, A. K. (2014). Ideophones: Between grammar and poetry. *Pragmatics and Society, 5*(3), 335–340. https://doi.org/10.1075/ps.5.3.01lah

Landsberg, M. E. (Ed.). (1995). *Syntactic iconicity and linguistic freezes: The human dimension.* Berlin: Mouton de Gruyter. https://doi.org/10.1515/9783110882926

Li, Y. (1991). On deriving serial verb constructions. In C. Lefebvre (Ed.), *Serial verbs: Grammatical, comparative and cognitive approaches* (pp. 103–136). Amsterdam: John Benjamins. https://doi.org/10.1075/ssls.8.05li

Malkiel, Y. (1959). Studies in irreversible binomials. *Lingua, 8*, 113–160. https://doi.org/10.1016/0024-3841(59)90018-X

McLean, B. (2021). Revising an implicational hierarchy for the meanings of ideophones, with special reference to Japonic. *Linguistic Typology 25*(3), 507–549. https://doi.org/10.1515/lingty-2020-2063

McVeigh, B. (2000). How Hello Kitty commodifies the cute, cool, and camp: 'Consumutopia' versus 'control' in Japan. *Journal of Material Culture, 5*, 225–245. https://doi.org/10.1177/135918350000500205

Meir, I., & Tkachman, O. (2014). Iconicity. In M. Aronoff (Ed.), *Oxford bibliographies in linguistics*. New York: Oxford University Press. https://doi.org/10.1093/OBO/9780199772810-0182

Miura, Y. (2018, July 24). [Blog post]. Retrieved from https://oceans-nadia.com/user/100026/recipe/325090

Mollin, S. (2014). *The (ir)reversibility of English binomials: Corpus, constraints, developments.* Amsterdam: John Benjamins. https://doi.org/10.1075/scl.64

Murata, T. (1984). Jinkō onomatope ni yoru nihongo onsei haierāki [Japanese sound hierarchy based on artificial onomatopoeia]. *Gengo Kenkyu: Journal of the Linguistic Society of Japan, 85*, 68–90.

Nasu, A. (2007). Onomatope no gengogakuteki tokuchō: Shiin no bunpu to yūhyōsei [Linguistic characteristics of mimetics: Consonant distribution and markedness]. *Nihongogaku, 26*(6), 4–15.

Nishi, K., Strange, W., Akahane-Yamada, R., Kubo, R., & Trent-Brown, S. A. (2008). Acoustic and perceptual similarity of Japanese and American English vowels. *Journal of Acoustical Society of America, 124*, 576–588. https://doi.org/10.1121/1.2931949

Nuckolls, J. B. (2019). The sensori-semantic clustering of ideophonic meaning in Pastaza Quichua. In K. Akita & P. Pardeshi (Eds.), *Ideophones, mimetics and expressives* (pp. 167–198). Amsterdam: John Benjamins. https://doi.org/10.1075/ill.16.08nuc

Oakeshott-Taylor, J. (1984). Phonetic factors in word order. *Phonetica, 41*, 226–237. https://doi.org/10.1159/000261729

Onēko. (2012, April 30). [Blog post]. Retrieved from https://ameblo.jp/hemenway/entry-11235273537.html

Oshima, D. Y., Akita, K., & Sano, S. (2019). Gradability, scale structure, and the division of labor between nouns and adjectives: The case of Japanese. *Glossa: A Journal of General Linguistics*, *4*(1), 41. 1–36. https://doi.org/10.5334/gjgl.737

O-tōfu. (2007, October 31). [Blog post]. Retrieved from https://cookpad.com/recipe/450710

Pinker, S., & Birdsong, D. (1979). Speakers' sensitivity to rules of frozen word order. *Journal of Verbal Learning and Verbal Behavior*, *18*, 497–508. https://doi.org/10.1016/S0022-5371(79)90273-1

Pitzl, M.-L. (2013). Creativity in language use. *Handbook of Pragmatics 2013*. Amsterdam: John Benjamins. https://doi.org/10.1075/hop.17.cre3

R Core Team. (2018). *R: A language and environment for statistical computing*. Vienna: R Foundation for Statistical Computing. Retrieved from http://www.R-project.org/

Roeper, T., & Siegel, M. E. A. (1978). A lexical transformation for verbal compounds. *Linguistic Inquiry*, *9*(2), 199–260.

Sánchez, I. R. (2013). Frequency and specialization in Spanish binomials *N y N*. *Procedia: Social and Behavioral Sciences*, *95*, 284–292. https://doi.org/10.1016/j.sbspro.2013.10.649

Sells, P. (2017). The significance of the grammatical study of Japanese mimetics. In N. Iwasaki, P. Sells, & K. Akita (Eds.), *The grammar of Japanese mimetics: Perspectives from structure, acquisition, and translation* (pp. 7–19). London: Routledge.

Shōki. (2016, October). [Blog post]. Retrieved from https://tabelog.com/kyoto/A2601/A260603/26008260/dtlrvwlst/B218391669/

Szatrowski, P. (2018). Sōgo sayō ni yoru onomatope no shiyō: Nyū seihin no shishokukai o rei ni shite [On the use of onomatopoeia in interaction: Examples from Japanese dairy taster brunches]. *NINJAL Research Papers*, *16*, 77–106.

Tachihara, K., & Goldberg, A. E. (2020). Cognitive accessibility predicts word order of couples' names in English and Japanese. *Cognitive Linguistics*, *31*(2), 231–249. https://doi.org/10.1515/cog-2019-0031

Toratani, K. (2013). Fukushiteki onomatope no tokushusei: Tagisei/jishōsei kara no kōsatsu [The uniqueness of adverbial mimetics in terms of polysemy and eventivity]. In K. Shinohara & R. Uno (Eds.), *Onomatope kenkyū no shatei: Chikazuku oto to imi* [Sound symbolism and mimetics: Rethinking the relationship between sound and meaning in language] (pp. 85–99). Tokyo: Hituzi Syobo.

Toratani, K. (2019). Classification of nominal compounds containing mimetics: A Construction Morphology perspective. In K. Akita & P. Pardeshi (Eds.), *Ideophones, mimetics and expressives* (pp. 101–133). Amsterdam: John Benjamins. https://doi.org/10.1075/ill.16.06tor

Uehara, S. (1998). *Syntactic categories in Japanese: A cognitive and typological introduction*. Tokyo: Kurosio.

Usugiri. (2019, May 8). [Blog post]. Retrieved from https://ameblo.jp/koichi-shoot/entry-12459862627.html

Utsunomiya. (2015, September 21). [Blog post]. Retrieved from https://minkara.carview.co.jp/userid/932446/blog/36467924/

Verhagen, J. V. (2007). The neurocognitive bases of human multimodal food perception: Consciousness. *Brain Research Reviews*, *53*(2), 271–286. https://doi.org/10.1016/j.brainresrev.2006.09.002

Williams, E. (1981). On the notions 'lexically related' and 'head of a word'. *Linguistic Inquiry*, *12*, 245–274.

Winter, B., Perlman, M., Perry, L. K., & Lupyan, G. (2017). Which words are most iconic? Iconicity in English sensory words. *Interaction Studies*, *18*(3), 433–454.

Appendix. A list of innovative binomial adjectives in Japanese

YX/XY stands for the reversibility of IBAs according to *Yahoo! Japan* (see Section 5).

	IBA	Gloss	Type	X	Y	Obst. const.	Voc. const.	Genre	YX/ XY
1	*aza-kawa*	clever-cute	Syn	A	A	Yes	N/A	Fashion	0.02
2	*daru-omo*	languid-heavy	Syn	A	A	No	Yes	Other	0.70
3	*ero-guro*	pornographic-grotesque	Syn	A	A	Yes	Yes	Fashion	0.02
4	*ero-kawa*	pornographic-cute	Syn	A	A	Yes	Yes	Fashion	0.20
5	*gachi-muchi*	sturdy-plump	Syn	M	M	No	No	Other	0.00
6	*gaku-buru*	shivering-trembling	Syn	M	M	N/A	No	Other	0.00
7	*gosu-rori*	Gothic-Lolita	Syn	A	A	No	N/A	Fashion	0.00
8	*gucha-doro*	squashed-muddy	Syn	M	M	N/A	Yes	Other	0.76
9	*fuwa-boke*	fluffy-senile	Syn	M	V	Yes	Yes	Other	0.52
10	*fuwa-pita*	fluffy-tight	Syn	M	M	Yes	No	Fashion	0.06
11	*fuwa-puru*	fluffy-jiggly	Syn	M	M	Yes	Yes	Food	0.34
12	*ike-kawa*	cool-cute	Syn	V	A	Yes	Yes	Fashion	0.10
13	*ira-oko*	irritated-angry	Syn	M	V	N/A	Yes	Other	0.01
14	*kari-pori*	crunchy-crunchy	Syn	M	M	N/A	Yes	Food	0.01
15	*kire-kawa*	beautiful-cute	Syn	A	A	N/A	No	Fashion	0.00
16	*mote-kawa*	poplar-cute	Syn	V	A	Yes	No	Fashion	0.01
17	*mochi-fuwa*	chewy-fluffy	Syn	M	M	Yes	N/A	Food	0.63
18	*nachu-kawa*	natural-cute	Syn	A	A	Yes	Yes	Fashion	0.00
19	*neba-toro*	sticky-creamy	Syn	M	M	Yes	Yes	Food	0.06
20	*pita-kawa*	tight-cute	Syn	M	A	N/A	N/A	Fashion	0.11
21	*sara-fuwa*	smooth-fluffy	Syn	M	M	No	No	Fashion	0.10
22	*sara-tsuya*	smooth-glossy	Syn	M	M	Yes	No	Fashion	0.25
23	*shuwa-furu*	fizzy-jiggly	Syn	M	M	N/A	N/A	Food	0.01
24	*toro-nama*	creamy-raw	Syn	M	A	No	No	Food	0.03
25	*tsuru-pika*	slippery-shining	Syn	M	M	N/A	No	Other	0.01
26	*tsuru-sube*	slippery-smooth	Syn	M	M	No	N/A	Fashion	0.00
27	*uru-sara*	moist-smooth	Syn	M	M	Yes	Yes	Fashion	0.02
28	*uru-tsuya*	moist-glossy	Syn	M	M	Yes	N/A	Fashion	0.01
29	*yuru-fuwa*	loose-fluffy	Syn	A	M	Yes	N/A	Fashion	0.04
30	*yuru-kawa*	loose-cute	Syn	A	A	Yes	Yes	Fashion	0.00
31	*aho-kawa*	fool-cute	Ant	A	A	Yes	N/A	Fashion	0.02
32	*atsu-mori*	hot-exciting	Ant	A	V	Yes	Yes	Other	0.02
33	*busa-kawa*	ugly-cute	Ant	A	A	N/A	Yes	Fashion	0.04
34	*chibi-kawa*	little-cute	Ant	A	A	N/A	N/A	Fashion	0.11
35	*dasa-kawa*	dowdy-cute	Ant	A	A	N/A	No	Fashion	0.83
36	*dasa-ike*	dowdy-cool	Ant	A	V	No	Yes	Fashion	0.10
37	*guro-kawa*	grotesque-cute	Ant	A	A	N/A	Yes	Fashion	0.06
38	*heta-uma*	unskilled-skillful	Ant	A	A	N/A	N/A	Other	0.18

	IBA	Gloss	Type	X	Y	Obst. const.	Voc. const.	Genre	YX/ XY
39	*ita-kimo*	pathetic-disgusting	Ant	A	A	Yes	Yes	Other	0.06
40	*kimo-kawa*	disgusting-cute	Ant	A	A	N/A	No	Fashion	0.03
41	*kowa-kawa*	scary-cute	Ant	A	A	N/A	Yes	Personality	0.35
42	*kū-kawa*	cool.headed-cute	Ant	A	A	N/A	No	Fashion	0.49
43	*mazu-uma*	bad.tasting-yummy	Ant	A	A	No	No	Food	0.02
44	*oji-kawa*	middle.aged.man-cute	Ant	N	A	Yes	No	Fashion	0.06
45	*pocha-kawa*	chubby-cute	Ant	M	A	N/A	Yes	Fashion	0.01
46	*tsuyo-kawa*	strong-cute	Ant	A	A	N/A	Yes	Fashion	0.09
47	*uza-kawa*	annoying-cute	Ant	A	A	Yes	Yes	Personality	0.10
48	*yan-dere*	depressed-lovestruck	Ant	V	M	Yes	No	Personality	0.00
49	*bari-boro*	crunched-crumbled	Seq	M	M	N/A	Yes	Food	0.03
50	*fuwa-puri*	fluffy-plump	Seq	M	M	Yes	N/A	Food	0.67
51	*fuwa-shuwa*	fluffy-fizzy	Seq	M	M	Yes	Yes	Food	0.14
52	*fuwa-toro*	fluffy-creamy	Seq	M	M	Yes	No	Food	0.18
53	*kari-fuwa*	crunchy-fluffy	Seq	M	M	No	Yes	Food	0.21
54	*kari-mofu*	crunchy-fluffy	Seq	M	M	No	Yes	Food	0.14
55	*kari-toro*	crunchy-creamy	Seq	M	M	N/A	No	Food	0.02
56	*kari-juwa*	crunchy-juicy	Seq	M	M	No	N/A	Food	0.11
57	*mochi-toro*	chewy-creamy	Seq	M	M	Yes	N/A	Food	0.08
58	*puri-toro*	plump-creamy	Seq	M	M	N/A	Yes	Food	0.20
59	*saku-shuwa*	crisp-fizzy	Seq	M	M	N/A	No	Food	0.15
60	*saku-toro*	crisp-creamy	Seq	M	M	Yes	Yes	Food	0.70
61	*saku-juwa*	crisp-juicy	Seq	M	M	N/A	No	Food	0.01
62	*tsun-dere*	cold-lovestruck	Seq	M	M	N/A	Yes	Personality	0.00
63	*muzu-kyun*	itchy-wrung	Seq	M	M	Yes	N/A	Other	0.00
64	*fuwa-uma*	fluffy-yummy	Caus	M	A	No	No	Food	0.01
65	*horo-uma*	crumbled-yummy	Caus	M	A	No	N/A	Food	0.02
66	*koku-uma*	full.bodied-yummy	Caus	N	A	No	No	Food	0.08
67	*kyun-jini*	wrung-dead	Caus	M	V	No	No	Fashion	0.00
68	*saku-uma*	crisp-yummy	Caus	M	A	No	No	Food	0.03
69	*waku-teka*	excited-shining	Caus	M	M	Yes	No	Other	0.00
70	*baku-ike*	bombing-cool	Dgr	P	V	No	No	Fashion	0.06
71	*bari-kata*	very-hard	Dgr	P	A	N/A	N/A	Food	0.00
72	*bari-kawa*	very-cute	Dgr	P	A	N/A	N/A	Fashion	0.10
73	*bari-uma*	very-yummy	Dgr	P	A	No	No	Food	0.02
74	*bachi-kuso*	tense-damn	Dgr	M	A	N/A	No	Other	0.01
75	*dera-uma*	very-yummy	Dgr	P	A	No	Yes	Food	0.02
76	*gan-guro*	face-black	Dgr	N	A	N/A	No	Fashion	0.00
77	*gachi-gire*	real-enraged	Dgr	P	V	N/A	No	Other	0.00
78	*geki-atsu*	violently-hot	Dgr	P	A	No	Yes	Other	0.01
79	*geki-oko*	violently-angry	Dgr	P	V	No	Yes	Other	0.00

	IBA	Gloss	Type	X	Y	Obst. const.	Voc. const.	Genre	YX/ XY
80	*geki-kawa*	violently-cute	Dgr	P	A	N/A	Yes	Fashion	0.02
81	*geki-mazu*	violently-bad.tasting	Dgr	P	A	No	Yes	Food	0.01
82	*geki-muzu*	violently-difficult	Dgr	P	A	No	Yes	Other	0.00
83	*geki-nae*	violently-discouraging	Dgr	P	V	No	Yes	Other	0.01
84	*gero-mabu*	vomiting-beautiful	Dgr	P	A	No	Yes	Fashion	0.00
85	*gero-mazu*	vomiting-bad.tasting	Dgr	P	A	No	Yes	Food	0.04
86	*gero-uma*	vomiting-yummy	Dgr	P	A	No	Yes	Food	0.03
87	*gū-kawa*	ugh-cute	Dgr	M	A	N/A	Yes	Fashion	0.00
88	*gū-sei*	ugh-saint	Dgr	M	A	No	No	Personality	0.00
89	*gū-sei*	ugh-right	Dgr	M	A	No	No	Other	0.03
90	*gū-chiku*	ugh-damn	Dgr	M	A	N/A	No	Personality	0.01
91	*gyan-kawa*	terribly-cute	Dgr	M	A	N/A	N/A	Fashion	0.01
92	*kuso-dasa*	damn-unfashionable	Dgr	P	A	N/A	Yes	Fashion	0.00
93	*kuso-deka*	damn-big	Dgr	P	A	N/A	No	Food	0.00
94	*kuso-nemi*	damn-sleepy	Dgr	P	A	No	No	Other	0.03
95	*kuso-uma*	damn-yummy	Dgr	P	A	No	N/A	Food	0.01
96	*kuso-yaba*	damn-risky	Dgr	P	A	No	Yes	Other	0.06
97	*maji-oko*	really-angry	Dgr	P	V	No	Yes	Other	0.02
98	*maji-yaba*	really-risky	Dgr	P	A	No	N/A	Other	0.00
99	*mecha-ike*	very-cool	Dgr	P	V	No	Yes	Fashion	0.07
100	*mecha-kawa*	very-cute	Dgr	P	A	Yes	No	Fashion	0.01
101	*mecha-mote*	very-popular	Dgr	P	V	N/A	Yes	Fashion	0.00
102	*mek-kawa*	very-cute	Dgr	P	A	Yes	Yes	Fashion	0.00
103	*neo-kawa*	neo-cute	Dgr	P	A	Yes	Yes	Fashion	0.51
104	*oni-yaba*	ogre-risky	Dgr	P	A	Yes	No	Other	0.65
105	*choi-waru*	a.bit-bad	Dgr	P	A	No	No	Fashion	0.01
106	*yaba-uma*	risky-yummy	Dgr	P	A	No	No	Food	0.13
107	*yume-kawa*	dream-cute	Dgr	N	A	Yes	Yes	Fashion	0.14
108	*don-biki*	bang-put.off	Dgr	M	V	N/A	No	Other	0.00
109	*horo-niga*	dropping-bitter	Dgr	M	A	Yes	No	Food	0.00
110	*dare-toku*	who-benefit	AP	N	V	N/A	Yes	Other	0.15
111	*fuk-karu*	foot-light	AP	N	A	Yes	Yes	Personality	0.03
112	*meshi-uma*	rice-yummy	AP	N	A	No	Yes	Other	0.69
113	*mune-atsu*	heart-hot	AP	N	A	Yes	Yes	Other	0.03
114	*mune-kyun*	hot-wrung	AP	N	M	Yes	N/A	Other	0.00
115	*ore-toku*	me-benefit	AP	N	V	Yes	N/A	Other	0.78

SECTION III

Change in the language of food

CHAPTER 5

Verbs of eating

From active zones, cultures, metonymy, and metaphor to withdrawal

Toshiko Yamaguchi
University of Malaya

The chapter explains how *kuu* and *taberu*, two major verbs of eating in Japanese, emerged, developed, and changed their literal and figurative meanings. Both verbs began their life distinctly. *Kuu* emerged from the active zone, while societal structures gave rise to *taberu*. This difference is reflected in two facets of culture, labeled Culture 1 and Culture 2, which embrace adversity and hierarchical society, respectively, revealing two social attributes that are historically prevalent in Japan. Today's usages of *taberu* and *kuu* show a shift in the selection of active zones and a shift from metonymy to metaphor. Drawing upon *kuu*'s current tendency to withdraw from figurative expression, the chapter suggests that metonymy and metaphor can effect a clear division of labor.

Keywords: active zones, cultures, metonymy, metaphor, verbs of eating, withdrawal

1. Introduction

Eating is a primary human activity in all cultures. In his monograph entitled *Everyone Eats*, Anderson (2005, p. 11) stated that one of the basic abilities humans originally possessed was to "live on anything they c[ould] bite," as well as two other abilities, to learn, reason and plan, and to live on society with other in respecting common customs. In this light, eating was not a basic, fixed, static, aspect of human life but one that developed alongside the evolution of human social life. Present-day Japanese has two major verbs to express the act of eating, namely *kuu* and *taberu*.[1] They did not originally have to do with eating but were derived from conceptually

1. They are written in Japanese by combining a Chinese character and syllabaries: *kuu* 食う and *taberu* 食べる. Both contain the same character 食, whose structure depicts the way food is served on a plate with a lid on top.

https://doi.org/10.1075/celcr.25.05yam

related senses, a fact in accord with Anderson's original statement. According to extant historical documents to which I have had access, the first verb, *kuu*, derived the meaning of eating during the Late Old Japanese (LOJ) period (800–1100) from holding an object in the mouth, an action reserved for animals and birds (Nakamura, Okami & Sakakura, 1984, p. 223). In my collection of data, *hamu* was the verb used for the human consumption of food (poem 802 in *Manyōshū* [*An Anthology of Ten Thousands Leaves*] ca. 770) in the Old Japanese (OJ) period (710–800). This verb did not come to be used widely as a verb of eating but is etymologically related to the present-day verb *kamu* 'to bite' (Kindaichi, Hayashi & Shibata, 1988, p. 726). The second verb discussed in this chapter, *taberu*, is the modern verb for eating, whose original form is the verb *tabu*, which developed the meaning of eating from the concept of receiving or, more precisely, "receiving an object with the respect of the giver." The shift from receiving to eating is reported by two authoritative Japanese dictionaries, the *Comprehensive Dictionary of the Japanese Language* (Editorial team of Shogakukan, 2001, p. 1088) and the *Kadokawa Comprehensive Dictionary of Classical Japanese* (Nakamura et al., 1984, p. 198). Like *kuu, tabu* existed in LOJ but was not used widely as a verb of consumption before the Late Middle Japanese (LMJ) period (1330–1610). According to these two dictionaries, *tabu* developed into *taberu* through the intermediate form *taburu* (Editorial team of Shogakukan, 2001, p. 748 and Nakamuea et al., 1984, p. 198, respectively). Besides historical documentation, this study also sourced examples from contemporary newspapers and websites. When the latter is concerned, it is striking to note that *kuu* is no longer used as the standard verb of eating; it is rather used either figuratively, to realize adversative meaning, or literally, to emphasize an uncouth and rude manner of eating. While I acknowledge that *kuu* is still accepted as a verb of eating, among speakers of regional dialects and particularly male speakers in informal settings, this chapter stands by the claim that in contemporary Japanese society, *taberu* is now the common verb for eating, used in the media and taught in formal education at school, and is no longer perceived to be a specifically polite term as it once was.

The point of departure for this chapter is the question of why there have been two verbs to express eating. In order to answer this question, I explore how they have emerged, developed, and changed meaning up to the present. I refer to active zones, metonymy, metaphor, and what I call "withdrawal." Culture is another notion with an important contribution to observed cognitive operations. In this study, culture is understood as the values, beliefs, or understandings shared by people in a society, and will be divided into Culture 1 and Culture 2. When *kuu* started to co-occur with inedible objects (e.g., *oitekibori* 'being left behind') in the Early Modern Japanese (EMdJ) period (1610–1870), it no longer meant 'to eat' but 'to receive'; that is, 'to receive (=experience) something unfortunate'. This suggests that our understanding of eating became contiguous with adversity (Culture 1).[2] When *tabu*, an earlier form of *taberu*, emerged as the verb of consumption (i.e., of drinking and eating), the concept of honorifics and its subordinate concept of receiving, then rooted deeply in Japanese society (Tsujimura, 1968), impelled *tabu* to supplant *kuu* (Culture 2). This substitution was natural in Japanese society since the use of *kuu*, which had retained the sense of biting for centuries, was perceived as too rough and rude for use as the verb of eating (Nakamura et al. 1984, p. 198). While *tabu* and *taberu* never yielded figurative meaning, the meaning of *taberu* has recently begun to be extended metonymically.[3] *Kuu* is also undergoing changes, in the sense that some of its metonymic extensions are on the way to becoming metaphorical. An important point here is that *kuu* is not itself involved in this process; while it metonymically attracted an inedible entity as its direct object, it was the inedible object itself that served to form metaphorical expressions.

The rest of the chapter is structured as follows. Section 2 summarizes what active zones are. Section 3 explains the two types of culture identified above. Section 4 presents selected examples, based on which the rise and development of *kuu, tabu*, and *taberu* as verbs of eating can be elaborated. Section 5 discusses the notion of "withdrawal" in the light of additional examples containing *kuu*. Section 6, the final section, concludes the chapter.

2. Active zones

The active zone is a notion proposed by Langacker (1987, 2009, among others). Taylor's (1989/2003, pp. 93–94) construct of "perspectivization" may encompass a similar idea in that both consider the meaning of words as "a person's total knowledge" (Taylor, 1989/2003, p. 92). Similarly, Evans and Green (2006) explained active zone phenomena in conjunction with the way in which encyclopedic knowledge is at work in discourse. The way our encyclopedic knowledge pinpoints its subparts or substructures leads to the construction of novel meaning, and this falls within the scope of metonymy (Langacker, 2009, p. 41). Croft (2002, 2006) had already suggested the term "domain highlighting" to locate metonymy as the tool to generate conceptual associations or, more specifically, "conceptual unities" (Croft, 2006). Thus, the fact that a sentence such as *This red pen is not red* (Langacker, 1987, p. 274; Evans and Green, 2006, p. 239) is not contradictory can be accounted for by

2. Newman considers intake of food as receiving (1997, p. 221).

3. I am using the expression "recently" here because these new metonymic meanings are not yet codified in Japanese dictionaries, and they are thus considered new, and hence, recent.

substructures in what Lakoff (1987) termed the idealized cognitive model (ICM).[4] The point is precisely that the active zones activated by the two constituents are not identical; that is, the active zone of *This red pen* profiles its outer surface, not the color of the ink, while that of the predicate *red* profiles the marks it leaves on paper. Given this, the active zone refers to a specific facet of a collection of several facets contained by objects (e.g., *pen* or *trumpet*); or, put differently, it is an aspect of the speaker's "encyclopaedic cultural knowledge" (Langacker, 2009, p. 45) about things and processes present in her environment. The examples in (1) show that the active zone of *the trumpet* is decided by the choice of the verb.

(1) a. We heard the trumpet.
(Langacker, 1987, p. 271, slightly modified by the author)
b. We saw the trumpet.

The active zone for (1a) is the sound emitted by the trumpet, not the physical object. It is evident that a specific aspect selected from the trumpet ICM is facilitated by the verb *hear*, which underlines the auditory properties of a musical instrument. This analysis is justified when *heard* is replaced by *saw*. the active zone of (1b) is not the sound but the visual properties of the trumpet (e.g., its shape or color) (Evans, 2007, p. 5). As Langacker declared (2009, p. 41), the active zone phenomenon is strong proof that the information coded linguistically provides mental access to certain other elements.

The aforementioned examples serve to demonstrate that a precise description of a predication is not possible if it relies solely on linguistic forms; there are almost always tacit cognitive operations germane to the interpretation. As Littlemore (2015, p. 4) wrote, language basically underspecifies its meaning. This point is illustrated by the examples in (2), where the means used for hitting can be interpreted in different ways.

(2) a. She hit me.
b. She hit me (with her left hand/her elbow/a stick). (Langacker, 2009, p. 44)

Consider (2a). A default active zone for the event described in an English-speaking culture might be the use of the fist, assumed here to be the right hand (Langacker, 2009, p. 44), but, as shown in (2b), there are several other possibilities. The first two means (*left hand* and *elbow*) are other body parts of the subject; according to Langacker (2009, p. 44), a stick, not part of the subject but an object she holds, can also be pinpointed as an active zone.

4. I agree with Littlemore (2015, p. 10) who prefers to use idealized cognitive models in place of domains or domain matrices to the extent that ICMs emphasize the encyclopedic, flexible, slightly idiosyncratic nature of the knowledge networks that we have in our heads. They are idealized because they are not necessarily real.

The perspective adopted from the discussions of this section is that the emergence and semantic development of verbs of eating make effective use of the ideas of the active zone and ICM. It will be shown that the selection of an active zone has shifted from one substructure (e.g., holding food) to another (e.g., mastication of food). When eating is regarded as a part of life, the ICM itself has shifted. These shifts are tied intricately to cultural values that have themselves undergone shifts. A very noticeable cultural shift is that the sense of adversity is no longer a characteristic value of Japanese culture in our time. In other words, a sense of happiness appears to be superseding our old habits of submitting to adversity.

3. Cultures

Culture is viewed as a pattern or patterns of behavior, values, beliefs, or understandings that characterize groups of people in a given society (Boyd & Richerson, 1985, p. 33; for a similar conception of culture, see also Kövecses, 2005, p. 1; Lange & Paige, 2003, p. x). In what follows, I will use the short expression "cultural values" or simply "culture." The ways in which the meaning of *kuu* has been extended and supplanted by the honorific verb *tabu*, which developed into *taberu*, cannot be accounted for without taking into consideration the cultural values that people shared at different stages in the history of Japanese society.[5] As noted earlier, I take the view that there were two kinds of cultural values influencing the formation of verbs of eating. One is what I call "Culture 1," which embraced adversity, a feeling of negativity and unhappiness enshrined in the Japanese psyche. The other is what I call "Culture 2," which embraced the hierarchical structure of ancient Japanese society that used honorifics. This partition is, first of all, drawn from my observation of the data I have collated; that is, examples extracted from extant historical materials and contemporary authentic materials (articles in newspapers and magazines). I discerned a pattern, and hypothesized that there are two types of subcultures that underlie the use of verbs of eating. In other words, verbs of eating required cultural input for the development of their meanings. As we all know, language is closely related to various cultural forms. One can surely argue that these subcultures did not exist in a vacuum, in that while adversity was central to the psychology of people in ancient societies, another cultural value, awareness of hierarchical structure, would

5. At the urging of one reviewer, I note that cultural values should be treated differently from cognitive linguistics terms such as "frames" (defined as a "schematization of a knowledge structure," Evans, 2007, p. 85), "world knowledge," or "background knowledge," in that "value," as used in this chapter, is a kind of appraisal assigned to the use of a language. Appraisal may not be equated with a knowledge system. One can say, however, that cultural values form a constituent of an ICM.

have been operational concurrently. The presence of the latter can be proven by the wealth of honorific forms that were already firmly established in the OJ period (Tsujimura, 1971). My point is that the Japanese language, unlike Japanese society, required two forms of culture in different diachronic phases for its evolution over time: first adversity and then hierarchical social structure, never both at the same time. In what follows, I explain the contexts/significance of these forms of culture.

I have profited hugely from reading Minami's (1971 [1953]) monograph, originally published in Japanese eight years after the end of the Second World War (1945). Therein Minami declares that a sense of adversity was representative of the mentality of the Japanese people. That is to say, unhappiness, rather than happiness, is an essential characteristic of the Japanese psyche. Minami goes on to say that unhappiness is grounded deeply in the psychology of the Japanese people because they have long shared the belief that the state of unhappiness offers a good opportunity for self-cultivation and service, while "happiness is hazardous and transient" (p. 72). When one considers himself unhappy, he strives to work hard to achieve a better life. This is what Minami calls the aesthetics of imperfection and incompletion. In Japanese literature, just as in popular songs at the time Minami wrote his monograph, expressions correlated with unhappiness (e.g., *namida* 'tears'; *sabishisa* 'loneliness'; *wakare* 'separation, farewell') abound and are much more frequent than those correlated with happiness (Minami, 1971 [1953], pp. 60–62). In my preliminary study on verbs of eating (Yamaguchi, 2009), I stated that *kuu* developed figurative expressions, all of which were associated with negativity. Since other languages do not necessarily do this (Newman, 2009), a natural question one can ask is why the Japanese opted for this. A reasonable response, as I have suggested (Yamaguchi, 2009), might be to refer to Minami's concept of adversity. The association of *kuu* with a variety of negative meanings is ascribed to the cultural value prevalent in the long history of Japanese society that gave priority to unhappiness. As will be discussed below in Section 4.3.2, however, this cultural value appears to be becoming obsolete in contemporary Japan.

Honorifics, mentioned above, refer to the system of lexical and grammatical forms whose essential function is to allow language users to show respect to their interlocutors. By employing respectful forms, one shows deference toward one's superior. By using humble forms, one also shows deference by humbling oneself. Honorifics were used at first to express self-respect in the OJ period, for example when the Emperor referred to himself (Tsujimura, 1968, pp. 86–89; Tsujimura, 1971, pp. 13–15), but came to be employed as a means to categorize spoken interactions according to participants' social roles.[6] For example, parents and administra-

6. As almost all scholars working in the field of honorifics have mentioned, social roles were not the only context in which honorifics were employed. Roles that emerged in spoken discourses

tors were categorized as higher than their children and peasants, respectively. Thus, everyday interactions were differentiated linguistically, first through two levels of honorific forms – that is, respect and humility – and later through polite forms, which were neutral in terms of expressing respect and were added to form a tripartite system. Some actions were assigned special lexical items to lexically designate honorifics. Going/coming and giving/receiving are examples. One of these was *tabu*, which meant to receive an object (e.g., food) in a humble manner as a way of showing respect toward a giver who is of a higher social status than the receiver. The use of honorifics in social interactions was predominant in Japan for centuries and is still integral to Japanese people's verbal interactions today, although the system itself has been simplified greatly (Miyaji, 1971). Alongside the sophistication of this language usage, the people constituting Japanese society gradually gave preference to sidelining rough expressions and enhancing gentle and courteous expressions. The emergence of *tabu* as the verb of eating occurred alongside this process of what Japanese grammarians call "beautification," which produced polite expressions. An activity of consumption and the presence of food that one consumes were both germane to this process,[7] which may be self-explanatory on the grounds that consumption was, and remains, a central aspect of human life, and this could account for why *tabu* and *taberu* were accepted as refined verbal expressions as opposed to *kuu*. Seen from a different angle, the sequence *tabu–taberu* is oriented toward the establishment of an agent, a person who acted upon an object, rather than a person being acted upon as a patient.[8] Thus, Culture 2 presents a new dimension of the Japanese social structure, and consequently Japanese linguistic structure. The fact that *taberu*, which emerged without recourse to adversity, did not yield figurative expressions must owe much to the operation of Culture 2, a form of culture that did not promote a patient orientation, a component central to the formation of *kuu*'s adversity-inducing figurative expressions.

were also important but this function of honorifics came about later than social roles. This fine differentiation of functions does not, in my opinion, play a role in explaining the use of *tabu*; therefore, I only refer to social roles in this chapter.

7. Japanese has a specific vocabulary for beautification, that is, 美化語 *bikago* "words of beautification." The prefix *o-* was added to nouns to make them sound polite. Examples include *o-mizu* 'water', *o-kome* 'rice', *o-cha* 'tea'. These words still exist in present-day Japanese and, interestingly, they are no longer perceived to be polite.

8. The depiction of agent and patient as contrasting notions in terms of eating is motivated by Newman's (2009) discussion.

4. Verbs of eating

The purpose of this section is twofold. First, it demonstrates representative examples from the data I have collected. Second, it explains how *kuu* and *taberu* (including *tabu*, an earlier form of *taberu*) emerged as verbs of eating and developed literal and figurative meanings. Some shifts in meaning can be neatly illustrated by drawing on the ideas of the active zone and ICM (Section 2). In other words, a semantic shift took place as a result of a shift from one substructure to another within an ICM. Given that metonymy is defined as an operation that allows the linguistic form to establish a natural association with a selected active zone, it is this process that played a major role in bringing forward semantic change in verbs of eating.[9] Besides active zones, Culture 1 and Culture 2, as discussed in Section 3, are intertwined with the metonymic process. Regarding the temporal sequence, our data reveal that metaphor arose posterior to metonymy and that this occurred when a more abstract concept was derived from the concrete action denoted by the expression headed by the verb of eating. Evans (2007, p. 142) illustrates, albeit briefly, how *ham sandwich* in the phrase *Be careful, the ham sandwich has wandering hands* receives a metaphorical interpretation. Metonymically, it pinpoints the customer in a restaurant ICM but when it evokes "human qualities" (e.g., "perverseness") motivated by the food item "ham sandwich" through conceptual metaphor, such as HUMAN QUALITY IS FOOD,[10] the utterance becomes metaphorical. To demonstrate a similar yet unidentical process, we look at examples with *oitekibori* 'being left behind' diachronically and synchronically (Section 4.1.3).

4.1 Kuu

4.1.1 *From holding to biting to eating*

As noted in the Introduction, the verb *kuu* originally referred to the act of holding an object, specifically by an animal or bird in its teeth or beak. The oldest example in my data set is extracted from a poem in *Nihon-shoki* (*The Chronicles of Japan*, 720), as in (3).

9. Note that this understanding of metonymy is not encapsulated by standing-for relations stipulated by Kövecses and Radden (1998, Section 2), although ICM and its parts equally play a role in these presentations.

10. The original conceptual metaphor proposed by Evans and Green (2006, p. 311) is AN INANIMATE ENTITY IS AN AGENT.

(3) … sono amu o akizu hayaku **kui** …
that horsefly ACC dragonfly quickly hold
'The dragonfly quickly flew away as soon as it **held** the horsefly in its mouth.'
(*Nihon-shoki* [*The Chronicles of Japan*], Poem 30, 720)

In this example, *kui* (the continuative form of *kuu*) carries the meaning of 'holding an object in one's mouth' and the subject is not human but a dragonfly.[11] About 250 years later, this usage of *kuu* had developed into the general verb of eating. The earliest example I have is from *Kagerō Nikki* (*Kagero Diary*, 974–995). The examples in (4) and (5) show that the subject of *kuu* is a person and what is eaten is food. In this text, *kuu* is used predominantly as the verb of eating. The objects consumed are either a specific item of food (that is, *fish*), as in (4), or a meal, which is expressed by the noun *mono* 'thing,' as in (5). *Kuu* in these examples was not yet perceived to be a coarse verb and this perception continued until around the beginning of the LMJ period according to my data set.[12]

(4) "mada io nado mo **kuwa**-zu. Koyoi-namu-owase-ba,
yet fish some also eat-NEG this.evening-PART-come.RES-COND
morotomoni-tote aru. izura" nado ii-te, mono mai-rase-tari.
together-PART exist EXCL etc. say-CONJP thing come.HUMB-PRF
Sukoshi **kui**-nado-shi-te, …
little eat-some-do-CONJP
'I have not yet **eaten** the fish. I thought we could eat it together if you came this evening. Shall we [eat now],' said [the person], having [the servants] prepare the meal. He **ate** a little, …
(Michizuna no haha, *Kagerō Nikki* [*Kagero Diary*], Passage 50, 974–995)

11. The continuative form is a translation of the *renyō* form in Japanese (Shirane, 2005, p. 25). It is one of the six word forms that are attached to the end of the verb to convey grammatical and semantic functions in Japanese classical grammar (the other five forms are *mizen* 'imperfective,' *shūshi* 'final,' *rentai* 'attributive,' *izen* 'perfective,' and *meirei* 'imperative'). The continuative form indicates that the action expressed by the verb has occurred or been carried out. It also precedes a conjunctive particle 接続助詞, indicating that the action is simultaneous or continuative. This way, Japanese verbs inflect their forms depending on what form the following item requires.

12. This observation tallies with what Yanase (1971, p. 124) states in his annotation of *Hōjōki* ('Visions of a Torn World', 1220), an essay written in the Early Middle Japanese (EMJ) period (1100–1330).

(5) mizu yari-taru hi no ue ni oshiki domo sue-te, mono
water flow-PRF pipe GEN upper-part LOC tray some put-CONJP food
kui-te, tezu kara suiha nado suru kokochi ito
eat-and own.hand from rice.in.cold.water some do heart very
tachiuki made are-do, …
hard.to.leave extent exist-CONCP
'Placing a tray on the water pipe, we **had a meal**. When I prepare water rice by myself (as I do on a journey), I do not feel like going back home, but …'
(Michizuna no haha, *Kagerō Nikki* [*Kagero Diary*], Passage 85, 974–995)

Kuu remained polysemous with meanings associated with mastication and consumption in the following centuries. At the beginning of the LMJ period, or more precisely, in the *Tsurezuregusa* (*Essays in Idleness*, ca. 1331), *kuu* was used in a scene in which two animals (*horse* and *dog*) bite humans, as shown in (6). Here, the component of chewing is pinpointed as a salient active zone, and hence, the emphasis on using teeth, foregrounding the act of biting.

(6) … hito **kuu** uma o-ba mimi o kiri-te … hito
person attack horse ACC-EMPHP ear ACC cut-CONJP person
kuu inu o-ba yashinai-kau-bekarazu
attack dog ACC-EMPHP look.after-keep-should.not
'When horses **bite** people, their ears are clipped as a warning sign. Dogs should not be kept when they **bite** people.'
(K. Yoshida, *Tsurezuregusa* [*Essays in Idleness*], Passage 183, c. 1331)

Note that *kuu* incorporates the sense of violent attack into the act of biting. The choice of this specific combination of attack and biting is likely to be a reflection of adversity (Culture 1) because biting itself as a bodily action does not necessarily lead to negativity universally. For example, Newman (1997) has shown that Greek culture perceives mastication as an aspect of acquiring new knowledge, which designates a positive quality. Adversity embodies the idea that the people affected are hurt or disadvantaged and therefore invokes the feeling of unhappiness.

4.1.2 *Eating and living*

Eating is an essential part of human life. Eating (and drinking) and living are thus closely associated. This association was already established in the EMdJ period. The *Comprehensive Dictionary of the Japanese Language* (Editorial team of Shogakukan, 2001, p. 748) refers to its first appearance in 1711, in a narrative ballad called *Imamiya no Shinjū* (*Suicide in Imamiya*). In modern Japanese, this usage of *kuu* is actively employed and it is codified as an intransitive verb in Japanese dictionaries. The example in (7), which is an extract from an interview with a Japanese novelist who lived in Manchuria as a young boy at the end of the Second World War. He describes the countless hardships he had to overcome, listing what he did ("working for the Soviet Troops," "stealing glasses and selling them," "acting as an agent to deal with abandoned children") to survive in life-threatening situations. Note that *kuu* in this usage belongs to the ICM of living, of which eating is a part. All the examples I obtained for this study have negative connotations – a reflection of Culture 1. A most typical case, like here, is the "lack of money" that makes life hard, as we will also discuss regarding examples in (15) and (16) in Section 4.3.1.

(7) jūsansai no boku ga kazoku o sasaeru-shika ari-mase-n.
thirteen.years.old GEN I NOM family ACC support-only exist-POL.NEG
Soren-gun no tokoro-de hataraku-koto mo ari-mashi-ta ga **kuu**
Soviet-troop GEN place-LOC work-NMLZ also exist-POL-PST but eat
tame no shudan wa eran-deir-are-nai. Shōnen no nakama-tachi
for GEN means TOP choose-ASP-POT-NEG boy GEN fellow.friend-PL
to hikōjō kara nusun-da garasu o yami-ichi de ur-u.
with airport from steal-PST glass ACC black-market LOC sell-PRS
Osana-go o tebana-zaruoenaku-nat-ta hōjin to ko
young-child ACC abandon-cannot.help-become-PST Japanese with child
o hoshi-garu genchi no nakadachi o shi-ta koto-sae
ACC want-MOOD local.area GEN go-between ACC do-PST NMLZ-even
ari-mas-u.
exist-POL-PRS
'I was thirteen years old and had to take care of my family. I even worked for the Soviet troops. There was no choice, I had to **live** (survive), by hook or by crook. With boys in the same situation I sold glasses that we stole from an airport on the black market. I even acted as a go-between for Japanese people who had to abandon their children and local people who wanted to adopt children.' ("Pyonyan de," 2018)

4.1.3 *Eating an inedible object as acceptance of adversity*

I stated in Section 1 that *kuu* is used largely figuratively in present-day Japanese in the sense that it takes an inedible object as its complement. This subsection focuses on *kuu*'s nonliteral expressions containing *oitekibori*, which was initially a nominal compound consisting of *oiteke* (an imperative form meaning 'leave x') and *hori* (meaning 'pond').[13] A famous myth of the EMdJ period speaks of a "talking pond" which cried, "Leave the fish behind!" to fishermen when they were about to leave with the fish they had caught. Hearing this voice, the fishermen were so scared that they rushed away without taking the fish. The result is obvious: the fish were left behind at the pond. This pond is mentioned in *Kisanjin ie no Bakemono* (*A Monster at the House of Kisanjin*, 1787). In this story, *oitekebori*[14] is used both to refer to the pond and to a person who is left alone. (8) is an extract in which *oitekebori* occurs twice: one use refers to a person who stayed behind and the other to the pond called *Oitekebori*. In this example, *oitekebori* does not occur with *kuu* and neither does it have a negative connotation.

(8) tomo-dachi no untsuku-mera ga ore o **oitekebori** ni shiot-ta
friend-PL GEN idiot-PL NOM I ACC leaving.behind DAT do-PST
ga ore ga shiawase ni nat-ta. Tomeyama wa
but I NOM happy DAT become-PST (personal.name) TOP
oitekebori nite okamochi ni kimo o
(name.of.the.pond) LOC (personal.name) DAT liver ACC
tsubu-sase-chi to kinodoku ni nari-kere-ba …
damage-CAUS-EMPH QUOT feel.sorry DAT become-PRF-CONJP
'Although my friends, the idiots, left me behind, I was fortunate. I felt sympathy for Tomeyama because he was terrified by Okamochi at the *Oitekebori* pond and …'[15] (*Kisanjin Ie no Bakemono* [*A Ghost at the House of Kisanjin*], p. 424, 1787)

When *oitekibori* co-occurs with *kuu*, as in today's usage, it describes unhappy scenarios. One instance is demonstrated by (9), a magazine article in which travelers

13. The change from /h/ to /b/ is an effect of sequential voicing, a phonological process that causes the initial voiceless consonant of the second element of a compound to become voiced. The glottal fricative /h/ becomes a voiceless bilabial stop /p/ due to the historical fact that /h/ was descended from /p/. That is to say, this phenomenon is reminiscent of the old pair /p/ and /b/ (Iwasaki, 2002, p. 22; Vance, 1987, p. 134).

14. The first part of the compound retained its original imperative form ending with *-e*.

15. The nickname of Okamochi is "Kisanjin," the expression found in the title of the story. This nickname consists of three characters (turtle+mountain+person) and Okamochi himself is seen as a *bakemono* 'monster', another expression found in the title, which is believed to reside in his psyche.

are trapped at the airport because the plane they were to board had taken off. In this example, unhappiness – or despair, to be more precise – is caused by the untimely take-off. An intriguing point is that the scene described in this article still entails an aspect of physical motion (=the take-off of a plane), an element enshrined in the original expression with *oitekibori* (=leaving of fishers from the pond).

(9) yagate tōjō-jikan ga ki-te bippu senyō basu ni
finally boarding-time NOM come-CONJP VIP exclusive bus DIR
norikomi-mashi-ta. Bippu wa hiroi chūkijō o guruguru mawari-masu
get.into-POL-PST VIP TOP large parking ACC round turn-POL
ga tōjōki ga mitsukari-mase-n. Basu no untenshu wa shikirini
but airplane NOM find-POL-NEG bus GEN driver TOP continusly
musen de kōshin shi-teimashi-ta ga totsuzen ōgoe de
wireless with communication do-PROG-PST but suddenly loud.voice with
sakebi-mas-u. Nanto! Tōjōki wa hokano kyaku to nimotsu o
shout-POL-PRS what! airplane TOP other passenger and luggage ACC
tsukete ririku. Bippu no jyōkyaku zenin ga **oitekibori** o **kut**-ta
load take.off VIP GEN passenger all NOM left.behind ACC eat-PST
to iu wake des-u.
QUOT say reason COP-PRS
'Boarding time finally arrived and we got into the bus reserved for VIPs. The bus was moving around the parking area but could not find the plane we were to board. The driver was constantly contacting the person in charge but he suddenly shouted: "What!" The plane had taken off with the other passengers and our luggage. This literally meant that all the passengers on the bus were left behind at the gate.' (Kurauchi, 2011)

Another instance from present-day Japanese is demonstrated by (10), an extract from an interview featuring a retiree who lost his wife. It is reported that he is unable to do housework (e.g., using washing machines, preparing meals at home) like his late wife had. By using *oitekibori*, the retiree expresses regret that in our modern times housework can easily be avoided by paying money. Instead of cooking at home, one can buy prepared meals or eat out. One can also take clothes to the dry cleaners instead of doing laundry at home. If one can afford to spend money, it can substitute major parts of one's daily routines. Despite this, the retiree recognizes the significance of housework accomplished by human hands and hence he cannot but regret his inability to do it. The combination of *oitekibori* and *ku* (the continuative form of *kuu*, see footnote 11) conveys the message that housework, whose value cannot be equated with money, is, ironically, eclipsed by it. Unlike (9), this unhappy situation is not caused by a physical action; it resides in the speaker's mind.

(10) nandemo kinsen ni okikaeru jidai dakara, kaji wa
everything money DAT replace time as household.affairs TOP
oitekibori o **ku**-ttei-masu. Hontō wa kane de kae-nai,
left-behind ACC eat-PRF-POL in.reality TOP money DAT buy-NEG
monosugoku kichōna koto nandes-u. Shakai-zentai ga kinsen ni
extremely valuable NMLZ EXPL-PRS society-whole NOM money DAT
okikaeru koto o yameta-ra kaji wa daijina sigoto
replace NMLZ ACC stop-COND household.affairs TOP important work
toshite, motto kurōzu-appu sa-reru no de-wa nai-deshō-ka
as more close-up do-CAUS NMLZ COP-TOP NEG-COP-Q
'Because we live in a time when everything is substitutable with money, housework has been neglected. The truth is that it is something valuable that cannot be bought with money. If our entire society would stop doing this substitution, I believe, housework would regain its value as an important routine.'
("Bentō ga," 2019)

In (11) *oitekibori* is used as an adverb suffixed by the adverbial marker *ni*. Where this example differs from (9) and (10) is in the use of *oitekibori* without the verb *kuu*, but the sense of adversity remains, namely, the negativity of Japanese politics failing to keep pace with the political advances elsewhere in East Asia.

(11) tayori no beikoku ni amerika daiichi-shugi no daitōryō
reliance GEN America LOC America number.one-principle GEN president
ga tōjō shi, chōsen hantō jōsei no henka ga
NOM appearance do Korea Peninsula circumstance GEN change NOM
nihon o **oitekibori**-ni susum-u. Kibishii kyokumen
Japan ACC being.left.behind-ADVZ advance-PRS severe aspect
ga tsuzuku.
NOM continue
'A president with "America First" appeared in the USA, which Japan relies on. The situation in the Korean Peninsula advances, which leaves Japan behind. Severe situations persist. ("Ushinawareta," 2018)

4.2 Tabu

The verb *tabu* is an earlier form of *taberu*. It initially expressed a situation in which a person receives an object (e.g., food) from a person of a higher social status. Because attention to the hierarchical structure of Japanese society, then an important of Japanese etiquette, was expressed by usage of *tabu*, it was considered to be a refined, and thus polite, counterpart to *kuu*, which was perceived as a coarse expression because of its emphasis on the use of the teeth, central to the crushing and cutting of food.[16] An attentive reader may notice that both *kuu* and *tabu* became a verb of consumption through their association with the idea of receiving; but they differed in terms of perspective: while for *kuu*, receiving derived from bodily action, for *tabu* it was part of social life. That is, receiving was activated in association with two different active zones, possibly in two different ICMs. Consider the examples below. (12) depicts a situation in which *tabu* was used as a verb of drinking in a sociocultural context in which a priest, regarded as a holy man, preached in front of ordinary people. During its early development, *tabu* incorporated both eating and drinking in its semantics. Since eating and drinking are evidently distinct physiologically (e.g., drinking typically lacks chewing), the coexistence of both meanings in a single word proves that *tabu* did not develop the semantics of eating based on bodily action, in contrast to *kuu*.

(12) Mata, "hito ni sake susumuru-tote, onore mazu
once.again person DAT alcohol recommend-INTENT self first
tabe-te, hito ni shii-tatematsura-n to suru wa ken nite
drink-CONJP person DAT force-HON-INTENT PART do TOP sword with
hito o kira-n to suru-ni ni-taru-koto-nari. ...
person ACC decapitate-INTENT PART do-CONJP resemble-PRF-NMLZ-COPUL
'Again, if, when offering *sake* to someone, you first drink some yourself and then try to force it on the other man, it is like trying to kill a man with a (double-edged) sword ...'
(K. Yoshida, *Tsurezuregusa* [*Essays in Idleness*], Passage 125, c. 1331)

What is interesting about (13) is that it shows that *tabu* is losing its honorific sense and merely designates an aspect of eating. According to Nakamura et al. (1984, p. 198), *tabu* appeared in reported speech. The purpose of reported speech is to convey propositional content; thus humility, which is the product of actual interactions, would not fit the situation described here. This example suggests that *tabu* started to become a genuine lexeme of consumption. The presence of the suffix of politeness, *-mashi-*, might be another piece of supporting evidence for this claim; *-mashi-* would not be used if *tabu* were itself an honorific marker. Furthermore, Nakamura et al. (1984) claimed that it was in the EMdJ period that *tabu* began to show a general tendency to lose its honorific status and became a lexical item in its own right. As *tabu* underwent this process, its form also changed, to *taburu*, and finally to *taberu*, a process that included a sound change in the middle vowel from /u/ to /e/.

16. An interesting point worth noting here is that *tabu* was used only when food, among other things, was given to the eater by someone else; *kuu* was preferred when the eater himself supplied and ate food (Kindaichi, et al. 1988, p. 726).

(13) sabishi sau naru koto kana. Chito sasa nado, kore yori
lonely look PRF NMLZ EXCL little alcohol some this from
tabe-mashi-te to iu mo iya-rashik-u, …
drink-POL-CONJP QUOT say also hesitant-seem-PRS
'"How lonely you look!" She was apparently hesitant to say, "I would start drinking alcohol (before Yonosuke, a male protagonist of this story, drank)", …'
(S. Ihara, *Kōshoku Ichidai Otoko* [*The Life of an Amorous Man*], Book I, Story 7, 1682)

4.3 Taberu

The verb *taberu* is used to express the consumption of edible objects in the sense of putting them in the mouth, chewing, and swallowing them, as exemplified by (14). Unlike *tabu*, discussed in Section 4.2, *taberu* is used solely for eating, not for drinking. In this extract, the featured person has a high opinion of Japanese sweets from Fukui Prefecture.

(14) kono okashi wa jimoto no meika. Taizai suru
this sweet TOP local.area GEN famous.confection stay do
tabini itadai-teimasu.[17] Hin ga yoku-te kinu
on.the.occasion.of eat(humble)-HABITUAL dignity NOM good-CONJP silk
no yōna shitazawari. Shita no naka de toroke-te iku kanji
GEN like taste tongue GEN inner.part LOC melt-CONJP go feeling
ga suki-des-u. Shōryō nanode tsui takusan
NOM like-COP-PRS little as undeliberately a.lot
tabe-teshimai-mas-u. Ōshū nado kaigai de-no sigoto mo ooku,
eat-PRF-POL-PRS Europe etc. overseas LOC-GEN Job too many
kakuchi de amai mono o **taberu**-no-des-u ga kēki ya
each.place LOC sweet thing ACC eat-NOMLZ-COP-PRS but cake and
chokorēto nado mukō no mono wa gatsunto hebī.
chocolate etc. over.there GEN thing TOP extremely heavy
'This sweet is a famous confection from Fukui. I eat (=*itadai-*) it every time I stay here. It is delicious and its texture is smooth as silk. I like the feeling as it melts in my mouth. As the pieces are small, I tend to **eat** a lot. I travel overseas a lot for work, such as in Europe, and **eat** sweets in every place I visit, but sweets over there, like cakes and chocolates, are quite heavy.' [17]
("(Otoko no betsubara). Hosokawa," 2019)

17. This verb *itadai* (the *renyō-* form of *itadaku*) is a humble form of *taberu* 'eat'. This verb may have been used instead of the standard *taberu* to sound polite and to underline the speaker's appreciation of sweets to the producer in Fukui Prefecture. It is grammatically correct to use *taberu* but the use of *itadaku* foregrounds the speaker's mental interaction with the food.

4.3.1 *Eating and living*

As discussed earlier (Section 4.1.2), *kuu* had already established metonymic usage in the EMdJ period to mean 'to live' and this intransitive usage is also found with *taberu*. As shown by (15), *taberu* is frequently used in present-day Japanese with this extended meaning and in both (15) and (16) the speaker uses *taberu* concurrently with synonymous words, which are underlined (e.g., *ikiru* 'to live', in (15); *seikatsu suru* 'to live' in (16)). Similar to *kuu, taberu* also developed this meaning on the grounds that eating is an integral part of human life – besides other central elements of life such as sleeping and working. That neither of these latter was chosen to stand for living might indicate that eating is conceptually the most prominent facet among all the substructures in the ICM of living.

(15) Ikiru tameni, **taberu** tameni watashi-tachi wa hatarai-teiru. Shigoto no
live for eat for I-PL TOP work-PROG work GEN
tameni inochi o otosu-no wa honmatsu-tentō-na
for life ACC lose-NMLZ TOP beginning.ending-overturn-ADJZ
hanashi desu ga, …
story COP but
'We work to survive and to live. It is a total mistake to ruin our lives by devoting ourselves entirely to our workplace, …' ("Kokkai-shingi," 2018)

(16) nishi-nihon zaichū no josei (42) wa … kō hanas-u.
West-Japan stay GEN woman (age) TOP this.way speak-PRS
Keiyaku- shain toshite no shūnyū wa 14-man-en
contract-employee as GEN salary TOP fourteen-ten.thousand-yen
hodo. "4 nin de **taberu** node seiippai. … "seikatsu suru dakede
about four person by eat as just.enough life do only
seiippai nonaka, jibun de seido o shirabe-rare-ru
just.enough while self by regulations ACC examine-POT-PRS
hitori-oya-katei wa kagir-areru-no-de-wa".
one.person-parent-family TOP limit-PASS-NMLZ-COP-Q
'A woman aged 42 living in western Japan reported the following: "My monthly salary as a contract employee is about ¥140,000. It is scarcely enough for a family of four to **live**. While maintaining our basic quality of life takes up all my time at present, it would hardly be possible for one-parent families to look into the rules and regulations (to find and apply for relevant allowances)."' ("Teishotoku," 2018)

4.3.2 *Eating an inedible object as an expression of enjoyment*

Another intriguing fact is that *taberu* occurs with inedible objects, creating figurative expressions. Consider (17), in which *taberu* is used to articulate enjoyment. The interviewee associates enjoyment with "eating" seasons, which means that he derives pleasure from tasting different foods and dishes associated with the four seasons in Japan. The four seasons and the foods typifying each are tightly connected in the ICM of eating. (18) is analogous to (17) in that *taberu* is used to express enjoyment of the referent of the object, a novel by Murakami in this case, but *taberu* includes the actual cooking of food mentioned in a novel. By personally cooking and tasting a dish, one enjoys what is written in the novel. What is new here is that eating represents enjoyment and happiness, a phenomenon that is not part of Japanese tradition.

(17) ... kisetsu-kan o **taberu**, shiki no henka o
season-flavor ACC eat four.seasons GEN change ACC
tanoshimu-no-ga nihon no shokumi no yoi tokoro desu.
enjoy-NMLZ-NOM Japan GEN quality.of.food GEN good point COP.PRS
'One **eats** the flavor of the seasons. It is wonderful that we can enjoy the changes in the four seasons in the quality of food in Japan.'
("(Otoko no betsubara). Ota," 2018)

(18) Ano shōsetsu ga **tabe**-tai: Hawai o **taberu**.
that novel NOM eat-want Hawaii ACC eat
'(I) want to **eat** a novel: I will **eat** Hawaii' (the title of a series of essays accompanied by a specific title concerning Hawaii, a place that appears in Haruki Murakami's novel *Dance Dance Dance*). ("Murakami Haruki," 2018)

4.4 Summary

Sections 4.1 to 4.3 have demonstrated, based on sixteen Examples (3)–(18), that the extensions of three verbs of eating, *kuu*, *tabu*, and *taberu*, are basically metonymic; that is, a specific active zone of an ICM is highlighted to be the new referent associated with the original referent. This finding coincides with the major consensus in the cognitive linguistics literature, that metonymy is ubiquitous and more fundamental than metaphor in constructing meaning (e.g., Barcelona, 2007; among others). The importance of metonymy and metaphor has also been emphasized by historical linguists (e.g., Allan, 2010; Fortson IV, 2003; Hopper, 1996; Kay & Allan, 2015; Nerlich, 2010; Ullman, 1962). For example, Nerlich (2010, p. 204) proposes what she calls "serial metonymy" (see also Nerlich & Clarke, 2001) to account for the lexical development of words. It underlines one-to-many relations between the vehicle and the target, in contrast to generally accepted relations that are one-to-one. To give a concrete example, she exemplifies several relations embodied in the development of *paper* in English in the following way: (a) a substance made from the pulp of wood or another fibrous material; (b) something used for writing or drawing on; (c) an essay or dissertation; (d) a document; and (e) the contents of an essay. The idea of taking into consideration a word's meanings at different stages actually illuminates the pillar of active zones. What makes the Japanese lexicon distinct from those of other languages might be the roles of culture therein; in Japanese, two forms of culture played a role in organizing the internal structure of ICMs and in determining the experiential link between the vehicle and the target within an ICM, and ultimately inducing a new meaning. As mentioned repeatedly above, the incorporation of a negative tone into the interpretation of *kuu* was motivated by the force of Culture 1, and the change from *kuu* to *taberu* is due to the force of Culture 2. Figurative expressions such as *oitekibori o kuu* 'to have the misfortune of being left behind' or the adverbial *oitekiborini* 'disadvantageously' are on the verge of becoming metaphoric (see Examples (10) and (11), respectively) in the sense that they are losing their original motional sense and establishing conceptual metaphors that can be formulated as IDEAS ARE ACTIONS because ideas are evoked in the speaker's mind through the image of someone or something being left behind. At first glance, this example may support the claim that metaphor arises from the metonymic base, which gives the impression that it coincides with the general direction of research in the cognitive linguistics literature (e.g., Goossens, 1990; Taylor, 1989/2003) as well as the historical linguistics literature that takes cognitive processes seriously. However, what we have not yet discussed in depth is the idea that the perspective that IDEAS ARE ACTIONS is actually based on the presence of *oitekibori*, not the verb *kuu*. This finding is grounded in the following interpretations. First, what contributes to the building of metaphor is the action itself, with motion or without, encoded in *oitekibori*, as indicated by (9) and (10). Second, ideas such as disappointment or regret evoked in the sentence are not derived from receiving, as evidenced by (9), (10), and (11). Third, the sense of adversity is retained even if *kuu* is not in use, as demonstrated by (11). All these empirical facts may suggest that operations of metonymy and metaphor can be differentiated. Here we come to the topic of "withdrawal," which might provide another argument in favor of the interpretations we have raised here.

5. *Kuu*'s withdrawal

There is a general consensus that metaphor and metonymy are conceptually related. Taylor (1989/2003, pp. 138–139 cited by Heine, Claudi & Hünnemeyer, 1991, p. 74) explains how metonymy acts as an intermediary in the formation of the conceptual metaphor MORE IS UP. The experience of the pile getting higher is metonymic in that height is literally correlated with quantity. Thus, metaphor emerges when the up-down schema, the base for metaphor, is dissociated from the piling-up image. When we talk about "prices getting higher," although prices cannot get higher in concrete terms, we are referring to the abstract concept of "addition." At the outset of Section 4, I cited an example of metonymy with *ham sandwich* from Evans (2007). The difference between Taylor's example and Evans' is that in the former, the vehicle and target set for metonymy are also valid in metaphor. The point is that the same metonymy-producing concepts become less concrete in metaphor. In Evans' example, metonymy is used to identify a reference in the real world. Metonymy and metaphor share only the vehicle (*ham sandwich*); the target is not shared. When *oitekibori o kuu*, the example in (10), loses its original spatial sense and develops the sense of "being left behind" in one's mind, a shift from the concrete to the abstract has taken place. This shift is similar to the case of *ham sandwich* since it also loses its concrete reference in the transition from customer to human quality. What is specific to Japanese is that the shift is not triggered by the word that forms a metonymy but another one present in the predication: not *kuu* but *oitekibori* is responsible for the shift, for the reasons I mentioned at the end of Section 4. In what follows, I deal with this aspect of *kuu*, namely its disappearance from the expression, which I label "withdrawal."

By considering two further examples in which *kuu* takes *monzenbarai* ('turning a visitor away (=*harai*) at the gate (=*monzen*)') as an inedible object, I demonstrate how and why *kuu* withdraws and what this phenomenon indicates for the relation between metonymy and metaphor. Note that *kurai* (the continuative form of *kurau*) derives morphologically from *kuu* to augment the effect of roughness in eating, thereby expressing harmfulness and roughness more strongly. Example (19) retains the sense of refusal that *monzenbarai* originally expressed.

(19) shokushu niyotte wa **monzenbarai** o **kurai** dansei ga
types.of.jobs according.to TOP turn.a.visitor.away ACC eat male NOM
uke-rare-ru kenshū ya kunren o uke-rare-nai
attend-POT-PRS workshop and training ACC attend-POT-NEG
'I (=Japanese woman) **was refused** permission to attend workshops and training for some jobs, which were offered to men only.' ("Nyonin-kinsei," 2018)

In Example (20), an article concerning reclamation work in Henoko, Okinawa Prefecture, *monzenbarai* is headed by the literal verb *uke* (the final form of *ukeru* 'accept') in place of *kuu*.

(20) Kōsoshin de Okinawa-ken … kuni ga kyoka
Appeal.hearing LOC Okinawa-prefecture government NOM permission
naku kōji o susume-teiru-no-wa ihō da-to
not construction.work ACC continue-PROG-NOMLZ-TOP illegal COP-QUOT
uttae-mashi-ta ga saibansho wa "shinri no taishō ni-wa
sue-POL-PST but court TOP trial GEN object DAT-TOP
nara-nai" toshite kōso o kikyaku-shi-mashi-ta. Futatabi,
become-NEG by.way.of appeal ACC dismiss-do-POL-PST again
Okinawa-ken wa kyūsai o motome-ta shihō no ba de
Okinawa-prefecture TOP help ACC request-PST justice GEN place LOC
monzenbarai o **uke**-ta to iu koto-des-u.
refusal.at the.gate ACC receive-PST QUOT say NMLZ-COP-PRS
'Okinawa Prefecture brought an action in court against the Japanese Government due to its continuous construction work without prefectural permission, but the court dismissed the appeal, saying that the government cannot be the defendant of a trial. This means that, once again, Okinawa Prefecture was turned down despite its appeal for support.' (Iwasaki, 2018)

(19) and (20) are semantically analogous in that both have an agent who is turned down by the authority. The question is why *kuu* is not used in (20). Keller (1997, p. 16) maintains that when politeness loses its markedness, that is, its exceptionality as compared to unmarked impolite expressions, it starts to disappear. Keller equates language change to a game; there is a winner (who is marked) and a loser (who is unmarked). What is happening to *kuu* can be explained by this line of argument. *Kuu* acquired the meaning of receiving and this caused inedible objects to be used nonliterally, thereby inviting adversity, a popular concept among Japanese people at that time. In the early stages of this development, *kuu*'s meaning was unequivocally that of receiving. One piece of evidence for this is that *kuu* with this meaning was substituted by *chōdai suru* (an honorific expression of receiving) in some expressions during the EMdJ period (Editorial team of Shogakukan, 2001, p. 993). When *kuu* was used frequently as the verb of receiving and conventionalized, its effect was reduced and, similar to the case of politeness, *kuu*'s marked meaning of receiving came to be superfluous and, consequently, lost its exceptionality; that is, its uniqueness to express receiving based on eating. It goes without saying that the degree of adversity might be stronger in (19) than (20) due to *kuu*'s overt presence, but adversity is undoubtedly conveyed in (20). This commonality indicates that when exception is not in demand, *kuu* withdraws, as a loser in Keller's game

metaphor. While I have not determined how this Kellerian competition correlates with the notion that IDEAS ARE ACTIONS, one thing that is palpably clear is that the conceptual metaphor is current regardless of the presence of the verb. This suggests that the Kellerian account illustrates only the physical disappearance of *kuu*. Refusal is an action, the same as leaving someone behind. Different thoughts and effects resulting from these actions in the speaker's mind (e.g., disappointment, despair, sadness, and regret) can be derived, and one can safely say that this process is concurrent with an underlining mental process such as that of IDEAS ARE ACTIONS.

6. Conclusion

This chapter has elaborated on a variety of meanings that two verbs of eating, *kuu* and *taberu* (including *tabu*, an earlier form of *taberu*), have yielded between the eighth century and the present. Let me briefly summarize the key points. First, *kuu* acquired the meaning of eating through shifting substructures (holding food, to mastication, to eating) within the eating ICM. Second, *kuu* appeared in figurative expressions when it shifted further, from eating to receiving. The role of *kuu* here was to invite inedible objects to construct new, adversative meaning, but it was not itself involved in the construction of IDEAS ARE ACTIONS. Third, expressions with an inedible object became more schematic in that they lost the original sense of motion. Fourth, when receiving was no longer marked (since the literal verb *ukeru* 'receive' supplanted *kuu*), *kuu* started to disappear from the predication. This can be explained with reference to Keller's game metaphor. Fifth, *taberu* emerged from *tabu*, whose original meaning was to receive food from a person of higher social rank. Sixth, *taberu* has recently started producing nonliteral expressions, focusing on eating as an expression of enjoyment/happiness, departing from our old cultural habit of prioritizing adversity/unhappiness. Seventh, both *kuu* and *taberu* have extended their meaning from eating to that of sustaining life.

At the outset of this chapter, we asked why there are two verbs of eating in the Japanese lexicon. The answer is twofold. The linguistic expression of consumption developed from imagery of holding and biting, connected later with negative emotion, and Japan's sociocultural system, whose role was the categorization of people, later connected with positive emotion. We have also confirmed that metaphor arose from the process in which the vehicle gradually loses its physical property. Although metaphor arose later than metonymy, this historical process may not corroborate the claim that metaphor is "based on" metonymy. The cases examined above have greater affinity with Evans' "ham sandwich" example than Taylor's "pile getting higher."

Contemporary scholars such as Littlemore (2015, p. 132) and Barnden (2010) have stated that metaphor and metonymy are intrinsically slippery. However, their discussions of metonymy underscore neither active zones nor subtypes of culture. Barnden's definition of metonymy centers on contiguity. While some active zone-based associations can be conceived of as contiguous to the extent that when two things are associated, they are contiguous (e.g., "a car" and "its fuel tank," resulting in *I filled up my car*) (e.g., Fortson IV, 2003, p. 649), contiguity itself is a problematic term in that not all that is contiguous is metonymically associative: *The house burned down* does not equate to "A dining room burned down" (Croft, 2006, p. 318). Many historical linguists share the view that semantic change is initiated by the operation of metonymy, resulting ultimately in the construction of metaphor (e.g., Allan, 2010; Heine et al., 1991; Hopper, 1996; Traugott & Dasher, 2001). Here, too, the focus is found to be far from substructures and subcultures. Despite this diversity of research directions, I hope that the present study, exclusively based on verbs of eating, has proven that there is another source of meaning construction, namely the interplay among three items, that is, active zone-based metonymy, subcultures, and what here is dubbed "withdrawal." Not all metonymic expressions have completely developed into metaphor but we have witnessed how abstract ideas gradually come into existence by stripping off concreteness from the source meaning. All the findings here lead to the conclusion that there is a clear division of labor between metonymy and metaphor.

Abbreviations

ADJZ	Adjectivializer	EMPHP	Emphatic particle
ADVZ	adverbializer	EXCL	Exclamation
ASP	Aspect	EXPL	Explanation
CONCP	Concessive particle	INTENT	Intention
CONJP	Conjunctive particle	PART	Particle
COPUL	copulative	PL	Plural
EMPH	Emphasis	PRS	Present

References

Allan, K. (2010). Tracing metonymic polysemy through time: MATERIAL FOR OBJECT mappings in the OED. In M. E. Winters, H. Tissari, & K. Allan (Eds.), *Historical cognitive linguistics* (pp. 163–196). Berlin: De Gruyter Mouton. https://doi.org/10.1515/9783110226447.163

Anderson, E. N. (2005). *Everyone eats: Understanding food and culture*. New York, NY: New York University Press.

Barcelona, A. (2007). The role of metonymy in meaning construction at discourse level: A case study. In G. Radden, K-M. Köpcke, T. Berg, & P. Siemund (Eds.), *Aspects of meaning construction* (pp. 51–75). Amsterdam and Philadelphia, PA: John Benjamins. https://doi.org/10.1075/z.136.06bar

Barnden, J. (2010). Metaphor and metonymy: Making their connections more slippery. *Cognitive Linguistics*, *21*(1), 1–34. https://doi.org/10.1515/cogl.2010.001

Bentō ga pan to ringo demo kodomo wa sodatsu Kaji no sokubaku sayonara [Children can grow with bread-and-apple bento – Goodby to housework]. (2019, January 29). *Asahi Shimbun*. Retrieved from https://digital.asahi.com/articles/ASM1X46PMM1XUPQJ009.html?iref=pc_ss_date

Boyd, B., & Richerson, P. J. (1985). *Culture and the evolutionary process*. Chicago, IL: Chicago University Press.

Croft, W. (2002). The role of domains in the interpretation of metaphors and metonymies. In R. Dirven & R. Porings (Eds.), *Metaphor and metonymy in comparison and contrast* (pp. 161–205). Berlin and New York, NY: De Gruyter Mouton. https://doi.org/10.1515/9783110219197.161

Croft, W. (2006). On explaining metonymy: Comment on Peirsman and Geeraerts, "Metonymy as a prototypical category". *Cognitive Linguistics*, *17*(3), 317–326. https://doi.org/10.1515/COG.2006.008

Editorial team of Shogakukan. (2001). *Nihon Kokugo Dai-jiten* [The comprehensive dictionary of the Japanese language]. Tokyo: Shogakukan.

Evans, V. (2007). *A glossary of cognitive linguistics*. Salt Lake City, UT: The University of Utah Press.

Evans, V., & Green, M. (2006). *Cognitive linguistics: An introduction*. Edinburgh: Edinburgh University Press.

Fortson , IV, B. W. (2003). An approach to semantic change. In B. D. Joseph & R. D. Janda (Eds.), *The handbook of historical linguistics* (pp. 648–666). Malden, MA: Blackwell. https://doi.org/10.1002/9780470756393.ch21

Goossens, L. (1990). Metaphonymy: The interaction between metaphor and metonymy in expressions for linguistic actions. *Cognitive Linguistics*, *1*(3), 323–340. https://doi.org/10.1515/cogl.1990.1.3.323

Heine, B., Claudi, U., & Hūnnemeyer, F. (1991). *Grammaticalization: A conceptual framework*. Chicago, IL: Chicago University Press.

Hopper, P. (1996). Some recent trends in grammaticalization. *Annual Review of Anthropology*, *25*, 217–236. https://doi.org/10.1146/annurev.anthro.25.1.217

Ihara, S. (1682). Kōshoku Ichidai Otoko [The life of an amorous man]. In Kingoro Maeda (Ed.), *Kōshoku ichidai otoko zen chūshaku* [A completely annotated edition of Kōshoku ichidai otoko]. Book I. Tokyo: Kadokawa, (1980).

Iwasaki, K. (2018, December 15). Abe-seiken ga tsuzuku kagiri Okinawa no min-i wa mushi-sare-tsuzukeru [Okinawa's public opinion will remain ignored as long as the Abe's political power continues]. *Web Ronza*. Retrieved from https://webronza.asahi.com/politics/articles/2018121400001.html?iref=pc_ss_date

Iwasaki, S. (2002). *Japanese*. Amsterdam/Philadelphia: John Benjamins. https://doi.org/10.1075/loall.5

Kay, C., & Allan, K. (2015). *English historical semantics*. Edinburgh: Edinburgh University Press.

Keller, R. (1997). In what sense can explanations of language change be functional? In J. Gvozdanović (Ed.), *Language change and functional explanations* (pp. 9–20). Berlin: Mouton de Gruyter. https://doi.org/10.1515/9783110813753.9

Kindaichi, H., Hayashi, O., & Shibata, T. (Eds.). (1988). *Nihongo hyakka Daijiten* [An encyclopedia of the Japanese language]. Tokyo: Taishukan.

Kisanjin ie no bakemono [A Monster at the House of Kisanjin]. (1787). In T. Suzuki (Ed.), *Kibyōshi hyakushū* [One hundred illustrated short stories] (pp. 419–428). Tokyo: Hakubunkan, (1901).

Kokkai-shingi wa tsuzuite imasu ga… Shōsetsu ga tou "hatarakikata kaikaku" [Diet deliberations continue … "Reforming how to work" which a novel questions]. (2018, June 19). *Asahi Shimbun*. Retrieved from https://digital.asahi.com/articles/ASL6M3CDLL6MOIPE004.html?_requesturl=articles%2FASL6M3CDLL6MOIPE004.html&rm=797

Kövecses, Z. (2005). *Metaphor in culture: Universality and variation*. Cambridge: Cambridge University Press. https://doi.org/10.1017/CBO9780511614408

Kövecses, Z., & Radden, G. (1998). Metonymy: Developing a cognitive linguistic view. *Cognitive Linguistics*, *9*(1), 37–77. https://doi.org/10.1515/cogl.1998.9.1.37

Kurauchi, T. (2011, July). *Tōjōki ni oitekibori o kutta hanashi* [A story about having the misfortune of being left behind by a plane]. *Topics Global*. Retrieved from https://www.ube-ind.co.jp/ube/jp/ad/topics/topics_403.html

Lakoff, G. (1987). *Women, fire and dangerous things: What categories reveal about the mind*. Chicago, IL: University of Chicago Press. https://doi.org/10.7208/chicago/9780226471013.001.0001

Langacker, R. W. (1987). *Foundations of cognitive grammar: Theoretical prerequisites*. Stanford, CA: Stanford University Press.

Langacker, R. W. (2009). *Investigations in Cognitive Grammar*. Berlin: De Gruyter Mouton. https://doi.org/10.1515/9783110214369

Lange, D. L., & Paige, R. M. (2003). *Perspectives on culture in second language learning*. Greenwich. CT: Information Age Publishing.

Littlemore, J. (2015). *Metonymy: Hidden shortcuts in language, thought and communication*. Cambridge: Cambridge University Press. https://doi.org/10.1017/CBO9781107338814

Michizuna no haha [the mother of Michizuna]. (974–995). *Kagerō Nikki* [Kagero Diary]. In Tsutomu Kakomoto (Ed.), *Kagero Nikki Zen Chūshaku* [A completely annotated edition of Kagoro Diary]. Tokyo: Kadokawa, (1966).

Minami, H. (1971 [1953]). *Psychology of the Japanese people*. (A. R. Ikoma, Trans.). Tokyo: University of Tokyo Press.

Miyaji, Y. (1971). Gendai no keigo [Honorifics in modern times]. In T. Tsujimura (Ed.), *Keigo-shi* [A history of honorifics] (pp. 367–425). Tokyo: Taishukan.

Murakami Haruki "Dansu dansu dansu" no hanbāgā o dōga de ajiwau [Tasting the hamburger from "Dance dance dance" by Haruki Murakami with a video clip]. (2018, July 28). *Good life with books*. Retrieved from https://book.asahi.com/article/11707198?iref=pc_ss_date

Nakamura, Y., Okami, M., & Sakakura, A. (Eds.). (1984). *Kadokawa kogo dai-jiten* [Kadokawa comprehensive dictionary of classical Japanese]. Tokyo: Kadokawa.

Nerlich, B. (2010). Metaphor and metonymy. In A. H. Jucker & I. Taavitsainen (Eds.), *Historical pragmatics* (pp. 193–215). Berlin: De Gruyter Mouton.

Nerlich, B., & Clarke, D. D. (2001). Serial metonymy: A study of reference-based polysemisation, *Journal of Historical Pragmatics*, *2*(2), 245–272. https://doi.org/10.1075/jhp.2.2.04ner

Newman, J. (1997). Eating and drinking as sources of metaphor in English. *Cuadernos de Filología Inglisa*, *6*(2), 213–231.

Newman, J. (Ed.) (2009). *Linguistics of eating and drinking*. Amsterdam: John Benjamins. https://doi.org/10.1075/tsl.84

Nihon-shoki [The chronicles of Japan]. (720). In Y. Tsuchihashi (Ed.), *Kodai kayō zen-chūshaku: Nihon-shoki-hen* [A completely annotated collection of ancient poems: An edition of the Chronicles of Japan]. Tokyo: Kadokawa, (1976).

"Nyonin-kinsei" Kabe koeru ni wa koe o age te Moriyama Mayumi san [Raise your voice to overcome the wall, "Women Not Admitted", Ms. Mayumi Moriyama]. (2018, May 5). *Asahi Shimbun*. Retrieved from https://digital.asahi.com/articles/ASL4L3DVPL4LUPQJ003.html?iref=pc_ss_date

(Otoko no betsubara). Hosokawa Toshio san. 'Aratama seika' no habutae-mochi [(Men's separate stomach) Mr. Toshio Hosokawa. Habutae-mochi by "Aratama seika" company. (2019, February 15). *Asahi Shimbun*. Retrieved from https://digital.asahi.com/articles/DA3S13894910.html?iref=pc_ss_date

(Otoko no betsubara). Ota Kazuhiko san. "Onkashitsukasa Shiono" no dōmyōji sakura-mochi" [(Men's separate stomach) Mr. Kazuhiko Ota. *Dōmyōji sakura-mochi* of "Japanese sweet shop *Shiono*"]. (March 30, 2018). *Asahi Shimbun*. Retrieved from https://www.asahi.com/articles/DA3S13428957.html?iref=pc_ss_date

Pyonyan de shūsen, kuitsume baiketsu mo. Itsuki Hiroyuki o osoi-tsuzuketa yūutsu [The end of WWII in Pyongyang – Sold even blood, being broke. The gloom that kept visiting Hiroyuki Itsuki]. (2018, 25 December). *Ashahi Shimbun*, Retrieved from https://digital.asahi.com/articles/ASLDK5K1KLDKUEHF00P.html?iref=pc_ss_date)

Shirane, H. (2005). *Classical Japanese: A grammar*. New York: Columbia University Press.

Taylor, J. (1989/2003). *Linguistic categorisation* (3rd ed.). Oxford: Oxford University Press.

Teishotoku-katei no gakuhi genmen Kōtōkyōiku, shōgakukin-kakujū Honebuto no hōshin [Tax reduction and exemption for low income families – High school education, scholarship expansion – Big-boned reform]. (2018, June 6). *Asahi Shimbun*. Retrieved from https://www.asahi.com/articles/DA3S13527810.html?iref=pc_ss_date

Traugott, E., & Dasher, R. B. (2001). *Regularity in semantic change*. Cambridge: Cambridge University Press. https://doi.org/10.1017/CBO9780511486500

Tsujimura, T. (1968). *Keigo no shiteki kenkyū* [Historical study of honorifics]. Tokyo: Tokyodo.

Tsujimura, T. (1971). *Keigo-shi no hōhō to mondai* [Methods and problems in the history of honorifics]. In T. Tsujimura (Ed.), *Keigo-shi* [History of Honorifics] (pp. 1–32). Tokyo: Taishukan.

Ullman, S. (1962). *Semantics: An introduction to the science of meaning*. Oxford: Blackwell.

Ushinawareta gaikō baransu [Lost diplomatic balance]. (2018, November 20). *Asahi Shimbun*. Retrieved from https://digital.asahi.com/articles/DA3S13777735.html?iref=pc_ss_date

Vance, T. J. (1987). *An introduction to Japanese phonology*. Albany, NY: State University of New York Press.

Yamaguchi, T. (2009). Literal and figurative uses of Japanese EAT and DRINK. In J. Newman (Ed.), *The linguistics of eating and drinking*. (pp. 173–193). Amsterdam: John Benjamins. https://doi.org/10.1075/tsl.84.09yam

Yanase, K. (1971). *Hōjōki chūshaku* [Annotation of Visions of a torn world]. Tokyo: Kadokawa.

Yoshida, K. (c. 1331). Tsurezuregusa [Essays in Idleness]. In K. Yasuraoka (Ed.), *Tsurezuregusa zen chūshaku* [A completely annotated edition of Tsurezuregusa]. Tokyo: Kadokawa. (1967–1968).

CHAPTER 6

Naturalization of the Japanese loanword *sushi* in English

A cognitive account

Kiyoko Toratani
York University

This chapter examines where the Japanese loanword *sushi* stands in its naturalization process into English. Application of Doi's (2014) scale to usage of *sushi* in the Oxford English Dictionary shows it is midway through naturalization. The chapter questions the finding, pointing out the problems of Doi's scale, including its unmotivated ordering of criteria (e.g., precedence of "compounding" over "semantic change"). To assess the degree of naturalization, the chapter suggests considering the degree of entrenchment, which is reflected in (i) token frequency, (ii) use of the loanword in constructions, including snowclones (e.g., *Sushi is the new pizza*), and (iii) the word's ability to expand the nomenclatural network. Examination of these points suggests *sushi* has already moved into the naturalized stage.

Keywords: Construction Morphology, entrenchment, frame-shifting, internet memes, lexical borrowing, snowclones, frequency, encyclopaedic

1. Introduction

Since around the turn of the 21st century, the academic literature on *sushi* has steadily grown, with several disciplines discussing its characteristics as a globally consumed commodity (Bestor, 2000; Edwards, 2012; Feng, 2012; House, 2018; Namimatsu, 2019; Sakamoto & Allen, 2011; Stano, 2016, etc.). Linguistic literature on *sushi* remains scarce, however. At best, the term is included as an example in the literature on borrowings (Cannon, 1994; Daulton, 2014; Durkin, 2014; Morrow, 2020; Takeshita, 2010; Yamamoto, 2020).[1] For instance, Durkin surveys loanwords from different

1. According to Haugen, borrowing refers to "the attempted reproduction in one language of patterns previously found in another" (1950, p. 212), while loanword "is ordinarily limited to terms ... in which speakers have imported not only the meaning of the form but also with more or less complete substitution of native phonemes" (1950, p. 214).

https://doi.org/10.1075/celcr.25.06tor

languages in the Oxford English Dictionary (OED). He reports Japanese ranks 10th in the production of loanwords, making it one of the "most prolific donor languages" (2014, p. 23), and he cites *sushi* as an example. The literature on borrowings (e.g., Durkin, 2014) illuminates an intriguing feature of the general characteristics of Japanese loanwords in English, but it pays scant attention to the characteristics of individual loanwords, a gap this chapter begins to fill by offering an in-depth study of the Japanese loanword *sushi*. More specifically, it explores where *sushi* stands in the naturalization process, from a cognitive perspective.

Doi (2014) posits a three-stage scale of the naturalization process, with "totally foreign" at one end and "fully incorporated" at the other (see Section 2.1). Application of this scale to *sushi* in the OED examples indicates that it is currently at Stage 2 and, thus, is not completely incorporated. This chapter questions the validity of this finding. First, it points out the problems of Doi's scale. Second, it argues that *sushi* has already moved into the naturalized stage. Drawing on Diamond (2016, p. 536), the chapter posits that a word is considered "naturalized" when it has "reached a level of general currency where it is unselfconsciously used with the expectation of being understood," proposing that "unselfconscious usage" (Diamond, 2016, p. 536) by native speakers reflects a highly entrenched degree of the word, and this degree of entrenchment should constitute a critical part of the standards to determine where the loanword stands in the process of naturalization. Further, it argues that the highly entrenched degree of the word is realized in (i) high token frequency, (ii) use of the loanword in constructions, including snowclones and Internet memes, and (iii) the word's ability to expand the nomenclatural network.

To put the discussion into perspective, the chapter parts company with past research on Japanese loanwords in English in terms of data and approach, thus positioning its argumentation as innovatively distinct. First, it breaks with the heavy reliance on dictionary entries as a data source (e.g., Cannon, 1981; Doi, 2014) by consulting data on social media platforms (e.g., blogs) and restaurant menus. Second, it foregrounds the elucidation of the mechanism of how a loanword is used, drawing on insights from Cognitive Linguistics, as an alternative to the descriptive tradition of past work, such as recording the year of the loanword's first reported appearance (e.g., Cannon, 1981; Doi, 2014) or determining the frequency count of the loanword in a given source (e.g., Morrow, 2020; Yamamoto, 2020). The chapter's approach is in the spirit of Cognitive Contact Linguistics (Zenner, Backus, & Winter-Froemel, 2019), an emerging research program in which Cognitive Linguistics is cross-fertilized with contact linguistics to cover the study of loanwords.

The remainder of the chapter proceeds as follows. Section 2 introduces Doi's (2014) scale. It then applies the scale to *sushi* in the OED, pointing out the problems of Doi's scale. Section 3 turns to one of the major problems in Doi: i.e., the unmotivated sequence of criteria (e.g., "compound formation" must precede "semantic change"), drawing on Construction Morphology (Booij, 2010) to explain. Sections 4 to 6 offer an account based on usage. Section 4 makes the case for "token frequency" as a valuable source of evaluation. Section 5 discusses how *sushi* is used in snowclones (e.g., *Sushi is the new pizza* < "X BE the new Y" (Traugott & Trousdale, 2014)) and Internet memes (e.g., *One Does Not Simply Make Sushi* < Does Not Simply X) (cf. Dancygier & Vandelanotte, 2017). Section 6 turns to speakers' ability to develop a nomenclatural network centering on *sushi*. The section also explains why this nomenclatural network develops differently in Japanese and English, drawing on the idea of frame-shifting (Coulson, 2001), whereby the Japanese word *sushi* is reanalyzed in a new "frame" (Fillmore, 1982, 1985), i.e., the sushi frame evoked by the word *sushi* in North American English, giving rise to novel construal and socio-cultural conventions not found in the sushi frame evoked by the word *sushi* in Japanese. The discussion implies our knowledge of words is encyclopaedic in nature, conforming to a view entertained by Cognitive Linguistics. Section 7 contains concluding remarks.

2. Naturalization process

2.1 Doi's (2014) scale

Doi posits that when Japanese words are borrowed into English, they go through different stages before they can be considered fully "naturalized." He proposes a scale of the naturalization process based on data drawn mainly from the OED. The essence of the scale is diagrammed in Figure 1 (Doi, 2014, p. 697).

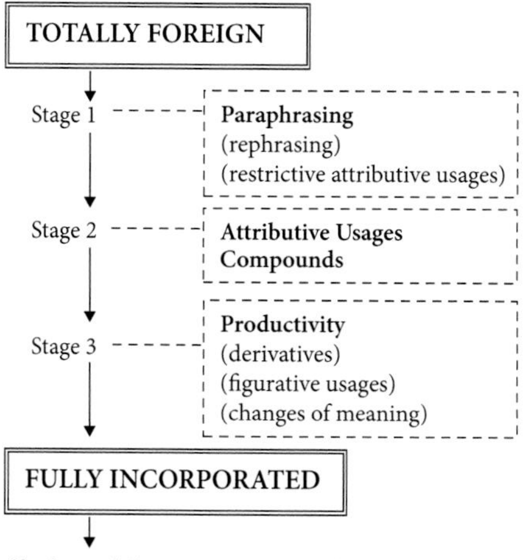

Figure 1. Doi's scale of naturalization process

As Figure 1 shows, the scale is linear. When a Japanese word is borrowed into English, the word is considered "totally foreign." The loanword then goes through three stages. In Stage 1, the loanword is accompanied by a paraphrase. In the example "the *amado* – wooden shutters" (an 1880 citation in the OED), the loanword accompanies a paraphrase (wooden shutters). Alternatively, a single-word paraphrase can be added after the loanword as in the example "the *shoji* screens" (an 1886 citation in the OED).

In Stage 2, a loanword occurs in a compound noun ("attributive usage"). For instance, in "*tatami* room" (a 1979 citation in the OED), the loanword is followed by the head noun, "room," meaning "a room with mats made of straws called *tatami*." The "attributive usages" are seen as distinct from Stage 1's "restrictive attributive usages," where the loanwords are paraphrased as a subset of the head noun. For instance, in a Stage 1 instance, *tatami* mat, the compound can be restated as "*tatami* is a kind of mat." In contrast, in a Stage 2 instance, *tatami* room, such paraphrasing is disallowed (**tatami* is a kind of room).

In Stage 3, loanwords demonstrate three types of "productivity."[2] The first refers to affixation: e.g., in "Kabukiesque" (a 1954 citation in the OED), *-esque* attaches to Kabuki (traditional form of Japanese drama), or in "tycoonish" (a 1958 citation in the OED), *-ish* attaches to tycoon ("the title by which the shogun of Japan was described to foreigners"). The second type of productivity refers to the figurative use of loanwords. An example is *hara-kiri* (suicide by disembowelment). In a passage reading "The Liberal Unionist party … will hesitate long before committing 'hari-kari' in that fashion" (an 1888 citation in the OED), the loanword is used to describe the act of a political party rather than an individual. The third type of productivity refers to a semantic change. One example Doi gives is *hibachi* (an earthenware container with charcoals used to heat the room). Citing an example from Internet, "Hibachi grill, $1. Perfect for grilling sausages, veggies, and other light barbeque," Doi argues that, in this instance, the meaning of *hibachi* "has been broadened to represent any container for charcoal" (2014, p. 686).

After going through the three stages, loanwords are considered "fully incorporated." After this, however, there is another process: "fresh word-formation processes that would apply equally to native and fully incorporated words [if applicable])" may take place (Doi, 2014, p. 697). But Doi neither specifies the type of word-formation nor provides examples.

2. Doi's use of the term "productive" seems inappropriate. First, "[w]e most often speak of productivity in connection with patterns of word-formation," usually referring to "[t]he degree of freedom with which a particular grammatical pattern can be extended to new cases" (Trask, 1999, p. 165). Accordingly, it seems inappropriate to place semantic processes (figurative usage, semantic change) under productivity and to classify the base noun with which the suffix is combined as "productive" rather than classifying the suffix as such.

2.2 *Sushi* in OED, the definition of "naturalization," and the problems of Doi's (2014) scale

Having observed Doi's scale, let us now examine at what stage *sushi* is positioned on the scale based on examples in the OED. The OED contains examples in addition to the definition. (1) shows a simplified version of all the quotations for the entry *sushi* by extracting the relevant parts, followed by the year of publication of the original in parentheses (underscores added).

(1) a. "sushi <u>or rice sandwiches</u>" (1893).
b. "*sushi*, <u>which is a lump of rice which has been pressed with the hand into a roundish form with a slight mixture of vinegar and covered on the top with a slice of fish or lobster, or a strip of fried egg, or rolled in a piece of laver</u>" (1910).
c. "His *sushi* … had to be eaten at the stall" (1928).
d. "Sushi has been made in many ways since olden times and is prized by rich and poor alike" (1936).
e. "We were standing at the <u>*sushi* buffet</u> of the train" (1967).
f. "Since sushi is nothing more than the equivalent of a sandwich, or fishy snack, the <u>sushi bar</u> can hardly be described as a den of iniquity" (1968).

Recall that on Doi's scale, Stage 1 loanwords accompany a paraphrase; Stage 2 loanwords form attributive compounds; Stage 3 loanwords provide evidence of productivity. Application of these criteria to (1) reveals *sushi* is at Stage 2; the first two instances accompany a paraphrase (e.g., sushi <u>or rice sandwiches</u> (1a)), indicating *sushi* is at Stage 1 in these examples; in the last two instances, *sushi* occurs at the attributive position of a compound noun (*sushi* buffet (1e); *sushi* bar (1f)), indicating it is at Stage 2. No examples show evidence of productivity (Stage 3).

While Doi's proposal prompts us to reflect on what it really means for a Japanese loanword to "naturalize" in English, it is not without flaws.

First, using the OED examples as the major source to determine the criteria for the naturalization process is problematic. The OED seems to provide more examples for earlier dates than recent ones, and some are not updated. If the entry remains un-updated, it raises a question about the current status of the word. This is precisely the case for *sushi*. As (1) shows, the last example is from about half a century ago (1968). This selection raises an obvious question: can we conclude that the naturalization process of *sushi* stopped at Stage 2? It is further questionable whether the cited examples can be credibly used as the standard of evaluation, since they are chosen on independent grounds, such as providing "enough context to give an idea of its meaning" (Diamond, 2016, p. 539); they are not gathered to represent the semantic or formal varieties Doi (2014) seeks.

Second, using the OED examples as a source to determine the criteria for the naturalization process is contradictory. Consider the following comment that appears in a section sub-headed, "Naturalization," where Diamond outlines the criteria for a word's inclusion in the OED:

> To be entered in the *OED*, a word needs to have reached a level of general currency where it is unselfconsciously used with the expectation of being understood: that is, we look for examples of uses of a word that are not immediately followed by an explanation of its meaning for the benefit of the reader. This would apply equally to loanwords from other languages and new English formations unfamiliar to a general English-speaking readership. (Diamond, 2016, pp. 536–537)

Doi never defines the term "naturalization."[3] From Diamond's comment, it seems reasonable to posit that "naturalization" refers to a state wherein the word has "reached a level of general currency where it is unselfconsciously used with the expectation of being understood" with its use "not immediately followed by an explanation of its meaning for the benefit of the reader" (Diamond, 2016, pp. 536–537). Furthermore, this clearly indicates that a word's appearance in the OED is already proof that it has been naturalized. It is conflicting to create criteria to measure to what extent a word is naturalized for a word already in the OED.

Third, the sequence of the criteria given in Doi seems unmotivated. Doi offers no account of why the criteria should be sequenced in the proposed order.[4] For instance, why should a semantic change follow the word's ability to form an attributive compound? The only justification is that "paraphrasing" (Stage 1) precedes other phenomena (cf. Cannon, 1994). If writers are aware that the meaning of a word is unknown to their readers, they are likely to add an explanation, but once the meaning is assumed to be known, this step will be skipped, unless there is a reason not to do so (cf. Diamond, 2016, pp. 536–537). Section 3 gives more details on why Doi's proposed sequence is problematic.

Fourth, Doi dismisses a critical aspect of data. On Doi's scale, the loanword used in a phrase or sentence as-is, such as *sushi* in (1c), "his *sushi*," and (1d), "Sushi has been made," plays no role in the evaluation of the status of naturalization. There are no reasonable grounds to state that the loanword's ability to participate in compound formation (e.g., *sushi bar*) can be used as evidence of naturalization, and its bare usage, such as "his sushi," plays no role. Counter to Doi, this chapter argues "usage" is an important aspect in the determination of the state of naturalization (see Sections 4 to 6).

3. Doi uses the spelling "naturalisation/naturalise." This chapter adopts American spelling, "naturalization/naturalize," following Cannon (1992) among others.

4. The criteria and their order seem a slight variation of Kimura (2000).

3. The sequence of criteria on Doi's scale

3.1 Semantics

3.1.1 *Semantic change*

On Doi's scale, semantic change is a criterion for Stage 3 status, suggesting that only the loanwords that have gone through Stage 1 and Stage 2 can go through semantic change. Differently stated, there should be evidence that a word's ability to form an "attributive compound" (Stage 2), such as *sushi restaurants* or *sushi chefs*, is a prerequisite for *sushi* to go through semantic change (Stage 3). To explore this point, let us first examine the meaning of *sushi*.

According to the Kōjien dictionary (Niimura, 2018), *sushi* originated in an adjective in Old Japanese, *sushi*, meaning 'sour' (cf. Shimizu, 2012, p. 104). The dictionary lists the following two senses of the word, translated from the Japanese original. The first is "fermented fish (and shellfish) or its rice-added version, known as *nare-zushi* 'aged sushi', in which the rice functions to accelerate fermentation" (cf. Mouritsen, 2009, p. 15). The second sense is more relevant to the present discussion: "rice with vinegar and seasoning, combined with ingredients, such as fish, shellfish and vegetables." A slightly different definition provided by Takeshita, "cold rice dressed with vinegar … garnished especially with bits of raw seafood or vegetables" (2010, p. 277), is adopted here as the Japanese sense of *sushi*, listed in (2d).

At the moment, *sushi* in English seems to be used predominantly in the following three senses (2a)–(2c):[5]

(2) a. SUSHI$_1$: "A Japanese dish consisting of small balls of cold boiled rice flavoured with vinegar and commonly garnished with slices of fish or cooked egg" (OED)
b. SUSHI$_2$: rolled sushi
c. SUSHI$_3$: raw fish
cf. d. SUSHI$_4$ (= one of Japanese senses of sushi): "cold rice dressed with vinegar, … garnished especially with bits of raw seafood or vegetables" (Takeshita, 2010, p. 277)

The first sense, (2a), cited from the OED, is judged close to one of the commonly accepted Japanese senses of *sushi* (2d) (cold rice with vinegar mixed with seafood and/or vegetables), which covers various shapes and culinary methods, *nigiri* (oval), *chirashi* (a pile), *makizushi* (rolled), *hakozushi* (box-shaped), among others. SUSHI$_1$ differs from this Japanese sense in that it specifies the shape of *sushi* as "small balls." This is an instance of "narrowing," whereby "[a] relatively general meaning becomes

5. For some connoisseurs, the term may refer to the Japanese sense, SUSHI$_4$.

more specific" (Traugott, 2006 p. 125). The essence of change can be represented as: Japanese SUSHI (n.) "vinegared rice with ingredients" > English SUSHI$_1$: (n.) "vinegared rice, shaped in a small size, with ingredients," where ">" stands for "becomes" or "is assigned the new meaning" (Traugott, 2006 p. 124).

The second sense, (2b), is a more overt case of "narrowing" (Japanese SUSHI (n.) "vinegared rice with ingredients" > English SUSHI$_2$: (n.) "rolled sushi"), where *sushi* is used to refer to a subtype of *sushi*: i.e., *sushi* rolls.[6] When native speakers of Japanese use *sushi* in conversations, as in *Sushi o tabeta* 'I ate sushi', they are usually referring to *nigiri*, "a bite-size of [oval-shaped] rice seasoned with vinegar, topped with a slice of seafood or cooked eggs" (Evans, 1997, p. 121). If a rolled version is intended, the Japanese native would use the specific term *makizushi* 'rolled sushi'. This differs from the use of *sushi* in English, as represented in the following examples, cited from blog entries (underscores added):

(3) a. "Homemade Sushi … Sushi is easy and fun to make at home, and you can put all your favorite ingredients into your perfect custom roll – here's how!" (Ozug, 2016)

b. "HOW TO MAKE SUSHI … Making your own sushi can be so much fun! You get to create your own rolls, add any type of filling, topping and sauce." (Nesteruk, n.d.)

In these examples, the headings say "sushi" (e.g., Homemade Sushi (3a)) but the actual instructions the bloggers offer are for the rolled version, as in "perfect custom roll" (3a).

The third sense, "raw fish" (2c), which is absent in the Japanese original, is another obvious example of narrowing (Japanese SUSHI (n.) "vinegared rice with ingredients (such as raw fish)" > English SUSHI$_3$: (n.) "raw fish"), where *sushi* stands for one of the typical ingredients included in different types of Japanese *sushi*, namely, 'raw fish'. Such usage is reported in Daulton: "sushi is commonly mistaken to denote raw fish only" (2014, p. 7).

These three senses constitute a "semantic change" (Stage 3), as they are instances of "narrowing." On Doi's scale, they are predicted to emerge after Stage 2, after the loanword has formed an attributive compound. However, this is untenable. Occurrence of semantic change is independent of the formation of an attributive compound. This point is substantiated by Blank's attempt to identify various

6. *Makizushi* can be translated as 'sushi rolls' or 'rolled sushi'. Typing "sushi rolls" in Google returns 5,690,000 hits vs. 893,000 hits for "rolled sushi." In the iWeb corpus (Davies, 2018), "sushi roll(s)" returns 2,366 hits vs. "rolled sushi", 91 hits. It seems more common to call the North American rolls such as California roll and its variants "sushi rolls." To differentiate, in this chapter, *makizushi* will be translated as "rolled sushi" whereas the North American rolls will be referred to as "sushi rolls."

conceptual relations that hold between two senses of a word when a person uses it in a sense that differs from the more accepted meaning. He calls one of these relations "blurred concepts":

> In some cases, … speakers make transfers without being aware of it, because their knowledge about the limits of these concepts and the respective categories is momentarily or permanently blurred. Confusions of this kind happen every day to almost everyone. (Blank, 1999, p. 77)

Returning to the topic at hand, it is very likely that establishment of the first sense (SUSHI$_1$) in English is a result of a "wrong" transfer when *sushi* was first borrowed into English. Of course, as Blank notes, confusions about a category of a concept can happen any time. It remains uncertain when exactly the different senses of *sushi* appeared. But there is certainly no evidence that a speaker's ability to form an attributive compound must precede semantic change.

3.1.2 *Figurative usage*

On Doi's scale, figurative uses of a loanword occur in Stage 3. This assumes such uses can occur only after the loanword completes Stage 2 (forming an attributive compound). There seems no justification for this sequencing. Creation of an attributive compound using the loanword and its figurative use simply cannot be compared. The former is formal, whereas the latter is semantic. It is entirely possible, for example, that an attributive compound is figuratively created (Benczes, 2005). In Doi's own example, "Japan's Sumo Bank (a headline: Time, 26 July 2004)" (2014, p. 688), *sumo* is used figuratively to express "something big" and occurs at the attributive position of the compound.

3.2 Morphology

Doi's scale considers two types of morphological processes as criteria to determine the stages of naturalization. One is formation of compounds, and the other is affixation. These processes are complex in their own right.

Cognitive Grammar (Langacker, 1987) assumes that when a person has knowledge of a word, the word become represented in his or her mind as a symbolic unit. Further, the realization of the symbolic unit obtains only after the word "has been used sufficiently frequently and has become **entrenched** (acquiring the status of a habit or a **cognitive routine**)" (Evans & Green, 2006, p. 501, emphasis in original).

Loanwords such as *sushi* are no exception (cf. Langacker, 2008, p. 468). The more frequently the loanword is used, the more it becomes entrenched in the minds of the users, rendering it recognizable by many interlocutors in the speech community. For instance, a speaker who recognizes that *sushi* is a noun referring to a type of food may apply a given morphological process (affixation, compounding, among others) that has been applied to other nouns, assuming the relevant affixes and compounds are already established as a symbolic unit.

To give an example, consider how people might have formed the compound *sushi bar*, which first appears in 1992 in the *Time Magazine* corpus (Davies, 2007). Its creators must have known the meaning of the compound "X *bar*," as represented in Figure 2.

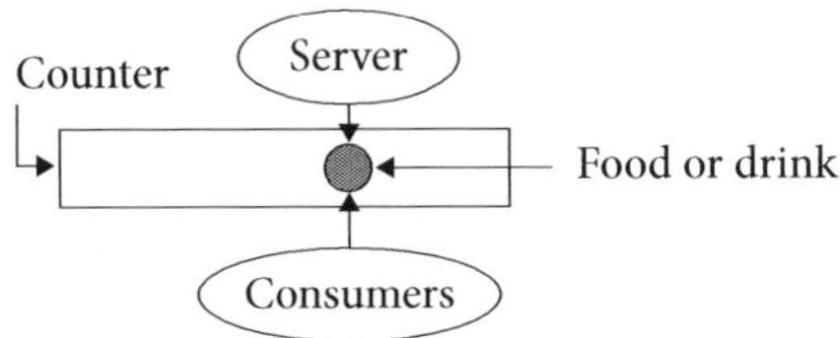

Figure 2. Image of the "X *bar*" compound

The user of the compound must have known that the *bar* in this case refers to "a barrier or counter over which drink (or food) is served out to customers, in an inn, hotel, or tavern, … etc." (OED). He or she must also have known that the item in the X slot refers to the food or drink served over the counter by a server to a customer, given the various compounds already in circulation, such as *coffee bar* (a 1956 citation in *Time*), *sandwich bar, burger bar*, and *wine bar* (1962, 1979, and 1982 citations in the Corpus of Historical American English, respectively).

To represent the relationship of the two components of the compound nouns more formally, we can refer to Booij and Hüning (2014); they posit a hierarchical lexicon (Booij, 2010) in which units called "constructional schemas" are hierarchically organized with different degrees of abstraction, as in (4).

(4) a. $\langle [X_i\ Y_j]_{Yk} \leftrightarrow [\text{SEM}_j \text{ with relation R to SEM}_i]_k \rangle$

|

b. $\langle [N_i\ [\text{bar}]_{Nj}]_{Nk} \leftrightarrow [\text{a place with a counter}_j \text{ over which SEM}_i \text{ is served}]_k \rangle$

|

c. $\langle [[\text{wine}]_{Ni}\ [\text{bar}]_{Nj}]_{Nk} \leftrightarrow [\text{a place with a counter}_j \text{ over which wine}_i \text{ is served}]_k \rangle$

(adapted from Booij & Hüning, 2014, p. 81)

Constructional schemas in (4a) consist of formal (the left side of the double arrow) and semantic structures (the right side of the double arrow), with co-indexation specifying correlation between two different types of information, formal properties and semantic properties. This schema is the most abstract, containing the most variables. (4b) is a schema for the compound "X *bar*," which means a place with a counter over which some consumable product (SEM_i) is served. If a speaker fills *Ni* with *wine* as in (4c), the compound *wine bar* yields the meaning of a place with a counter over which wine is served. A speaker with the knowledge of (4b) may extend the left item, creating a new compound *sushi bar* since *sushi* is something consumable served over the counter. The more frequently this compound is used, the more it becomes entrenched, rendering *sushi bar* more recognizable among the members of a speech community.

Doi seems to be concerned with only the superficial aspect of compound formation; i.e., a compound consists of two words. He leaves unaddressed the more complex aspects of compound formation: (i) the speakers must have access to the constructional schema $[N_i\ [\text{bar}]_{Nj}]_{Nk}$ (4b), and (ii) the speakers must have the knowledge that *sushi* is a kind of item that can take the slot of *Ni* therein, before yielding a compound such as *sushi bar*.

The attachment of an affix to the stem is equally complex. Consider the case of *-ish*, a suffix added to an adjective or a noun, meaning 'resembling the quality of' as in *ale-ish* ("Of or characteristic of ale" (OED), or *-esque*, a suffix added to a noun, meaning 'resembling the style of' as in "pizza-esque foods" (https://soyummy.com/26-pizzas-world-travel-food/). Following Booij (2010), the following constructional schema can be posited:

(5) a. $\langle[[N]_i\text{-ish}]_{Aj} \leftrightarrow [\text{resembling the quality of SEM}_i]_j\rangle$
b. $\langle[[N]_i\text{-esque}]_{Aj} \leftrightarrow [\text{resembling the style of SEM}_i]_j\rangle$

In both cases, the suffix occurs in an abstract schema [X-Y] where X is a noun and Y a suffix, with X replaceable by various different words. If a speaker creates a word like "sushi-ish dishes" (govisithawaii.com), or a "sushi-esque snack" (freepeople.com), it implies he or she has access to the constructional schemas in (5) and knows *sushi* is a kind of item that can take the noun slot (N).

Although the meaning of the component of the compound in (4) and those of the suffixes in (5) differ completely, the cognitive operations speakers adopt when using them are reasonably comparable. This comparability does not lend support to the idea implied by Doi that English speakers start creating a new word based on the loanword with an affix such as *sushi-ish* only after they have created sufficient compounds where the loanword occurs in the attributive position like *sushi bar*.

4. Token frequency

Token frequency, which Doi does not cover, constitutes important information for any discussion of naturalization. Token frequency refers to "the frequency with which specific instances are used in language" (Evans & Green, 2006, p. 118). Cognitive Linguistics assumes "linguistic units that are more frequently encountered become more **entrenched** (that is, established as a cognitive pattern or routine) in the language system" (Evans & Green, 2006, p. 114; emboldening in the original). That is, the higher the token frequency, the more likely a word is established as English (cf. Bybee, 1985, p. 117).

I argue *sushi* is already an established linguistic unit in English. Consultation of the OED's "frequency band," i.e., a word's frequency measured in terms of range, provides the basis for my argument. According to the OED, *sushi* currently belongs to band 4, where "most words remain recognizable to English-speakers, and are likely be used unproblematically in fiction or journalism." With this characterization, it seems safe to conclude that *sushi* is completely naturalized, a well-entrenched linguistic unit in English.[7]

This possibility is corroborated by Takeshita who gives *sushi* as an example of one of "[m]any 'foreign' words [that] have become part of 'standard' Englishes" (2010, p. 276). In other words, *sushi* has reached the "fully incorporated" status. The results of quantificational research on frequency corroborate this. Cannon includes *sushi* as one of the "110 High-Frequency Japanese Items in English" (1994, p. 395). Morton, who examines the frequency of *sushi* in the *New York Times*, reports: "Sushi … experienced a bullish and unabated increase in frequency" (2010, p. 7), occurring "633 times in the first decade of the twenty-first century" (2010, p. 6). Daulton reports *sushi* is "the most frequent Japanese loanword" (2014, p. 6) in the Corpus of Contemporary American English (COCA).

5. *Sushi* in constructions

This section discusses use of *sushi* in constructions with a focus on snowclones and Internet memes to show it is entrenched deeply enough to be utilized in these constructions.

5.1 *Sushi* in snowclones

"Snowclones" is the term proposed by Glen Whitman (Whitman, 2004) in a reply to a post by Geoff Pullum. One day, Pullman notes that the sequence "If Eskimos have N words for snow, then X have Y words for Z" has been numerously changed by writers replacing variables, thus producing sentences like "If Eskimos have N words for snow, then Santa Cruzans must have even more for surf"; he

7. Band levels of other food terms are as follows: 5 (*pizza, hamburger*), 4 (*tofu*), 3 (*edamame, wasabi, sukiyaki, yakitori, tempura*), 2 (*panko, teppan-yaki*). The frequency of *sushi* does not reach the level of familiar Western food such as *pizza* but is higher than other Japanese food.

comments that there should be an appropriate term for this "reusable customizable easily-recognized twisted variant of a familiar but non-literary quoted or misquoted saying" (Pullman, 2003). It should be no surprise to find *sushi* mentioned in snowclones, as the food item *sushi* is commonly found in North America, at least in cities, and its visual images appear in blogs and online restaurant reviews, regardless of physical location.

An early example of *sushi* appearing in a snowclone is built on the formulaic sequence, "X BE the new Y" (Traugott & Trousdale, 2014), a sequence which has produced numerous snowclones, especially in the field of fashion ("Grey is the new black" (Slay Magazine, 2017)) and food ("Coffee is the new wine" (Aubrey, 2012)). The example in (6a) comes from a web newspaper article (underscore added) and is arguably one of the earliest snowclones containing *sushi*; (6b) gives a more recent example.

(6) a. "We're talking big – sushi is the 'Japanese tapas', sushi is the new pizza, sushi is the sandwich of the 21st century. It's healthy, Zen, stylish". (Renton, 2006)

b. "Sushi is the new sandwich" . (Feng, 2012, p. 218)

The basic process of creating snowclones parallels that of creating compounds (cf. Traugott & Trousdale, 2014, pp. 270–272). How speakers arrive at the snowclone "*sushi* is the new pizza" based on the formulaic sequence "X BE the new Y" is elaborated below by applying constructional schemas from Construction Morphology (Booij, 2010).

(7) a. <[X_i BE the new Y_j]$_k$ ↔ [A characteristic position enjoyed by SEM_j for a while is now replaced by SEM_i]$_k$>
Pragmatics: SEM_i and SEM_j must belong to the same semantic category. The trend has been that SEM_j is perceived to occupy a characteristic position that dominates the category, as in the topmost item in popularity, acceptability, and so forth. This trend changes with the appearance or re-appreciation of a different item (SEM_i), which takes over the position.

b. <[Sushi is the new pizza] ↔ [A characteristic position enjoyed by pizza for a while is replaced by sushi]>

The snowclone "*sushi* is the new pizza" is instantiated by the constructional schema shown in (7a). The speaker must know the form (the syntactic representation on the left of the double-headed arrow, <[X_i BE the new Y_j]$_k$), the meaning (the semantic representation on the right of the double-headed arrow, "<[A characteristic position enjoyed by SEM_j for a while is now replaced by SEM_i]$_k$>"), and the pragmatic condition, elaborated below the representation in carets, which clarifies the relationship between X and Y. To sum up: (a) the referents replacing the two variables must be comparable in the mind of the speaker, belonging to the same semantic category (e.g., food), and (b) the speaker must perceive that Y used to occupy a distinguishing position dominating the category, as in the most popular item, but this position was recently taken by a newer or a re-appreciated item X.

When two items satisfy this pragmatic condition, (7b) instantiates (7a), yielding the snowclone "*sushi* is the new pizza." Given the context of (6a), where *sushi* is compared to tapas, pizza, and sandwich, the writer must have hoped to convey that *sushi* is trendier to eat than pizza as a light meal (but is a healthier option) eaten casually, perhaps using fingers.

The minimum requirements for the speaker to be able to use the construction are: (i) the constructional schema (7a) is deeply entrenched, and (ii) the speaker certainly knows the meaning of the words replacing the variables. Otherwise, s/he would not be able to create a snowclone conveying what s/he intends to convey. In other words, the speaker's ability to use a loanword in a snowclone shows s/he has firmly internalized its semantics. Furthermore, the fact that the meaning of the snowclone is well understood by the Internet community supports how solidly the loanword is naturalized in English.

This point can be applied to any snowclone based on an idiom, a cliché, a movie title, and so forth. (8) gives some more examples.

(8) a. "Sushi is not everyone's cup of tea" (< X isn't one's cup of tea). (Oliver Maki, 2018)

b. "My Big Fat Sushi Dinner" (< My Big Fat X (a 2002 movie, My Big Fat Greek Wedding). (Pang, 2005)

c. "once a sushi lover, always a sushi lover" (< Once a Y, always a Y). (Le, 2010)

d. "Don't cry over spilt sushi." (< Don't cry over spilt milk, a variant of "It is no use crying over spilt milk"). (Sushi Euphoria, 2011)

To create these expressions, the respective speakers must know the meaning of formulaic sequences such as "X isn't one's cup of tea" (8a). They must also know that the variable (or one of the variables) can be replaced by *sushi*. If the writers of the phrases in (8) knew people would have a hard time understanding the meaning of *sushi*, there is very little chance that they would have created them. Accordingly, the snowclones in (8) can be seen as evidence of the accelerated naturalization of the loanword *sushi*.

5.2 *Sushi* in Internet memes

Another instance which can be argued to illustrate "unselfconscious usage" by native speakers is use of *sushi* in Internet memes, which are "multimodal constructions" (Dancygier & Vandelanotte, 2017) (D&V, henceforth) consisting of an image and text.

The text in Internet memes typically comes in two parts, an upper text and a lower text. An example from D&V (2017) uses a phrase, "one does not simply" (upper text) with an image of Boromir (Sean Bean), taken from a scene from the film, *The Lord of the Rings*, in which Boromir looks determined but distressed, making a hand gesture of a shape that looks like a ring (cf. https://makeameme.org/character/one-does-not-simply). According to D&V, in that scene, "characters are deciding on the best course of action, especially the idea of walking into the deadly land of Mordor. In the discussion, Boromir says: 'One does not simply walk into Mordor'" (2017, p. 574). In this context, the line implies the immense difficulty and danger of going into Mordor, or to put it more clearly, the task is "futile and bound to fail" (D&V, 2017, p. 575). In Internet memes, the first part usually appears in the upper text, as in "ONE DOES NOT SIMPLY," and the remaining part (walk into Mordor) is replaced by various phrases. The upper text is "often formulaic and easily recognizable" (D&V, 2017, p. 578), while the lower text "often delivers the punch line of the meme" (D&V, 2017, p. 578), thus governing the implication of the message.

A keyword search for images in Google, typing in "meme, one does not simply, sushi" returns various lower texts.

(9) ONE DOES NOT SIMPLY
  a. Say no to sushi
  b. Make sushi
  c. Get a la carte sushi
  d. Only get one roll of sushi
  e. "Walk home" after all you can eat sushi

To be able to use *sushi* in this multimodal construction, the creator must be certain the text with *sushi* in (9) perfectly complements the image (in the creator's own view): for instance, in (9b), sushi-making is categorized as a "futile undertaking" (D&V, 2017, p. 568). The multimodal construction invites the construal that a tremendous amount of consideration and preparation is required to make *sushi*, but this effort does not guarantee success. The viewers will appreciate the humor, as the image of *sushi* does not match the image of Boromir but is presented at the same level of seriousness as walking into Mordor.

Use of *sushi* is not limited to the "one does not simply" meme. It also appears in a meme with the image of "The Most Interesting Man in the World." The upper text reads: "I don't always eat sushi." And the lower text adds: "But when I do, I post a picture of it on Instagram." Another example is a "Willy Wonka Sarcasm Meme" saying, "Oh, you eat sushi?" (upper text) and then commenting, "You must be so cultured" (lower text).

It is unimaginable that the word *sushi* could be used in such a fashion if the loanword were still progressing through naturalization. People's unselfconscious ability to use *sushi* in multimodal constructions or to appreciate those constructions is a clear indicator of how well the word is incorporated into English.

6. Expansion of a nomenclatural network

6.1 Background

Another aspect of loanwords not considered in Doi is the word's ability to expand a word network. If the term *sushi* is not fully part of English as Doi's scale predicts, it seems reasonable to posit that the term *sushi* is borrowed as is, or with the same expansion of hyponyms as the Japanese original noted in Section 3.1.1, possibly in their translations, such as *nigiri* (oval shaped *sushi* with raw fish on top), *chirashi* (*sushi* rice with vegetables and raw fish), *makizushi* (rolled *sushi*), and *hakozushi* (box-shaped *sushi*). But if the word *sushi* is already established, it will have a unique network different from the Japanese original, as native speakers can freely create new words based on well-entrenched native words or long-settled loanwords, resulting in expansion of a word network, just like a well-entrenched word such as *pizza* has a word network of its own, with various hyponyms, from *Neapolitan* to *Chicago*, or names of different ingredients from *pepperoni* to *spinach*, and, notably, new variants can be created any day.

This section discusses how *sushi* participates in the creation of such a nomenclatural network. The argument is that native speakers' ability to freely expand a nomenclatural network centering on *sushi* is evidence of the highly entrenched degree of the term.

Two types of processes contribute to the development of *sushi*'s nomenclatural network. The first is the creation of dish names frequently observed on North American restaurant menus. I focus on a subset of *sushi, sushi* rolls, which have a striking range of varieties with unique names (cf. Stano, 2016). The second is the creation of new food names, dubbed "hybrid sushi" here (see Figure 7 for a partial nomenclatural network).

In what follows, to show how the word network develops differently in North American English and Japanese, I draw on the idea of "frame-shifting" (Coulson, 2001). Before launching into my discussion, however, it is first necessary to give a brief history of how the food commodity "California roll" has come to be popularized in the U.S.,[8] as this creation arguably sparked the expansion of the nomenclatural network centering on *sushi*.

6.2 On California roll

Although who invented the California roll is debated, two authors (Issenberg, 2007, Chapter 5; Kamp, 2009) credit two men, Chef Ichiro Mashita and his assistant, Teruo Imaizumi, working for a Japanese restaurant in Los Angeles in the 1960s.[9] To comply with the management's request to "make *sushi* for the Caucasians" (Issenberg, 2007, p. 90), they created the California roll through trial and error. The key features of the California roll are the following: (i) avocado is included as an alternative to tuna, providing a similar texture and ensuring availability; (ii) it uses an inside-out rolling technique to hide "black paper" (*nori* 'dried seaweed') an ingredient often removed when Americans eat Japanese *makizushi* 'rolled sushi', and (iii) creamy mayonnaise is added to provide an accent to the accompanying crabmeat.

Importantly, the creation of the California roll was the result of a conscious effort to enact broader acceptance. To create their envisioned *sushi*, the two chefs made a drastic conceptual revision, knocking down the prototype (cf. Lakoff, 1987) of *makizushi*, an integral part of Japanese food culture. Coulson calls this type of revision, *frame-shifting*, saying it "reflects the operation of a semantic reanalysis process that reorganizes existing information into a new frame" (2001, p. 34). In the case of the California roll, existing information about *makizushi* 'rolled *sushi*' was reorganized to meet the expectations of a new frame, i.e., the sushi frame evoked by the word *sushi* in North American English. This frame-shifting can be seen as responsible for yielding differences between the English nomenclatural network centering on *sushi* and its Japanese counterpart.

---

8. One encyclopedia (Mariani, 2014) defines California roll as: "A form of sushi made with avocados, crabmeat, cucumbers, and other ingredients wrapped in vinegared rice." As discussed hereinafter, this description lacks one of the most important characteristics; i.e., it is *ura-maki* 'rolled inside-out'.

9. A Vancouver-based Japanese chef claims he created it in the 1970s (cf. The Canadian Press, 2016).

6.3 Frame-shifting

6.3.1 *Sushi frame evoked by the Japanese word* sushi

In the sushi frame evoked by the Japanese word *sushi*, Japanese people structure expectations of traditional *sushi*, including *makizushi* (rolled *sushi*), compatible with Japanese culture, aesthetics, and conventions. A prototypical image of *makizushi* and its features is presented in Figure 3.[10]

- Origin: mid-18th century
- Conceived as a subtype of sushi
- Naming convention: conservative
- Typical image of *makizushi*

- Ingredients in the center: those going well with vinegared rice (e.g., cucumber)
- Shape: cylindrical
- Rolling method: prototypical outer layer: *nori* 'dried seaweed'
- Rice: vinegared rice
- Plating: cross-section, faceup
- …

Figure 3. A prototypical image of *makizushi* and its features

Makizushi is postulated to have originated in the mid-18th century and is considered a staple traditional Japanese food, often home-made and consumed on festive occasions (Maki-zushi no hanashi henshū iin-kai, 2012, Chapter 1). Typical *makizushi* has the following characteristics for Japanese. First, *makizushi* is conceived as a subset of *sushi*, and it should consist of vinegared rice and ingredients – however rudimentary this may seem. Second, the rolling technique is such that a thinner layer, typically dried seaweed, is the outer layer, and the layer holds the vinegared rice, which, in turn, wraps around the ingredient in the center, typically a single ingredient, such as pickled radish, tuna, or cucumber, which "goes well" with the flavor of vinegared rice (from the Japanese standard). This becomes very relevant to naming in the sushi frame evoked by the Japanese word *makizushi*. Third, when served on a dish, the roll, cut into several pieces, is placed with the

10. Illustrations in Figure 3 and 5: Copyright (-2020) by Irasutoya (https://www.irasutoya.com/). Reprinted with permission.

cut sections facing up. The sections are consumed as-is or dipped into soy sauce served in a small dish.

The naming method of *makizushi* is rather conservative. Mitsukan's survey of representative names of *makizushi* (Maki-zushi no hanashi henshū iin-kai, 2012, Chapter 1) suggests *makizushi* is first categorized into two types based on shape: *hosomaki* 'thin roll' and *futomaki* 'thick roll' (see Figure 4).

Hosomaki 'thin roll' has various hyponyms, all of which refer to an ingredient. The first subtype refers to the ingredient of the outer layer, such as *wakame* 'seaweed', *datemaki* 'omelet mixed with fish paste', or *Hiroshima-na* 'Hiroshima greens'. This subtype has only a handful of co-hyponyms. The other subtype refers to the ingredient placed in the center, such as *shinko* 'pickled radish', *kanpyō* 'dried gourd', *tekka* 'tuna', or *kappa* 'cucumber',[11] and has more co-hyponyms. Although there are exceptions,[12] most form a compound *X-maki* 'X-roll', where X refers to the name of an ingredient. Figure 4 shows the partial nomenclatural network of *sushi* in Japanese, with more details on the hyponyms of *makizushi*.

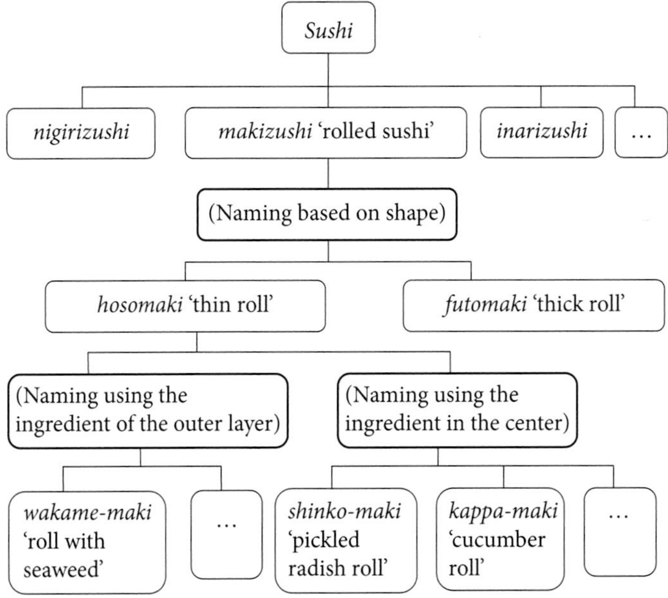

Figure 4. Partial nomenclatural network of *sushi* in Japanese

11. *Tekka* literally means 'red-hot-iron'. This naming is based on the metonymic relevance of the red color of the iron to the color of tuna (Encycropedia Nipponika, 2001). *Kappa* refers to "an imaginary creature with a plate on its head living in the river" which metonymically relates to cucumbers, allegedly the favorite food of *kappa*. (Yamaguchi & Bates, 2014).

12. This includes: *ehō-maki* [lucky direction-roll], which is eaten for good luck during *Setsubun* (the last day of the winter according to the old calendar), facing the direction of *ehō* 'lucky direction'.

6.3.2 *Sushi frame evoked by the word* sushi *in North American English*

After the California roll was created, it quickly became the prototype for *sushi* rolls in the sushi frame evoked by the word *sushi* in North American English, as summarized in Figure 5.

- Origin: latter half of 1900s
- Conceived as a subtype of rolled food
- Naming convention: liberal
- Prototypical image of *sushi rolls*

- Ingredients in the center: items familiar to the locals but categorically unrestricted.
- Shape: typically cylindrical
- Rolling method: typically inside-out
- Rice: typically vinegared rice
- Plating: various techniques
- …

Figure 5. A prototypical image of *sushi* rolls and their features

As noted in Section 6.2, North American *sushi* rolls were created sometime during the latter half of the 1900s by restaurant chefs. Naturally, consumption is dominantly in restaurants with no tie to Japanese construal of *makizushi* as traditional food. One of the distinguishing features of *sushi* rolls in the sushi frame evoked by the word *sushi* in North American English is that they are created using an inside-out rolling technique (*ura-maki* 'lit. back rolling'), as seen in many images of *sushi* rolls in online media. Another is that the ingredients placed in the center are food items familiar to locals and seen as palatable, but categorically, no restrictions are imposed on which ingredients should be employed. It goes without saying that they do not have to be what Japanese consider "a match," i.e., an ingredient that goes well with vinegared rice.

Freed from the strict constraints of the sushi frame evoked by the Japanese word *sushi*, innumerable types of *sushi* rolls have been created based on the California roll, especially in restaurants. They naturally result in the creation of innumerable co-hyponyms for *sushi* rolls. An informal observation of a few dozen North American restaurant menus indicates the North American method of naming *sushi* rolls is much more liberated than the Japanese method. While both Japanese *makizushi* and North American *sushi* rolls employ a naming strategy used in branding (Danesi, 2011), Japanese basically uses a single strategy referring to "ingredients," interpreted here as a type of a "product constitution" (a subset of "descriptor names," such as *shinko-maki* 'pickled radish roll'). North American English uses a few more strategies referring to: (a) ingredients (a subset of "descriptor names"), such as *Bulgogi roll, Crispy cream cheese roll, Mango roll*, covering many ingredients that substantially deviate from the traditional Japanese standard; (b) place names (a subset of "descriptor names"), such as *Philadelphia roll, Texas roll, Tokyo roll*; or (c) suggestive names, i.e., "those that connect the consumer by allusion to certain lifestyles or psychological domains of meaning" (Danesi, 2011, p. 179), although what is suggested often remains a mystery, as in *American Dream roll, Cowboy roll*, and *Kamikaze roll*. These constitute only partial naming methods. More work is necessary to obtain a fuller range of name types.

6.3.3 *Hybrid sushi*

Another nomenclatural expansion is found in a category for new types of food involving *sushi*, "hybrid sushi," as exemplified below.

(10) a. Sushi + Pizza → Sushi Pizza
b. Sushi + Burrito → Sushi Burrito; Sushirrito; Sushitto
c. Sushi + Doughnut → Sushi Donut; Doshi
d. Sushi + Tacos → Sushi Tacos
e. Sushi + Burger → Sushi Burger

They are created via compounding as in *sushi pizza* (10a) or via morphological blend as in *doshi* (10c). As for compounds, since the right element is usually the head in English (Williams, 1981), we may imagine that in these food types, the element on the right determines the food category. For instance, we may think that *sushi pizza* is a type of pizza. However, this is not the case. In all cases in (10), the carbohydrate comes from *sushi* rice (not from the head), while the shape of the food comes from the head. Accordingly, hybrid *sushi* is a type of *sushi* where *sushi* rice is molded to form the shape of the non-*sushi* food, arguably through conceptual blending (Fauconnier & Turner, 1998). For instance, in *sushi pizza* (see Figure 6),[13] *sushi* and *pizza* have a carbohydrate as a commonality (a requirement

13. The photo in Figures 6 is by courtesy of the author.

Figure 6. Sushi pizza

for blending to be projected into a mental space called "generic space"); furthermore, only selected elements from each component are brought together, resulting in a new creation, with the rice molded into the pizza shape, fried and garnished with a *sushi* topping, such as salmon and *tobiko* (roe).

Once again, the point is that unless both component words are highly entrenched, the speaker will not be able to use them to create a new name.

A partial nomenclatural network that centers on English *sushi* is diagrammed in Figure 7.

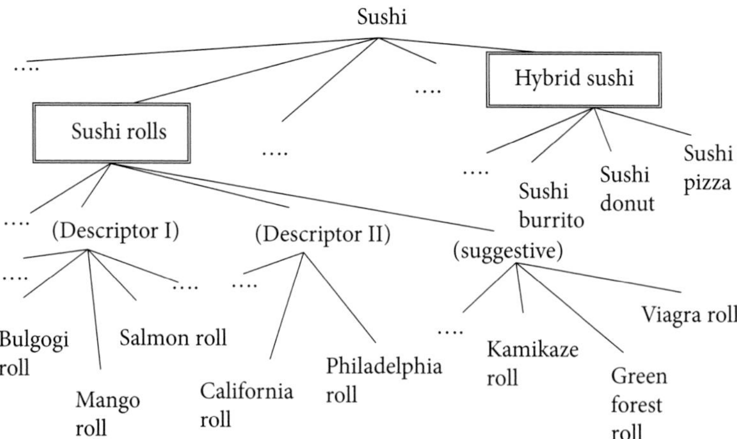

Figure 7. Partial nomenclatural network of *sushi* in English

Two critical differences from its Japanese counterpart (Figure 4) are that first, English *sushi* has an emerging category, hybrid *sushi*, and second, the *sushi* roll category has many more hyponyms than the Japanese original, *makizushi* 'rolled sushi'.

The fact that the shades of the meaning of the term *sushi* differ, as does how the term expands its nomenclatural network in the sushi frame evoked by the word *sushi* in North American English and the frame evoked by the Japanese word *sushi*, suggests the word meaning is dynamic, compatible with the position that frames in frame semantics incorporate an encyclopedic view of word meanings.

7. Conclusion

This chapter has presented an in-depth study of the Japanese loanword *sushi* in English, evaluating where it stands in the naturalization process and arguing Doi's (2014) scale is inadequate to make this determination. It has suggested a high degree of entrenchment (or speakers' "unselfconscious use" of the word) should be a criterion of the extent to which a word is naturalized and used this understanding to argue *sushi* is highly entrenched, as reflected in (i) its high token frequency, (ii) its use in constructions such as snowclones, and (iii) its ability to extend the nomenclatural network. In short, *sushi* has already reached the maximal level of naturalization, contra the midway stage predicted by Doi's scale.

The chapter's use of a cognitive perspective shed light on how the loanword *sushi* behaves in the target language. More specifically, the use of Construction Morphology (Booij, 2010) revealed the unsoundness of the ordered sequence of Doi's criteria (Section 3). As an alternative, the chapter suggested the process of forming compounds applies to forming a construction (snowclones) (cf. Booij, 2010). Thus, *sushi* used as-is (something neglected by Doi, 2014) can be a valuable indication of the degree of entrenchment within speech communities (Sections 4 and 5). The chapter's subsequent application of the concepts of frames (Fillmore, 1982) and frame-shifting (Coulson, 2001) indicated the meaning of *sushi* is encyclopaedic in nature (Section 6) and showed how the word has developed an associated network differently in Japanese and North American English because of differences in frame-specific information. The section concluded by briefly explaining how conceptual blending (Fauconnier & Turner, 1998) can help account for the creation of some of the names of hybrid *sushi*.

The chapter's theoretical discussion was substantiated by examples of *sushi* found in various online media. The web search not only revealed the linguistic characteristics of *sushi* in English, but the findings also hinted at how the word *sushi* (and naturally the denoted food item) is perceived in North American English-speaking communities. Instances of *sushi* in blogs, online newspapers, and magazines give a glimpse of how people interact with *sushi* socially and culturally. Its frequent appearance implies the full penetration of its meaning as a food commodity into English. For instance, a statement like "Sushi is easy and fun to make at home, and you can put all your favorite ingredients into your perfect custom roll" (3a) indicates the blogger's experience of home *sushi*-making and his/her perception of the cooking experience. The online instances also give a clue as to how people construe the meaning of *sushi* – in this case, it is used to mean a subset of *sushi* (in the original Japanese sense), a *sushi* roll. Meanwhile, an examination of menus suggests that because they are detached from the Japanese ideals of *makizushi* 'rolled sushi', North American chefs create all sorts of variants of California rolls (itself a new variant), arguably conceiving *sushi rolls* as a kind of rolled food and naming them in a variegated way.

The chapter has focused on one loanword, *sushi*, and, as such, is limited in its scope. Arguably, however, the study of even a single word can help us better understand how Japanese loanwords assimilate into English. An interesting topic for future research would be to determine whether the loanword *sushi* displays the same level of naturalization in other languages as it does in North American English.

Acknowledgements

Part of this article was presented at the Conference on the Language of Japanese Food, held at York University, on May 5, 2018, and at the 15th International Cognitive Linguistics Conference, held at Kwansei Gakuin University, on August 9, 2019. I thank the audiences for their questions and comments. I am also grateful to reviewers, for giving me valuable and constructive comments. I thank Elizabeth Thompson for her editorial assistance. All remaining errors, omissions, and shortcomings are, of course, my responsibility.

References

Aubrey, A. (2012, August 16). Coffee is the new wine. Here's how you taste it. *npr*. Retrieved from https://www.npr.org/sections/thesalt/2012/08/16/158932704/coffee-is-the-new-wine-heres-how-you-taste-it

Benczes, R. (2005). Metaphor- and metonymy-based compounds in English: a cognitive linguistic approach. *Acta Linguistica Hungarica, 52*(2–3), 173–198. https://doi.org/10.1556/ALing.52.2005.2-3.3

Bestor, T. (2000). How sushi went global. *Foreign Policy*, November/December, 54–63. https://doi.org/10.2307/1149619

Blank, A. (1999). Why do new meanings occur? A cognitive typology of the motivations for lexical semantic change. In A. Blank and P. Koch, *Historical semantics and cognition* (pp. 61–90). Berlin & New York: De Gruyter Mouton. https://doi.org/10.1515/9783110804195.61

Booij, G. (2010). *Construction Morphology*. Oxford: Oxford University Press.

Booij, G., & Hüning, M. (2014). Affixoids and constructional idioms. In R. Boogaart, T. Colleman, & G. Rutten (Eds.), *Extending the scope of Construction Grammar* (pp. 77–106). Berlin: De Gruyter Mouton. https://doi.org/10.1515/9783110366273.77
Bybee, J. L. (1985). *Morphology: A study of the relation between meaning and form*. Amsterdam: John Benjamins. https://doi.org/10.1075/tsl.9
Cannon, G. (1981). Japanese borrowings in English. *American Speech*, *56*, 190–206. https://doi.org/10.2307/454433
Cannon, G. (1992). Malay(sian) borrowings in English. *American Speech*, *67*, 134–162. https://doi.org/10.2307/455451
Cannon, G. (1994). Recent Japanese borrowings into English. *American Speech*, *69*, 373–397. https://doi.org/10.2307/455856
Corpus of Contemporary American English. (1990–2017). Retrieved from https://www.english-corpora.org/coca/
Corpus of Historical American English. (1810s–2000s). Retrieved from https://www.english-corpora.org/coha/
Coulson, S. (2001). *Semantic leaps: Frame-shifting and conceptual blending in meaning construction*. Cambridge: Cambridge University Press. https://doi.org/10.1017/CBO9780511551352
Dancygier, B., & Vandelanotte, L. (2017). Internet memes as multimodal constructions. *Cognitive Linguistics*, *28*(3), 565–598. https://doi.org/10.1515/cog-2017-0074
Danesi, M. (2011). What's in a brand name? A note on the onomastics of brand naming. *Names*, *59*(3), 175–85. https://doi.org/10.1179/002777311X13082331190119
Daulton, F. (2014). Boutique words for the culturally savvy: The common Japanese loanwords in American English. *The Kyoto JALT Review*, *2*, 1–13.
Davies, M. (2007). *TIME Magazine Corpus*. Retrieved from https://www.english-corpora.org/time/
Davies, M. (2018). *The iWeb corpus*. Retrieved from https://www.english-corpora.org/iWeb/
Diamond, G. (2016). Making decisions about inclusion and exclusion. In P. Durkin (Ed.), The Oxford Handbook of Lexicography (pp. 532–545). https://doi.org/10.1093/oxfordhb/9780199691630.013.38
Doi, S. (2014). The naturalisation process of the Japanese loanwords found in the Oxford English Dictionary. *English Studies*, *95*(6), 674–699. https://doi.org/10.1080/0013838X.2014.942100
Durkin, P. (2014). *Borrowed words: A history of loanwords in English*. Oxford: Oxford University Press. https://doi.org/10.1093/acprof:oso/9780199574995.001.0001
Edwards, P. A. (2012). Global sushi: eating and identity. *Perspectives on Global Development and Technology*, *11*(1), 211–225. https://doi.org/10.1163/156914912X620842
Encyclopedia Nipponica. (2001). Tokyo. Shogakkan.
Evans, T. M. (1997). *A dictionary of Japanese loanwords*. Westport, Connecticut and London: Greenwood Publishing Group.
Evans, V., & Green, M. (2006). *Cognitive Linguistics: An introduction*. Edinburgh: Edinburgh University Press Ltd.
Fauconnier, G., & Turner, M. (1998). Conceptual integration networks. *Cognitive Science*, *22*, 133–187. https://doi.org/10.1207/s15516709cog2202_1
Feng, C. H. (2012). The tale of sushi: History and regulations. *Comprehensive Reviews in Food Science and Food Safety*, *11*(2), 205–220. https://doi.org/10.1111/j.1541-4337.2011.00180.x
Fillmore, C. J. (1982). Frame semantics. In the Linguistic Society of Korea (Ed.), *Linguistics in the morning calm* (pp. 111–137). Seoul: Hanshin.

Fillmore, C. J. (1985). Frames and the semantics of understanding. *Quaderni di Semantica, 6*(2),222–254.

Haugen, E. (1950). The analysis of linguistic borrowing. *Language, 26*(2), 210–231. https://doi.org/10.2307/410058

House, J. (2018). Sushi in the United States, 1945–1970. *Food and Foodways, 26*(1), 40–62. https://doi.org/10.1080/07409710.2017.1420353

Issenberg, S. (2007). *The sushi economy: Globalization and the making of a modern delicacy*. New York: Gotham Books.

Kamp, D. (2009). *The United States of arugula: The sun dried, cold pressed, dark roasted, extra virgin story of the American food revolution*. New York: Broadway Book.

Kimura, M. (2000). The naturalization process of Japanese loanwords as reflected in English dictionaries: The four-stage hypothesis and associated problems. In J. E. Mogensen, V. H. Pedersen, & A. Zettersten (Eds.), *Proceedings of the Ninth International Symposium on Lexicography* (pp. 293–303). Tübingen: Max Niemeyer Verlag. https://doi.org/10.1515/9783110915044.293

Lakoff, G. (1987). *Women, fire, and dangerous things*. Chicago: The University of Chicago Press. https://doi.org/10.7208/chicago/9780226471013.001.0001

Langacker, R. (1987). *Foundations of Cognitive Grammar: Theoretical prerequisites*, Volume 1. Stanford, California: Stanford University Press.

Langacker, R. (2008). *Cognitive grammar: A basic introduction*. Oxford: Oxford University Press. https://doi.org/10.1093/acprof:oso/9780195331967.001.0001

Le, C. (2010, April 24). Reasons to eat sushi [Blog post]. Retrieved from https://www.thepetite-adventurer.com/eatsushi/

Maki-zushi no hanashi henshū iin-kai [Editorial committee of stories of rolled sushi]. (Ed.). (2012). *Nihon no dentō-shoku makizushi no hanashi: Kabushikigaisha Ajikan Sōgyō 50-shūnen kinenshi* [Stories of rolled sushi, Japanese traditional food: Commemorative publication to cerebrate the 50-year anniversary of Ajikan company inauguration]. Hiroshima: Ajikan.

Mariani, J. F. (2014). California roll. *The encyclopedia of American food and drink*, 2nd ed. London, UK: Bloomsbury.

Morrow, P. R. (2020). Japanese loanwords in English: A corpus-based study. *Journal of Nagoya Gakuin University; Humanities and Natural Sciences, 57*(1), 1–13. https://doi.org/10.15012/00001260

Morton, M. (2010). *Times* tables. *Gastronomica: The Journal of Critical Food Studies, 10*(2), 6–8. https://doi.org/10.1525/gfc.2010.10.2.6

Mouritsen, O. (2009). *Sushi: Food for the eye, the body, & the soul*. New York: Springer.

Namimatsu, N. (2019). Transformation and globalization of traditional food "sushi". *The Bulletin of the Institute of Japanese Culture Kyoto Sangyo University, 24*, 37–78. Retrieved from https://ksu.repo.nii.ac.jp/

Nesteruk, N. (n.d.). How to make sushi [Blog post]. Retrieved from https://tatyanaseveryday-food.com/recipe-items/make-sushi/

Niimura, I. (2018). (Ed.). *Kōjien*, 7th ed. Tokyo: Iwanami Shoten.

Oliver Maki – Soho. (2018, July 22). [Blog post]. Retrieved from https://steakandteeth.com/2018/07/22/olivermaki/

Oxford English Dictionary Online. Oxford University Press.

Ozug, J. (2016, June 9). Homemade Sushi [Blog post]. Retrieved from https://www.fifteenspatulas.com/homemade-sushi/

Pang, A. S.-K. (2005, June 30). My big fat sushi dinner in Paddington station [Blog post]. Retrieved from http://www.askpang.com/?m=200506

Pullman, G. (2003, October 27). Phrases for lazy writers in kit form. *Language Log*. Retrieved from http://itre.cis.upenn.edu/~myl/languagelog/archives/000061.html

Renton, A. (2006, February 26). How sushi ate the world. *The Guardian*. Retrieved from https://www.theguardian.com/world/2006/feb/26/japan.foodanddrink

Sakamoto, R., & Allen, M. (2011). There's something fishy about that sushi: how Japan interprets the global sushi boom. *Japan Forum*, *23*(1), 99–121. https://doi.org/10.1080/09555803.2011.580538

Shimizu, K. (2012). *Tabemono gogen jiten* [Food etymology dictionary]. Tokyo: Tokyodo.

Slay Magazine. (2017, January 10). Grey Clothing: Why Grey is the New Black. Retrieved from https://www.theslaymagazine.com/blog/grey-clothing-why-grey-is-the-new-black

Stano, S. (2016). Lost in translation: Food, identity and otherness. *Semiotica*, *211*, 81–104. https://doi.org/10.1515/sem-2016-0100

Sushi Euphoria. (2011, April 24). [Blog post]. Retrieved from http://sushieuphoria.blogspot.com/2011/06/april-24-2011.html

Takeshita, Y. (2010). East Asian Englishes: Japan and Korea. In A. Kirkpatrick (Ed.), *The Routledge handbook of world Englishes* (pp. 265–281). London & New York: Routledge.

The Canadian Press. (2016, June 13). Chef Tojo of Vancouver honoured as Goodwill ambassador for Japanese food. *News 1130*. Retrieved from https://www.citynews1130.com/2016/06/13/chef-tojo-of-vancouver-honoured-as-goodwill-ambassador-for-japanese-food/

Trask, R. L. (1999). *Key concepts in language and linguistics*. London & New York: Routledge.

Traugott, E. C. (2006). Semantic change: Bleaching, strengthening, narrowing, extension. In K. Brown (Ed.), *Encyclopedia of language and linguistics*, 2nd ed., vol. xi (pp. 124–131). Oxford: Elsevier. https://doi.org/10.1016/B0-08-044854-2/01105-6

Traugott, E. C., & Trousdale, G. (2014). Contentful constructionalization. *Journal of Historical Linguistics*, *4*(2), 256–283. https://doi.org/10.1075/jhl.4.2.04tra

Whitman, G. (2004, January 16). Snowclones. *Agoraphilia: The Center for Blurbs in the Public Interest*. Retrieved from http://agoraphilia.blogspot.com/2004_01_11_agoraphilia_archive.html#107412842921919301

Williams, E. (1981). On the notions 'lexically related' and 'head of a word'. *Linguistic Inquiry*, *12*, 245–274.

Yamaguchi, M., & Bates, S. (2014). *A Japanese-English dictionary of culture, tourism, and history of Japan [revised edition]*. Tokyo: Sanshusha.

Yamamoto, M. (2020). English words of Japanese origin: A study of dictionaries and corpora (Master's thesis, Tampere University). Retrieved from https://trepo.tuni.fi/

Zenner, E., Backus, A., & Winter-Froemel, E. (2019). *Cognitive contact linguistics: placing usage, meaning and mind at the core of contact-induced variation and change*. Berlin: De Gruyter Mouton.

SECTION IV

Taste terms

CHAPTER 7

Clear is sweet

Defining aesthetic *sake* taste terms with a usage-based approach

Hiroki Fukushima
Tainan University of Technology

Taste terms such as *soft* for wine often have a special meaning that differs from their general definition. This chapter proposes a way to define terms of Japanese *sake* taste by employing (1) a usage-based approach, (2) "encyclopedic semantics" rather than a "dictionary view," and (3) sense-making theory (Fukaya & Tanaka, 1996; Tanaka & Fukaya, 1998), drawing on data from a "*sake* tasting description corpus." Sixteen high-frequency adjectivals (e.g., *yawarakai* 'soft') are selected and their sense(s) defined in a bottom-up and abductive fashion based on scores indicating the strength of co-occurrence between terms. The suggestion is that the target terms can have a sense related to taste, flavor, texture, time flow, etc. not normally provided by an ordinary dictionary.

Keywords: sense-making theory, encyclopedic semantics, taste, flavor, corpus, Japanese

1. Introduction

Taste terms have attracted a great deal of scholarly attention, especially with respect to English wine taste (e.g., Caballero, 2007, 2017; Lehrer, 1978, 2009; Lopez-Arroyo & Roberts, 2014; Paradis & Eeg-Olofsson, 2013, among others). Japanese scholars have produced some linguistic studies on *sake* taste terms (e.g., Matsuura, 1992; Otsuka, 2004; Utsunomiya, 2006; Otsuka, Suwa & Yamaguchi, 2015), but the investigation is in its infancy, largely because of the historical context of the *sake* brewing industry.

Sake (Japanese *sake*, also spelled *saké*) is a fermented alcoholic beverage made from rice and is commonly referred to as Japanese rice wine. *Sake* is a fermented food product like soy sauce, miso, and *katsuobushi* 'dried bonito', standard seasonings for Japanese foods. Premium *sake* uses special rice called *sakamai* '*sake* rice'

https://doi.org/10.1075/celcr.25.07fuk

that is especially suitable for brewing premium *sake* (Gauntner, 2011). Just as there are various types of wine, there are various types of *sake*. Red wine can be roughly divided into three categories: full-bodied, medium-bodied, and light-bodied. For white wine, the gradation from sweet to dry is generally used. In the case of Japanese *sake*, sweet types (*amakuchi*) and dry types (*karakuchi*) are the most common. Light, pale types (*tanrei*), and full, rich types (*nōjun*) are also available. In the 1980s and 1990s, pale and dry (*tanrei-karakuchi*) types of *sake* were popular (and remain so). However, around 2000, there was a boom in *ginjō-shu* (premium *sake* made from highly polished rice using a special technique). *Ginjō-shu* has a floral and fruity flavor.

The basic taste terms for *sake* are (1) umamiful acidity, (2) bitterness, and (3) astringency:

(1) Jōhin-na san-mi ga shita o arai…
'Elegant acidity washes the tongue…'
for *'Hakurakusei Premium-Junmai'* (SSI, 2010)

(2) Jukuseikan no naka, nigami sanmi ga kōgo ni kao o nozokase
'In the aging flavor, bitterness and acidity appear alternately'
for '*Hanano Tsuyu, Junmai-Ginjo*' (Matsuzaki, 1995)

(3) Fukunda sai ni sanmi to shibumi ga kurosu suru
'When I put *sake* in the mouth, acidity and astringency crosses'
for '*Kagami yama, limited Ginjo*' (Matsuzaki, 1995)

As the flavors of *sake* have expanded, more expressions have been required. However, the study of the development of verbal expressions for *sake* has generally been neglected. Technical terms for brewing and descriptive terms used to indicate some of the off-flavors of a *sake* are emphasized, leaving terms to describe appealing flavors unstudied. In response, Fukushima (2013) compiled a small encyclopedia, listing *sake* taste words. Considered epoch-making in the *sake* industry,[1] this work has inspired other work, leading to the development of a method for defining taste terms.

This chapter advances this line of research by examining the technical details of how to define taste terms, drawing on insights from Cognitive Linguistics (Langacker, 2008) and the theory of sense-making (Fukaya & Tanaka, 1996; Tanaka & Fukaya, 1998), a theory in phenomenology of communication. First, I propose a new model of expressing *sake* taste that relies on a subjective construal which I call an "emergence-motivated event construction." Then, I apply it to a "*sake* tasting comment corpus" (*Sake* Corpus) consisting of approximately 120,000 words, containing texts compatible with the "emergence-motivated event

1. In 2014, this work received the Good Design Award in Japan.

construction." Specifically, I propose a method to define *sake* taste terms based on the co-occurrence patterns between the target term and the other terms in the construction, defining 16 adjectivals (a combined group of adjectives and adjectival nouns),[2] such as *karui* 'light' and *marui* 'round', considered "aesthetic" in the sense of Sibley (1959). This method allows me to offer a richer analysis of taste terms, covering both off-flavors and appealing flavors.

The remainder of the chapter is organized as follows: Section 2 introduces the theoretical notions upon which the chapter draws and explains the epistemological stance taken to describe the taste; Section 3 describes the method; Section 4 contains an analysis of 16 taste terms; Section 5 offers a discussion, followed by concluding remarks in Section 6.

2. Theoretical background

2.1 Sense-making theory and epistemological background: How is taste as an event constructed in the mouth?

To define the aesthetic *sake* taste terms, I draw on "sense-making theory" (Fukaya & Tanaka, 1996; Tanaka & Fukaya, 1998), arguing that the meaning of a word is determined through various levels of interaction. The interaction includes the relationships among words (i.e., co-occurrence), between words and sentence or context, and even between humans (i.e., communication level). Fukaya and Tanaka claim the sense of a single word cannot be determined *a priori*; rather, the sense is cooperatively "made" during the communication process. The chapter concurs with sense-making theory on this dynamic aspect of word sense.

I propose to define *sake* taste by focusing on adjectivals as an alternative to a dominantly used method focusing on nouns. I call this latter way of verbalization an "object-motivated event construction," where the experiencer primarily uses nouns to describe the event of tasting. This is commonly found in English tasting comments by wine sommeliers, as in, "I realize a note of black cherry, cassis, and the rich flavor of the oak," where the sommelier detects the elements of the flavor and verbalizes them, perhaps selecting the terms from his or her list of tasting words.

This is analogous to "audio" or "visual event construction," where an event is reported objectively. For instance, if an individual witnesses a traffic accident, he or she might construct the event as follows:

2. Japanese adjectives end in /i/, as in *yawarakai aji* (soft taste), whereas adjectival nouns require /na/ (a derived form of copular) to be placed at the prenominal position, as in *odayaka na aji* (calm *taste*).

(4) "there are two cars" → "two cars collide"

The example in (4) is illustrative of "object-motivated event construction," where the focus is placed on identifying the event participants (i.e., cars), in the same manner as the sommelier identifies the flavors.

An alternative way of reporting the same scene is shown in (5). I call this "emergence-motivated event construction."

(5) "something happened!" → "something crashed!" → "Oh, two cars crashed."

This sequence might be thought of as merely a playful flipping of things. However, the portrayal of the scenes in (4) and (5) is epistemologically distinct. Object-motivated event construction (4) and emergence-motivated event construction (5) take opposite approaches. If language interacts with cognition, or if language forms our thoughts, then having the correct cognition theory is indispensable to proper language analysis.

In what follows, I adopt emergence-motivated event construction to define *sake* taste. Modeling (5), the sequence of cognizing tasting experience can be presented as in (6):

(6) "taste emerges" → "I wonder what this taste is." → "I can taste X and Y."

The proposed analysis of the event construction of tasting is not the same as that of the visual event construction. When we taste something – that is, when we have an event construction of tasting or when we conceptualize what we taste in our mouths – what we realize first is not the element of taste, such as sweetness, acidity, apple flavor, or other flavors in *sake* (as expressed by nouns), but the emergence of the tasting event itself.

Supporting emergence-motivated event construction means that adjectives, adjectival nouns, and verbs (but not nouns) take the leading role in the tasting description. The recognition of the emergence of an event is primarily expressed by adjectives and adjectival nouns. They are no longer merely modifiers but play a critical role, enabling us to encode the inceptive stage of our tasting experience.

To make the image of this process more concrete, let us consider an example of a dark, haunted house attraction. In that dark space, an experience arises suddenly:

"Something happened!" → "Chilly!" → "Oh, a wet sponge!"

You can see that it is nonsense to take the existence of "myself" and "sponge" as a starting point in this haunted house experience. This model represents a way of cognition that starts from the "experience itself" rather than describing the situation from an "objective," subject-independent perspective.

The starting point of the gustatory representation construction is the experience itself; that is, how a drink "emerges" on the perception of the subject. Simply put, "emerging" is knowing "something happened!".

Then, when does the wet sponge (and the subject, "I"), or the two cars in the example of the collision, come out after the "emergence"? After the emergence, the "object" (and the "self") will stand out by asking reflectively (introspectively) what has happened. To quote Ichikawa (1990, p. 192), the emergence of immediate experience (unmittelbare Erfahrung) (i.e., "Something happened!") is an event before reflection, but through the reflection (i.e., by thinking about what happened, or what it tastes like) our connection to the world itself is grasped. In this point, the two terms of connection, "object" and "self," will stand out.

2.2 Usage-based approach

The chapter's proposed method of defining taste terms has the following characteristics, in harmony with the themes of Cognitive Linguistics:

- the dynamic aspect of word senses
- usage-based
- "encyclopaedic semantics" rather than a "dictionary view"

The meaning of a taste term is often different from the word's general definition. For example, when *tōmei* 'clear' is used to express the taste of Japanese *sake*, it could represent (or modify) the lightness of the body, or its clean sweetness, or a quick fading of the aftertaste. However, 'light body', 'sweetness', or 'aftertaste' would never be listed in the definition of *tōmei* 'clear' in general dictionaries. As illustrated in this example, I am emphasizing the dynamic aspect of word senses. The "sense of a word" is not fixed and static as in a dictionary. It varies, depending on the context; it is *made* dynamically in communication. This is the dynamic aspect of a word's meaning.

To clarify the dynamic sense of a word, I apply a method called the "usage-based approach" (Langacker, 2008). In the usage-based approach, the sense of a word is determined, in a bottom-up way, from the language used. The usage-based approach is wholly compatible with corpus linguistics and other quantitative approaches (Tummers, Heylen, & Geeraerts, 2005). In the lexicon of the domain of taste, Lehrer's (2009) study on wine terms is a milestone in the development of quantitative techniques and the usage-based approach. Lehrer argues:

> Although someone unfamiliar with wine talk may be perplexed, amused, or even irritated by some of the metaphors, people can learn to figure out their meanings via the intralinguistic relationships of words. (Lehrer, 2009, p. 256)

By "the intralinguistic relationships," Lehrer means the semantic relations of such terms as synonyms, antonyms, association, and hyponyms. For instance, a "feminine" wine can be associated with descriptors such as "*soft, perfumed*, and *delicate*" (Lehrer, 2009, p. 256).

I agree with Lehrer's point that the meaning of words can be understood from "the intralinguistic relationships of words," but I depart from Lehrer's intention to cover such relationships as antonyms and synonyms. I propose defining the terms of taste based on the co-occurrence relationships of the terms appearing in a *sake* tasting comment. Stated differently, the meaning of a term is defined based on what words are used with the term and what words are modified by the term in a *sake* tasting comment.

2.3 The terms under investigation: Aesthetic terms

The expressions that appear as taste descriptors include adjectivals that can be characterized as "aesthetic terms" or as representing the "quality of taste," especially the aesthetic quality of taste.

What is "beauty" as we feel it? Alternatively, how can we appreciate an aesthetic quality? Frank Sibley has proposed a methodology to answer such questions. His method is to interpret aesthetic concepts using words. In "Aesthetic Concepts" (1959), he discusses the kinds of words used when experts appreciate paintings and asks how they put their appreciation into words or explain it to novices who do not understand the focal point of their appreciation.

Sibley calls terms that express aesthetic concepts "aesthetic terms." An aesthetic term (or an aesthetic expression) is a word requiring *taste* or perceptiveness in order to be applied.[3] For example, aesthetic terms include terms such as *unified, balanced, integrated, dynamic, vivid*, etc. Note that "blue line" or "straight line" or "good picture" is not an aesthetic term (each of these is a "non-aesthetic term"), because no *taste* or perceptiveness is needed to apply it.

Aesthetic terms can be found in a description of taste, as well as in the explanatory notes of drawings. Aesthetic terms for the sense of taste exist in various parts of speech, including verbs and mimetics (see also Fukushima, 2019), but adjectives and adjectival nouns are dominant. Table 1 shows adjectivals (adjectives and adjectival nouns) that frequently appear in *sake* descriptions (*Sake* Corpus, see Section 3). The aesthetic terms appear in bold text.

Among the adjectivals, some terms are regarded as aesthetic, but others are not. According to Sibley's (1959) definition, such terms as *nai* 'not exist', *amai* 'sweet', and

3. "Taste" in this context is an academic term in the domain of philosophy and aesthetics (it does not mean the sense of taste). Rather, "taste" is the ability to make an intellectual judgment of an object's aesthetic merit.

Table 1. Frequent adjectivals in *Sake* Corpus

N	Adjectives			Adjectival nouns		
	Japanese	English trans.	freq.	Japanese	English trans.	freq.
1	nai	no	329	**kirei**	**clean**	**140**
2	amai	sweet	297	**odayaka**	**calm**	**134**
3	yoi	good	283	**sawayaka**	**fresh**	**106**
4	**yawarakai**	**soft**	**239**	**fukuyoka**	**plump**	**96**
5	**karui**	**light**	**172**	**tōmei**	**clear**	**96**
6	tsuyoi	strong	137	yuruyaka	slow and soft	66
7	**katai**	**hard**	**103**	**maroyaka**	**mellow**	**62**
8	takai	high	98	**hanayaka**	**gorgeous**	**55**
9	karai	dry	95	**fukuzatsu**	**complex**	**47**
10	**marui**	**round**	**94**	**sumāto**	**smart**	**46**
11	usui	thin	94	**shāpu**	**sharp**	**43**
12	**futoi**	**bold**	**83**	kasuka	faint	41
13	koi	dense	74	**sumūzu**	**smooth**	**38**
14	**kōbashii**	**roasted aromatic**	73	**nōmitsu**	**dense**	**37**
15	nagai	long	72	**furesshu**	**fresh**	**35**
16	**mizumizushii**	**fresh**	71	**nameraka**	**smooth**	**35**
17	**yasahii**	**tender**	**66**	**tansei**	**neat**	**35**
18	**wakai**	**young**	57	**nobiyaka**	**easy**	**34**
19	**wakawakashii**	**youthful**	55	**keikai**	**jaunty**	**30**
20	**chikarazuyoi**	**powerful**	54	**sunao**	**smooth**	**30**

yoi 'good' are not aesthetic terms because no *taste* or perceptiveness is needed to call a *sake* 'sweet' or 'good'. Likewise, *takai* 'high' is not an aesthetic term; it merely indicates the percentage of alcohol.

Of course, there are some problematic cases. One example is *tsuyoi* 'strong'. In the general case, *tsuyoi* 'strong' is used as the indicator of the alcohol percentage (*tsuyoi* 'strong' means a high percentage). However, *tsuyoi* 'strong' can be used as an aesthetic term, as in (7).

(7) Aji no oshi wa tsuyoi ga atokire wa yoku…
'The volume of the taste is strong, but the finishing is clear…'
for '*Nishinoseki, Honjōzō*' (Matsuzaki, 1995)

On the one hand, in this case, *tsuyoi* 'strong' may represent an aesthetic quality as it refers to perceptiveness, although in most usages, *tsuyoi* 'strong' just describes the degree. On the other hand, a word with a similar meaning, *chikarazuyoi* 'powerful', has more expressive meanings than its core meaning, 'high degree', as shown in (8).

(8) oku kara oshiage-te kuru yō na chikarazuyoi umami
'powerful umami pushing up from the back of the mouth'
for '*Azuma-ichi, Super Premium Ginjo*' (Matsuzaki, 1995)

In this chapter, I analyze the meanings of 16 adjectivals. In their description of the taste of *sake*, these words produce more complex meanings than their literal meanings.

(9) Adjectives:
karui 'light', *katai* 'firm', *marui* 'round', *futoi* 'bold', *yawarakai* 'soft', *kōbashii* 'roasted aromatic', *yasashii* 'tender', and *chikarazuyoi* 'powerful'

(10) Adjectival nouns:
kirei 'clean', *odayaka* 'calm', *sawayaka* 'fresh', *tōmei* 'clear', *fukuyoka* 'plump', *hanayaka* 'gorgeous', *maroyaka* 'mellow', and *fukuzatsu* 'complex'.

Note that these 16 adjectivals do not constitute the entire list of the aesthetic terms for *Sake* tasting. As we have seen in the example of strong and powerful, whether an adjectival word is an aesthetic term can depend on the context. I have listed 16 terms based on their (high) frequency in the *Sake* tasting corpus. But of course, other words (e.g., slow, balanced, thick, and so on) can be listed as aesthetic terms.

3. Method

3.1 Corpus and text coding (mining) tool

3.1.1 *Corpus*

For this analysis, I use a *Sake* Corpus, a corpus of Japanese *sake* tasting expressions primarily taken from *sake*-reviewing books and magazines written in Japanese. The *Sake* Corpus also includes tasting comments and expressions provided by six tasters, myself included. Table 2 summarizes the details. Note that the paragraphs refer to the different *sake* brand descriptions. In total, the *Sake* Corpus consists of 120,789 words.

Table 2. Details of the *sake* corpus

	Details
Tokens	120,789
Types	6,018
Type Token Ratio	20.07
Sentences	5,582
Paragraphs (brands of *sake*)	2,388
Average Frequency	10.50
Standard Deviation	64.55

The *Sake* Corpus draws on data from 11 books and magazines, as well as data from a tasting experiment. At first glance, the number of consulted books may seem limited. However, the books or magazines for *sake* tend to introduce the brewing method of *sake* brands, not the taste or flavor. Thus, eliciting the "tasting comment data" from published material is a difficult task. (11) is a typical example of flavor description in a *sake* magazine. Figure 1 shows an image where such descriptions appear (basic translations are given in the bottom part of the image).

(11) a. Kajitsukei no hanayaka-na kaori to,
'Fruity, elegant flavor and'
b. pukkuri-to-shita umami ga kōchū de fukurami,
'pulump-umami swells in the mouth,'
c. taoyaka ni nagare-te iku. Hōrei na *sake* o jikkan.
'then it calmly flows. (I) realized the rich, splendid taste.

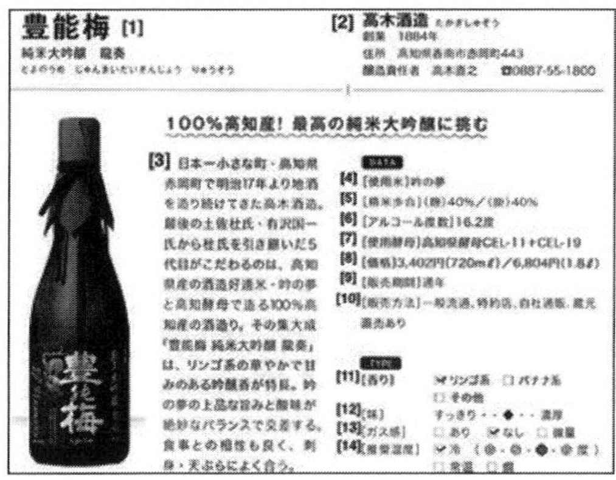

Figure 1. A standard style of tasting comment description in Japanese *sake* books and magazines.[4]

Note. [1] Brand name, [2] Brewery info, [3] Introduction of the brewery and flavor descriptions, [4] Sake rice, [5] Rice-polishing ratio, [6] Alcohol content, [7] Yeast, [8] Price, [9] Seasons on the market, [10] How to buy, [11] Flavor: Apple-type / Banana-type / other types, [12] Taste: Fresh type- Rich type, [13] Gas: Yes / No / slightly, [14] Recommended temperature range: Chilled – room – hot

3.1.2 *Coding tool*

As a text-mining tool, I used KH Coder (Higuchi, 2004) for the entire process of corpus analysis (i.e., word extraction with ChaSen, PoS tagging, listing word frequency, making KWIC concordance, and drawing word networks).[5]

4. Captured from *Sake Competition 2019*. Copyright (2019) by Pia Corporation. Adapted with permission.

5. KH Coder is free software for quantitative content analysis or text mining. It is also used for computational linguistics and can be used to analyze Catalan, Chinese (simplified), Dutch, English, French, German, Italian, Japanese, Korean, Portuguese, Russian, Slovenian, and Spanish text ("KH Coder Index Page," 22-09-2019).

3.2 How to define adjectives and adjectival nouns

3.2.1 *Calculation of the co-occurrence score with KWIC*

Using KWIC, we can calculate the "score" for determining what words most frequently co-occur with the target term. The calculated "score" is used to indicate the strength of co-occurrence relationships. For a detailed explanation of KWIC, see Appendix 1; the protocol for calculating a score is shown in Appendix 2.

In this analysis, I considered the words with a score of over 1.000 in defining the target term (i.e., approximately the top 30 words in the concordance list). As an example, Table 3 (excerpt from Table 4) shows the words that co-occur with the term *yawarakai* 'soft'. From left to right, the columns in the table give the (1 through 21) ranking of the score (N) of the co-occurring words, the co-occurring words (Word), the English translation of the co-occurring words (Eng. Trans.), pronunciation of the co-occurring words (Pron.), the part of speech (PoS) of the words, the total number of co-occurrences (Total), the number of occurrences to the left of the target term (LT), the number of occurrences to the right side of the target term (RT), and the scores.

Table 3. Concordance list for *yawarakai* 'soft' (excerpt from Table 4)

N	Word	Pron.	Eng. Trans.	PoS	Total	LT	RT	Score
1	甘み	amami	sweetness	noun	10	4	6	5.617
2	口当たり	kuchiatari	mouthfeel	noun	5	2	3	2.95
3	舌	shita	tongue	noun	7	2	5	2.767
4	舌先	shitasaki	tip of tongue	noun	7	4	3	2.733
5	甘味	amami	sweetness	noun	4	1	3	2.7
6	甘い	amai	sweet	adj.	4	2	2	2.667
7	丸い	marui	round	adj.	4	1	3	2.583
10	酸味	sanmi	acidity	noun	6	3	3	2.35
12	口腔	kōkū	oral cavity	noun	5	1	4	2.233
13	酸っぱい	suppai	sour	adj.	3	1	2	2
15	香り	kaori	flavor	noun	3	1	2	1.833
16	辛味	karami	dryness	noun	3	0	3	1.833
20	包む	tsutsumu	wrap	verb	2	1	1	1.333
21	優しい	yasashii	tender	adj.	2	1	1	1.333

Table 3 shows that *yawarakai* 'soft' co-occurs with several different types of words, including words for flavor (*kaori* 'flavor' [15]), taste (*amami* 'sweetness' [1] [5] [6], *sanmi* 'acidity' [10], *suppai* 'sour' [13], *karami* 'dryness'[16]), parts of the mouth (*shita* 'tongue' [3] [4], *kōkū* 'oral cavity'[12]), and organoleptic feel (*kuchiatari* 'mouthfeel' [2], *marui* 'round' [7], *tsutsumu* 'wrap').

These semantic categories are important to the model of "emergence-motivated event construction," introduced in Section 2.1. In this model, the taste (of a cup of *sake*) is described as a personal experience. The emergence of the taste is experienced in the mouth cavity of the taster, and the experience of the taste unfolds in time and space in his or her mouth. If a taster wants to describe the personal story, the words for time and space, namely, the words for describing the timeline of the changing process of the taste and the words for pointing out the spot (where the taste is felt), are indispensable.

In this chapter, I shed light on the "story of the taste." To describe the story of taste is to tell the personal experience, including organoleptic feelings, texture, structure, and movements of the taste. These feelings are never objectively measured with taste sensor machines.

3.2.2 *Defining the target terms*

The terms to be used to define the target term are selected from the list of the top words in the concordance. This task relies on the knowledge and skill of the individual producing the definition. If the person knows very little about *sake* or lacks tasting skill or does not understand the meaning of the words in the list, he or she will clearly be unable to define the target term properly. Moreover, a different person is likely to define the same term differently.[6]

Although the method is not fixed or rigidly defined, I set the following tags (in square brackets and bold text) as the point to be defined.

[Flavor] or [Taste]: [Flavor] or [Taste] terms describe which the target term tends to modify, taste, or flavor (e.g., Words for [Taste] include: taste, sweetness, bitterness, acidity, etc.; Words for [Flavor] include: flavor, scent, floral, fruity flavor, etc.).

[Dominance]: [Dominance] describes which tastes among the basic tastes (i.e., sweetness, acidity, umami, bitterness, astringency, and dryness) are more likely to co-occur with the target term.[7]

[Structure]: [Structure] terms include words for the structure or physical texture of the *sake* (e.g., *bodī* 'body', *waku* / *wakugumi* / *kokkaku* 'frame', *rinkaku* 'contour',

6. This type of subjective approach may be avoided in some research fields such as experimental psychology and cognitive science. However, the sense of taste itself is firmly in the subjective domain. It cannot be shared directly with another person, nor can it be represented by sensor information from a "tasting machine," as the sense of taste cannot be reduced to the sum of its component elements.

7. Astringency and dryness are not basic tastes in an anatomical context (they are algesthesia), but in this chapter, I regard them as "basic tastes." Note that a salty taste will almost never be noted in the taste of *sake*.

katamari 'lump', *futoi* 'bold'). Examples of the usage of the [**Structure**] terms include instantiations of a "conceptual metaphor" (Lakoff & Johnson, 1980), "TASTE IS BUILDING" or "TASTE IS BODY."

An example of the two conceptual metaphors is given in (12), where *kokkaku* literally means the skeleton structure.

(12) kokkaku ga shikkari-shita, futoi umami
'(I feel) the firm-framed, bold umami'

The first part of the phrase *kokkaku ga shikari-shita* 'firmly framed, or firm physique' involves the equation of "building" or "human body" with "taste," where the elements of "taste" are conceptualized as corresponding to (or "mapped onto") those of "building." Stated differently, the taste is conceptualized as having a frame, just like a building or human body has a frame, and the stability of the "frame" of the taste is expressed by *shikari-shita* 'firm'. The conceptual metaphor takes over in the latter part of (12), where the elements of "taste" are conceptualized as corresponding to those of the "human body." Because of this correspondence, the taste term *umami* can accompany a modifier *futoi* '(lit.) fat' (See Sakaguchi, this volume, for the opposite direction of metaphorical mapping: i.e., to use taste terms such as *amai* 'sweet' to express a concept in other domains such as emotion).

[**Organoleptic Feelings**]: [Organoleptic Feelings] terms include terms on

[**Texture**]: The majority of [Organoleptic Feelings] are words for [Texture] or mouthfeels (e.g., *kanshoku* 'feeling', *tacchi* 'touch', *sofuto* 'soft', *kurīmī* 'creamy'). Words like *marui* 'round', *tsutsumu* 'wrapping', *naderu* 'stroking', and other words for stimulus are not tagged as [Texture], but as [Organoleptic Feelings]. For [Organoleptic Feelings], mimetics are often used (e.g., *zara-zara* 'rough texture', *suru-suru* 'smooth').[8]

[**Parts of the mouth**]: [Parts of the mouth] terms refer to the words for the parts of mouth used to indicate the point or the place where the taste or flavor is felt (e.g., *kuchi* 'mouth', *oku* 'back (of the mouth)', *hanasaki* 'nose tip', *shita* 'tongue'). These words can be found in expressions like the one in (13), an instance of *shitasaki* 'tip of the tongue'.

(13) Shitasaki de amami o kanjiru
'(I feel) sweetness on the tip of the tongue.'

8. Note that mimetics (also known as 'ideophones') depict broad sensory imagery that involve auditory, visual, tactile, or other types of perception (cf. Dingemanse, 2011, 2012).

[Timeline]: [Timeline] terms describe the timeline of the tasting experience, from beginning to end (i.e., in my "emergence-motivated event construction" model, from the emergence of the taste to its disappearance). In the tasting comment, describing the way the taste or flavor appears and disappears is very important. The words for appearance are, for example, *saisho* 'beginning', *arawareru* 'appear', *tatsu* 'stand' (cf. Section 4.2.6), and *hanasaki* 'tip of the nose'. The words for disappearance include *kieru* 'fade', *kireru* 'finish', *nokoru* 'remain', and *atokuchi* 'aftertaste'. It is notable that some words for the part of the mouth often (indirectly) refer to the point of the timeline (e.g., 'nose tip' = 'the starting point', or 'back of the mouth' = 'the last point').

[Movement]: [Movement] terms include verbs modified by adjectivals expressing the movement of the taste. Representative examples include: *fukuramu* 'swell', *hirogaru* 'spread', *nagare* 'flow', *tadayou* 'drift', and *osamaru* 'subside' (see Yoshinari, this volume, for motion verbs in Japanese wine taste descriptions).

[Characteristic Words]: [Characteristic Words] terms include words that supplement the information of the target terms but are important to feature the characteristics of the taste, such as *sukoshi* 'a little'.

[Related Words] : If the PoS of the word is the same as the PoS of the target term (i.e., adjectives or adjectival nouns in the concordance list), and if the word has an intralinguistic relationship with the target term, such as synonymy, antonymy, hyponymy, or gradable antonymy (cf. Lehrer, 2009), then the word should be included. For example, if the description includes *yawarakaku marui* 'soft and round', and the target term is *yawarakai* 'soft', *marui* 'round' should be listed as a related word, as it expresses a synonymous meaning as 'soft' in the *sake* tasting context.

4. Results

This section reports the results of my analysis of the target aesthetic taste terms (shown in italics as in *yawarakai* 'soft'), applying the method described in Section 3. Each subsection starts with a table showing a concordance list containing the top 20 words that co-occur with the target term,[9] followed by the definitions under the tagged categories such as **[Taste]** and **[Dominance]**. Within the descriptions of the definitions, square brackets are used to indicate the rank of the word score ("N" in Table 3), as in *amai* 'sweet' [6]. Due to space limitations, not all terms are listed in the tables (the full concordance list can be seen on my website),[10] but some are

9. If there is a "tie score" for the 20th word, all words with the same score are listed.

10. http://www.hiroki.fukushima.jp

included in the descriptions with the ranks, as in *haneru* 'spring' [27], for specificity, although the table may list just up to [20] or so. Wherever appropriate, sentence examples are included. Section 4.1 provides the results for eight adjectives and Section 4.2, the results for eight adjectival nouns.

4.1 Adjectives

4.1.1 Yawarakai *'soft'*

Table 4. Concordance list for *yawarakai* 'soft'

N	Word	Pron.	Eng. Trans.	PoS	Total	LT	RT	Score
1	甘み	amami	sweetness	noun	10	4	6	5.617
2	口当たり	kuchiatari	mouthfeel	noun	5	2	3	2.95
3	舌	shita	tongue	noun	7	2	5	2.767
4	舌先	shitasaki	tip of tongue	noun	7	4	3	2.733
5	甘味	amami	sweetness	noun	4	1	3	2.7
6	甘い	amai	sweet	adj.	4	2	2	2.667
7	丸い	marui	round	adj.	4	1	3	2.583
8	一瞬	isshun	momentary	adv.	3	3	0	2.5
9	感じる	kanjiru	feel	verb	5	2	3	2.5
10	酸味	sanmi	acidity	noun	6	3	3	2.35
11	塊	katamari	lump	noun	3	0	3	2.25
12	口腔	kōkū	oral cavity	noun	5	1	4	2.233
13	酸っぱい	suppai	sour	adj.	3	1	2	2
14	入る	hairu	enter	verb	4	2	2	2
15	香り	kaori	scent	noun	3	1	2	1.833
16	辛味	karami	dryness	noun	3	0	3	1.833
17	細い	hosoi	thin	adj.	3	1	2	1.7
18	上品	jōhin	elegance	AN	3	1	2	1.7
19	主張	shuchō	assertion	noun	2	0	2	1.333
20	包む	tsutsumu	wrap	verb	2	1	1	1.333
21	優しい	yasashii	tender	adj.	2	1	1	1.333

Note:
"AN" stands for "adjectival noun."

As Table 4 shows, *yawarakai* 'soft' co-occurs with a variety of taste terms (e.g., *yawarakai amami* 'soft sweetness'), flavor terms (e.g., *yawarakai kaori* 'soft flavor'), or words that express an aesthetic sense (e.g., *yawarakaku jōhin* 'soft and elegant'). (13) provides a sentence example from the corpus.

(13) Kome no yawarakai umami ya amami to kankitsukei no yōna sanmi…
'Soft umami and sweetness of rice, and the citrus-like acidity…'
for *Tatenokawa, Super premium Ginjo* (Hasegawa, 2015)

Given the co-occurrence pattern, *yawarakai* 'soft' can be defined as follows:

[Flavor or Taste] The term *yawarakai* 'soft' is used more frequently to describe "taste" than "flavor," as evidenced by the higher token frequency of the taste terms covering 'sweetness' [1, 5, 6] and 'acidity' [10, 13] versus one use of *kaori* 'flavor' [15].

[Dominance] Among the taste descriptors, sweetness and acidity are the dominant tastes for the feelings of 'soft', as indicated by the higher token frequency of the terms expressing 'sweetness' [1, 5, 6] and 'acidity' [10, 13], versus one use of 'dryness' [16].

[Organoleptic feel] *Yawarakai* 'soft' describes texture in the entire oral cavity and on the tongue, as indicated by terms such as *kuchiatari* 'mouthfeel' [2] (*kuchiatari ga yawarakai* 'it has soft mouthfeel'), *shitasaki* 'tip of the tongue' [4], and *kōkū* 'oral cavity' [12]. It may represent the mouthfeel as a liquid stream (e.g., *yawarakai seiryū* 'soft clear stream' [24]) or as a sense of springing (*yawarakaku haneru* 'springs up softly' [27]).

[Related words] *Yawarakai* 'soft' is considered to be related to words expressing similar quality, such as *marui* 'round' [7] (e.g., *yawarakaku marui* 'soft and round'), *hosoi* 'thin' [17], *jōhin* 'elegance', and *yasashii* 'tender' [21].

4.1.2 Karui *'light'*

Table 5. Concordance list of *karui* 'light'

N	Word	Pron.	EngTrans	PoS	Total	LT	RT	Score
1	刺激	shigeki	stimulus	noun	23	1	22	19.933
2	感じる	kanjiru	feel	verb	32	8	24	9.75
3	舌	shita	tongue	noun	32	26	6	9.483
4	痺れ	shibire	numbness	noun	8	0	8	8
5	奥	oku	back	noun	18	15	3	7.567
6	苦味	nigami	bitterness	noun	7	1	6	6.25
7	上顎	uwaago	maxilla	noun	18	14	4	6.217
8	甘み	amami	sweetness	noun	8	1	7	6.2
9	引く	hiku	fade	verb	9	9	0	5.917
10	左右	sayū	right and left	noun	12	11	1	4.917
11	酸味	sanmi	acidity	noun	6	2	4	4.75
12	全体	zentai	full	adv.	10	7	3	4.2
13	香り	kaori	scent	noun	12	9	3	3.65

(*continued*)

Table 5. *(continued)*

N	Word	Pron.	EngTrans	PoS	Total	LT	RT	Score
14	印象	inshō	impression	noun	7	4	3	3.5
15	飲む	nomu	drink	verb	7	2	5	3.45
16	痺れる	shibireru	numbness	verb	4	1	3	3.333
17	口中	kōchū	mouth	noun	8	5	3	3.167
18	ピリピリ	piripiri	stimulus	onoma	3	0	3	3
19	後口	atokuchi	aftertaste	noun	5	2	3	3
20	その後	sonoato	later	adv.	11	8	3	2.967

[Organoleptic Feelings] *Karui* 'light' represents a lesser degree of sensations. It can describe 'alcohol' (*arukōru* [41]), 'stimulus' (*shigeki / piripir*i [1, 18]), and numbness (*shibire / shibireru* [4, 16]) to the 'tongue' (*shita* [3]), as seen in (14).

(14) Akarui inshō ga hirogari, uwa-ago ni <u>karui shigeki</u> ga hirogaru
'Bright impression expands, and <u>light stimulus</u> spread on the maxilla'
(comment from tasting experiment data, 2017)

[Taste] Among basic tastes, *karui* 'light' represents the degree of 'stimulus' (*shigeki* [1]). Here it means the 'bitterness' (*nigami* [6]) and 'acidity' (*sanmi* [11]) felt on the 'tongue' (*shita* [3]). (15) is illustrative of this taste definition.

(15) nōmitsu na tōn no naka de <u>karui sanmi</u> ga akusento ni…
'during the dense tone, the <u>light acidity</u> gives some accent…'
for 'Aratama, DEWA33' (Matsuzaki, 1995)

[Related words] *Karui* 'light' is considered related to words such as *sawayaka* 'refreshing [25] and *kirei* 'fine' [37]. Note that *karui* 'light' is used as a euphemistic expression for thin (*usui* 'thin' [43]) or weak *sake.*

4.1.3 Katai *'firm'*

Table 6. Concordance list of *katai* 'firm'

N	Word	Pron.	Eng Trans.	PoS	Total	LT	RT	Score
1	感じる	kanjiru	feel	verb	10	2	8	3.65
2	香り	kaori	scent	noun	8	3	5	3.55
3	苦味	nigami	bitterness	noun	5	2	3	3.45
4	印象	inshō	impression	noun	5	0	5	3.4
5	少々	shōshō	a little	adv.	4	3	1	3.333
6	触手	shokushu	tentacle	noun	2	0	2	2
7	水	mizu	water	noun	2	0	2	2
8	味	aji	taste	noun	4	2	2	1.95

Table 6. (*continued*)

N	Word	Pron.	Eng Trans.	PoS	Total	LT	RT	Score
9	少し	sukoshi	a little	adv.	5	3	2	1.65
10	刺激	shigeki	stimulus	noun	3	1	2	1.583
11	鼻腔	bikū	nasal cavity	noun	4	2	2	1.583
12	舌	shita	tongue	noun	4	2	2	1.367
13	全体	zentai	full	adv.	4	3	1	1.333
14	冷たい	tsumetai	cold	adj.	2	2	0	1.333
15	立つ	tatsu	stand	verb	2	2	0	1.2
16	引き締まる	hikishimaru	tighten	verb	1	0	1	1
17	岩	iwa	rock	noun	1	0	1	1
18	中央	chūō	middle	noun	2	2	0	1
19	透明	tōmei	transparent	AN	1	0	1	1
20	平板	hiraban	flat plate	AN	1	0	1	1
21	螺旋	rasen	spiral	noun	1	0	1	1
22	立方体	rippōtai	cube	noun	1	0	1	1

[Dominance] [Taste] *Katai* 'firm' seems to primarily describe the quality of [Taste]. It characteristically co-occurs with *nigami* 'bitterness' [3] and *sanmi* 'acidity' [23].

[Parts of the mouth] Words expressing the parts of the mouth include: *bikū* 'nasal cavity' [11], *shita* 'tongue' [12], *zentai* 'whole' [13], and *uwaago* 'maxilla' [25]. These words indicate the points in the mouth where elements such as 'bitterness', 'acidity', and other 'stimuli' (*shigeki* [10]) emerge. (16) shows one example, with 'the top of the mouth cavity' as the focus.

(16) kuchi no ue no hō ni aru <u>ita no yō na katai aji</u>
'<u>board-like firm taste</u>, existing at the top of the mouth cavity'
(comment from a tasting experiment data, 2017)

[Characteristic words] Other characteristic words are adjectival nouns such as *shōshō / sukoshi* 'a little' [5, 9]. Basically, *katai* 'firm' is not a word to use when speaking well of a *sake*. Thus, adverbs that mitigate the degree are used with *katai* 'firm' to modify the tone of the description (giving a less harsh nuance).

To describe "firmness" in more detail, similes such as 'like a rock' (*iwa* 'rock' [17]) or mimetics (sound symbolic words) such as *gigigi* (scratching sound) [34] or *zara-zara* (rough texture) [35] are used.

[Related words] *Katai* 'firm' is considered related to words such as *hikishimaru* 'tighten' [16], *tōmei* 'transparent' [19], and *heiban* 'flat plate' [20].

A few more notes on related words are in order:

- *Tsumetai* 'cold' [14] has an important relationship with *katai* 'firm'. *Sake* that feels too firm at a cold temperature may lose its firmness and soften when warmed.
- *Tōmei na sake* 'transparent *sake*' (cf. [19]) would not mean the color of the *sake*, but would refer to a clear, clean, and light type of *sake* (see also the definition of *tōmei* 'clear' in Section 4.2.4). Transparency has the nuance of being ineffectual or simplistic. In general, a pure taste is welcomed for the taste of *sake*, but too much simplicity may mean *katai* 'firm' *sake* that will not swell in the mouth and be felt like a 'flat plate [20]' in the mouth (note that *heiban* 'flat plate' [20] is a metaphor for 'dead' in Japanese, indicating flatness or monotony).

4.1.4 Marui *'round'*

Table 7. Concordance list for *marui* 'round'

N	Word	Pron.	EngTrans	PoS	Total	LT	RT	Score
1	味	aji	taste	noun	13	5	8	6.417
2	甘味	amami	sweetness	noun	7	2	5	4.917
3	甘い	amai	sweet	adj.	5	0	5	4.333
4	広がる	hirogaru	spread	verb	5	1	4	3.583
5	収まる	osamaru	subside	verb	4	1	3	3.5
6	輪郭	rinkaku	contour	noun	4	0	4	3.25
7	残る	nokoru	remain	verb	5	2	3	3.2
8	練れる	nereru	knead	verb	3	0	3	3
9	甘み	amami	sweetness	noun	5	3	2	2.75
10	丸い	marui	round	adj.	4	2	2	2.667
11	柔らかい	yawarakai	soft	adj.	4	3	1	2.583
12	口	kuchi	mouth	noun	5	1	4	2.033
13	ふっくら	fukkura	plump	noun	2	0	2	2
14	厚み	atsumi	thickness	noun	2	0	2	2
15	留まる	tomaru	stay	verb	2	0	2	2
16	舌	shita	tongue	noun	6	3	3	1.867
17	感じる	kanjiru	feel	verb	6	2	4	1.7
18	増す	masu	increase	verb	4	3	1	1.667
19	後口	atokuchi	aftertaste	noun	4	4	0	1.533
20	口先	kuchisaki	lips	noun	2	1	1	1.5

[Dominance] [Taste] As indicated by the higher token frequency of the terms expressing *amai / amami* 'sweetness' [2, 3, 9], the target term *marui* 'round' primarily expresses taste, especially sweet taste: e.g., *marui amami* 'round sweetness'.

[Structure] *Marui* 'round' represents the physical form of *sake* in the mouth: e.g., *kyūtai* 'sphere' [31], *katamari* 'lump' [30], *rinkaku* 'contour' [6], or *atsumi* 'thickness' [14].

[Movement] As well as the physical form, *marui* 'round' represents the way the *sake* moves: e.g., *hirogaru* 'spread' [4], *osamaru* 'subside' [5].

[Timeline] Words describing the last part of the mouth are characteristic: e.g., *nokoru* 'remain' [7], *todomaru* 'stay' [15], *atokuchi* 'aftertaste' [19], and *oku* 'back' [29]. An example expressing timeline with *nokoru* 'remain' is given in (17).

(17) saigo, marui karami ga shita ni nokoru
'finally, round-shaped dryness stays on the tongue'
(comment from a tasting experiment data, 2017)

[Related words] *Marui* 'round' is considered related to expressions such as *nereru* 'matured' [8], *yawarakai* 'soft' [11], and *fukkura fukuyoka* 'plump' [13, 28].

4.1.5 Futoi *'bold'*

Table 8. Concordance list for *futoi* 'bold'

N	Word	Pron.	EngTrans	PoS	Total	LT	RT	Score
1	味	aji	taste	noun	24	15	9	11.867
2	味わい	ajiwai	taste	noun	11	1	10	9.75
3	酸味	sanmi	acidity	noun	11	3	8	7.233
4	練れる	nereru	knead	verb	6	1	5	5.25
5	香り	kaori	scent	noun	11	5	6	5.067
6	力強い	chikarazuyoi	forceful	adj.	5	2	3	3.533
7	旨味	umami	umami	noun	3	0	3	2.333
8	醇味	junmi	rich taste	noun	3	0	3	2.25
9	酒	sake	*sake*	noun	9	3	6	2.183
10	音色	neiro	tone	noun	2	0	2	2
11	口中	kōchū	in the mouth	noun	6	4	2	1.9
12	流れ	nagare	flow	noun	4	2	2	1.783
13	気流	kiryū	airflow	noun	3	1	2	1.75
14	酸	san	acid	noun	4	2	2	1.65
15	練る	neru	knead	verb	5	2	3	1.583
16	伸びやか	nobiyaka	smooth	AN	2	1	1	1.5
17	濃密	nōmitsu	dense	AN	2	1	1	1.5
18	コク	koku	knock	noun	2	0	2	1.333
19	横たわる	yokotawaru	lie down	verb	2	0	2	1.333
20	強い	tsuyoi	strong	adj.	2	2	0	1.333

Futoi 'bold' co-occurs with terms such as *junmi* 'rich' [8] and *nōmitsu* 'dense' [17], or is used to describe full-body [31] type *sake* with 'acidity' (*san / sanmi* [3, 14]) and *umami* [7] (e.g., *umami ga futoi* 'umami is bold (rich)'). This term is especially well-used for *junmai* 'pure rice' [21], a kind of rice with rich umami.

[Structure] *Futoi* 'bold' is used to note the terms covering structure or "body-build" of *sake*, co-occurring with terms such as *body* 'body' [31], *rinkaku* 'contour' [23], and *kokkaku* 'frame' [37].

[Movement] *Futoi* 'bold' co-occurs with the words describing the fluid movement of the *sake*. This is evidenced by the higher token frequency of such words as *nagare* 'flow' [12], *kiryū* 'airflow' [13], and *nobiyaka* 'smooth' [16]. (18) shows an example with *nagare* 'flow'.

(18) zentai ni tappuri to shita futoi nagare o miseru
'on the whole, a full-bold stream is felt' for *Kinmon-Aizu* (Matsuzaki, 1995)

[Related words] *Futoi* 'bold' is considered related to terms such as *chikarazuyoi* 'forceful' [6], *nōmitsu* 'dense' [17], *tsuyoi* 'strong' [20], and *koi* 'thick' [35].

4.1.6 Kōbashii *'roasted aromatic'*

Table 9. Concordance list for *kōbashii* 'roasted aromatic'

N	Word	Pron.	EngTrans	PoS	Total	LT	RT	Score
1	香り	kaori	flavor	noun	13	1	12	11.7
2	風味	fūmi	flavor	noun	9	0	9	8.2
3	甘味	amami	sweetness	noun	16	4	12	6.283
4	甘い	amai	sweet	adj.	6	5	1	5.333
5	ナッツ	nattsu	nuts	noun	11	10	1	3.7
6	タッチ	tacchi	touch	noun	4	0	4	2.75
7	味	aji	taste	noun	3	0	3	2.25
8	酒	sake	*sake*	noun	7	5	2	2.15
9	ヨーグルト	yōguruto	yogurt	noun	2	0	2	2
10	様	sama/yō	-like	noun	4	3	1	2
11	旨味	umami	umami	noun	3	2	1	1.833
12	感触	kanshoku	feel	noun	3	1	2	1.583
13	アーモンド	āmondo	almond	noun	3	2	1	1.5
14	抜ける	nukeru	go through	verb	5	2	3	1.4
15	ふくよか	fukuyoka	plump	AN	2	1	1	1.25
16	感じる	kanjiru	feel	verb	4	3	1	1.25
17	深み	fukami	depth	noun	2	0	2	1.2
18	果実香	kamika	fruit fragrance	noun	1	0	1	1
19	甘み	amami	sweetness	noun	1	0	1	1
20	甘酸っぱい	amazuppai	sweet and sour	adj.	1	0	1	1
21	香味	kōmi	flavor	noun	1	0	1	1
22	旨い	umai	delicious	adj.	1	1	0	1
23	複雑	fukuzatsu	complex	AN	1	0	1	1
24	余韻	yoin	aftertaste	noun	1	0	1	1

[Dominance] *Kōbashii* 'roasted aromatic' is used to describe the total experience in the mouth, both flavor (*kaori / fūmi*) and taste (*aji*) [1, 2, 7]: e.g., *jukusei shita kōbashii kaori* 'aged, roasted-aroma'.

[Texture] *Kōbashii* 'roasted aromatic' co-occurs with words expressing texture (*tacchi* 'touch' [6], *kanshoku* 'feel' [12]), but *kōbashii* 'roasted aromatic' itself does not directly modify the texture: e.g., **kōbashii tacchi* (intended: 'roasted aromatic touch').

[Taste] As for the basic tastes, *kōbashii* 'roasted aromatic' mainly represents sweetness and umami, as indicated by *amai* 'sweet' [3], *amami* 'sweetness' [4], *amazuppai* 'sweet and sour' [20], and *umami* [11, 22].

[Flavor] *Kōbashii* 'roasted aromatic' tends to co-occur with concrete words that specify the meaning of fragrance (*nattsu* 'nuts' [5], *yōguruto* 'yogurt' [9], and *āmondo* 'almond' [13]). *Jukusei* 'aging' [29] and *kogasu* 'burn' [30] are also words specifying fragrance. (19) is illustrative.

(19) <u>Goma o abutta yō na kōbashii kaori</u> ni meron no fūmi ga nozoku
'Flavor like melon peeks out from the <u>roasted sesame-like aroma</u>'
for *Kunimare Juku* (Matsuzaki, 1995)

[Parts of the mouth] *Hana* 'nose' [27] and *nukeru* 'go through' [14] suggest fragrance is perceived retro-nasally; "retro-nasal olfaction" refers to the perception of odors emanating from the oral cavity during eating and drinking, as opposed to *orthonasal olfaction*, which occurs during sniffing.

[Related words] *Kōbashii* 'roasted aromatic' is considered related to *fukami* 'depth' [17], *fukuyoka* 'plump' [15] (see also the definition of 'plump' in Section 4.2.5), and *fukuzatsu* 'complex' [23] (similar but only mildly related).

4.1.7 Yasashii *'tender'*

Table 10. Concordance list of *yasashii* 'tender'

N	Word	Pron.	EngTrans	PoS	Total	LT	RT	Score
1	甘味	amami	sweetness	noun	12	2	10	10.2
2	舌	shita	tongue	noun	7	5	2	4.333
3	タッチ	tacchi	touch	noun	5	2	3	3.75
4	口あたり	kuchiatari	mouthfeel	noun	5	2	3	3.4
5	きれい	kirei	clean	AN	5	3	2	3.167
6	広がる	hirogaru	spread	verb	5	3	2	3
7	引く	hiku	fade	verb	4	1	3	2.533
8	酒	sake	*sake*	noun	6	2	4	2.533
9	包み込む	tsutsumikomu	wrap	verb	4	3	1	2.533
10	撫でる	naderu	stroke	verb	3	1	2	2.25

(*continued*)

Table 10. (*continued*)

N	Word	Pron.	EngTrans	PoS	Total	LT	RT	Score
11	甘み	amami	sweetness	noun	3	1	2	2.2
12	全体	zentai	full	adv.	5	3	2	2.2
13	包む	tsutsumu	wrap	verb	2	0	2	2
14	感触	kanshoku	feel	noun	3	2	1	1.833
15	柔らかい	yawarakai	soft	adj.	2	1	1	1.333
16	印象	inshō	impression	noun	2	0	2	1.25
17	感じる	kanjiru	feel	verb	4	1	3	1.25
18	可憐	karen	pretty	AN	2	0	2	1.2
19	舌先	shitasaki	tip of tongue	noun	3	2	1	1.2
20	流れ	nagare	flow	noun	4	2	2	1.117

[Taste] *Yasashii* 'tender' is exclusively modified by one of the basic taste terms, *amami* 'sweetness' [1, 11]. *Sanmi* 'acidity' [21] appears on the list, but its rank is rather low. Generally speaking, if *amami* 'sweetness' is on a concordance list, *umami* is also expected, because sweetness and umami are both the primary tastes of *sake*. The fact that only sweetness appears on the list means sweetness is characteristically modified by the target term, *yasashii* 'tender'.

[Organoleptic Feelings] Describing a texture-related word seems to be a significant function of *yasashii* 'tender'. *Tacchi* 'touch' [3], *kuchiatari* 'mouthfeel' [4, 30], and *kanshoku* '(haptic) feeling' [14] are directly related to the texture of *sake* (e.g., *yasashii kanshoku* 'tender feeling').

The taste elements are sometimes felt as something moving, and *yasashii* 'tender' is used to detail the manner of the movements, expressed by such verbs as *tsutsumu* 'wrapping' [9, 13] (e.g., *shita o yasashiku tsutsumu* 'wrap the tongue tenderly') or *naderu* 'stroking' [10], both of which express the feelings on the tongue. Related to texture, *yasashii* 'tender' refers to a weakness of the *shigeki* 'stimulus' [31] of the *arukōru* 'alcohol' [22].

[Related words] *Yasashii* 'tender' is considered related to *kirei* 'clean' [5], *yawarakai* 'soft' [15], *kurīmī* 'creamy' [24], and *jūnan* 'flexible' [34]. It may be further noted that *karen* 'pretty' [18] and *josei* 'lady (feminine)' [35] may be considered synonymous in the context of a *sake* description.

4.1.8 Chikarazuyoi *'powerful'*

Table 11. Concordance list of *chikarazuyoi* 'powerful'

N	Word	Pron.	EngTrans	PoS	Total	LT	RT	Score
1	味	aji	taste	noun	5	1	4	4.25
2	押し	oshi	pushing	noun	4	0	4	4
3	切れ	kire	clearing	noun	6	4	2	4
4	感じる	kanjiru	feel	verb	11	4	7	3.617
5	太い	futoi	thick	adj.	5	3	2	3.533
6	切れ味	kireaji	sharpness	noun	5	2	3	3.333
7	押し上げる	oshiageru	push	verb	6	5	1	3.117
8	飲む	nomu	drink	verb	3	1	2	2.2
9	旨味	umami	umami	noun	3	0	3	2.2
10	酸味	sanmi	acidity	noun	3	2	1	1.45
11	辛い	karai	dryness	adj.	3	0	3	1.45
12	全体	zentai	full	adv.	5	2	3	1.317
13	渋味	shibumi	astringency	noun	4	1	3	1.167
14	酒	sake	*sake*	noun	5	1	4	1.05
15	コク	koku	rich taste	noun	1	0	1	1
16	ボリューム感	boryūmukan	volume	noun	1	0	1	1
17	圧す	assu	press	verb	1	0	1	1
18	応える	kotaeru	respond	verb	2	0	2	1
19	押し味	oshiaji	lasting taste	noun	1	0	1	1
20	甘み	amami	sweetness	noun	1	0	1	1
21	剛直	gōchoku	fortitude	AN	1	0	1	1
22	持つ	motsu	hold	verb	1	1	0	1
23	切り口	kirikuchi	cut	noun	1	0	1	1
24	側面	sokumen	Sides	noun	1	0	1	1
25	張り	hari	tension	noun	1	0	1	1
26	入る	hairu	enter	verb	1	0	1	1
27	抜ける	nukeru	go through	verb	1	1	0	1
28	密度	mitsudo	density	noun	1	0	1	1
29	立ち上がる	tachiagaru	rise	verb	1	0	1	1

[Dominance] *Chikarazuyoi* 'powerful' tends to be used to describe taste [1] rather than flavor [102].

[Taste] Along with *futoi* 'bold', *chikarazuyoi* 'powerful' is used to describe the dense, plump (*boryūmukan* 'volume' [16]) *sake* with *umami* [9], *sanmi* 'acidity' [10], or *shibumi* 'astringency' [13]. (20) gives one of the characteristic usages.

(20) Gut-to semaru sanmi to chikarazuyoi ajiwai ga nihonshu fan ni ureshii
'pressing acidity and the powerful taste are the joy of the *sake* funs'
for *Tabito* (SSI, 2010)

[Timeline] It is interesting that *chikarazuyoi* 'powerful' co-occurs with expressions for a clear finish, as indicated by *karai* 'dryness' [11], *kire* 'breaking' [3], and *kireaji* 'sharpness'[6], and with expressions for a long aftertaste, as indicated by *oshi-aji* 'lasting taste' [19].

[Related words] *Chikarazuyoi* 'powerful' is considered related to *futoi* 'bold' [5] and *gōchoku* 'fortitude' [21].

4.2 Adjectival nouns

4.2.1 Kirei *'clean'*

Table 12. Concordance list of *kirei* 'clean'

N	Word	Pron.	EngTrans	PoS	Total	LT	RT	Score
1	味	aji	taste	noun	24	9	15	10.05
2	甘味	amami	sweetness	noun	17	4	13	8.2
3	香り	kaori	scent	noun	14	8	6	6.183
4	酒	*sake*	sake	noun	16	5	11	5.9
5	果実香	kajitsuka	fruit fragrance	noun	8	4	4	3.75
6	口	kuchi	mouth	noun	10	6	4	3.617
7	流れ	nagare	flow	noun	8	5	3	3.2
8	優しい	yasashii	tender	adj.	5	2	3	3.167
9	引き	hiki	fading	noun	6	3	3	3
10	たなびく	tanabiku	trail	verb	5	4	1	2.95
11	良い	yoi	good	adj.	6	4	2	2.933
12	口あたり	kuchiatari	mouthfeel	noun	6	4	2	2.75
13	広がる	hirogaru	spread	verb	5	1	4	2.75
14	飲む	nomu	drink	verb	7	4	3	2.7
15	少ない	sukunai	less	adj.	4	4	0	2.583
16	旨味	umami	umami	noun	7	0	7	2.533
17	引く	hiku	fade	verb	6	1	5	2.333
18	後口	atokuchi	aftertaste	noun	6	6	0	2.15
19	引き方	hikikata	way of fading	noun	5	4	1	1.783
20	漂う	tadayou	drift	verb	4	4	0	1.783

[Dominance] *Kirei* 'clean' co-occurs with both [Taste] and [Flavor].

[Taste] Taste expressions include: *aji* 'taste' [1], *amami* 'sweetness' [2], *umami* 'umami' [16], *sanmi* 'acidity' [30], and *shibumi* astringency [34] (e.g., *kirei na shibumi ga kokochi ii* 'the clean astringency is comfortable').

[Flavor] Flavor expressions include: *kaori / kōmi* 'flavor' [3] [29], *kajitsuka* 'fruity fragrance' [5], *kōki* 'aroma' [26] (e.g., *kirei na kōki ni michiru* 'clean flavor fills my mouth'), and *fukumiga* 'first flavor' [27].

[Movement] *Kirei* 'clean' often co-occurs with words expressing a metaphorical motion, in particular, of fluidity and airy movement, such as *nagare* 'flow' [7], *tanabiku* 'trailing' [10], *hirogaru* 'spread' [13], *tadayou* 'drift' [20], and *fukuramu* 'swell' [21]. One instance of *tanabiku* 'trailing' is shown in (21).

(21) honnori tanabiku <u>kireina ringo-ka</u>
'slightly trailing, <u>clean flavor of apple</u>'
for *Ohmon Tojinohana* (Matsuzaki, 1995)

[Timeline] *Kirei* 'clean' modifies a smooth and quickly fading sensation (*hiki / hiku / hikikata* 'fading' [9, 17, 19]) at the last point of taste (*atokuchi* 'after taste' [18]).

[Texture] As well as modifying taste, *kirei* 'clean' modifies texture, as in *kuchiatari* 'mouthfeel' [12] and *tacchi* 'touch' [31]. In this case, it represents the smoothness and low stimulation of alcohol; e.g., *kirei na kuchiatari* 'clean mouthfeel'.

[Related Words] *Kirei* 'clean' is considered related to *yasashii* 'tender' [8], *karui* 'light' [22], and *kihin* 'elegant' [28].

4.2.2 Odayaka *'calm'*

Table 13. Concordance list for *odayaka* 'calm'

N	Word	Pron.	EngTrans	PoS	Total	LT	RT	Score
1	香り	kaori	flavor	noun	36	29	7	16.233
2	酒	sake	*sake*	noun	19	13	6	5.9
3	甘み	amami	sweetness	noun	11	3	8	4.533
4	酸味	sanmi	acidity	noun	9	4	5	3.65
5	味	aji	taste	noun	8	0	8	3.45
6	落ち着く	ochitsuku	calm	verb	6	3	3	2.667
7	印象	inshō	impression	noun	7	2	5	2.5
8	果実香	kajitsuka	fruit fragrance	noun	5	0	5	2.5
9	熟成感	jukuseikan	ripening	noun	6	2	4	2.45
10	甘味	amami	sweetness	noun	6	2	4	2.15
11	引く	hiku	fade	verb	4	3	1	2.083
12	共に	tomoni	together	adv.	2	2	0	2
13	口あたり	kuchiatari	mouthfeel	noun	6	2	4	2
14	香味	kōmi	flavor	noun	4	2	2	2
15	帯びる	obiru	wear	verb	4	2	2	2
16	流れ	nagare	flow	noun	5	0	5	2
17	酸	san	acid	noun	4	2	2	1.667
18	ゆったり	yuttari	slow	adv.	4	1	3	1.533
19	口	kuchi	mouth	noun	4	1	3	1.5
20	奥	oku	back	noun	6	2	4	1.45

[Dominance] *Odayaka* 'calm' can modify almost any domain, as seen in the section on [Taste] and [Flavor].

[Taste] In the taste domain, various kinds of taste co-occur with *odayaka* 'calm', such as *aji* 'taste' [5], *amami* 'sweetness' [3, 10], *sanmi / san* 'acidity' [4, 17], *umami* 'umami' [33], *shibumi* 'astringency' [34], and *karami* 'dryness' [35] (e.g., *Odayaka na sanmi to umami* 'Calm acidity and umami').

[Flavor] Flavor terms include *kaori / kōmi / kōki* 'flavor' [1, 14, 24] and *kajitsuka* 'fruity fragrance' [8]. *Odayaka* 'calm' can express the overall impression (*insho* 'impression' [7], *tōn* 'tone' [30]) rather than the detailed flavor.

[Timeline] In addition to denoting tastes and flavors, *odayaka* 'calm' denotes the states of the timeline flow (*nagare* 'flow' [16]) of the taste, as evidenced by the higher token frequency of the following words: *hiku* 'fading' [11], *yuttari* 'slow' [18], and *shūshi* 'whole time' [26]. It is also used for the overall spatial points (*kuchi* 'mouth' [19], *oku* 'back' [20], *hanasaki* 'nose tip' [38]). (22) gives an example of a case of *shūshi* 'from start to finish'.

(22) atokuchi ni sanmi ga o o hiku mono no shūshi odayaka na…
'Acidity aftertaste lasts longer, but it's calm from first to last…'
for *Mansaku no Hana, Nama* (Matsuzaki, 1995)

4.2.3 Sawayaka *'fresh'*

Table 14. Concordance list for *sawayaka* 'fresh'

N	Word	Pron.	EngTrans	PoS	Total	LT	RT	Score
1	香気	kōki	aroma	noun	20	3	17	8.3
2	香り	kaori	flavor	noun	16	4	12	6.4
3	リンゴ	ringo	apple	noun	17	10	7	5.767
4	酸味	sanmi	acidity	noun	10	2	8	3.833
5	甘み	amami	sweetness	noun	7	0	7	3.25
6	果実香	kajitsuka	fruity fragrance	noun	6	0	6	3
7	メロン	meron	melon	noun	8	6	2	2.65
8	酒	sake	*sake*	noun	6	5	1	2.533
9	感じる	kanjiru	feel	verb	7	3	4	2.25
10	軽い	karui	light	adj.	3	3	0	2.25
11	口中	kōchū	mouth	noun	7	3	4	2.233
12	広がる	hirogaru	spread	verb	6	3	3	2.233
13	果実	kajitsuka	fruit	noun	6	4	2	1.983
14	思う	omou	think	verb	5	5	0	1.95
15	立つ	tatsu	stand	verb	7	2	5	1.833
16	飲む	nomu	drink	verb	4	1	3	1.7
17	甘味	amami	sweetness	noun	4	0	4	1.7
18	口	kuchi	mouth	noun	6	3	3	1.7
19	大吟醸	daiginjō	daiginjo	noun	4	3	1	1.583
20	梨	nashi	pear	noun	4	1	3	1.5

[Dominance] *Sawayaka* 'fresh' describes both flavor [1, 2, 6] and taste [4, 5, 17, 22]. In the context of *sawayaka* 'fresh', *sanmi* 'acidity' [4] means fruity [6, 13] acidity, as in (23).

(23) Gurēpufurūtsu no yō na sawayaka na sanmi ga tanoshimeru
'fresh acidity like grapefruit can be enjoyed'
for *Atagonomatsu, Hitonatsu no Koi* (Hasegawa, 2015)

[Flavor] Many words describe the kind of fruit: *ringo* 'apple' [3], *meron* 'melon' [7], *nashi* 'pear' [20], *aoringo* 'green apple' [37], *ichigo* 'strawberry' [46], and *kankitsu* 'citrus' [77].

[Characteristic words] As well as names of fruits, the names of other foods are listed: *ramune* 'ramune-soda' [32], *minto* 'mint' [74], and *yōguruto* 'yogurt' [75]. These fruits and foods in the collocation list are typically linked with *sawayaka* 'fresh'.

[Related words] *Sawayaka* 'fresh' is considered related to *ereganto* 'elegant' [30], *karui* 'light' [10], *wakai* 'young' [21], *uiuishii* 'innocent' [23], *keikai* 'nimble' [27], *syāpu* 'sharp' [31], *hosoi* 'thin' [35], and *wakawakashii* 'youthful' [36].

4.2.4 Tōmei *'clear'*

Table 15. Concordance list of *tōmei* 'clear'

N	Word	Pron.	EngTrans	PoS	Total	LT	RT	Score
1	味	aji	taste	noun	24	6	18	8.85
2	感じる	kanjiru	feel	verb	16	8	8	5.05
3	甘い	amai	sweet	adj.	6	4	2	3.45
4	甘味	amami	sweetness	noun	5	2	3	2.5
5	甘み	amami	sweetness	noun	7	2	5	2.283
6	清らか	kiyoraka	cleanness	AN	5	4	1	2.2
7	糖	tō	sugar	noun	5	1	4	2.083
8	辛味	karami	dryness	noun	5	2	3	1.95
9	液体	ekitai	liquid	noun	4	1	3	1.75
10	清流	seiryū	clear stream	noun	4	1	3	1.75
11	酒	sake	*sake*	noun	5	4	1	1.7
12	サステイン	sasutein	sustain	noun	3	2	1	1.5
13	消える	kieru	disappear	verb	4	4	0	1.4
14	薄い	usui	thin	adj.	3	2	1	1.333
15	否や	inaya	soon	noun	2	2	0	1.333
16	まとまり	matomari	unit	noun	3	1	2	1.25
17	少し	sukoshi	a little	adv	2	1	1	1.25
18	あっさり	assari	simple	adv.	3	2	1	1.167
19	広がる	hirogaru	spread	verb	3	2	1	1.083
20	層	sō	layer	noun	3	1	2	1.033
21	粒子	ryūshi	particle	noun	4	2	2	1.033

Tōmei 'clear' in a *sake* description has three usages: (1) as a description of the transparent appearance of the liquid, (2) as a synesthetic expression of the taste of the *sake*, and (3) as a metaphorical expression of cleanness. Of course, the boundaries of these classifications are often fuzzy.

Tōmei literally means the visual appearance of the liquid of the *sake* in the glass, i.e., 'transparent', 'colorless', or (liquid being) 'not cloudy'. In the evaluation of a *sake*, transparency is often emphasized, for transparency indicates good quality and condition. A special small cup called *janome* (meaning 'double circle', or literally, 'snake-eye') is used to judge the condition of *sake* (see Figure 2). A navy-blue double circle is painted on the bottom of a *janome. Sake* tasters check the color (i.e., colorlessness) and transparency of *sake* by setting it against the whiteness of the bottom of the *janome*. They judge its condition by checking the sharpness of the boundary of the double circle. If the boundary contrast is sharp, the *sake* is in sound condition.

Figure 2. *Janome*: A traditional *sake* tasting cup[11]

[Taste] As a metaphorical expression, *tōmei* 'clear' primarily represents the cleanness (*kiyoraka* [6]) of the sweet taste [3, 4, 5]. The sweetness is often directly called 'caster (superfine) sugar' [7] ('brown sugar' [37] implies a roasted sweet aroma).

Note that *tōmei* 'clear' is often used as a euphemistic expression for a taste which is too light, thin, or faint.

[Characteristic words] The image of *seiryōkan* 'cooling' [28] or *seiryū* 'clear stream' [14] is included in this category.

[Related Words] *Tōmei* 'clear' is considered related to expressions such as *assari* 'simple' [18], *karui* 'light' [25], and *awai* 'faint' [31].

11. Photo: Copyright (2019) by shige hattori / PIXTA. Adapted with permission.

4.2.5 Fukuyoka *'plump'*

Table 16. Concordance list for *fukuyoka* 'plump'

N	Word	Pron.	EngTrans	PoS	Total	LT	RT	Score
1	旨味	umami	umami	noun	16	0	16	7.4
2	味	aji	taste	noun	17	2	15	7.183
3	香り	kaori	scent	noun	16	3	13	5.983
4	甘い	amai	sweet	adj.	8	4	4	4.45
5	口あたり	kuchiatari	mouthfeel	noun	8	1	7	3.5
6	やわらかい	yawarakai	soft	adj.	6	4	2	3.1
7	香味	kōmi	flavor	noun	7	3	4	2.75
8	印象	inshō	impression	noun	6	1	5	2.7
9	広がる	hirogaru	spread	verb	5	2	3	2.4
10	厚み	atsumi	thickness	noun	7	2	5	2.283
11	感触	kanshoku	feel	noun	5	1	4	2.2
12	酒	sake	*sake*	noun	6	4	2	2.067
13	立つ	tatsu	stand	verb	8	5	3	1.8
14	生	nama	raw	noun	5	3	2	1.75
15	甘味	amami	sweetness	noun	4	2	2	1.7
16	思う	omou	think	verb	4	4	0	1.583
17	感じる	kanjiru	feel	verb	5	4	1	1.533
18	広がり	hirogari	spread	noun	5	2	3	1.533
19	味わい	ajiwai	taste	noun	3	0	3	1.5
20	純米	junmai	pure rice	noun	5	5	0	1.417

A scent expressed by *fukuyoka* 'plump' may be associated with a floral scent. However, in the description of *sake* taste, *fukuyoka* 'plump' mainly represents the umamiful [1] taste or flavor of the fermented rice and koji [24]. In this respect, *fukuyoka* 'plump' may be considered a technical term. (24) gives an example.

(24) Omachi naradewa no **kome no ajiwai** no fukuyoka-sa
'the plumpness of the **rice-taste**, unique for *Omachi* (a rice variety)'
for *Seikō* (SSI, 2010)

[Texture] *Fukuyoka* 'plump' co-occurs with words expressing texture and structure, as shown in (25). For texture, it mainly describes a texture of softness (*yawarakai* 'soft' [6]), roundness (*marui* 'round' [22]), and mouthfeel [5, 11].

[Structure] For structure, *fukuyoka* represents the swelling and spreading (*hirogari* [18]) or feelings of thickness (*atsumi* [10]) associated with a umamiful taste.

(25) ***marumi*** ga ari <u>fukuyoka na ajiwai</u> no naka ni mizumizushii san ga…
'(I feel) **roundness**, and juicy acidity in the <u>plump taste</u>…'
for *Sekai-Ittō*, Kumakusu (Matsuzaki, 1995)

4.2.6 Hanayaka *'gorgeous'*

Table 17. Concordance list for *hanayaka* 'gorgeous'

N	Word	Pron.	EngTrans	PoS	Total	LT	RT	Score
1	香り	kaori	scent	noun	22	0	22	9.7
2	香気	kōki	aroma	noun	15	1	14	7.033
3	立つ	tatsu	stand	verb	12	6	6	6.95
5	イチゴ	ichigo	strawberry	noun	6	3	3	1.9
6	印象	inshō	impression	noun	5	2	3	1.75
7	口中	kōchū	mouth	noun	6	3	3	1.65
8	香味	kōmi	flavor	noun	3	0	3	1.5
9	甘み	amami	sweetness	noun	3	1	2	1.25
10	メロン	meron	melon	noun	3	2	1	1.083
12	若々しい	wakawakashii	youthful	adj.	1	1	0	1
13	桃	momo	peach	noun	3	2	1	1
14	インパクト	inpakuto	impact	noun	4	0	4	0.95
15	感じる	kanjiru	feel	verb	3	0	3	0.95
16	とばくち	tobakuchi	beginning	noun	3	3	0	0.833
17	みずみずしい	mizumizushii	juicy	adj.	2	0	2	0.75
18	鼻先	hanasaki	nose tip	noun	2	2	0	0.75
19	ふくらむ	fukuramu	bulge	verb	2	2	0	0.667
20	最初	saisho	first	noun	2	2	0	0.667

[Dominance] *Hanayaka* 'gorgeous' is mainly used for flavor [1, 2, 8] rather than taste (*amami* 'sweetness' [9]).

[Flavor] In the context of a *sake* description, *hanayaka* 'gorgeous' implies the 'sharp' (*shāpu* [24]) and 'fresh' (*furesshu* [25]) flavor of the 'fruit' (*kajitsuka* [28]). There are many names for fruits on the concordance list: *ichigo* 'strawberry' [5], *meron* 'melon' [10], *momo* 'peach' [13], *ringo* 'apple' [26] (e.g., *hanayaka na meron no kaori* 'gorgeous flavor of melon').

[Timeline] The words for indicating time, especially the beginning point of the taste, are characteristic: *tobakuchi* 'beginning' [16], *saisho* 'first' [20]. *Tatsu* [3] (literal translation = stand) means the appearance of the flavor. *Hanasaki* 'tip of the nose' [18] indicates the entrance point of the flavor, that is, the first point of the chronological order of the flavor. An example is given in (26).

(26) **Hanasaki ni tatsu** ringo no yo na hanayaka de shāpu na kaori
'**around the tip of the nose**, apple-like gorgeous and sharp flavor **appear**'
for *Wakamidori, Nama* (Matsuzaki, 1995)

[Related words] *Hanayaka* 'gorgeous' is considered related to *shāpu* 'sharp' [24] and *furesshu* 'fresh' [25].

4.2.7 Maroyaka *'mellow'*

Table 18. Concordance list for *maroyaka* 'mellow'

N	Word	Pron.	EngTrans	PoS	Total	LT	RT	Score
1	旨味	umami	umami	noun	6	0	6	2.833
2	酒	sake	*sake*	noun	6	5	1	2.833
3	感じる	kanjiru	feel	verb	6	3	3	2.25
4	印象	inshō	impression	noun	4	0	4	1.7
5	甘味	amami	sweetness	noun	4	0	4	1.5
6	風味	fūmi	flavor	noun	3	0	3	1.5
7	味わい	ajiwai	taste	noun	3	1	2	1.5
8	酸味	sanmi	acidity	noun	4	1	3	1.45
9	熟成	jukusei	aging	noun	4	4	0	1.417
10	少ない	sukunai	less	adj.	2	2	0	1.333
11	くるりと	kururito	kururi	onoma	2	2	0	1.2
12	甘み	amami	sweetness	noun	4	0	4	1.15
13	そのもの	sonomono	itself	noun	1	0	1	1
14	なんとなく	nantonaku	vaguely	adv.	1	1	0	1
15	もたらす	motarasu	bring	verb	1	1	0	1
16	甘い	amai	sweet	adj.	2	0	2	1
17	口当たり	kuchiatari	mouthfeel	noun	2	2	0	1
18	思う	omou	think	verb	2	1	1	1
19	小さい	chiisai	small	adj.	1	1	0	1
20	流れ	nagare	flow	noun	2	0	2	1

[Dominance] In its literal meaning, *maroyaka* 'mellow' is a word for texture [17].

[Taste] When *maroyaka* 'mellow' modifies the basic taste, it represents a 'well-united' (e.g., *matomaru* [21]) taste with multiple elements, e.g., *umami* [1], *amami* 'sweetness' [5, 12, 16], and *sanmi* 'acidity' [8]. (27) gives an example with *ketsugō suru* 'unite'.

(27) **amami to sanmi** ga umaku ketsugō shite maroyaka na atokuchi…
'**sweetness and acidity** are well-united and mellow aftertaste (lasts)…'
for *Shokō* (Matsuzaki, 1995)

[Related words] *Maroyaka* 'mellow' is considered related to *odayaka* 'mild' [30] and *yawarakai* 'soft' [32].

4.2.8 Fukuzatsu *'complex'*

Table 19. Concordance list for *fukuzatsu* 'complex'

N	Word	Pron.	EngTrans	PoS	Total	LT	RT	Score
1	味	aji	taste	noun	15	2	13	7
2	香味	kōmi	flavor	noun	4	0	4	1.7
3	酸味	sanmi	acidity	noun	4	2	2	1.533
4	現われる	arawareru	appear	verb	2	2	0	1.5
5	なんだか	nandaka	somehow	adv.	1	1	0	1
6	含む	fukumu	contains	verb	1	1	0	1
7	香ばしい	kōbashii	fragrant	adj.	1	1	0	1
8	細かい	komakai	fine	adj.	1	1	0	1
9	多面性	tamensei	multifaceted	noun	2	0	2	1
10	感じる	kanjiru	feel	verb	3	1	2	0.917
11	混ざる	mazaru	mix	verb	2	2	0	0.833
12	印象	inshō	impression	noun	3	3	0	0.783
13	旨い	umai	delicious	adj.	2	1	1	0.75
14	苦味	nigami	bitterness	noun	3	2	1	0.733
15	渋味	shibumi	astringency	noun	3	3	0	0.733
16	見る	miru	look	verb	2	2	0	0.7
17	味わい	ajiwai	taste	noun	2	1	1	0.7
18	香り	kaori	scent	noun	2	2	0	0.667
19	少し	sukoshi	a little	adv.	2	0	2	0.667
20	混じる	majiru	mix	verb	2	2	0	0.533

[Dominance] *Fukuzatsu* 'complex' co-occurs with both taste [1, 3, 13, 14, 15, 17] and flavor [2, 7, 18, 26], e.g., *fukuzatsu na umami to shibumi* 'complex umami and astringency'.

[Taste] Terms expressing acidity, bitterness, and astringency often co-occur with the basic taste terms. These tastes may be thought of as the off-flavor. However, a small amount of 'acidity' (*sanmi* [3]), 'bitterness' (*nigami* [14]), and 'astringency' (*shibumi* [15]) can be 'mixed' (*mazaru* [11]) to produce a complex taste in an advantageous sense. One example with a few taste terms is given in (28).

(28) **sanmi, nigami ga karan-de** fukuzatsu na tenshon o…
'**acidity and bitterness are mixed**, and (rise) complexed tension'
for *Bizen no Sake-hitosuji, Hiden* (Matsuzaki, 1995)

[Related words] Several words to describe the delicacy of the *sake* are found in the list: *komakai* 'fine' [8], *sensai* 'delicate' [33], and *meikai* 'with clarity' [37]. At first sight, these words seem contradictory to a 'complex' (*fukuzatsu*) taste. However, to produce well-mixed [11], 'interlocked' (*irikun-da* [35]), multifaceted tastes and flavors, delicacy and fineness are essential. If a complex-taste *sake* loses its delicacy, the taste will have a complicated, cluttered feeling.

4.3 Summary

The chapter gives specialized definitions for 16 adjectives and adjectival nouns, clarifying their peripheral senses. It finds that aesthetic terms (the target terms in this chapter) can have a sense related to taste, flavor, dominance, structure, organoleptic feelings, texture, parts of the mouth, timeline, and movement. Although an ordinary dictionary does not provide these peripheral senses, understanding them is key to building up encyclopedic semantics.

5. Discussion

5.1 Clear is sweet

This chapter proposes a new method to abductively define the sense of aesthetic terms using words co-occurring with the target terms (the terms to be defined, i.e., aesthetic terms). More specifically, I adopt a *usage-based approach* to analyze the meanings of words depending on their domain (object), co-occurrence relationships, cultural backgrounds, or context.

What my corpus-based study shows is that in the domain of *sake* taste terms, the target term can acquire a nuanced meaning when one term frequently co-occurs with another. For example, if the word *tōmei* 'clear' has a strong co-occurrence tendency with the word *amami* 'sweetness', *tōmei* is expected to obtain the meaning of "sweet taste," beyond the literal meaning of "clear" or "transparent." This point is elaborated below in a comparison of the sense of *futoi* 'bold' and *tōmei* 'clear'. I argue there are two steps in these types of sense extensions (see Figure 3).

The Japanese word *futoi* 'bold' is a basic adjective, literally meaning "large in diameter or width," as in *futoi kubi* 'a thick neck'. It also has a metaphoric usage, *futoi koe* 'bold voice'. This usage suggests *futoi* is first extended to mean "large in degree"; in the next step, this is applied to the quality of voice to achieve the meaning "low and grave." If *futoi* is used to describe a taste, *futoi* must first refer to "strong in degree (of something)," assuming the same metaphoric extension takes place. So if we say *futoi umami* '(lit.) thick *umami*', we mean the *umami* taste is strong. If we disregard the frequency, it is possible to describe various degrees of taste, such as *futoi sanmi* 'bold acidity' or *futoi shibumi* 'bold astringency'. These expressions are generally understandable and not very poetic.

Interestingly, when these uses are encountered in the speech community of *sake*, *futoi* obtains the meaning of the word that frequently co-occurs with it. For instance, *futoi* 'bold' inherits the sense of *umami* from the entrenched use of *futoi umami* 'bold *umami*' or *tōmei* 'clear', the sense of sweetness from the entrenched use of *tōmei na amami* 'clear sweetness'.

This is not simply speculation but is corroborated by the following examples.

(29) marumi no aru futoi aji
'bold taste with roundness' For 'Tenpo-isui, Junmai-Ginjo' (Matsuzaki, 1995)

(30) zentai ni dosshiri to shita futoi aji
'massive and bold taste as a whole' For 'Ten-on, Ginjo' (Matsuzaki, 1995)

These examples are taken from reviews of *sake* in books and magazines. They are not very poetic, and readers can readily grasp their meaning. Notably, *futoi* 'bold' does not co-occur with *umami* (*futoi umami* 'bold umami') but with *aji* (*futoi aji* 'bold taste'). Critically, *futoi aji* 'bold taste' implies "*umami*," or to be more precise, "a strong degree of *umami*," showing that the sense of *umami* in *futoi* cannot be explained if only the first step of the metaphoric extension has been taken.

With some certainty, I can say readers in the *sake* community will agree the use of *futoi* 'bold' in (29) and (30) represents the sense of *umami*. Whether the use actually signifies *umami* itself must be verified by interviewing the tasters. Notably, this pattern of sense extension is not limited to *sake*. For example, in wine descriptions, *smooth* expresses that the degree of astringency is mild, whereas *rough* expresses that the astringency is strong. Likewise, *delicate* indicates a (low) degree of astringency, not saltiness or sweetness in wines, although none of the terms literally denotes the sense of "astringency" (cf. Broadbent, 1975/2020). In Cognitive Linguistics, this phenomenon is called conventionalization (or entrenchment in a person); that is, a word conventionally acquires a special meaning in the language use of a speech community (cf. Langacker 1987).

The process of how *futoi* 'bold' and *tōmei* 'clear' acquire new meanings is summarized in Figure 3.

As shown in Figure 3, the sense extension process has two stages. First a regular metaphor is used. Then, as a certain collocation (e.g., *futoi* 'bold' and *umami*, or *tōmei* 'clear' and sweetness) is more frequently used by the speech-community, a new shade of meaning "slides" from the word (umami; *amami* 'sweetness') that co-occurs with it. This becomes conventionalized, yielding a new meaning (*futoi* 'bold'; *tōmei* 'sweet'). As it is conventionalized, it becomes jargon.

The important point is that *futoi* 'bold' is jargon, and its meaning comes from the word *umami* (umamiful) that co-occurs with it. When the meaning of *futoi* 'bold' develops from the literal meaning via a metaphor, the meaning of "strong degree of taste" can be understood even by those unfamiliar with *sake* tasting.

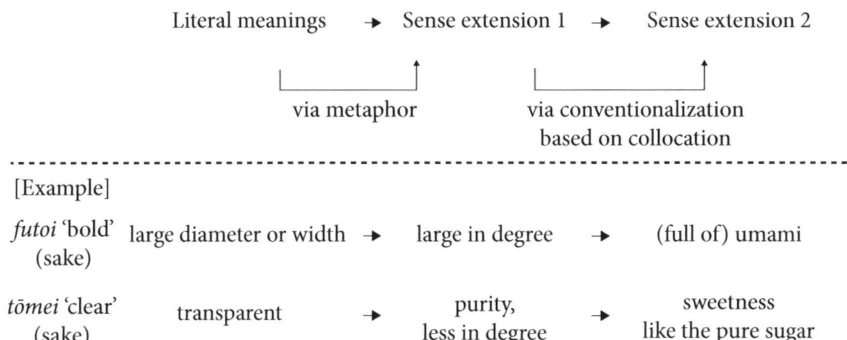

Figure 3. Sense extension when creating jargon

However, the nuance generated by "*umami*" appearing with *futoi* 'bold' cannot be understood by those outside the *sake* community, making it community-specific jargon. Similarly, when they use the wine-tasting term *rough*, wine tasters intend "tannic (not alcoholic) taste" and by *sharp wine*, they mean "fresh acidity." These meanings are jargon and, as such, are only valid in the wine community. Thus, in the context of wine, *futoi* 'bold' does not have a meaning of *umami*, although it can have the regular metaphorical sense of 'strong' or another specialized meaning in the wine community. In short, *tōmei* '(literally) clear can mean 'sweet' in the *sake* community, but this may not necessarily apply to a coffee community.

5.2 On Lehrer's approach to lexical relationships

This study seeks to grasp the peripheral senses of 16 adjective and adjectival nouns, meanings not likely found in a general dictionary. Relevant words for the target terms can be identified using a concordance list (i.e., words that co-occur with the target term). In general, the relevant words tend to be adjectivals on a concordance list; e.g., *karui* 'light' or *wakai* 'young' for the target term *furesshu* 'fresh' are both adjectives.

Lehrer (2009) points out that among the wine terms, those involving lexical relationships (synonymy, antonymy, class inclusion, and association) play a major role in understanding the meanings of wine vocabulary. I argue that the type of relationship is not especially critical in defining the tasting term. The important thing is that there is **some** relationship. The type of relationship cannot be determined *a priori* by the co-occurrence patterns or general determination. It might be argued that the specific relationship is not in one's knowledge, but can be understood through an experience of drinking a cup of *sake*. For a certain *sake*, *ereganto* 'elegant' may be a synonym of *furesshu* 'fresh', but for another, it may represent the opposite quality. We cannot determine the type of relationship unless we drink the *sake*, and we cannot tell whether there are any relationships at all in a couple of words without actually drinking. For this reason, I have used only the "relative words" for each target term.

6. Conclusion

In the description of taste, a word often has a unique sense in a specific context; e.g., *fukuyoka* 'plump' means 'umamiful flavor' in descriptions of *sake*. Applying a usage-based approach, in this chapter, I investigated whether the meaning of adjectives and adjectival nouns can be defined by examining a co-occurrence relationship of the terms that appear in a *sake* description corpus (120,000 words in Japanese). I first calculated the strength of the co-occurrence between the target term (the term to be defined) and the other words in the text. To measure the strength, I computed a concordance "score" using KH Coder, a text mining software package. Then, based on the computed co-occurrence scores, I defined the referent and the sense of the target term in a bottom-up and abductive fashion.

Using this approach, I defined 16 target terms (adjectives and adjectival nouns). Nearly all of the definitions are consistent with my language intuition for the target term in the context of *sake* description, affirming (at least in a subjective way) the validity of the approach. At the same time, the defining process described here depends on my (i.e., the taster's) language sense and tasting sense. Another individual may well give an alternative definition based on the same concordance list. However, if we accept a sense-making theory (Fukaya & Tanaka, 1996; Tanaka & Fukaya, 1998), such variation in making language sense is natural to human communication. The new approach presented in this chapter can be readily extended to an analysis of other drinks (and food), including wine and coffee, both Japanese and non-Japanese.[12]

Through its analysis of *sake* tasting terms, this chapter supports the idea that the definitions of terms are "encyclopaedic" rather than dictionary-based, a major theme of Cognitive Linguistics. It also corroborates the view that food-related media, such as *sake* tasting comments, function as a valuable source of information, especially in the domain of aesthetics.

12. I have been building corpora of *sake* (in Japanese), wine (JP / EN), chocolate (JP), ramen: also known as 'Chinese noodle'(JP), and perfumes (EN). These corpora can be shared with other researchers under particular conditions.

The sense of taste has long been neglected by aesthetic studies, and research on "verbalizing the sense of taste" seems to have taken a wrong turn. The tasting words lists created by sommeliers may help us articulate the tacit feelings of the taste, but their "object-motivated event construction" or "nominal way" of describing something (cf. Section 2.1) trivializes our personal experience of taste. To better describe the aesthetic quality (Sibley, 1959) of taste, I argue that we should use the theoretical lens of "emergence-motivated event construction" and study the functions of adjectives (and adjectival nouns). I believe the usage-based, encyclopaedic semantics of the adjectives for taste will open the door to the aesthetics of taste.

Funding

This work was supported by JSPS KAKENHI Grant Number 20K20127.

References

Broadbent, M. (1975/2020). *Wine Tasting* (English Edition). Academie du Vin.

Caballero, R. (2007). Manner-of-motion verbs in wine description. *Journal of Pragmatics*, *39*(12), 2095–2114. https://doi.org/10.1016/j.pragma.2007.07.005

Caballero, R. (2017). From the glass through the nose and the mouth: Motion in the description of sensory data about wine in English and Spanish. *Terminology*, *23*(1), 66–88. https://doi.org/10.1075/term.23.1.03cab

Dingemanse, M. (2011). The meaning and use of ideophones in Siwu (Unpublished doctoral dissertation). Max Planck Institute for Psycholinguistics/Radboud University, Nijmegen.

Dingemanse, M. (2012). Advances in the cross-linguistic study of ideophones. *Language and Linguistics Compass*, 6, 654–672. https://doi.org/10.1002/lnc3.361

Fukaya, M., & Tanaka, S. (1996). *<Kotoba> no Imizuke ron* [The sense-making theory of <words>]. Tokyo: Kinokuniya.

Fukushima, H. (2013). *Encyclopedia of sake terms*. Keio University.

Fukushima, H. (2019, August). Aesthetic terms for taste appreciation in Japanese. Paper presented at the 28th International Joint Conference on Artificial Intelligence (IJCAI-19), Macao.

Gauntner, J. (2011). *Sake handbook*. Retrieved from http://qut.eblib.com.au/patron/FullRecord.aspx?p=876525

Hasegawa, K. (2015). *Nihonshu techō* [Sake Handbook]. Tokyo: Gakken Publishing.

Higuchi, K. (2004). Quantitative analysis of textual data: differentiation and coordination of two approaches. *Sociological Theory and Methods*, *19*(1), 101–115. https://doi.org/10.11218/ojjams.19.101

Higuchi, K. (2016). *KH Coder 3 Reference Manual*. Retrieved from https://khcoder.net/en/manual_en_v3.pdf

Lakoff, G., & Johnson, M. (1980). *Metaphors we live by*. Chicago: University of Chicago Press.

Langacker, R. W. (2008). *Cognitive grammar: A basic introduction*. Oxford/New York: Oxford University Press. https://doi.org/10.1093/acprof:oso/9780195331967.001.0001

Lehrer, A. (1978). We drank wine, we talked, and a good time was had by all. *Semiotica*, *23*(3–4). https://doi.org/10.1515/semi.1978.23.3-4.243

Lehrer, A. (2009). *Wine & conversation* (2nd ed). Oxford/New York: Oxford University Press. https://doi.org/10.1093/acprof:oso/9780195307931.001.0001

López-Arroyo, B., & Roberts, R. P. (2014). English and Spanish descriptors in wine tasting terminology. *Terminology*, *20*(1), 25–49. https://doi.org/10.1075/term.20.1.02lop

Matsuura, T. (1992). Sake o ajiwau kotoba [Terms for tasting sake]. In I. Tajima & K. Niwa (Eds.), *Gendai Nihongo no kenkyū (Shohan)* [Contemporary Japanese study (first edition)]. Osaka: Izumi Shoin.

Matsuzaki, H. (1995). *Sake guidebook: Tastes of 1212*. Tokyo: Shibata-Shoten.

Otsuka, H. (2004). *Analysis for evaluated expressions of tasting Japanese sake*. Retrieved from: https://www.jstage.jst.go.jp/article/pjsai/JSAI04/0/JSAI04_0_147/_pdf/-char/ja

Otsuka, H., Suwa, M., & Yamaguchi, K. (2015). *Studies of expressions to taste Japanese sake by creating onomatopoeia*. Retrieved from: https://www.jstage.jst.go.jp/article/pjsai/JSAI2015/0/JSAI2015_2N5OS16b5/_pdf/-char/ja

Paradis, C., & Eeg-Olofsson, M. (2013). Describing sensory experience: the genre of wine reviews. *Metaphor and Symbol*, *28*(1), 22–40. https://doi.org/10.1080/10926488.2013.742838

Sibley, F. (1959). Aesthetic concepts. *The Philosophical Review*, *68*(4), 421–450. https://doi.org/10.2307/2182490

SSI. (2010). *Nihonshu encyclopedia for gourmet*. Tokyo: Tokyo-shoseki.

Tanaka, S., & Fukaya, M. (1998). *<Imizukeron> no tenkai* [The evolvement of the <sense-making theory>]. Tokyo: Kinokuniya.

Tummers, J., Heylen, K., & Geeraerts, D. (2005). Usage-based approaches in Cognitive Linguistics: A technical state of the art. *Corpus Linguistics and Linguistic Theory*, *1*(2), 225–261. https://doi.org/10.1515/cllt.2005.1.2.225

Utsunomiya, H. (2006). Flavor terminology and reference standards for sensory analysis of sake. *Journal of the Brewing Society of Japan*, *101*(10), 730–739. https://doi.org/10.6013/jbrewsocjapan1988.101.730

Appendix 1

In order to clarify what words co-occur with the target words (the adjectives and adjectival nouns listed above), KWIC (Key Words in Context), or simply "concordance," is used. With KWIC, we can analyze how a target word is used in the corpus. In this appendix, an example of KWIC using KH Coder, a text mining application, is shown. Figure AP-1 illustrates the KWIC for the word "flavor" in a wine tasting corpus.

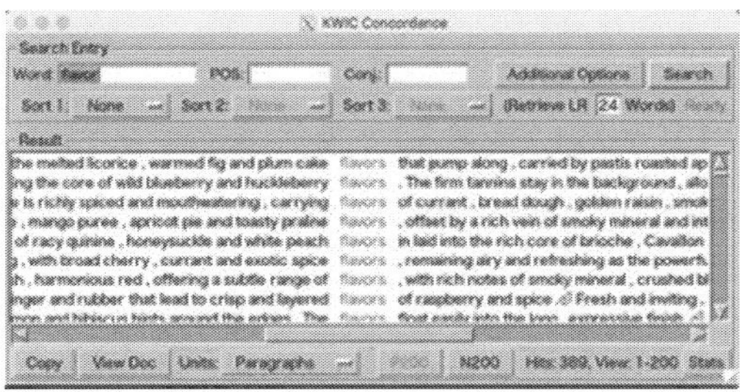

Figure AP-1. Window showing KWIC concordance results[13]

KH Coder is a very useful text mining tool. It provides statistics, multi-dimensional scale (MDS), word networks, and other helpful visuals.

> Using the Collocation Stats window in KH Coder (Figure AP-2), it is easy to determine which words frequently appear before and after the target word (or node word). In Figure AP-2, the statistics show that the word "hear" appears thrice in a position two words before (L2) and twice just before (L1) the node word "say." In addition, we see clearly that words like "Red," "Shirt," and "Porcupine" are often used in association with "say." (*KH Coder Reference Manual*: Higuchi, 2016, Revised)

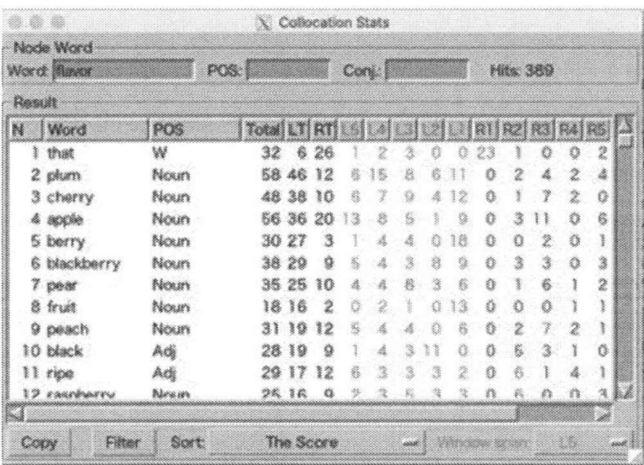

N	Word	POS	Total	LT	RT	L5	L4	L3	L2	L1	R1	R2	R3	R4	R5
1	that	W	32	6	26	1	2	3	0	0	23	1	0	0	2
2	plum	Noun	58	46	12	6	15	8	6	11	0	2	4	2	4
3	cherry	Noun	48	38	10	6	7	9	4	12	0	1	7	2	0
4	apple	Noun	56	36	20	13	8	5	1	9	0	3	11	0	6
5	berry	Noun	30	27	3	1	4	4	0	18	0	0	2	0	1
6	blackberry	Noun	38	29	9	5	4	3	8	9	0	3	3	0	3
7	pear	Noun	35	25	10	4	4	8	3	6	0	1	6	1	2
8	fruit	Noun	18	16	2	0	2	1	0	13	0	0	0	1	1
9	peach	Noun	31	19	12	5	4	4	0	6	0	2	7	2	1
10	black	Adj	28	19	9	1	4	3	11	0	0	5	3	1	0
11	ripe	Adj	29	17	12	6	3	3	3	2	0	6	1	4	1

Figure AP-2. Collocation statistics window

13. AP-1 and AP-2 are the screenshots of KH coder, captured by the author.

Appendix 2

Concordance *score* is calculated following. In the function *f(w)* shown below (from Higuchi, 2016, pp. 39–40), where l_1 is the frequency of a certain word *w* that appears just before the node word; l_2 is its frequency, two words before the node word; r_1 is its frequency just after the node word; and r_2 is its frequency, two words after the node word.

$$f(w) = \sum_{i=1}^{5} \frac{(li + ri)}{i}$$

In general, the greater the frequency that a certain word *w* appears before or after the node word ($l_i + r_i$), the larger the value *f(w)*. In calculating the value *f(w)*, frequencies ($l_i + r_i$) are divided by "*i*," which weighs the frequencies according to their distance from the node word. Thus, words that appear nearer to the node word (i.e., with a smaller "*i*") have greater weight than those that occur five words before or after the node word. In this formula, the frequencies of words that appear just before and after are simply added, since they are divided by unity.

CHAPTER 8

A frame-semantic approach to Japanese taste terms

Kei Sakaguchi
Tohoku Gakuin University

This chapter offers a frame-semantic account of the meanings of Japanese taste terms, analyzing 5,620 instances of collocations, consisting of an adjectival taste term and a noun, such as *shibui kao* 'lit. astringent face'. It first defines the literal sense of the taste terms, identifying what frame is evoked by not only using but also adjusting the definitions and set of arguments from FrameNet (an English resource) to fit the case of Japanese. It then considers the sense extensions. The findings include the following: both the literal and the extended senses can imply (un)desirability; the semantic change can be accounted for by identifying frames of both literal and figurative uses that prop up the lexical meanings.

Keywords: taste terms, adjectives, frame semantics, metaphor, pejoration

1. Introduction

The literature abounds with studies on the meanings of taste terms (Backhouse, 1994; Muto, 2002a, 2002b, 2015; Seto, 2003, among others). Some investigate the semantic relation of taste terms (e.g., Kim, 2018; Kunihiro, 1982; Yamada, 1972) or polysemous senses of taste terms (e.g., Minashima, 2005; Muto, 2001, 2002a, 2002b, 2015; Sakaguchi, 2014, 2015; Seto, 2003), whereas others attempt to verify Williams's (1976) hypothesis on the unidirectionality of synaesthetic metaphors whereby a certain directionality of semantic extension obtains among the terms belonging to a specific sense modality, including taste (e.g., Kusumi, 1988; Seto, 2003; Sakai, 2008; Shinohara & Nakayama, 2011; see also Tsujimura, this volume).

It is generally agreed that Japanese taste terms, such as *amai* 'sweet', are polysemous, with at least some of their extended senses attributed to figuration. Many of the details, however, remain unsettled. These include: which taste terms bear a particular relation with other taste terms, such as antonymy; whether such a relation applies only to the basic senses of the taste terms or can cover the extended

https://doi.org/10.1075/celcr.25.08sak

senses; which theory can most effectively explain the (in)validity of Williams's (1976) unidirectionality hypothesis on synaesthetic metaphor; which concept is best suited to elucidate the nature of polysemy; and how the mechanisms of semantic extensions are best captured.

This chapter investigates how Japanese taste terms are used in written language, identifying how they acquire extended or metaphorical meanings. Six Japanese taste terms (cf. Backhouse, 1994) are chosen for investigation:[1] *oishī* 'delicious', *amai* 'sweet', *nigai* 'bitter', *suppai* 'sour', *shibui* 'astringent' and *shoppai* 'salty'. *Oishī* 'delicious' is not a taste term proper – in Seto (2003), it is classed as a term of a taste evaluation – but it is included here as it is a term expressing savoriness, commonly used as a taste term in the field of physiology.

The chapter departs from previous work in the following ways. First, it uses frame semantics (Fillmore, 1982, 1985) as the basic analytical framework, thus enabling me to detail the speakers' encyclopedic knowledge associated with the taste term. It partly builds on Sakaguchi (2014, 2015), but refines the details of the definitions specific to the evoked frame, given a taste term, such as "the `Chemical-sense_description` frame."

Second, the chapter pays special attention to characterizing implicit desirability or undesirability ("(un)desirability," henceforth) of taste terms, little discussed in the literature (cf. Muto, 2015). The chapter empirically shows the involvement of implicit (un)desirability in taste terms, drawing on data from the Balanced Corpus of Contemporary Written Japanese (see Section 2). Specifically, it examines the collocational patterns of the target taste term, X, that appears in the [X *te* Y] construction (e.g., *amaku te umai ichigo* 'sweet [X] and delicious [Y] strawberries') and uses the context of this construction to determine whether the target taste term implies (un)desirability. It discusses implicit (un)desirability for both the basic and the extended senses; some of the latter are considered in terms of melioration and pejoration (see Winter (2019) for an evaluative function of sensory adjectives in English).

Third, the chapter discusses metaphor, modeling after Sullivan (2013), who offers a novel account of the nature of metaphoric language, integrating various insights, in particular, from frame semantics (Fillmore, 1982, 1985) and conceptual

1. Backhouse (1994) suggests there are four basic taste terms (*amai* 'sweet', *karai* 'pungent', *nigai* 'bitter', and *shibui* 'astringent') and one borderline case *suppai* 'sour', whose distinction is determined on the basis of Berlin and Kay's (1969) criteria for defining basic color terms. *Suppai* is classed "borderline" as the judgements involve both "accepted" and "rejected." This chapter does not investigate *Karai* 'pungent' because pungent is not classified as a taste, but a sensation physiologically.

metaphor theory (CMT) (Lakoff, 1993; Lakoff & Johnson, 1980), thereby offering a different perspective on the much discussed issue of metaphors of taste terms.[2]

The remainder of the chapter is organized as follows: Section 2 describes the data; Section 3 introduces the basic notions of frame semantics; Section 4 offers an analysis of taste terms; Section 5 recasts the findings from the perspective of frame semantics and conceptual metaphor; finally, Section 6 contains a conclusion.

2. Data

Data were collected from the Balanced Corpus of Contemporary Written Japanese (BCCWJ) constructed by the National Institute for Japanese Language and Linguistics (NINJAL). The corpus contains as many as 104.3 million words covering genres such as weblogs, novels, and white papers. BCCWJ covers a wide range of written Japanese, including some food-related media. Since the chapter analyzes not only literal meanings, but also figurative meanings, this corpus matches its goal. To be precise, I collected [Adj+N] collocations of *oishī* 'delicious', *amai* 'sweet', *nigai* 'bitter', *suppai* 'sour', *shibui* 'astringent' and *shoppai* 'salty' to investigate how these words are used both literally and figuratively in daily language. Table 1 shows the distribution of the data.

Table 1. List of collected data

Lexical Unit	Translation	Tokens [A+N]	Types of N	Figurative use
oishī	delicious	2,805	672	35 (5%)
amai	sweet	1,899	491	269 (55%)
nigai	bitter	484	138	65 (47%)
shibui	astringent	287	128	116 (91%)
suppai	sour	112	54	1 (2%)
shoppai	salty	33	21	3 (14%)
	Total:	**5,620**	**1,504**	**489 (33%)**

Table 1 shows the token frequency of collocations consisting of a taste term and a noun such as *oishī hanashi* 'delicious story' (indicated under "Tokens [A+N]") and the type frequency of the noun (indicated under "Types of noun"). For the latter,

2. This chapter focuses on metaphorical uses of taste terms. It is possible to use adjectives from other sematic type (e.g. *yawarakai* 'soft') as a taste term, as discussed in Fukushima (this volume), who examines metaphorical usages of adjectives to describe the taste of *sake*. In our case, taste terms are in the source domain, whereas in Fukushima's case, non-taste terms are in the source domain, indicating that the direction of mapping is opposite.

I manually counted the type frequency of the figurative usage (indicated under "Figurative use").

As shown in Table 1, *amai* 'sweet', *nigai* 'bitter' and *shibui* 'astringent' have a higher frequency of figurative use. Interestingly, literal use of *shibui* 'astringent' is quite rare. The figurative case of *suppai* 'sour' is also infrequent but is often found in its variant form *sui* used in idioms such as *sui mo amai mo* (lit. both sourness and sweetness), which means good and bad experiences.

3. Framework: What does it mean to take a frame-semantic approach?

To consider the data I collected, shown in Table 1, I employ a frame-semantic approach, whose basic concepts are outlined below.

3.1 Two types of frame: Cognitive and linguistic

As noted in Fillmore and Baker (2009), there are two types of frames: cognitive frames and linguistic frames. The former is 'invoked' to make sense of given information (Fillmore & Baker, 2009, pp. 314–316). This encyclopedic knowledge includes cultural settings or experiences which cannot be directly associated with linguistic forms. For example, when we see and make sense of a post on Twitter with the #MeToo hashtag, the post may invoke in us a certain cognitive frame whereby we understand that it expresses someone's voice about sexual harassment. The linguistic form 'me too' has never had such a meaning, and the form itself does not help our interpretation. To understand it, we need to associate with it our knowledge about the recent chain of news and the contemporary movement against sexual harassment. The second frame, the linguistic frame, is 'evoked' directly by linguistic forms. For example, when we read the sentence, *I bought the book for $10*, we understand who the buyer was, what he or she bought, how much it cost, and the existence of an implicit seller. Evocation of the linguistic frame enables the interpreter to understand the whole structure of the event. Even if one participant is not verbalized in the sentence, we may know it exists. This process of understanding the sentence is facilitated by the linguistic clues, i.e., the linguistic frame. To better understand the difference between frame invocation and evocation, let us observe the following statement by Fillmore, which comes from an interview done by Andor (2010):

> when humans face particular situations, they can "invoke" frames (from their personal *mental framicon* – I just made that up, adapted from 'mental lexicon') to help them make sense of those situations, but the words we encounter can "evoke" frames by virtue of their conventional association with them.
>
> (Andor, 2010, p. 158)

The structured knowledge that we use to understand language is automatically determined if frames are "evoked" by linguistic forms. On the other hand, conventional (or cultural) knowledge to understand the situation must be "invoked" by people's actively, and is not determined automatically by a given situation. By this distinction, it can be said that the aim of frame semantics is to investigate the structured knowledge that is evoked by linguistic forms and used by human to understand languages.

3.2 Components of frames

In frame semantics, participants in a particular event are called frame elements (FEs). FEs are classified into two types: core and non-core FEs. A core-FE is a participant that must occur within the construction of the sentence and "instantiates a conceptually necessary component of a frame,[3] while making the frame unique and different from other frames" (Ruppenhofer et al., 2016, p. 23). In contrast, non-core FEs do not "introduce additional, independent or distinct events from the main reported event" (Ruppenhofer et al., 2016, p. 24).[4]

FEs can be identified in the definition of each frame, as provided by FrameNet (https://framenet.icsi.berkeley.edu/fndrupal/). In the case of *I bought the book for $10*, the word *bought (buy)* evokes a frame called `Commerce_buy`,[5] defined by FrameNet as follows:[6]

> `Commerce_buy` frame definition:
> These are words describing a basic commercial transaction involving a Buyer and a Seller exchanging Money and Goods, taking the perspective of the Buyer. The words vary individually in the patterns of frame element realization they allow. For example, the typical pattern for the verb BUY: Buyer buys Goods from Seller for Money. (FrameNet)

The `Commerce_buy` frame has two core FEs {Buyer, Goods}, and other props such as Money, Seller, and Place are non-core FEs. The definition above shows the relation among FEs.

3. Because of some constructional effects, core frame elements may not be verbalized in the sentence.

4. Non-core frame elements are also called peripheral frame elements.

5. In the literature of frame semantics, the name of the frame is written in courier_new font, and the names of frame elements are given in small capitalized letters as follows: FRAME_ELEMENTS.

6. FrameNet is an ongoing project to make an online dictionary of frames and provides detailed information on frames.

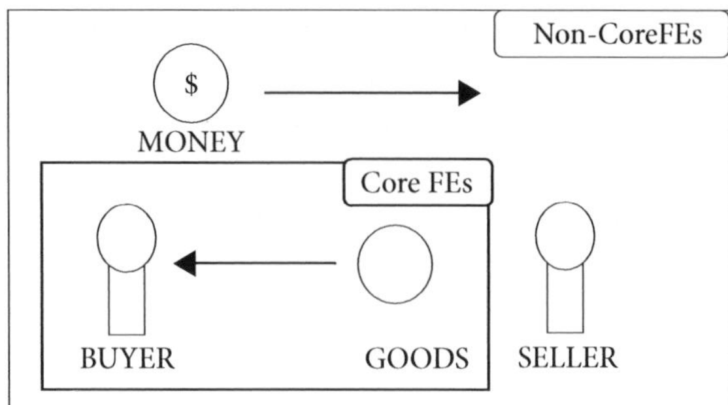

Figure 1. `Commerce_buy` frame (simplified)

Figure 1 shows the simplified relation in the above example. The inner box gives the set of core FEs; these are the central components of the commercial transaction, with the perspective on the buyer. The outer box shows the set of non-core FEs; these are not central to the event but are crucial to understand the whole structure of the event. By using these definitions, it is possible to annotate the sentence to clearly indicate which arguments are realized in it:

(1) [$_{\text{BUYER}}$ I] bought^{Target} [$_{\text{GOODS}}$ the book] [$_{\text{MONEY}}$ for $10].

3.3 Words-frames-meanings relation and frame-to-frame relation

In frame semantics, polysemy is analyzed in terms of divergence in the frames evoked (cf. Ruppenhofer et al., 2016). This relation among words, frames, and meanings is described in Figure 2.

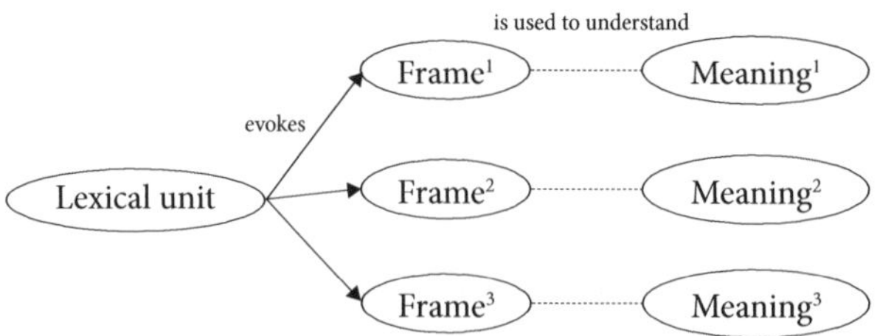

Figure 2. Words-frames-meanings relation

As the figure suggests, if one lexical unit has three different meanings, that lexical unit can evoke three different frames. Once we focus on the relation among frames, however, this relation will be represented differently, as in Figure 3, which shows the relation among frames, or the frame-to-frame relation, and this relation demonstrates the hierarchical structure of frames. In this figure, Frame^1 works as a mother node, and all the core FEs are inherited by Frame^2. Therefore, Frame^1 and Frame^2 have the relation of a so-called "is-a relation." Meanwhile, Frame^1 and Frame^3 have a "using" relation, showing that the child frame (Frame^3) is a specific case of a mother frame without the need to inherit the FEs of the mother frame (Frame^1). Higher level frames in this hierarchy are more abstract than lower level ones.

In addition to the hierarchical relation, there is a horizontal relation among frames. One of these is the relation between Frame^2 and Frame^4, also called a metaphor relation. Frame^2 works as a source domain and Frame^4 as a target domain. This relation is well analyzed by Sullivan (2013), reinforcing the conceptual metaphor theory (cf. Lakoff, 1993; Lakoff & Johnson, 1980).

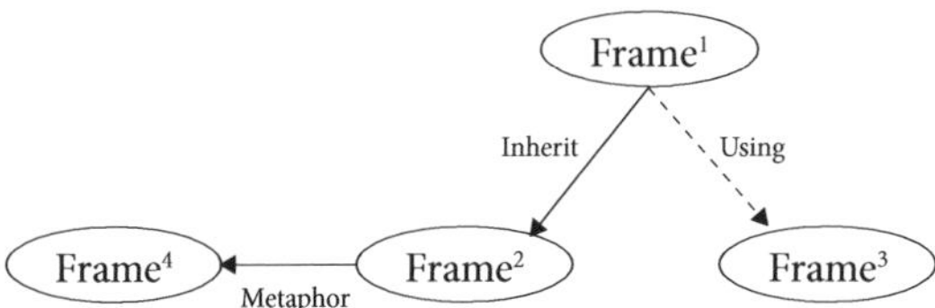

Figure 3. Frame-to-frame relation

The next section identifies which frames are evoked by taste terms, applying the concepts from frame semantics described above.

4. Analysis

This section has four subsections. Subsection 4.1 identifies which frames are evoked by basic taste terms. Subsection 4.2 demonstrates how basic taste terms used literally have implicit (un)desirability from a constructional point of view. Subsection 4.3 examines how implicit (un)desirability is preserved in the extended meanings, arguing that (un)desirability becomes the core component of extended meanings. Subsection 4.4 proposes a possible theory for semantic extension of taste terms by detecting frames that also prop up the understanding of figurative meanings of taste terms.

4.1 A frame for taste terms

4.1.1 *Literal usage*

As a first step of the frame-semantic approach to lexical meaning, it is essential to identify the frame evoked by words in literal usage. For example, Sakaguchi (2014, 2015) proposes taste adjectives evoke the `Chemical-sense_description` frame. The following definition of this frame is taken from FrameNet:

> `Chemical-sense_description` frame definition:
> This frame covers the descriptions of tastes and smells, and has one main frame element, PERCEPTUAL_SOURCE. The frame element SENSORY_ ATTRIBUTE occurs mainly with the words taste, flavour, and smell.
> Core Fes: PERCEPTUAL_SOURCE, SENSORY_ATTRIBUTE
> Core FE definitions:
> PERCEPTUAL_SOURCE is used for the entity that is being described. A recipe can stand in for a PERCEPTUAL_SOURCE which is a kind of food.
> SENSORY_ATTRIBUTE is used for words that describe the perception itself.
> (FrameNet)

This frame has one non-core FE, DEGREE, and it is possible to add the intensifier *totemo* 'very' as shown in (2). The definition above also suggests that nouns like *recipe* can be modified by words evoking this frame (see (3)), even if they do not denote direct perceptual sources, such as foods, meals, or drinks. This construal is possible via a metonymic reference (cf. Radden & Kövecses, 1999), where the recipe stands for the dish it produces, which can be delicious. In addition, the frame element SENSORY_ATTRIBUTE explains some cases of synesthetic metaphors (cf. Seto, 2003), shown in (4), where the taste term is used to describe *nioi*, the term expressing smell.

(2) oishī niku
delicious meat
[$_{\text{DEGREE}}$ totemo] oishī^{Target} [$_{\text{PERCEPTUAL\_SOURCE}}$ niku] 'very delicious meat'

(3) oishī reshipi
delicious recipe
oishī^{Target} [$_{\text{PERCEPTUAL\_SOURCE}}$ reshipi] 'delicious recipe'

(4) oishī nioi
delicious smell
oishī^{Target} [$_{\text{SENSORY\_ATTRIBUTE}}$ nioi] 'delicious smell'

In the data I examined, *suppai* 'sour', *nigai* 'bitter', *shoppai* 'salty', and *amai* 'sweet' occur in the collocational patterns that parallel (2) and (4), but metonymic type collocations such as (3) do not.

4.1.2 *Delicious face and delicious restaurant?*

In English, the phrases *delicious face* and *delicious restaurant* seem unnatural (see footnote 8). However, the literal word-for-word translations into Japanese, (5) and (6) respectively, sound completely natural.[7]

---

7. The string of letters and digits indicates the identification number of the example of BCCWJ.

(5) oishī kao (lit. delicious face)
torotoro no shokkan ni oishī kao (OY03_09510)
fluffy GEN texture DAT delicious face
'the face of feeling delicious for the food which has fluffy texture'

(6) oishī resutoran (lit. delicious restaurant)
mura de ichiban oishī resutoran no na wa shaa da
village in the best delicious restaurant GEN name TOP Shaa COP
'the name of the best restaurant (which serves the most delicious foods or drinks) in the village is Shaa.'

It is difficult to detect what frame elements are borne by the nouns in (5) and (6) using the `Chemical-sense_description` frame. Instead, I argue (5) involves an `Emotion_directed` frame, following the insight from previous literature, which considers SENSORY adjectives such as TASTE adjectives to be a subcase of EMOTION adjectives (cf. Nishio, 1972; Yakame, 2008). The `Emotion_directed` frame is evoked by emotion-related lexical units, as indicated by the FrameNet definition below:

> `Emotion_directed` frame definition:
> The adjectives and nouns in this frame describe an EXPERIENCER who is feeling or experiencing a particular emotional response to a STIMULUS or about a TOPIC. There can also be aCIRCUMSTANCE under which the response occurs or a REASON that the STIMULUS evokes the particular response in the EXPERIENCER.
> Core FEs: EVENT, STIMULUS, TOPIC, EXPERIENCER, EXPRESSOR, STATE, REASON
> Core FE definitions (selected):
> EXPERIENCER is the person or sentient entity that experiences or feels the emotions.
> EXPRESSOR marks expressions that indicate a body part, gesture or other expression of the EXPERIENCER that reflects his or her emotional state. They describe a presentation of the experience or emotion denoted by the adjective or noun. (FrameNet)

In other words, this frame explains the understanding of a human's emotion-related event, stimuli, and reaction. As noted above, in Japanese, some taste terms have characteristics similar to those of EMOTION adjectives. However, the sensation triggered by some perceptual stimuli should be distinguished from emotions, and it is impossible to add the frame element EXPRESSOR to the `Chemical-sense_description` frame. Accordingly, I combine the two frames, `Emotion_directed` and `Chemical-sense_description`, to account for (5). I call this presumptive frame the `Sensation_directed` frame. The frame-to-frame relation is shown below:

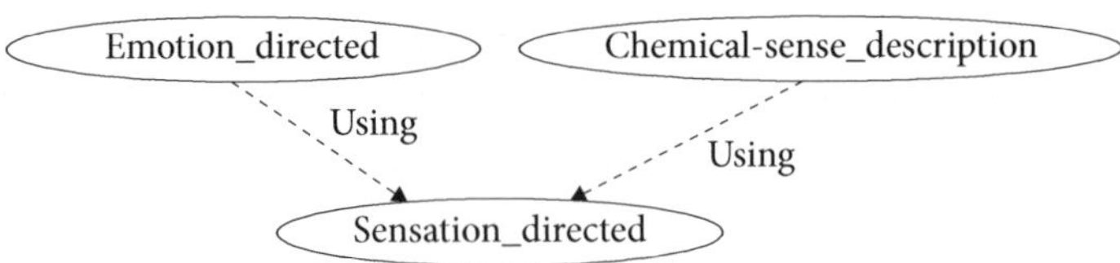

Figure 4. `Sensation_directed` frame and its frame-to-frame relation

> `Sensation_directed` frame definition:
> The adjectives that evoke this frame describe an EXPERIENCER who is experiencing a sensation and response to a STIMULUS (PERCEPTUAL_SOURCE). There can also be a CIRCUMSTANCE under which the response occurs or a REASON that the STIMULUS evokes the particular response in the EXPERIENCER. In addition, EXPRESSOR reflects the sensation of EXPERIENCER.
> Core FEs: EVENT, STIMULUS (PERCEPTUAL_SOURCE), TOPIC, EXPERIENCER, EXPRESSOR, STATE, REASON

This combinational frame uses the two frames introduced previously. Based on this definition, (5) can be annotated as below:

(5′) oishī kao
delicious face
oishī ^{Target} [$_{\text{EXPRESSOR}}$ *kao*]

Turning next to the case of (6), I argue that this can be accounted for by an addition of non-core FEs to the `Chemical-sense_description` frame. In English, it sounds unnatural when *delicious* is placed as part of the predicate to denote positive evaluation of the restaurant: cf. (7a) vs. (7b/c).[8]

(7) a. ?This restaurant is delicious.
b. This restaurant serves delicious meals.
c. The meals of this restaurant are delicious.

Frames on FrameNet are constructed based on naturally occurring English data recorded in the British National Corpus (BNC); consequently, they reflect the selection and the natural combination of the target lexical unit and its subject or modified nouns. For instance, *delicious* naturally occurred with nouns which stands for something to eat or drink, and not with nouns of places or time.

8. An anonymous reviewer pointed out that "delicious restaurants" are attested expressions on blogs. However, I treat the phrase as unnatural based on the fact that it was verified as such by one of my native speaker informants; furthermore, the BNC corpus contains no tokens of "delicious restaurant"/"restaurant is/was [and other be-verbs] delicious."

Therefore, non-core FEs, such as Place and Time, are not propped up by the `Chemical-sense_description` frame. In contrast, Japanese taste adjectives can modify words which bear the role of these FEs as seen in (6). These collocations can be analyzed by adding a set of non-core FEs (cf. Ruppenhofer et al., 2016, p. 24), Place, Manner, Means, and Time. Accordingly, (6) can be annotated as follows:

(6′) oishī ^{Target} [$_{\text{Place}}$ resutoran] (lit. delicious restaurant)

With the aid of this addition of non-core FEs, other examples can be similarly analyzed:

(8) oishī ^{Target} [$_{\text{Time}}$ kisetsu] (lit. delicious season)
nihon wa ima tottemo oishī kisetsu desu.
Japan TOP now very delicious season COP.POL
'Japan is now in the season of delicious foods'

These examples are similar to the setting-subject construction explained in Langacker (1990, 2008). In frame semantics, the "setting" of cognitive grammar is not used as a concept, but non-core FEs may function as a substitute. As seen above in (6′) and (8), Place and Time can be head nouns modified by taste terms. Superficially, they are in the position of an argument of an adjective. In cognitive grammar, the appearance of a word such as *kisetsu* 'season' is explained as a case of profile-shift. The frame-semantic approach makes it much clearer what part of the setting is profiled. In (6′), the Place of the event, the restaurant, is profiled, while the particular season, namely Time, is profiled in (8). This type of profile-shift cannot occur in English TASTE adjectives, as seen in the infelicity of (7a).

4.2 Implicit (un)desirability of taste terms

This section argues that each basic taste term (*amai* 'sweet', *suppai* 'sour', *nigai* 'bitter', and *shoppai* 'salty') has implicit (un)desirability in its literal meanings, drawing on the [Adj-*te*-Adj] construction to make the argument.

Odani (2012) suggests the concatenation of adjectives in the [Adj-*te*-Adj] (hereinafter A^1 refers to the first Adj, and A^2 refers to the second) construction, such as (9), follows two different semantic patterns.

(9) a. chīsaku-te akai ichigo
small-CONJ red strawberry
'small and red strawberry'

b. amaku-te umai ichigo
sweet-CONJ delicious strawberry
'sweet and thus delicious strawberry'

The first pattern is co-occurrence, in which a meaning or sensation of A^1 co-occurs with that of A^2. (9a) is an example of this type; it expresses that *a strawberry is small* and *a strawberry is red*, with the meanings of *small* and *red* co-occurring. The second pattern is order, in which the construction expresses the iconic order of the sensation or construal by the experiencer; i.e., A^1 is conceptualized first and A^2 follows, and as a subtype of this pattern, A^1 causes A^2. (9b) reflects the order of the conceptualization of the experiencer. The experiencer first profiles the meaning of A^1 and then shifts to A^2. In this example, A^1 (sweetness) functions as a reason for A^2 (deliciousness).

Drawing on the characteristic whereby adjectives with a -*te* form can reflect a causal relation, as in (9b), I will take this constructional meaning as a testing ground to examine the (un)desirability of taste terms. If one taste term (say X) has desirability in the literal usage, this taste term X is predicted to collocate with positive words much more often than with negative words, and vice versa if X has undesirability.

I examined the frequency of [X *te* Y] with each taste adjective using the BCCWJ and classified the value of Y (positive or negative). The result is shown in Table 2; in the table, "frequency" refers to the token number of the literal use of [X-*te* Y]; [X-*te*-Y(+)] indicates a collocation of an adjectival taste term with words of positive evaluation, wherein all the counted examples are taste-related; the evaluation of [X-*te*-Y(−)] is the opposite of [X-*te*-Y(+)].

Table 2. Co-occurrence in the [X-*te*-Y] construction

Lexical unit	Translation	[X-*te*-Y(+)]	[X-*te*-Y(−)]	Frequency
amai	sweet	87	6	196
shibui	astringent	0	1	34
nigai	bitter	2	15	33
suppai	sour	2	6	8
shoppai	salty	2	5	196

As shown in Table 2, *amai* 'sweet' tends to have desirability and to collocate with positive words. The other taste terms, *nigai* 'bitter', *shibui* 'astringent', *suppai* 'sour', and *shoppai* 'salty', tend to have undesirability. Needless to say, sourness, bitterness, and saltiness may not be the only reason for undesirable taste, and there are many delicious sour/bitter/salty foods.

Kim (2018) points out that these terms have negative/positive images that occur alongside their sensory meanings. As Kim's (2018) note is based on introspection, the result summarized in Table 2 can lend support to Kim's (2018) description.

The next step is to examine whether the implicit (un)desirability is preserved in the extended meanings. In frame semantics, positive/negative evaluation is marked as a parameter called "semantic type" (cf. Ruppenhofer et al., 2016, p. 15). For example, the English *delicious* always denotes positive evaluation of foods or drinks, and, therefore, its semantic type is marked as Positive_judgment. Although this parameter is not fully applied to the present FrameNet database, it is useful to clarify one aspect of Japanese taste terms.

To sum up, this section has argued that all the taste terms evoke the `Chemical-sense_description` frame and the `Sensation_directed` frame, but the semantic type should be differentiated as shown in Table 3.

Table 3. Frames and semantic type for literal usages of Japanese taste terms

Lexical Units		Semantic Type	Frames
oishī	delicious	Positive_judgement	• `Chemical-sense_description` • `Sensation_directed`
amai	sweet		
shibui	astringent	Negative_judgement	
nigai	bitter		
suppai	sour		
shoppai	salty		

As discussed above, *oishī* 'delicious' and *amai* 'sweet' tend to have implicit desirability, and, therefore, their semantic type can be marked as Positive_ judgement. In contrast, *nigai* 'bitter', *shibui* 'astringent', *suppai* 'sour', and *shoppai* 'salty' tend to have undesirability and are thus marked as Negative_judgement.

4.3 Preservation of (un)desirability in figurative usages

As argued in Subsection 4.2, basic taste terms tend to have implicit (un)desirability along with their sensory meanings. This section shows how implicit (un)desirability is preserved in some examples of figurative use of taste terms. Consider the examples below:

(10) nigai keiken
bitter experience

(11) nigai omoide/kioku
bitter memory

(12) nigai kao
bitter face
'face that reflects unpleasant feeling'

As shown in (10) and (11), *nigai* 'bitter' is used figuratively to denote the undesirability or unpleasantness of abstract things or to express uncomfortableness towards those things. This sense is similar to the figurative use of *bitter* in English. In (12), *nigai* 'bitter' occurs with *kao* 'face', and it denotes not only the face of a person eating bitter food, but also a face that expresses the experiencer's unpleasant feeling. Hence, *nigai kao* 'bitter face' can be interpreted both literally and figuratively.[9] The data I examined reveal 65 different types of figurative use of *nigai* (see Table 1), all with negative meanings.

As seen in Section 4.2, *shoppai* 'salty', used literally, tends to have undesirability. Its figurative use also has negative meanings, as exemplified below:

(13) shoppai uriage
salty sales
'disappointing sales'

(14) shoppai kao
salty face
'a face that shows discomfort'

As illustrated in (13), *shoppai* 'salty' means disappointment in figurative usage. Example (14) has some similarity with (12), and it denotes the discomfort experienced by a person. This possibility of multiple interpretations in this instance is the same as for *nigai kao* 'bitter face'. *Shoppai* or *shio* 'salt' connotatively implies some kind of deficiency. This point is reiterated in the following example, where *shio* 'salt' appears as part of a compound:

(15) shio taiō
salt response
'cold reception'

Shio-taiō can be translated as 'cold reception', following the definition of an online dictionary of Japanese (JapanDict).[10] It is a relatively new expression to denote an unwelcoming reaction to others. This negative meaning/image is similar to the figurative use of *shoppai* 'salty'.

As noted in Section 2, figurative usage of *suppai* 'sour' is quite rare, and only one example appears in the data:

9. The former interpretation is based on the metonymy. In this respect, this meaning results from metonymic extension, so it can be classified as a figurative, but it still relates to taste. Hereinafter, literal meaning includes the sense which relates to taste.

10. https://www.japandict.com [Accessed on August 16, 2019]

(16) *suppai omoi* (lit. sour feeling) 'disconsolate feeling'
seikaku no ran o miru-to mata suppai omoi ni nattari
personality GEN field ACC see-CONJ again sour feeling DAT become
shimasu (LBp4_00027)
do.POL
'When I read the field of my personality (of personality assessment), it made me feel disconsolate.'

In (16) *suppai* expresses disconsolateness, suggesting a semantic extension toward a negative side.[11] A disconsolate feeling is often expressed by the adjectival compound *ama-zuppai* (sweet-sour). This compound has a meaning similar to *bitter-sweet* in English. These words denote an indescribable mixture of good and bad feelings or memories. In this compound, *ama* (the stem of *amai*) expresses the positive side, and *suppai* expresses the negative side.

Amai 'sweet' also preserves its desirability in its extended senses. Its range of extended meanings is wider than other taste terms, some of which can be translated naturally and meaningfully in English (e.g., *sweet voice* (18)). Consider the following:

(17) amai kao (lit. sweet face) 'sweet(beautiful) face'
manga no kare wa yaya ronge no, moo-chotto amai kao nano
cartoon GEN he TOP a.little long-hair GEN, little more sweet face FP
'In the cartoon, he has a little long hair and a little more sweet face.' (OY15_04680)

(18) amai koe
sweet voice
'sweet(beautiful) voice'

(19) amai seikatsu
sweet life
'lovely life'

(20) amai fun'iki
sweet mood
'good mood'

(21) a. amai kotoba
sweet words
'tempting words'
b. amai yūwaku
sweet temptation
'strong temptation'

11. Kim (2018) collected data from BCCWJ, arguing that *suppai* is not polysemic. However, the example in (19) clearly shows that *suppai* is polysemous.

(22) amai kangae
sweet idea
'immature idea'

In (17), *amai* modifies *kao* 'face' to denote a positive evaluation of someone's face, and *amai* in (18) evaluates someone's voice in a positive way. In (19) and (20), *amai* is used to modify more abstract things, such as *seikatsu* 'life' and *fun'iki* 'mood'. *Amai* can also mean temptation, as shown in (21a), and can be used to intensify the meaning of *yūwaku* 'temptation' as illustrated in (21b). *Amai* in (21) can be interpreted as a word that conveys desirability but also conveys some dangerousness. As shown here, *amai* can be interpreted as a word with a positive image, but it can have negative meanings in figurative usages. Example (22) shows that *amai* has a negative meaning. In this usage, *amai* denotes someone's immaturity or lack of consideration.

Shibui 'astringent' also has figurative meanings. Similar to *amai*, the extended meaning can have either a positive or a negative connotation, as the following examples demonstrate:

(23) shibui otoko
astringent man
'a cool man'[12]

(24) shibui kao
astringent face
'a face expressing unpleasant feeling'

As seen earlier in Table 2, *shibui* 'astringent' has undesirability in its literal meaning, but in one of its figurative usages, it can have a positive meaning. In (23), for example, *shibui* 'astringent' denotes a positive evaluation and has a meaning similar to *cool* in English. In contrast, undesirability is preserved in the other extended meaning illustrated in (24). As with *nigai* 'bitter', *suppai* 'sour', and *shoppai* 'salty', *shibui* 'astringent' also modifies *kao* 'face' to denote an unpleasant feeling.

Involving a semantic change in opposite directions of desirability is unique to *amai* 'sweet' and *shibui* 'astringent' among taste terms and is not found in the figurative usages of other basic taste terms in the data consulted.

12. Actually, this translation is very simplified, and the sense of figurative *shibui* is bleached. This usage is used in the sense of 'a coolness that comes from age'.

4.4 A case of semantic pejoration

Semantic pejoration is a type of semantic change/extension. This semantic change may occur not only at the lexical level, but also at the syntactic, prosodic, and all other grammatical levels (cf. Finkbeiner, Meibauer & Wiese, 2016). In this type of semantic extension, words acquire negative meaning through the process of semantic change. The opposite process is called melioration. As Feist (2016, p. 47) has shown, *knave* and *churl* originally meant 'a man' or 'a young man', but these words today have negative meanings, such as 'a rude, unpleasant or dishonest person', as a result of pejoration. As has already been shown by Backhouse (1994); Minashima (2005); Jantra (1999); Kihara (2010), and Muto (2015), *amai* 'sweet' has negative meanings, such as *not enough, incomplete*, or a *lack of* something. Muto (2015) suggests that the origin of these negative meanings is the meaning of *amai* 'sweet' as an antonym of *suppai* 'sour', *shoppai* 'salty', *shibui* 'astringent', and *karai* 'spicy'. With this character, *amai* can be shown to be polysemic in the domain of taste, as it can modify *sake* as in *amai sake* to mean 'not-too-dry *sake*', even if the drink is not literally sweet, or, in other words, it lacks a dry taste or flavor. Foregrounding this sense of 'lack', the meaning of *amai* can be represented schematically as in 'lack of X',[13] thus motivating many figurative meanings of *amai*. Muto (2015) suggests the direction of the semantic extension: 'lack of dry taste' > 'lack of accuracy' > 'lack of consideration' and so on. I examined the path of semantic change of *amai* using the Corpus of Historical Japanese (NINJAL), and there is no supporting evidence for Muto's (2015) hypothesis. Nevertheless, it seems plausible to posit that 'lack of X' is preserved in the extended senses, even though the sense about taste may have become bleached. This point is illustrated in the following examples:

(25) amai kijun (lit. sweet standards) 'not strict (lenient) standards'
amai kijun o tsukureba, shōhisha kara tsuyoi hanpatsu o
lenient standart ACC make-but consumer from strong resistance ACC
ukeru (LBh6_00001)
have
'If we make a lenient standard, consumers will resist strongly.'

(26) amai keikaku (lit. sweet plan) 'not enough(ambiguous) plan'
imamadedōri no amai keikaku
like before GEN ambiguous plan
'ambiguous plan like before'

13. This 'X' simply indicates *something*, as used in algebra.

(27) amai oya (lit. sweet parents) 'indulgent parents'
watashi no oya wa binbōnin deari, sorehodo amai
my GEN parents TOP poor COP.CONJ not.so.much indulgent
oya demonai (PM11_01447)
parents COP.NEG
'My parents are poor, so they are not so much indulgent to me.'

In (25), *amai* denotes a lack of strictness in *kijun* 'standard', and *amai* in (26) indicates a lack of effort in planning or simply means not enough or ambiguity. In these examples, *amai* is understood as a negative evaluation despite its original use to denote positive meaning. In addition, it is not relevant to the sense of taste.

Example (27) is another case of pejorative use of *amai*, in this case meaning 'not strict' or 'spoiling'. These negative meanings can be explained by examining the perspective/viewpoint, and these usages can even preserve desirability in a certain way. Figure 5 illustrates this possibility; in the figure, the icon of the eye indicates the arrangement of the perspective.

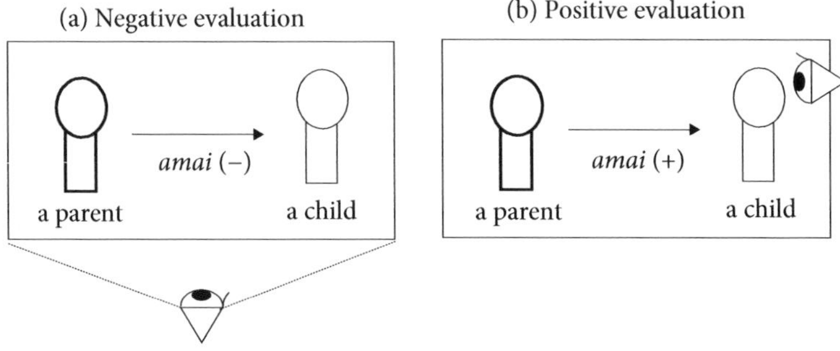

Figure 5. Perspective variation

Each box in the figure contains a parent and a spoiled child (hence the arrow from parent to child – the child is the object of the parent's attention). In Figure 5a), the perspective is from the outside. This allows the negative connotation as the external observer sees the parent spoiling the child. But if the perspective is from inside the figure and we are considering the parent's perspective of the child, *amai* can denote positive evaluation, as in Figure 5b).

As illustrated above, (un)desirability is determined by the difference in viewpoint. In other words, the desirability of literal *amai* is not preserved when the schematic sense of 'lack of' motivates the semantic extension. This problem is similar to the problem of '*Is the glass half full or half empty?*' typically considered to differentiate pessimists (the latter glass) from optimists (the former). This different construal is determined by the interpreter's mind, belief, and characteristics, along with the situation. An interpretation of 'lack of something' also differs based on the perspective. In (25) and (26), the beneficiary is the person who sets the standard or the person who makes the plan. The benefit is the easy job of the outcome of the lack of consideration or effort. These examples are not usually understood positively. However, in the next example, the lack of strictness is clearly understood as positive:

(28) *amai shiken* (lit. sweet examination) 'easy examination'

In (28), *amai* serves to express the lack of difficulty of the examination. This schematic sense of 'lack of X' is much like the cases of (25) to (27). In this usage, the perspective is always that of a beneficiary, so it is naturally understood positively.[14] This means that the sense of 'lack of X' does not account for every semantic extension of *amai*. The need to analyze the viewpoint is reinforced by the next example, often used in the context of baseball:

(29) a. amai tōkyū
sweet ball
'an easy ball (for the batter)'
b. amai tōkyū
sweet ball
'a careless throw (of the pitcher)'

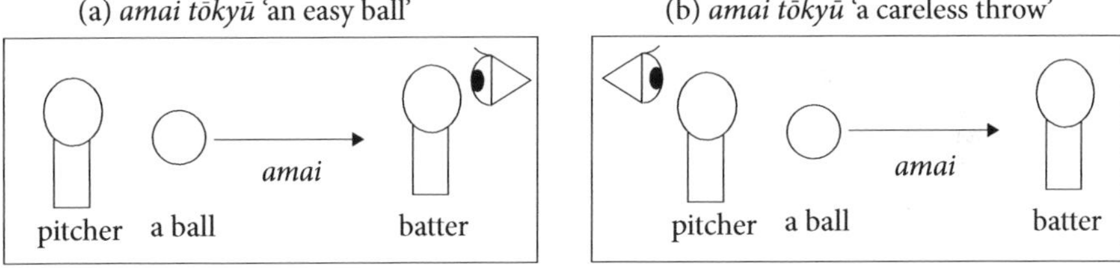

Figure 6. *Amai* meaning '*easy*' and its perspectives

In the context of baseball, especially in the scene of pitching/batting, *amai tōkyū* can have a double meaning, and its evaluation is differentiated by the perspective. If the perspective is the batter's, *amai tōkyū* is interpreted as 'an easy ball to hit', as shown in (29a) and Figure 6a). In contrast, if the perspective is the pitcher's, *amai tōkyū* denotes 'a careless throw' and has a negative sense, as illustrated in (29b) and the Figure 6b).

In previous studies by Jantra (1999) and Muto (2015), the change of scale or gradient was considered the core component of the semantic extension, but the change of the scale does not explain pejorative semantic extension, because some usages of positive 'lack of X' can be easily found.

14. Of course, if the perspective is that of the teacher who wants to give a strict grading, it is understood negatively.

This section has analyzed the extended meaning of *amai* 'sweet' in terms of differences in perspective. As the sets of antonyms are included in a single frame in frame semantics, the analysis offers an alternative solution to the analysis of figurative meanings of *amai* 'sweet' as both negative and positive.

4.5 A case of melioration

The literal meaning of *shibui* is astringent, implying undesirability, but, as mentioned in Section 4.3, *shibui* also has a positive meaning in its extended usage. Consider the following examples:

(23) shibui otoko (repeated)
astringent man
'a cool man'

(30) shibui midori
astringent green
'austere green'

In (23), *shibui* 'astringent' expresses a positive evaluation of appearance; it does not mean that the 'man' is experiencing undesirability. In (30), *shibui* does not imply a positive or negative evaluation; it simply denotes the austere tone of the color. It is possible to assume that in the process of semantic extension, the undesirability of *shibui* 'astringent' becomes bleached, and its range as an epithet is expanded by the effect of a synesthetic metaphor (cf. Williams, 1976). Speculatively, the synesthetic metaphor of *shibui* acquires positive meaning, although this path of semantic change must be studied more closely in the future.

5. Figurative usage of taste terms and patterns of semantic extension: Listing the frames for the figurative meanings of Japanese taste adjectives

To contribute to the theory of frame semantics, it would be useful to list all the frames that cover the various meanings of Japanese taste terms. This manual process may ultimately contribute to contrastive or typological studies, machine translation (cf. Hasegawa, Lee-Goldman & Fillmore, 2016), and the Japanese FrameNet (JFN), as well as the original FrameNet.

As shown in Section 4.1, all the taste terms can evoke the `Chemical-sense_description` frame and the `Sensation_directed` frame to make sense of their usages. Therefore, these two frames can be defined as original frames of taste terms. In CMT and the frame-semantic approach to figurative languages (cf. Sullivan,

2013), these frames serve as a part of the source domain. The following subsections examine how these original frames are mapped or linked to the other frames to clarify the figurative meanings of taste terms.

5.1 *Oishī* 'delicious'[15]

As discussed in Sections 4.1.1 and 4.1.2, *oishī* can evoke two basic frames. But *oishī* also evokes two additional frames: the `Luck` frame and the `Desirability` frame. Because of space considerations, definitions of frames for figurative taste terms are listed in the Appendix. In (31), *oishī* evokes the `Luck` frame, and its meaning in this collocation is roughly equivalent to the English *lucky*. In (32), *oishī* evokes the `Desirability` frame and simply denotes a positive evaluation of the noun.

(31) oishī ^{Target} [$_{\text{STATE\_OF\_AFFAIRS}}$ chansu] 'lucky opportunity'

(32) oishī ^{Target} [$_{\text{EVALUEE}}$ kankei] 'good relation'

According to Sullivan (2013), what is mapped in the conceptual metaphor is a frame, and frame elements of both the target domain and the source domain correspond to each other. If these expressions are the result of a conceptual metaphor, the source domain should be TASTE and the mapped frame should be the `Chemical-sense_description` frame. The target domain is assumed to be STATE, and the original frame functions as either the `Luck` frame or the `Desirability` frame. One of the core FEs of the original domain is PERCEPTUAL_SOURCE; this FE is mapped and comes to function as a STATE_OF_AFFAIRS or EVALUEE. Nevertheless, the data do not yield any figurative usages in which nouns that correspond to the FE of SENSORY_ATTRIBUTE are realized in the collocation. This is a case of a gap in mapping.

When frame semantics are adapted to CMT, the analysis of what is mapped and what is not mapped becomes more transparent conceptually. The frame-to-frame relation of frames evoked by *oishī* is illustrated in Figure 7.

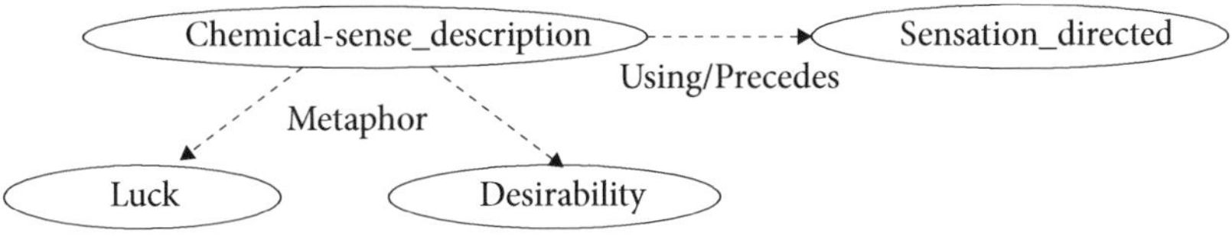

Figure 7. Frame-to-frame relation of *oishī*

15. This section of the analysis is part of a previous study, Sakaguchi (forthcoming).

As I noted above, the Sensation_directed frame is using the Chemical-sense_description frame to specify its FE (STIMULUS > PERCEPTUAL_SOURCE). Therefore, in Figure 4, only the "using" relation is shown, but a relation of contiguity between original frames can be drawn because the event of ingestion and the reaction to ingested objects are in a sort of sequential relation. It is also possible to suppose a sequential relation between these two frames, called a 'Precedes' relation in FrameNet, as shown in Figure 7.

5.2 *Amai* 'sweet'

The polysemy of *amai* is more varied and complicated for taste terms in Japanese, evoking Aesthetic, Difficulty, Emotion_directed, Mental_property, Accuracy, Desirability, and Color_qualities, as well as the original two frames. In the examples below, the evoked frame is shown in parentheses:

(33) amai ^{Target} [$_{\text{ENTITY}}$ kao] 'beautiful face' (Aesthetic)

(34) amai ^{Target} [$_{\text{TOPIC}}$ omoide] 'sweet memory' (Emotion_directed)

(35) amai ^{Target} [$_{\text{ENTITY}}$ kimochi] 'happy feeling' (Emotion_directed)

(36) amai ^{Target} [$_{\text{ACTIVITY}}$ mondai] 'easy question' (Strictness)

(37) amai ^{Target} [$_{\text{PROTAGONIST}}$ oya] 'spoiling parents' (Mental_property)

(38) amai ^{Target} [$_{\text{MEANS/ACTIVITY}}$ tōkyū] 'easy ball/careless throw' (Difficulty/Accuracy)

(39) amai ^{Target} [$_{\text{ENTITY}}$ kankei] 'good relation' (Desirability)

(40) amai ^{Target} [$_{\text{ENTITY}}$ iro] 'light color' (Color_qualities)

The frame-to-frame relation is illustrated in Figure 8. Space does not permit a detailed discussion of the mapping relation among those frames and the original frames. However, it is crucial to look at one frame, Position_on_a_scale. The outline of the frame in Figure 8 is a broken line, indicating it is not directly evoked by *amai* and it works as a via-point of mapping to more specific frames. This frame comes from the sense of 'lack of saltiness or bitterness' in the taste-related meaning of *amai* (see Section 4.4). In (38), the sentence is annotated multiply to reflect the possibility of different perspectives, as concluded in Section 4.4.

The extended meanings of *amai* which are understood by Mental_property and Accuracy tend to have negative connotations. This does not derive directly from the sense of 'lack of saltiness or bitterness' but is the result of a specification of the abstract sense of 'lack of X'. One possible interpretation of (38) is that *amai* is specified in terms of 'lack of accuracy', evoking the Accuracy frame, which may have a negative sense. However, if the perspective is transferred to another

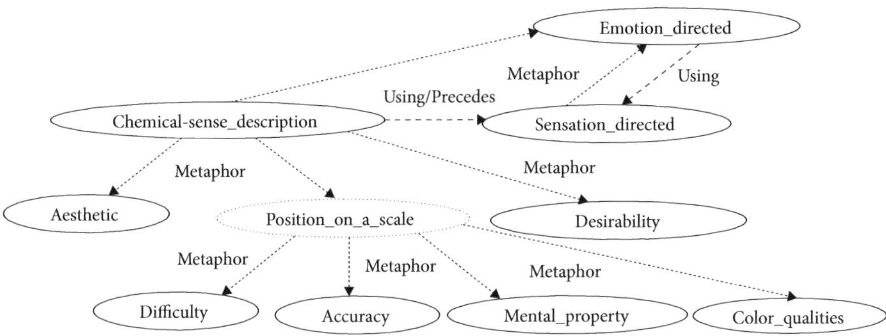

Figure 8. Frame-to-frame relation of *amai*

participant in the whole event, this negative meaning may reverse. In Example (40), *amai* is used to qualify the tone of the color. This meaning may also derive from the sense of 'lack of X'.

5.3 *Shibui* 'astringent'

As discussed in Section 4.5, *shibui* takes on extended meanings as a result of melioration. The extended meanings of *shibui* evoke `Aesthetic`, `Emotion_directed`, `Desirability`, and `Color_qualities`, as shown below:

(41) shibui ^{Target} [$_{\text{EXPRESSOR}}$ kao] 'frowning face' (`Emotion_directed`)

(42) shibui ^{Target} [$_{\text{EVALUEE}}$ otoko] 'a cool man' (`Desirability`)

(43) shibui ^{Target} [$_{\text{EVALUEE}}$ iro] 'austere color' (`Color_qualities`)

Like *amai*, *shibui* can also function as a color qualifier, in this case meaning 'dark' or 'austere'. Arguably, such a sense motivates the extended meaning (42), and this relation may be the Precedes relation introduced in Subsection 4.1.1. The frame-to-frame relation is illustrated in Figure 9.

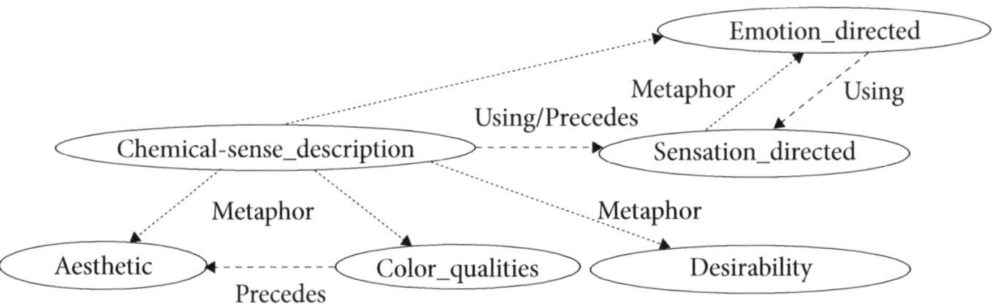

Figure 9. Frame-to-frame relation of *shibui*

5.4 *Suppai* 'sour', *nigai* 'bitter' and *shoppai* 'salty'

Suppai, nigai, and *shoppai* have varied extended meanings, but the variation is less wide than for other taste adjectives. `Desirability`, `Emotion_directed`, and the original two frames can be evoked by these taste terms. Consider the following:

(44) suppai ^{Target} [$_{\text{TOPIC}}$ omoi] 'bad feeling' (`Emotion_directed`)

(45) shoppai ^{Target} [$_{\text{EVALUEE}}$ uriage] 'bad sales' (`Desirability`)

(46) nigai ^{Target} [$_{\text{EXPRESSOR}}$ kao] 'sour face' (`Emotion_directed`)

Interestingly, Japanese *nigai kao* (lit. bitter face) in (46) is roughly equivalent to English *sour face*. It is unclear why these words do not function as a color qualifier. Clarification may come from fields outside linguistics where the topic of relation between colors and tastes has been given more attention (cf. Spence et al., 2015). According to Spence et al. (2015), *sour* associates with yellow, *salty* white, and *bitter* black. This association dovetails with my intuition, so it seems possible to say *nigai iro* 'bitter color' to denote dark colors. However, such examples are not found in the naturally occurring data I consulted.

6. The pattern of semantic extension and conceptual metaphor

This section offers an alternative characterization of the findings, using the terms used in the classic studies of adjectives and conceptual metaphors (cf. Dixon, 1982; Lakoff & Johnson, 1980), in an attempt to demonstrate the patterns of semantic extension of Japanese taste terms.

6.1 Simplified summary of the patterns of semantic extension

In the taxonomic notations of Dixon (1982), taste terms are categorized as words of PHYSICAL PROPERTY (hereinafter, capitalized words indicate semantic domains or conceptual metaphors). Figurative usages of *amai* 'sweet' and *shibui* 'astringent' are located in the COLOR domain. *Amai* 'sweet' has a meaning in the HUMAN PROPENSITY domain. All the taste terms have metaphorical usages denoting VALUE. The pattern of semantic extension can be drawn using Dixon's category terms, as shown in Figure 10.

The Japanese examples discussed in the previous sections accompany English translations. Interestingly, some figurative usages of Japanese taste terms coincide with those of English. For example, Japanese *amai kioku* could be literally translated, and its figurative meaning would be identical to English *sweet memory*. This

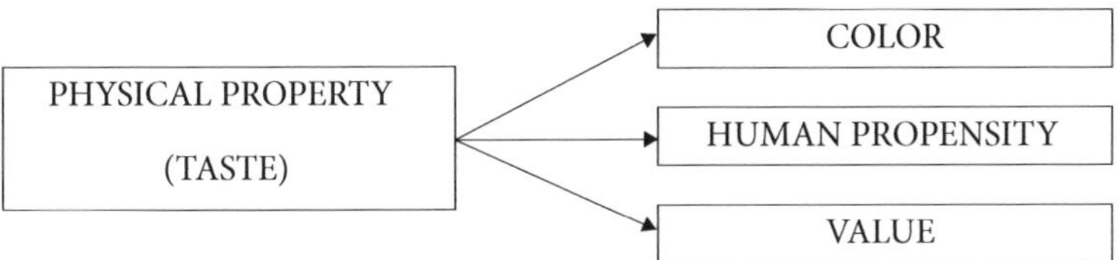

Figure 10. The pattern of semantic extension of taste terms in Japanese

coincidence shows that semantic extension from PHYSICAL PROPERTY (TASTE) to VALUE is found in English as well. A future study will determine whether the semantic extension pattern illustrated in Figure 10 is cross-linguistically valid.

6.2 Conceptual metaphors of Japanese taste terms

This section identifies what kind of conceptual metaphors underlie the variety of usages of Japanese taste terms. An example of a higher level conceptual metaphor is THE MIND IS A BODY, the basis of various figurative usages investigated in this chapter. As discussed in Section 6.1, taste terms have extended meaning in HUMAN PROPENSITY (which includes EMOTION, HUMAN CHARACTERISTICS and so on). These semantic domains are the sub-domain of the MIND domain, which is much more abstract than the TASTE domain, a sub-domain of the BODY domain. More precisely, a sub-metaphor of THE MIND IS A BODY metaphor, PERCEIVING IS EATING, triggers the figurative usages of taste terms. Such a metaphor is often found in Japanese, as illustrated below:

(47) nigai omoi o kami-shimeru
bitter feeling ACC bite-tightly
'think deeply about (lit. bite tightly) my bitter feelings'

In Japanese, EAT related verbs, such as *kamu* 'bite', can be used metaphorically (cf. Yamaguchi, this volume), taking an abstract entity, such as feeling, as their object because as a result of "metaphorical eating," the "eater" can perceive the taste of the abstract entity. In this case, the lowest and instantiated metaphors are FEELING IS TASTE, and VALUE IS TASTE. The source domain, TASTE, is evoked by taste terms, and the target domain is evoked by nouns which occur with adjectives. Those metaphors are not listed in the Master Metaphor List by Lakoff, Espensen & Schwartz (1991), but it is reasonable to posit them as conceptual metaphors. The extension from taste to color is more commonly explained under the notion of synaesthetic metaphors (Williams, 1976), but the examples discussed above suggest that conceptual metaphor serves as an alternative account.

7. Conclusion

This chapter has analyzed taste terms in Japanese from the standpoint of Cognitive Linguistics, adopting a frame-semantic approach. The main arguments can be summarized as follows:

1. Japanese TASTE terms have various figurative meanings related to COLOR, HUMAN PROPENSITY, and PHYSICAL PROPERTY.
2. Each taste term has a tendency to bear desirability or undesirability in its literal meaning. *Amai* 'sweet' tends to have positive meanings, and *suppai* 'sour', *nigai* 'astringent', *shoppai* 'salty', and *shibui* 'astringent' tend to have negative meanings.
3. Implicit (un)desirability is preserved in extended meanings in most cases. Notably, *amai* 'sweet' and *shibui* 'astringent' denote a negative or positive evaluation in their figurative usages through "pejoration" and "melioration" respectively.
4. Even if *amai* 'sweet' may be construed negatively in figurative usage, such a meaning may be interpreted positively if the perspective is that of the beneficiary (see Figure 6). The schematic meaning of *amai* 'lack of X' does not explain all negative cases, contra previous studies (e.g., Jantra, 1999); instead, they can be explained as a shift in perspective.

The chapter also suggests that frame semantics can be effectively applied to an analysis of metaphoric language. While the basic point about the involvement of metaphor in the semantic extension of taste terms is compatible with the argumentation of descriptive linguistics (cf. Dixon, 1982) (see Section 6.1), a reliance on frame semantics and CMT, as proposed in Sullivan (2013), can offer a richer and more refined discussion.

A cursory inspection of the figurative usage of English taste terms shows that in some cases, the expressions are semantic equivalents of Japanese (e.g., *sweet memory* vs. *amai kioku*), whereas in other cases, they are not (e.g., in English, *salty gossip* denotes 'sexual scandal' but in Japanese,[16] *shoppai* 'salty' cannot be used as its equivalent (**shoppai goshippu* is nonsensical)). It is left for future studies to investigate how the semantic extension of taste terms corresponds in English and Japanese, and beyond. Hopefully, some of the chapter's findings and its analytical method can be extended in other typological studies of taste terms.

16. This was pointed out to me by Professor Eve Sweetser.

Acknowledgements

First of all, I deeply thank the anonymous reviewers for their careful reading of my manuscript and their insightful comments and suggestions; they put my discussion on the right track and helped me create a cohesive flow. This study is part of my dissertation research in progress at the University of Tokyo. I am grateful to Professor Seiko Fujii, my supervisor, for her constructive comments, which substantially improved the quality of the chapter. A part of this chapter and some ideas derive from a presentation at a workshop, "Figurative Language and Grammar," organized and chaired by Professor Seiko Fujii and Professor Eve Sweetser at the 20th annual conference of Japanese Cognitive Linguistics Association. I was able to draw on helpful comments from the audience and discussants and am deeply grateful for this. I also thank Nicholas Hallsworth for his useful comments and careful correction of this paper.

References

Andor, J. (2010). Discussing frame semantics: the state of the art (An interview with Charles J. Fillmore) In *Review of Cognitive Linguistics, 8*(1), 157–176. https://doi.org/10.1075/rcl.8.1.06and

Backhouse, A. E. (1994). *The lexical field of taste: A semantic study of Japanese taste terms.* New York: Cambridge University Press. https://doi.org/10.1017/CBO9780511554322

Berlin, B., & Kay, P. (1969). *Basic color terms: Their universality and evolution.* California: University of California press.

Dixon, R. M. W. (1982). Where have all the adjectives gone? In R. M. W. Dixon (Ed.), *Where have all the adjectives gone?: and other essays in semantics and syntax* (pp. 1–62). Berlin: Walter de Gruyter. (Original work published 1977). https://doi.org/10.1515/9783110822939.1

Feist, J. (2016). *Semantic structure in English.* Amsterdam: John Benjamins. https://doi.org/10.1075/sfsl.73

Fillmore, C. J. (1982). Frame semantics. In the Linguistic Society of Korea (Ed.), *Linguistics in the morning calm* (pp. 111–137). Seoul: Hanshin.

Fillmore, C. J. (1985). Frames and the semantics of understanding. *Quaderni di Semantica, 6*(2), 222–254.

Fillmore, C. J., & Baker, C. (2009). A frames approach to semantic analysis. In H. Bernd and H. Narrog (Eds.) *The Oxford handbook of linguistic analysis* (pp.313–339). Oxford: Oxford University Press.

Finkbeiner, R., Meibauer, J., & Wiese, H. (Eds.). (2016). *Pejoration.* Amsterdam: John Benjamins. https://doi.org/10.1075/la.228

FrameNet. Retrieved from https://framenet.icsi.berkeley.edu/fndrupal/

Hasegawa, Y., Lee-Goldman, R., & Fillmore, C. J. (2016). On the universality of frames: Evidence from English-to-Japanese translation. In M. Hilpert, & J-O. Östman (Eds.) *Constructions across grammars* (pp. 35–66). Amsterdam: John Benjamins. https://doi.org/10.1075/bct.82.03has

Jantra, J. (1999). An analysis of the meaning extension of the Japanese adjective "*amai*" and its double meaning in advertisements-Contrasted with English "*sweet*" and Thai "*wăan.*" *Departmental Bulletin Paper of University of Kyoto, 3*, 142–193.

Japanese FrameNet. Retrieved from http://jfn.st.hc.keio.ac.jp/ja/home-ja/

Kihara, M. (2010). The Japanese adjective 'amai' and the English adjective 'sweet': Antonymous transfer of 'amai'. *Bulletin Paper of Nakamura Gakuen University, 42*, 55–61.

Kim, Y. M. (2018). Mikaku o hyōgen suru keiyōshi no imi kōzō to goi taikei [Semantics and the lexical organization of adjectives expressing taste] (Unpublished doctoral dissertation). Chuo University, Tokyo.

Kunihiro, T. (1982). *Imiron no hōhō* [Methodology of semantics]. Tokyo: Taishūkan shoten.

Kusumi, T. (1988). Comprehension of synaesthetic expressions: Cross-modal modifications of sense adjectives [in Japanese]. *Japanese Journal of Psychology, 58*(3), 373–380. Retrieved from https://www.jstage.jst.go.jp/article/jjpsy1926/58/6/58_6_373/_pdf

Lakoff, G. (1993). Contemporary theory of metaphor. In A. Orthony (Ed.), *Metaphor and thought*, 202–251. New York: Cambridge University Press. https://doi.org/10.1017/CBO9781139173865.013

Lakoff, G., Espensen, J. & Schwartz, A. (1991). Master metaphor list. Second draft copy. Technical report, Cognitive Linguistics Group, University of California Berkeley.

Lakoff, G., and M. Johnson. (1980). *Metaphors we live by*. Chicago: University of Chicago Press.

Langacker, R. W. (1990). *Concept, image, and symbol: The cognitive basis of grammar*. Berlin: Walter de Gruyter.

Langacker, R. W. (2008). *Cognitive grammar: A basic introduction*. New York: Oxford University Press. https://doi.org/10.1093/acprof:oso/9780195331967.001.0001

Minashima, H. (2005). Nichieigo no mikaku keiyōshi: *amai* and *sweet* [Taste adjectives in English and Japanese: *amai* and *sweet*]. *Departmental Bulletin Paper of Faculty of Education and Regional Studies of University of Fukui I, 60*, 11–29.

Muto, A. (2001). Mikaku keiyōshi *amai* to *karai* no tagi kōzō. [The semantic structure of the taste adjectives *amai* and *karai*]. *Journal of Japanese language teaching Nihongo Kyōiku, 110*, 42–51.

Muto, A. (2002a). *Oishī* no atarashii imi to yōhō: *umai mazui* to hikaku shite. [On the meaning of the taste adjective *oishī*--compared with *umai* and *mazui*]. *Nihongo Kyōiku* (Journal of Japanese language teaching), *112*, 25–34.

Muto, A. (2002b). Mikaku keiyoushi *suppai* no imi. [On the meaning of TASTE adjective *suppai*]. *Bulletin of Nagoya Meitoku Junior College, 16*, 73–89.

Muto, A. (2015). *Nihongo no kyōkankakuteki hiyu*. [Synesthetic Metaphors in Japanese].

National Institute for Japanese Language and Linguistics. (2018). Balanced Corpus of Contemporary Written Japanese (BCCWJ). Retrieved from https://chunagon.ninjal.ac.jp/

National Institute for Japanese Language and Linguistics. (2018). Corpus of Historical Japanese. Retrieved from https://chunagon.ninjal.ac.jp/

Nishio, T. (1972). *Keiyoushi no imi yōhō no kijutsuteki kenkyu:* [A descriptive study of the meaning and uses of Japanese adjectives]. Tokyo: Shūei Shuppan.

Odani, M. (2012). Sōtei yōhō ni okeru keiyōshi heichi kōbun ni kansuru ichi kōsatsu: Sōgōtekininchi to risantekininchi no kanten kara [On the construction of concatenative use of adjectives in attributive use: From a viewpoint of integrate/discrete schema]. In Yamanashi, M. (Ed.) *Ninchi gengogaku ronkō* [Studies in Cognitive Linguistics], *10* (pp. 105–141). Tokyo: Hituzi Syobo.

Radden, G. P., & Kövecses, Z. (1999). Towards a theory of metonymy. In K-U. Panther & G. P. Radden (Eds.), *Metonymy in language and thought* (pp. 17–59). Amsterdam: John Benjamins. https://doi.org/10.1075/hcp.4.03rad

Ruppenhofer, J., Ellsworth, M., Petruck, M. R. L., Johnson, C. R., Baker, C. F., & Scheffczyk, J. (2016). *FrameNet II: Extended theory and practice*. Berkeley, California: International Computer Science Institute.
Sakaguchi, K. (2014). The polysemy of Japanese adjectives "oishī", "umai" and "mazui" revisited: Frame semantics approach to the description of polysemy. *Papers from the National Conference of the Japanese Cognitive Linguistics Association, 14*, 323–335.
Sakaguchi, K. (2015). Frame semantics based contrastive studies of Japanese and English adjectives. *Papers from the National Conference of the Japanese Cognitive Linguistics Association, 15*, 458–470.
Sakaguchi, K. (Forthcoming). Figurative meanings of sensory and emotional adjectives in Japanese: Semantic patterns of [-i adjective + noun] constructions. In *Papers from the National Conference of the Japanese Cognitive Linguistics Association, 20*.
Sakai, A. (2008). Examination in "One direction hypothesis of 'Synesthesia metaphor'": From the result of preliminary research on "Words indicating sight" in seven different languages [in Japanese]. In *Bulletin of University of the Ryukyu, 5*, 1–18.
Seto, K. (2003). Gokan-de ajiwau [Tasting with five senses]. In Seto, K. (Ed.)., *Kotoba-wa aji-o koeru* [Words exceed taste] (pp. 62–78). Tokyo: Kaimeisha.
Shinohara, K., & Nakayama, A. (2011). Modalities and Directions in Synaesthetic Metaphors in Japanese. *Cognitive Studies, 18*(3), 491–507. Retrieved from https://www.jstage.jst.go.jp/article/jcss/18/3/18_3_491/_pdf
Spence, C., Wan, X., Woods, A., Velasco, C., Deng, J., Youssef, J., & Deroy, O. (2015). On tasty colours and colourful tastes? Assessing, explaining, and utilizing crossmodal correspondences between colours and basic tastes. *Flavour, 4*(1), 23. https://doi.org/10.1186/s13411-015-0033-1
Sullivan, K. (2013). *Frames and constructions in metaphoric language*. Amsterdam: John Benjamins Publishing Company. https://doi.org/10.1075/cal.14
Williams, J. M. (1976). Synesthetic adjectives: A possible law of semantic universals. In *Language, 52*(2), 461–478. https://doi.org/10.2307/412571
Winter, B. (2019). *Sensory linguistics: language, perception and metaphor*. Amsterdam/Philadelphia: John Benjamins. https://doi.org/10.1075/celcr.20
Yakame, H. (2008). *Nihongo keiyōshi no kijutsuteki kenkyū* [A descriptive study of contemporary Japanese adjectives: From a typological view]. Tokyo: Meiji Shoin.
Yamada, S. (1972). Gendai miyako hōgen mikaku goi kō: tōkyō hōgen tono hikaku o chūshin ni. [Taste terms in the contemporary Miyako language]. *Okinawa Bunka, 39*, 30–37.

Appendix. Frame definitions (alphabetical order)

The Appendix lists definitions of frames used in the chapter. For details, see the FrameNet online database (https://framenet.icsi.berkeley.edu/fndrupal/).

Accuracy

An AGENT is involved in an activity whose degree of success is dependent on a parameter of the action matching a particular set of values of a continuous variable or variables (e.g. quantity, location, time). The AGENT, or metonymically the INSTRUMENT or MEANS action, is described in terms of the actual or expected DEVIATION between the location, time, or quantity in the activity and the location, time, or quantity which is necessary for the intended event.

`Aesthetic`

An ENTITY is judged to be sensually pleasing or intellectually interesting to a (generally implicit) VIEWPOINT.

`Color_qualities`

This frame contains words that describe specific aspects of a COLOR. The DEGREE to which the COLOR being discussed deviates from the prototype may be marked. The description may also target a specific aspect of color.

`Desirability`

This frame concerns an EVALUEE being judged for its quality, i.e. how much it would probably be liked. In many cases, the EVALUEE is implicitly judged good or bad relative to other instances of its type. The EVALUEE's desirability is determined by one or more PARAMETERS, which are scalar properties of the EVALUEE. The evaluation may also explicitly be relativized to a set of CIRCUMSTANCES, a COMPARISON_SET of entities that belong to the same class as the EVALUEE, or an AFFECTED_PARTY. The DEGREE of goodness or badness may also be expressed. Note: With some targets, desirability is conventionally aligned with quantity, i.e., GOOD is MORE.

`Difficulty`

An EXPERIENCER has an easy or difficult time carrying out an ACTIVITY. The ease or difficulty associated with the ACTIVITY seems to often be associated with a prominent participant. However, we consider this impression to be due to the syntax and pragmatics of the relevant sentence constructions and employ no special FE for such participants. The DEGREE of ease or difficulty is often specified as well as a set of CIRCUMSTANCES. A PARAMETER may be mentioned that indicates in which respect the ACTIVITY is judged to be easy or difficult.

`Emotion_directed`

The adjectives and nouns in this frame describe an EXPERIENCER who is feeling or experiencing a particular emotional response to a STIMULUS or about a TOPIC. There can also be a CIRCUMSTANCES under which the response occurs or a REASON that the STIMULUS evokes the particular response in the EXPERIENCER.

`Luck`

A STATE_OF_AFFAIRS is evaluated as good (or bad), against a background assumption that previously, the STATE_OF_AFFAIRS was thought to be unlikely to occur. The STATE_OF_AFFAIRS holds for a particular PROTAGONIST.

`Mental_property`

The adjectives and nouns in this frame are all based on the idea that mental properties may be attributed to a person (PROTAGONIST) by a (usually implicit) JUDGE on the basis of that person's BEHAVIOR, as broadly understood. Though on a conceptual level these words always attribute mental properties to people, they may be applied to PROTAGONIST's BEHAVIORS as well, with the understanding that the BEHAVIOR is revealing a (usually temporary) property of the PROTAGONIST responsible for it. (the rest of the information is omitted)

`Position_on_a_scale`

This frame contains words that describe an ITEM's static position on a scale with respect to some property VARIABLE.

SECTION V

Motion and force in the language of food

CHAPTER 9

Verbs of seasoning in Japanese, with special reference to the locative alternation in English

Daisuke Nonaka
Kogakuin University of Technology & Engineering, Academic Support Center

This chapter identifies verbs of seasoning from the Balanced Corpus of Contemporary Written Japanese and divides them into two types: those taking the seasoning as direct object (e.g., *shio o furikakeru* 'sprinkle salt') and those marking the seasoning with the instrumental case (e.g., *shio de ajituke suru* 'season (something) with salt'). While some verbs of seasoning in English participate in the locative alternation (e.g., *Sprinkle salt over the meat* vs. *Sprinkle the meat with salt*), Japanese has considerably fewer alternating verbs, requiring the use of different verbs in the realm of seasoning. The difference is accounted for in light of "fashions of speaking" (e.g., Ikegami, 1985).

Keywords: culinary expression, recipe, verbs of seasoning, Balanced Corpus of Contemporary Written Japanese (BCCWJ), locative alternation, English-Japanese comparison

1. Introduction

Many languages have a wide variety of expressions to describe cooking procedures. In English, for example, culinary verbs that denote cutting up ingredients include *chop*, *mince*, and *slice*, while *broil*, *fry*, and *stew* specify methods of cooking. Listed in (1) and (2) are the respective Japanese counterparts of these verbs.

(1) *kizamu* 'chop', *mijin-giri ni suru* [fragment-cut do] 'mince', *usu-giri ni suru* [thin-cut do] 'slice'

(2) *aburu* 'broil', *ageru* 'deep-fry', *niru* 'stew'

While Japanese verbs such as those in (1) and (2) have been discussed in the literature (e.g., Kunihiro, 1981; Ikarashi, Fukutome & Tsuyukubo, 2016), those used to describe the addition of seasoning (salt, pepper, and other spices) to food, i.e., verbs of seasoning, have yet to be examined.

https://doi.org/10.1075/celcr.25.09non

This chapter offers a usage-based account of Japanese verbs of seasoning, examining the construction types in which they occur, with a special focus on the case marking patterns of the verbs' semantic arguments. To achieve this end, I first identify the Japanese verbs of seasoning, drawing on the Balanced Corpus of Contemporary Written Japanese (BCCWJ). Then, I discuss their characteristics, comparing them to their English counterparts with respect to their participation in the locative alternation. I consider how Japanese differs from English in conveying the action of seasoning; I elucidate the nature of the differences drawing on the idea of "fashion of speaking" (Ikegami, 1985; Whorf, 1956).

My analysis of the corpus data reveals an unexpected characteristic of Japanese verbs of seasoning, indicating the importance of looking into how verbs of seasoning are actually used. More specifically, *suru* '(lit.) do', which I do not consider to be a verb of seasoning in itself, ranks high in the statistical distribution and intricately interacts with other morphological elements, forming unique complexes to express the act of adding seasoning to food.

The rest of the chapter is organized as follows. Section 2 offers a foundational discussion of culinary terms, reviewing the literature. Section 3 describes the data; Section 4 gives a descriptive account of verbs of seasoning, reporting the results of statistical analysis and introducing Japanese verbs of seasoning; Section 5 turns to the constructions in which the verbs of seasoning appear, referring to locative alternation in English. Finally, Section 6 concludes the chapter.[1]

2. Cooking and grammar

2.1 Why study culinary expressions?

Let me start by explaining why I believe culinary expressions are important to linguists, particularly those investigating grammar. After all, as some might argue, culinary expressions, which pertain only to specific registers, behave in idiosyncratic ways, bearing little relevance to grammar. In point of fact, however, analyzing culinary expressions can provide insight into the behavior of some verbs.

Take the verb *furu*, for instance. *Furu* is a polysemous verb with multiple uses (cf. Kunihiro, 1997, pp. 235–238), as shown in the following examples.

1. This paper is a partially updated version of © Nonaka (2017a), which was written in Japanese. The present chapter reproduces some of the content in English. Section 5.2 is completely new.

(3) a. hata o furu
flag ACC wave
'wave a flag'
b. saikoro o furu
dice ACC throw
'throw dice'
c. shio o niku ni furu
salt ACC meat DAT sprinkle
'sprinkle salt over the meat'

What these uses have in common is the concept of moving something rapidly up and down or left and right. In (3a), *furu* means moving something in one's hand from side to side. Example (3b), which literally means shaking the dice, is a fixed expression used to mean rolling the dice. *Furu* in (3c) also involves shaking something, but this time, it conventionally stands for seasoning something else with it. Interestingly, only the use of *furu* illustrated in (3c) takes a goal argument (the dative case particle *ni* is often used for the goal argument), in this case, the meat where the salt ends up. (We can say *hata o sayū ni furu* 'wave a flag from side to side', but here *sayū* specifies in which direction the flag moves, rather than where it ends up. We cannot say **saikoro o yuka ni furu* to mean 'throw the dice on the floor'.) In other words, the goal argument is restricted to the use of *furu* as a verb of seasoning. This is a good illustration of how closely a verb's behavior can be related to our conception of cookery.

2.2 Previous studies on culinary expressions

How the category of cooking verbs is structured is one of the most discussed areas in the study of culinary expressions in both English and Japanese. Lehrer's (1974) study is an early and representative work on cooking verbs. Revising Lehrer, Kunihiro (1981) presents a contrastive study of English and Japanese cooking verbs by analyzing them in terms of the methods with which the action is conducted: cooking in liquid, cooking with oil, and cooking just by applying heat. Kunihiro (1981) further characterizes these verbs in terms of, for example, the kind of object or substance on which the action is performed, the utensil involved, or the kind of change the action is meant to achieve. The English verb *fry* denotes cooking food in hot fat (or oil) with a pan, while the act designated by *toast* is heating food such as bread to become brown and crisp. By the same token, the Japanese verb *niru* encodes cooking food in liquid with seasonings in a closed dish. Kunihiro also shows English and Japanese cooking verbs are differently lexicalized to represent cooking methods. The English verb *fry* is a cover term for cooking food in hot fat, but Japanese doesn't have such a superordinate verb and has to use more specific verbs like *itameru* 'stir-fry' or *ageru* 'deep-fry'.

Levin (1993) lists more than 40 cooking verbs and identifies the constructions in which they occur. She reports that some participate in both transitive (causative) and intransitive (inchoative) constructions (a phenomenon called the causative/inchoative alternation), as exemplified in (4) for *bake*.

(4) a. Jennifer baked the potatoes.
b. The potatoes baked. (Levin, 1993, p. 243)

The corresponding phenomenon in Japanese involves different but morphologically related verbs. The Japanese counterparts of (4) are given in (5), where "*yak*" is shared by the transitive form *yaku* 'bake' and the intransitive form *yakeru* 'bake'.

(5) a. Tarō ga jagaimo o yai-ta.
Taro NOM potato ACC bake-PST
'Taro baked the potatoes.'
b. Jagaimo ga yake-ta.
potato NOM bake-PST
'The potatoes baked.'

Other examples of transitive-intransitive verb pairs include *ageru* – *agaru* 'deep-fry', and *wakasu* – *waku* 'boil'.

Although cooking verbs in Japanese have been analyzed (e.g., Kunihiro, 1981; Yoshikawa, 1995), little attention has been paid to verbs of seasoning. Where does this difference come from? The vast majority of cooking verbs (e.g., *aburu* 'broil', *itameru* 'fry', *niru* 'stew') encode actions specific to cookery, such as broiling and frying, making it straightforward to identify the verbs and list them in this class. Some of them occur in both intransitive and transitive constructions, as seen in (5), whose alternating pattern has attracted the interest of many linguists (e.g., Haspelmath, 1993; Maruta & Suga, 2000). By contrast, Japanese has no verbs exclusively used for the addition of seasonings. As seen above, although *furu* can be used to denote a particular type of act of seasoning, this represents only one of its multiple senses. This is also true of other verbs used to describe the addition of seasonings. For example, verbs like *ireru* 'put (in)' and *kuwaeru* 'add' take a wide variety of nouns, as well as nouns expressing seasonings, as their objects.

To fully characterize the category of verbs of seasoning, we need detailed contextual information. Such information can easily be accommodated in the usage-based model, generally adopted in Cognitive Linguistics (Langacker, 2000; Taylor, 2006, 2012). The usage-based approach takes the view that linguistic structure is formed by language use; frequently occurring expressions are stored as linguistic units with contextual profiles (lexical items with which they collocate and texts in which they occur). Such lower-level units coexist with higher-level generalizations, or rather, are an integral part of linguistic knowledge. As Taylor (2006, p. 51) aptly puts it, "[K]nowing a word involves knowing the usage range of the word." On this view, it is reasonable to say that native speakers record as units seasoning expressions like *shio o furu* "sprinkle salt" along with conventional cookery scenarios. The category of verbs of seasoning is thus grounded on the usage-based model.

Obviously, different languages are composed of different conventional units, including verbs of seasoning. One important thing to note is that conventionalization in each language has accumulated to display a certain tendency. Preferred ways to conventionalize units found across different grammatical structures within a language are called "fashions of speaking" (Whorf, 1956). Naturally, fashions of speaking fall under the scope of the usage-based model (Nishimura and Hasegawa, 2016).

Now let us turn our attention to the syntactic behavior of verbs of seasoning. First, the act of seasoning can be conceived as a particular type of caused-motion event where something is caused to move. For instance, in (3c) with *furu*, 'salt' is caused to move onto the 'meat'. This means the verb of seasoning is associated with three event participants: agent, seasoning (e.g., salt, pepper), and goal (e.g., meat, fish). When describing the cooking procedure, the agent is not expressed overtly in either English or Japanese. The procedure is usually expressed in imperatives in English (e.g., *Sprinkle salt over the meat.*), while in Japanese, it is described using the non-past form of a verb (i.e., *shimasu* 'do [polite]' or *suru* 'do'), with the agent left unexpressed (e.g., *Niku ni shio o kakemasu* 'Sprinkle salt over the meat') (Mikami, 1969, p. 28).

An important question to ask, then, is how seasoning and goal entities are expressed in Japanese. Example (3c) shows that *furu* marks the seasoning with the particle *o* and the goal with *ni*. Does this mean that *furu*'s pattern is the only possibility? In other words, we need to identify what verbs are used to describe the addition of seasonings, as well as which case particles are used to mark the seasoning and goal nouns. To consider this question, I draw on the observation that English verbs of seasoning like *sprinkle* participate in the locative alternation (Nonaka, 2016, 2017b).

In locative alternation, verbs relating to putting some substance on a goal can occur in two constructions. Locative alternation in English is illustrated in (6) and (7): the (a) examples contain the substance (e.g., *hay*) as the direct object, whereas the (b) examples take the goal (or the location where the substance is placed such as *wagon*) as the direct object.

(6) a. Bill smeared paint on the wall.
    b. Bill smeared the wall with paint.

(7) a. John loaded hay onto the wagon.
    b. John loaded the wagon with hay.

Interestingly, locative alternation verbs in English are often found in recipes (Nonaka, 2016, 2017b; see also Iwata, 2008, p. 73; Matsumoto, 1999, pp. 32–33). For example, the alternating verbs *sprinkle* and *brush* express either seasoning or goal participants as their direct object.

(8) a. Sprinkle salt over the meat.
    b. Sprinkle the meat with salt.

(9) a. Brush melted butter over the potatoes.
    b. Brush the potatoes with melted butter.

While a substantial number of verbs participate in the locative alternation in English, the phenomenon is less common in Japanese. That is, the construction where the goal participant is marked with the accusative *o* is relatively rare in Japanese. (10) and (11) respectively show the Japanese counterparts of (6) and (7).[2]

(10) a. kabe ni penki o nuru
        wall DAT paint ACC apply.paint
        'smear paint on the wall'
     b. kabe o penki de nuru
        wall ACC paint INST apply.paint
        'smear the wall with paint' (Fukui, Miyagawa & Tenny, 1985, p. 5)

(11) a. hoshikusa o niguruma ni tsumu
        hay ACC wagon DAT load
        'load the hay on the wagon'
     b. *niguruma o hoshikusa de tsumu
        wagon ACC hay INST load
        'load the wagon with hey' (Fukui et al., 1985, p. 10)

Although the verb *nuru* 'smear' alternates (see (10)) just as *smear* does in English, the [NP *o* NP *de* V] construction is not available for *tsumu* 'load' (cf. (11a) vs. (11b)). In fact, Fukui et al. (1985); Okutsu (1980), and Matsumoto (1997) report that far fewer verbs allow alternation in Japanese than in English. The verb *furu* is a non-alternating verb as well, as shown in the contrast in acceptability in (12).

(12) a. shio o niku ni furu
        salt ACC meat DAT sprinkle
        'sprinkle salt over the meat'
     b. *niku o shio de furu.
        meat ACC salt INST sprinkle
        'sprinkle the meat with salt'

2. For an early analysis of the locative alternation in Japanese, see Kageyama (1980) and Okutsu (1981).

To investigate the characteristics of the verbs of seasoning like *furu* 'sprinkle', I chose *shio* 'salt' and *koshō* 'pepper' as representative seasonings and searched the BBCWJ to identify the verbs co-occurring with them. The next section describes the data and the method in more detail.

3. Data

The BCCWJ was used as the data source. The BCCWJ includes 100 million words of written Japanese from a large range of genres. The texts in the BCCWJ are analyzed into "short unit words" or the smallest linguistic units that carry meaning. Short unit words approximate word entries of Japanese dictionaries.[3] They are provided with part-of-speech information, allowing users to search for words by part-of-speech tag. I used the online search system of the BCCWJ, Chunagon, to retrieve data.

As a first step, I selected *shio* 'salt' and *koshō* 'pepper' as target words (node words) and searched the BCCWJ for verbs co-occurring with them. The question is: how many words should be included within the scope of the search conducted with respect to the node word? It has been argued that collocates occurring within four words to the left or right of the node are sufficient for discovery of significant collocates in English (cf. Sinclair, 1991, p. 175; Stubbs, 2002, p. 29). In studies on collocations in Japanese, however, no proposal has been made as to how many words should be examined to determine whether a given word is a significant collocate (Ishikawa, 2012, p. 89). As more than one noun of seasoning can occur in juxtaposition, and the positions of seasoning verbs can be quite distant from the node words (*shio* 'salt' or *koshō* 'pepper'), I decided to add two more words to the English model, and searched for verbs occurring within six words to the right of the nouns, *shio* 'salt' and *koshō* 'pepper'.[4] I went to the right because in Japanese, a verb final language, verbs are most likely to occur to the right of the node word. I used lemmatized tagging to find the different forms (inflectional and written forms) of the same word. Square brackets are used in the subsequent discussion to indicate that the item is a lemma. For example, "こしょう" (*hiragana*), "コショー"

3. The BCCWJ texts are also analyzed into "long unit words." Long unit words treat compound words (e.g., compound nouns, compound verbs, and compound particles) as whole units.

4. I used the following search formula to obtain verbs co-occurring with [shio]. When "塩" is replaced with "胡椒", those co-occurring with [koshō] are retrieved.

(i) キー: 品詞 LIKE "動詞%" AND 前方共起: (語彙素="塩" AND 品詞 LIKE "名詞%") WITHIN 6 WORDS FROM キー WITH OPTIONS tglKugiri="" AND tglBunKugiri="#" AND limitToSelfSentence="1" AND tglFixVariable="2" AND tglWords="20" AND unit="1" AND encoding="UTF-16LE" AND endOfLine="CRLF" (*katakana*), and "胡椒" (Chinese characters, *kanji*) are different realizations of the same lemma [koshō].[5]

Using this method, I obtained 3,997 tokens (432 types) of verbs co-occurring with [shio] and 1,210 tokens (139 types) of verbs with [koshō]. The top 15 verbs are presented in Tables 1 and 2 (two verbs co-occur with [shio] at rank 14). The headings "With [shio]" and "With [koshō]" in the tables indicate the number of verbs co-occurring with [shio] and [koshō], while "All" represents the number of all the verbs found in the corpus.

Table 1. Verbs co-occurring with [shio] ('salt')

Rank	Verb (LEMMA)	With [shio]	All
1	[suru] 'do'	631	2563860
2	[furu] 'sprinkle'	334	8003
3	[kuwaeru] 'add'	312	14785
4	[ireru] 'put (in)'	260	38409
5	[totonoeru] 'arrange'	176	3169
6	[aru] 'be, exist'	124	956900
7	[mazeru] 'mix'	112	3491
8	[tsukeru] 'attach'	89	44215
9	[iru] 'be, exist'	85	1121183
10	[iu] 'say'	71	803148
11	[taberu] 'eat'	66	32739
12	[oku] 'put (on)'	61	61241
13	[tsukuru] 'make'	55	57888
14	[mabusu] 'coat'	47	489
14	[tsukau] 'use'	47	68889

Note that the range of context where [shio] occurs differs from that of [koshō]. Most examples of [koshō] are found in cookery contexts, while [shio] is used in a large variety of registers, including scientific and religious contexts, as in (13)–(15). (I used the lemma without considering the difference in the reading of the orthography. For instance, the Chinese character "塩" has two readings /shio/ and /en/, the latter of which is mainly used for compounds like *shōsan-en* in (15).) Hence, verbs unrelated to food descriptions are found in my data.[6] Throughout the rest of

5. Typically, Chinese characters (*kanji*) are used for content words; *hiragana*, for words of Japanese origin and function words (e.g., case particles and inflectional endings); and *katakana*, for loan words, but the same concept can sometimes be written in the three ways, with slightly different nuances.

6. *Iru* is combined with *-te* to form a stative marker in (13). In addition, *aru*, following *de*, is used as the copula in (15). Both are treated as phrasal lexical items from the viewpoint of long unit words.

Table 2. Verbs co-occurring with [koshō] (‘pepper’)

Rank	Verb (LEMMA)	With [koshō]	All
1	[suru] ‘do’	260	2563860
2	[totonoeru] ‘arrange’	161	3169
3	[furu] ‘sprinkle’	154	8003
4	[kuwaeru] ‘add’	76	14785
5	[tsukeru] ‘attach’	56	44215
6	[ireru] ‘put (in)’	52	38409
7	[mazeru] ‘mix’	49	3491
8	[furikakeru] ‘sprinkle’	29	454
9	[kakeru] ‘put (on), pour’	20	40469
10	[itameru] ‘stir-fry’	20	2069
11	[aru] ‘be, exist’	17	956900
12	[taberu] ‘eat’	16	32739
13	[oku] ‘put (on)’	15	61241
14	[iru] ‘be’	13	1121183
15	[kiku] ‘take effect’	11	5431
15	[mazeawaseru] ‘mix in’	11	773

the chapter, I italicize [shio] and [koshō] and underline verbs which co-occur with the word of seasoning in the examples from the BCCWJ. [7]

(13) *shio* no kesshō kara deki-te.iru chisō
salt GEN crystal from made-STATIVE stratum
‘a stratum composed of crystallized salt’

(14) “Iyana hito ga tazune-te kita toki wa genkan ni *shio* o
disgusting people NOM visit-CONJ come when TOP entrance DAT salt ACC
make” to īmasu. Tsumari, *shio* ni wa “kiyome” no pawā ga
sprinkle QUOT say namely salt DAT TOP purifying GEN power NOM
aru no.desu.
exist COP
‘It is said that you should sprinkle salt in the entrance when disgusting people visit you. This is because salt has a purifying effect.’[8]

(15) shizengen kara no sono jūyōdo wa shōsan.*en* ryūshi to
natural.source from GEN its importance TOP nitrate particle and
hobo dōtō de.aru
almost equal COP
‘from the viewpoint of natural sources, it is almost as important as a nitrate particle’

7. Examples (13)–(31) and (34)–(36) are cited from the BCCWJ.

8. In Japan, salt is used in a religious practice for purification.

To extract significant collocates of [shio] and [koshō] from my data, I calculated the Dice coefficient, t-score, and MI score.[9] The Dice coefficient is calculated by using the overall occurrences of two items in a corpus and the co-occurrences of the two. The t-score and MI score take corpus size into account. Collocates with high frequency tend to obtain a high t-score. The value of the MI-score for a given word is high when, although its frequency is low in a corpus, it occurs almost exclusively in combination with certain other words. The value of the Dice coefficient lies between those of the t-score and MI-score (Ishikawa, 2008a, p. 116). Note that [shio] occurs 5,488 times and [koshō], 1,699 times in the BCCWJ, and the total number of words in the BCCWJ is 104,911,460. I made a statistical calculation for words co-occurring with [shio] or [koshō] ten times or more in the corpus. Tables 3 and 4 show the result for the statistical measures of verbs co-occurring with [shio] and [koshō] respectively. ("R" in Tables 3 and 4 stands for "rank".)

Table 3. Statistical measures of verbs co-occurring with [shio]

Dice coefficient			t-score			MI score		
R	**Verbs**	**Value**	**R**	**Verbs**	**Value**	**R**	**Verbs**	**Value**
1	[furu] 'sprinkle'	0.0495	1	[suru] 'do'	19.781	1	[mabusu] 'coat'	10.843
2	[totonoeru] 'arrange'	0.0407	2	[furu] 'sprinkle'	18.253	2	[furikakeru] 'sprinkle'	10.718
3	[kuwaeru] 'add'	0.0308	3	[kuwaeru] 'add'	17.620	3	[suru] 'do'	10.445
4	[mazeru] 'mix'	0.0249	4	[ireru] 'put (in)'	16.000	4	[totonoeru] 'arrange'	10.052
5	[mabusu] 'coat'	0.0157	5	[totonoeru] 'arrange'	13.254	5	[furu] 'sprinkle'	9.640
6	[furikakeru] 'sprinkle'	0.0135	6	[mazeru] 'mix'	10.566	6	[mazeru] 'mix'	9.260
7	[ireru] 'put (in)'	0.0118	7	[tsukeru] 'attach'	9.189	7	[mazeawaseru] 'mix in'	8.950
8	[mazeawaseru] 'mix in'	0.0064	8	[taberu] 'eat'	7.913	8	[momu] 'rub'	8.842
9	[momu] 'rub'	0.0063	9	[oku] 'put (on)'	7.400	9	[kuwaeru] 'add'	8.656
10	[yuderu] 'boil'	0.0062	10	[tsukuru] 'make'	7.008	10	[tokasu] 'melt'	8.479

9. See Hunston (2002); Chujo and Uchiyama (2004), and Ishikawa (2008a, 2008b) for my three statistical measures.

Table 4. Statistical measures of verbs co-occurring with [koshō]

Die coefficient			t-score			MI score		
R	Verbs	Value	R	Verbs	Value	R	Verbs	Value
1	[totonoeru] 'arrange'	0.0661	1	[suru] 'do'	13.550	1	[furikakeru] 'sprinkle'	11.946
2	[furu] 'sprinkle'	0.0317	2	[totonoeru] 'arrange'	12.685	2	[totonoeru] 'arrange'	11.615
3	[furikakeru] 'sprinkle'	0.0269	3	[furu] 'sprinke'	12.399	3	[furu] 'sprinkle'	10.215
4	[mazeru] 'mix'	0.0189	4	[kuwaeru] 'add'	8.690	4	[mazeawaseru] 'mix in'	9.779
5	[itameru] 'stir-fry'	0.0106	5	[tsukeru] 'attach'	7.388	5	[mazeru] 'mix'	9.759
6	[kuwaeru] 'add'	0.0092	6	[ireru] 'put (in)'	7.125	6	[itameru] 'stir-fry'	9.221
7	[mazeawaseru] 'mix in'	0.0089	7	[mazeru] 'mix'	6.992	7	[kuwaeru] 'add'	8.310
8	[kiku] 'take effect'	0.0031	8	[furikakeru] 'sprinkle'	5.384	8	[kiku] 'take effect'	6.967
9	[ireru] 'put (in)'	0.0026	9	[itameru] 'stir-fry'	4.465	9	[ireru] 'put (in)'	6.385
10	[tsukeru] 'attach'	0.0024	10	[kakeru] 'put (on)'	4.326	10	[tsukeru] 'attach'	6.289

I expected that semantically "heavy" verbs like [furikakeru] 'sprinkle' would be significant collocates of [shio] 'salt' and [koshō] 'pepper', assuming that a noun and a verb would naturally collocate if the latter's specific semantic content is compatible with the meaning of the former. It turns out, however, that [suru] 'do', which is semantically "light" but with a wider variety of uses, has a high t-score (the raw frequency of [suru] 'do' is the highest in both Tables 1 and 2). It is also interesting that the verb [totonoeru] 'arrange' obtains a high value in the three statistical measures.

4. Verbs of seasoning

This section discusses the characteristics of selected verbs from Tables 1–4. Section 4.1 looks at verbs expressing addition, coating, rubbing, and mixing; Section 4.2 turns to the usage of *suru* 'do', and Section 4.3 discusses verbs for arranging and attaching.

4.1 Verbs expressing addition, coating, rubbing, and mixing

The results of the three statistical measures in Tables 3 and 4 show that those verbs expressing "addition (of seasoning)," such as [furu] 'sprinkle', [kuwaeru] 'add', and [ireru] 'put (in)', are significant collocates of both [shio] and [koshō]. The following examples show how these verbs are used in a recipe: (16) gives an example with *furu* 'sprinkle', (17) with *ireru* 'put (in)', and (18) with *kuwaeru* 'add'. As in (16) and (17), [shio] and [koshō] are often juxtaposed (sometimes separated by a comma) within the same sentence.

(16) Kajikimaguro wa *shio*, *koshō* kaku shōshō o furu.
billfish TOP salt pepper each a little ACC sprinkle
'Sprinkle the billfish with a little salt and pepper.'

(17) Bōru ni tomato, bajiru no ha, ninniku, orību oiru, *shio*, *koshō* o
bowl DAT tomato basil GEN leaves garlic olive oil salt peper ACC
ire-te aeru.
put-CONJ mix
'Put tomato, basil leaves, garlic, olive oil, salt and pepper into the bowl and mix well.'

(18) Asuparagasu wa itame-zu.ni, yu ni *shio*, futsū no abura
asparagus TOP stir.fry-instead hot.water DAT salt ordinary GEN oil
o kuwae-te yuderu dakedemoyoi.
ACC add-CONJ boil be.all.right.to
'Instead of stir-frying asparagus, it is all right to add salt and ordinary oil and just boil asparagus.'

Another verb expressing an addition of seasoning, [furikakeru] 'sprinkle' (a compound verb consisting of *furu* 'sprinkle' and *kakeru* 'put (on)'), obtained a high Dice coefficient and MI-score.[10] (19) is an example containing *furikakeru*.

(19) Shiromi no sakana ni *shio*, *koshō*, sake o furikake-te,
white.meat GEN fish DAT salt pepper sake ACC sprinkle-CONJ
sanjuppun hodo oi-te aji o najimase-te shiruke o
30.min. about leave-CONJ taste ACC bring.out.flavor-CONJ liquid ACC
kit-te oku.
drain-CONJ put
'Sprinkle salt, pepper and sake over the white-meat fish and leave it for thirty minutes to bring out the flavor and drain excess liquid.'

10. One of the components of *furikakeru*, [kakeru] 'put (on)', is also listed among the top 10 collocates but only in the t-score column of Table 4, making it a less significant collocate for both [shio] 'salt' and [koshō] 'pepper' than I expected (an example which immediately comes to my mind is *kakeru*). I leave for future research to determine why [kakeru] does not co-occur so frequently with [shio] or [koshō] in the corpus.

As shown in Table 3, verbs expressing coating [mabusu] and rubbing [surikomu] come high on the MI lists. The two verbs are also strongly associated with [koshō] in terms of MI-score, but they do not make the top list in Table 4 because they co-occur with [koshō] fewer than ten times. The following examples show how these verbs occur in the text: (21) includes *mabusu* 'coat', and (22) includes *surikomu* 'rub'.

(20) Okura wa *shio* o mabushi-te yude, heta o otoshi-te hanbun
okura TOP salt ACC coat-CONJ boil calyx ACC remove-CONJ half
ni kirimasu.
into cut
'Sprinkle salt over the okra, boil it, remove the calyx and cut it into half.'

(21) Butaniku ni *shio*, *koshō* o surikomimasu.
pork DAT salt pepper ACC rub
'Rub salt and pepper over the pork.'

Lastly, as Tables 3 and 4 show, verbs expressing mixing, [mazeru] 'mix' and [mazeawaseru] 'mix together', occur high on the Dice coefficient and MI lists. They may be used to express the addition of seasoning to food, but they can also be used when two or more spices are combined.

(22) Tamago wa toki, *shio*, *koshō* kaku shōshō o mazeru.
egg TOP beat salt pepper each a.little ACC mix
'Beat the egg and add (lit. 'mix') a little bit each of salt and pepper into the egg.'

(23) Tori-niku ni, *shio* to kuro-*koshō* o mazeawase-ta mono
chicken-meat DAT salt and black-pepper ACC mix.together-PST thing
o surikomu.
ACC rub
'Rub the mixture of salt and black pepper over the chicken.'

As a final note, the verbs discussed in this section are all semantically "heavy." Not surprisingly, in all examples, the terms for 'salt' and 'pepper' are accusative-marked.

4.2 Suru

The verb [suru] 'do' is the top collocate with both [shio] and [koshō] in terms of raw frequency and t-score. Based on an informal observation that 'salt' is a more basic seasoning than 'pepper', I focused on the usage of [shio] 'salt' and extracted examples of [suru] describing the act of seasoning. Table 5 shows the four most frequently occurring types of expressions.[11]

11. This list is not exhaustive. Another expression is *shio o hito-maze suru* [salt ACC a.pinch-mix do] 'mix a little salt in'.

Table 5. [shio] + [suru] as verbs of seasoning

Type	Frequency	Variation (written forms, with or without the accusative marker *o*)
shio-koshō-suru type 'season with salt and pepper'	142	"塩, 胡椒する", "塩コショウする" "塩・こしょうをする", etc.
chōmi-suru type 'season (something)'	66	"調味する"
aji-tsuke-suru type 'season (something)'	42	"味付けする", "味つけをする", etc.
shio-suru type 'salt (something)'	32	"塩をする", "ひと塩する", etc.
Total	**282**	

As Table 5 shows, *shio-koshō suru* type verbs (meaning 'season with salt and pepper') occur most frequently. They have two basic variations: *shio-koshō o suru* and *shio-koshō-suru.*[12] (24) gives an example of the former and (25) of the latter.

(24) Gyū-sutēki-niku no ryōmen ni *shio-koshō* o shi-te karuku
beef-steak-meat GEN both.sides DAT salt-pepper ACC do-CONJ lightly
osaetsuke-te kanagushi o 4–5-hon utsu.
press-CONJ metal.skewer ACC 4–5-CL put
'Salt and pepper the beef steak on both sides, press it and put four or five metal skewers into the meat.'

(25) Koushi no niku ni *shio-koshō*-suru.
calf GEN meat DAT salt-pepper-do
'Salt and pepper the calf meat.'

The difference between the two examples is the presence or absence of the accusative case marker *o* before *suru*. This contrast is arguably motivated by pragmatics, a topic for future study. An important point here is that with or without the case marker *o*, the food onto which the seasoning is added is marked by the dative case particle *ni*.

The second type listed in Table 5 is *chōmi-suru* 'season (something)'. *Chōmi* is composed of two Chinese characters "調 (/*chō*/)" 'arrange' and "味 (/*mi*/)" 'flavor',[13]

12. They contain further variations if orthographical differences are considered.

13. The pronunciation /mi/ is the Chinese style reading. Chinese characters in Japanese can typically be read in multiple ways, these readings broadly being split into Chinese-style readings (*on-yomi*) mainly used in Sino-Japanese vocabulary items and Japanese-style readings (*kun-yomi*) mainly used in words of native Japanese origin.

the semantic equivalent of the English verb *season*. One example with this verb comes from a recipe and is given in (26).

(26) 1 ni gohan o ire-te maze, *shio*, *koshō* de chōmi-shimasu.
1 DAT rice ACC put-CONJ mix salt pepper INST season-do
'Put rice into the ingredients of step 1, mix them, and season with salt and pepper.'

What is particularly interesting about this example is that the phrase for salt and pepper appears in the instrumental case *de*, which differs from the first type, where 'salt' and 'pepper' constitute part of the complex predicate.

The third type also includes the Chinese character "味". In this case, however, "味" is pronounced as /aji/ (the Japanese-style reading). Like the first type, *aji-tsuke o suru* [flavor-attach ACC do] has a variant without *o* [X-*suru*], *aji-tsuke-suru*; both are equivalent in meaning to the English *season*. (27) gives an example of *aji-tsuke-suru* 'season'.

(27) Kono sōsu o *shio koshō* de aji-tsuke-shi-ta oniku ya
this sauce ACC salt pepper INST flavor-attach-do-PST meat and
shīfūdo ni kakete itadaku to
seafood DAT put HUMB if
'If you pour this sauce over the meat or seafood seasoned with salt and pepper'

Note here that the word for 'pepper' appearing in juxtaposition with 'salt' is also marked with the instrumental case, analogously to the second type.

The last item on the list is *shio-suru* 'salt (something)'; it is similar to the first type but without *koshō* 'pepper'. It is interesting to note that its 'pepper' variant, *koshō-suru* 'pepper (something)', does not seem commonly used, although a Google search indicates that it is attested.

Other variants of the *shio-suru* type found in the BCCWJ include *shio o suru* [salt ACC do] and *hito-shio suru* [a-pinch-of-salt do]. (28) provides an example of the former.

(28) Ko-tamanegi wa karuku *shio* o shi-te icchūya oi-ta mono o
small-onion TOP lightly salt ACC do-CONJ all.day put-PST thing ACC
shōyu-eki ni tsukekomu.
soy.sauce-liquid DAT soak
'Salt the small onion, leave for all day and soak in soy-sauce-based sauce.'

In this example, the target item onto which the salt is added is 'small onion'. Here it is marked by *wa* 'topic', but if it were un-topicalized, it would be marked by *ni* 'dative', much like with the pattern of the first type (*shio-koshō-suru* 'season with salt and pepper').

4.3 Verbs for arranging and attaching

A verb for arranging, [totonoeru] 'arrange', obtains a high MI-score in Tables 3 and 4. Most of the examples appear in the phrase *aji o totonoeru* [flavor ACC arrange] 'season'. In 176 instances, [shio] 'salt' is collocated with [totonoeru] 'arrange'; of these, 171 belong to this type (*aji o totonoeru*). The verb can be represented by the Chinese character "調", as in *aji o totonoeru* "味を調える".[14] (29) shows one example of this complex predicate.

(29) Shītake no kawari.ni masshurūmu o tsukai, *shio*, *koshō* de aji
shitake GEN instead mushroom ACC use salt pepper INST flavor
o totonoe
ACC arrange
'Use mushrooms instead of shitake, and season with salt and pepper'

(29) is similar to (26) and (27), in that the phrase for 'salt'/'pepper' is marked by the instrumental case *de*. Furthermore, the two characters in the phrase can be put together, forming a different expression, *chōmi-suru* "調味する." The two expressions have essentially the same meaning (i.e., to season).

The verb [tsukeru] '(lit.) attach' also appears in both Tables 3 and 4. This verb is used as part of the phrase *aji o tsukeru* [flavor ACC attach], another semantic equivalent of the verb *season* in English. *Aji o tsukeru* has a morphologically related variant, *aji-tsuke o suru*. This form also has a counterpart without the case particle *o*, as in *aji-tsuke-suru* (Section 4.2). In this form, the verb *suru* 'do' attaches to the compound noun [NV], *aji-tsuke*, which consists of a noun [N] (*aji* 'taste') and an infinitival form of the verb [V] (*tsuke* 'attach). This association is quite common in Japanese (cf. Yumoto, 2010), wherein [NV] (e.g., *aji-tsuke*) serves as an input to create a complex phrase [[NV] *o suru*] (e.g., *aji-tsuke o suru*), which, in turn, is further associated with the case-less counterpart [[NV]-suru] (e.g., *aji-tsuke-suru*). The BCCWJ also contains *shita-aji o tsukeru* [pre-flavor ACC attach] 'season prior to cooking', a slight variation depicting an act of seasoning in the preparatory stage of cooking. Examples of these expressions appear in (30) and (31).

(30) Goma-abura to *shio*, shoyu de aji o tsukere-ba dekiagari
sesame-oil and salt soy.sauce INST flavor ACC attach-COND completion
'Season with sesame oil, salt and soy sauce before serving'

(31) Wakasagi ni *shio*, *koshō* de shita.aji o tsukeru.
pond.smelt DAT salt, pepper INST pre-flavor ACC attach
'Season the pond smelt with salt and pepper beforehand.'

14. Other written forms for *totonoeru* are "整える" and "ととのえる." The three forms are found in the BCCWJ.

Table 6 shows the token frequency of these two types of predicates. As the table indicates, the *aji o tsukeru* (season) type occurs more frequently than the *shita-aji o tsukeru* (season prior to cooking) type.

Table 6. [shio] + [tsukeru] as verbs of seasoning

Type	Frequency	Variation (written forms, with or without the accusative marker *o*)
aji o tsukeru type 'season'	30	"味をつける", "味付ける", etc.
shita-aji o tsukeru type 'season prior to cooking'	23	"下味を付ける" "下味をつける"
Total	53	

5. Constructions

5.1 Japanese verbs of seasoning and their English counterparts

This section explains the behavior of verbs observed so far in the context of locative alternation. It is widely accepted that the two constructions of locative alternation in English differ in construal. Pinker (1989) shows that they reflect different ways of construing the same event, characterizing them as "change of location" and "change of state." (32) shows relevant sentences reflecting the different construals: (32a) is associated with "change of location" and (32b) with "change of state." The two sentences in (33) are their respective Japanese equivalents.

(32) a. He smeared paint on the wall.
b. He smeared the wall with paint.

(33) a. penki o kabe ni nuru
paint ACC wall DAT smear
'smear paint on the wall'
b. kabe o penki de nuru
wall ACC paint INST smear
'smear the wall with paint'

According to Pinker, the sentence in (32a) focuses on the description of the action the agent performs on the paint, implying that the paint ended up on the wall (change of location). In contrast, (32b) highlights what the agent does to the wall. This naturally yields an interpretation that the wall is covered with paint (change of state) (cf. Anderson, 1971). Ikegami (1985) explains this contrast in terms of process-oriented and result-oriented construal. Process-oriented construal concentrates on the action itself, paying little attention to the result the action brings about, while result-oriented construal focuses on the resultant state achieved by the action, backgrounding the process. Japanese locative alternation can be analyzed in a parallel fashion (cf. Fukui, et al., 1985; Kishimoto, 2001).

With this in mind, we turn to the constructions in which verbs of seasoning occur. Verbs of seasoning in Japanese can be divided into two types: those taking seasoning as their object (marked with the accusative particle *o*) and those marking seasoning with the instrumental case particle *de*. I will refer to the constructions as the seasoning-as-object construction (cf. (16), (17)) and the seasoning-as-instrument construction (cf. (26), (27)) respectively. In this chapter, I treat some complex expressions like *aji o tsukeru* 'season' as one verb. Note that the verb's arguments are sometimes omitted when they are contextually recoverable in Japanese.[15] In recipes, the goal argument is frequently unexpressed and sometimes marked with the topic particle *wa* rather than a case-marking particle.[16] Table 7 summarizes Japanese verbs of seasoning and the constructions in which they occur.

Table 7. [shio]/[koshō] and verbs

Verbs	*shio/koshō*	Goal item	Example
kuwaeru 'add', *furu* 'sprinkle', *ireru* 'put', *furikakeru* 'sprinkle'	Marked by *o*.	Marked by *ni*.	*Shio, koshō o nabe ni kuwaeru.* 'Add salt and pepper to the pan.'; *Shio, koshō o niku ni furikakeru.* 'Sprinkle salt and pepper over the meat.'
aji o tsukeru, *aji-tsuke-suru*, *aji o totonoeru*, *chōmi-suru* (all mean 'season')	Marked by *de*.	Often unexpressed. If expressed, marked by *ni* or *o*.	*Niku wa shio, koshō de aji o totoneru* 'Season the meat with salt and pepper.'; *Niku wa shio, koshō de aji-tsuke-suru.* 'Season the meat with salt and pepper.'
shio-koshō-suru 'to salt and pepper'	Expressed as verb	Usually marked by *ni*, sometimes by *o*	*Niku ni shio-koshō-suru.* 'Salt and pepper the meat.'

Verbs like *kuwaeru* 'add', *furu* 'sprinkle', *ireru* 'put (in)', *furikakeru* 'sprinkle' mark the seasoning participant with *o*, and the goal participant, when expressed, with *ni*. These verbs encode some aspects of a motion event. *Ireru* 'put (in)' specifies the type of goal, in this case, the container, and *furikakeru* 'sprinkle' specifies the means of moving the seasonings.

15. In some frameworks, this phenomenon is called "PRO drop."

16. The omission of verb arguments in recipes is dealt with by Takano and Ueshima (2003). English generally does not allow the omission of arguments, but it does in recipes (Brown & Yule, 1983). See Mikami (1969) and Aoyama (1987) for the use of *wa* in recipes.

The verbs listed in Table 5 and 6 mark the seasoning participant with *de*. As seen in Sections 4.2 and 4.3, they all include the Chinese character "味" 'flavor', clearly showing that they encode giving flavor to food. In the BCCWJ, the goal participants of these verbs are either omitted or marked with the topic marker *wa* in most cases. If they are expressed, they differ as to which case particle is employed. As for *aji o tsukeru* and *aji o totonoeru*, the goal participant is unexpressed in the clause in which they occur, because in Japanese, the occurrence of more than one accusative-marked object in a simplex clause is not permitted (the so-called double-*o* constraint) (Harada, 2000[1973]; Shibatani, 1990, pp. 310–311). The goal participant can be marked by *ni* (the case particle for the goal), as with *Niku ni shio de aji o tsukeru* 'Season the meat with salt', because *tsukeru* 'attach' is associated with the goal participant. There are, in fact, examples of the strings [NP *ni aji o tsukeru*] and [NP *ni shita-aji o tsukeru*] in the BCCWJ (cf. (31)).

Yumoto (2015) reports that both [NP *ni*] and [NP *o*] are possible with *aji-tsuke-suru*. One reason why *aji-tsuke-suru* can take a goal participant as its object is that it is not in conflict with the double-*o* constraint. What is more, as Yumoto argues, the goal argument can be seen as the entity which undergoes the change of state (change of flavor) in the act of seasoning; as a result, it is marked with the accusative *o*. The same line of reasoning can be applied to *shio-koshō-suru*. The *shio-koshō-suru* type verbs usually mark the goal participant with *ni* (29 tokens in the BCCWJ), but accusative-marked nouns are also found with them (3 tokens).[17] Although examples in which the goal participant is marked with the accusative *o* are not common, they suggest that the accusative *o* is used more easily in culinary expressions. A similar phenomenon is found in English. Pinker (1989) classifies the verb *drizzle* as non-alternating (not allowed to occur in the construction where the goal participant is expressed as direct object), but it can participate in the locative alternation when used as a verb of seasoning (e.g., *Drizzle dressing over the salad* vs. *Drizzle the salad with dressing*). *Dribble*, another supposedly non-alternating verb, sometimes, if not often, alternates when used in recipes (*dribble* is less common in recipes than *drizzle*). See Iwata (2008) and Nonaka (2016, 2017b) for these uses of *drizzle* and *dribble*.

17. One example violates the double-*o* constraint.

reitō	no	mikkusu	bejitaburu	o	*shio,*	*koshō*	o	shi-te	1.pun
frozen	GEN	mixed	vegetable	ACC	salt	pepper	ACC	do-te	1.minute

hodo	itameru.
about	stir-fry.

'salt and pepper the frozen mixed vegetable and stir-fry for about 1 minute'

Let us turn our attention to English verbs of seasoning. I extracted verbs of seasoning from Ichikawa's (1995) dictionary of English collocations, which presents verbs co-occurring with *salt* and *pepper*. The verbs are summarized in Table 8.

Table 8. Salt/pepper and verbs

Verbs	Salt/pepper	Goal item	Examples
add/put	Expressed as object	*to* (add), *on*, *onto* (put), *over* (sprinkle)	*Add salt and pepper to the pan.* *Put salt and pepper on the meat.*
sprinkle	Expressed in a *with* phrase	Expressed as object	*Sprinkle salt and pepper over the meat.* *Sprinkle the meat with salt and pepper.*
season			*Season the meat with salt and pepper.*
salt/ pepper	Expressed as verb		*Salt the meat.* *Pepper the meat.* *Salt and pepper the meat.*

What is of crucial importance is that English has verbs occurring in both the seasoning-as-object construction and the seasoning-as-instrument construction: i.e., they participate in the locative alternation. Locative alternation verbs specify what kind of entity moves and how it moves, as well as what change is brought about for the goal participant. The property of *sprinkle* is shared by *furu* 'sprinkle' and *furikakeru* 'sprinkle' on the one hand and *aji-tsuke-suru* 'season' and *chōmi-suru* 'season' on the other.

In Japanese, verbs occurring in the seasoning-as-object construction are sometimes syntactically linked to those occurring in the seasoning-as-instrument construction by *-te* (V-*te* V complex predicates) in recipes (e.g., *shio o fut-te aji-tsuke-suru* 'Season by sprinkling salt.'). In English, the verb *sprinkle* alone is enough to describe the same event (e.g., *Sprinkle the meat with salt*). (34)–(36) show complex predicates with *te*.

(34) goma to *shio* o fut-te aji o totonoe-te, taki-tate
sesame and salt ACC sprinkle-CONJ flavor ACC arrange-CONJ cook-freshly
no gohan ni maze-te
GEN rice DAT mix-CONJ
'sprinkle it with sesame seeds and salt and add to freshly cooked rice'

(35) Atsui gohan ni *shio* shō-shō o ire-te aji-tsuke-shi
warm rice DAT salt a.little ACC put-CONJ flavor-attach-do-and
'season the hot rice, by sprinkling (lit. putting-in) salt and pepper, and'

(36) shashin no yōni abura ga ue ni bunri.suru gurai ni
picture GEN like oil NOM upper.side at separate about COP
nat-tara *shio* o kuwae-te aji-tsuke-suru.
become-when salt ACC add-CONJ flavor-attach-do
'when the oil becomes separated (floating) on the top (part of the food) as shown in the picture, add salt to season it.'

Fukui et al. (1985) argue locative alternation is less common in Japanese than in English, but V-V compounds sometimes provide a way for non-alternating verbs to participate in the alternation: specifically, the attachment of a verb such as *-tsukusu* '(lit.) exhaust' to the base verb renders it possible for the verb to alternate (see also Kishimoto, 2001; Iwata, 2008, pp. 186–192). This point is illustrated below.

(37) a. John loaded hay onto the wagon.
b. John loaded the wagon with hay.

(38) a. hoshikusa o niguruma ni tsumu
hay ACC wagon DAT load
'load the hay on the wagon'
b. *niguruma o hoshikusa de tsumu
wagon ACC hay INST load
'load the wagon with hey'
c. niguruma o hoshikusa de tsumi-tsukusu
wagon ACC hay INST load-exhaust
'load the wagon with hey' (Fukui et al. 1985, p. 12)

(37), repeated from (7), shows that the English *load* alternates. Meanwhile, in Japanese, *tsumu* 'load' cannot alternate, as in (38a) and (38b) (repeated from (11)). However, the addition of *-tsukusu* 'exhaust', as in (38c), makes it possible for *tsumu* 'load' to occur in the [NP *o* NP *de* V] construction.

This observation is insightful, but *tsumi-tsukusu* in (38c) is not a conventional expression in Japanese, giving the impression that the expression is artificially created for the sake of argument. Fukui et al. (1985) themselves admit that some native speakers might judge *tsumi-tsukusu* in (38c) not perfectly acceptable, even though it is more acceptable than *tsukusu* in (38b). From a usage-based point of view, it is important to identify conventional expressions in each language. Comparison of the locative alternation in English to the V-*te* V predicates in Japanese, as in (34)–(36), provides insight into the differences between English and Japanese. Differently stated, the pattern in (34)–(36) shows that the natural way of expressing in Japanese what the [V NP with NP] construction does in English is not by changing the verb form (using a compound verb as in (38c)) but by expressing the semantic content using a complex phrase with *-te*, a conjunct.

To state this more generally with a focus on verbs of seasoning, Japanese and English differ as to which form the semantic component of the method in a seasoning action is mapped onto: i.e., Japanese prefers to use a complex predicate with *-te* (e.g., *shio o kuwae-te* '(by) adding salt' (36), while English tends to employ the [V NP with NP] construction. This difference leads to a further question: Why does this difference obtain? That is the topic of the next subsection.

5.2 From the viewpoint of fashions of speaking

The difference between English and Japanese noted in Section 5.1 is arguably motivated by their respective fashions of speaking (Ikegami, 1981, 1985, 2008; Whorf, 1956). Whorf (1956) notes:

> They [= the concepts of 'time' and 'matter'] do not depend so much upon any one system (e.g., tense, or nouns) within the grammar as upon the ways of analyzing and reporting experience which have become fixed in the language as integrated "fashions of speaking" and which cut across the typical grammatical classifications, so that such a "fashion" may include lexical, morphological, syntactic, and otherwise systemically diverse means coordinated in a certain frame of consistency.
> (Whorf, 1956, p. 158)

Although Whorf mentions "fashions of speaking," he does not explain the concept in detail, leaving Ikegami (1981, 1985, 2008) to develop it in a series of publications. Ikegami presents a contrastive study of English and Japanese, applying the concept of "fashions of speaking" to a wide variety of phenomena. Ikegami (1985) argues that English tends to use result-oriented expressions, while Japanese has a strong tendency to employ process-oriented expressions. For example, the English causative verb *burn* implies the achievement of the goal, making (40a) contradictory. However, its Japanese counterpart *moyasu* does not necessarily imply the resultant state brought about by the action; hence, the Japanese sentence (40b) ('I burned it, but it didn't burn.') can be used depending on the context (the subject and the object are omitted in (40b)).

(40) a. *I burned it, but it didn't burn.
b. moyashi-ta keredo, moe-nakat-ta
burn-PST though burn-NEG-PST

(Ikegami, 1985, p. 273)[18]

18. The word-for-word gloss and the romanization convention for (40) and (41) are modified from the original to be consistent with the rest of the examples.

The differences between a result-oriented and a process-oriented nature can be observed in the usage of the resultative construction. Both English and Japanese have the resultative construction, but English has a wider range of usage (see Kageyama (1996) and Washio (1997) for more discussion of English and Japanese resultatives). (41) gives a contrasting pair.

(41) a. John hammered the metal flat.
b. ??John ga kinzoku o pechanko.ni tatai-ta.
John NOM metal ACC flat pound-PST
'John hammered the metal flat.' (Washio, 1997, p. 5)

(41a) shows that the English verb *hammer* can occur in the resultative construction, where the adjective *flat* refers to a state resulting from the action. In contrast, the corresponding Japanese sentence (41b) is judged unnatural, suggesting a more restricted distribution of verbs entering the resultative construction in Japanese than in English. English further permits resultatives involving intransitive verbs, and these are systematically missing from Japanese.

(42) a. I danced (with her).
b. I danced her weary. (Ikegami, 1985, p. 291)

(42) shows that the originally intransitive verb *dance* can occur in the resultative construction. Its Japanese equivalent is naturally disallowed, as (43) shows.

(43) a. Watashi wa (kanojo to) odot-ta.
I TOP she with dance-PST
'I danced (with her).'
b. *Watashi wa kanojo o kutakuta.ni odot-ta.
I TOP she ACC weary dance-PST
'(intended) I danced her weary.'

In short, the differences between English and Japanese in the distribution of the verbs in the resultative constructions are evidenced in the different fashions of speaking.

Ikegami (1985, 2000) further notes that this difference is reflected in the rarity of the [NP *o* NP *de* V] construction, a construction of concern in our discussion of locative alternation. English extends the meaning of verbs denoting caused-motion events to include the change of state undergone by the goal, allowing the verbs to participate in the locative alternation. English has a variety of alternating verbs, including some verbs of seasoning (e.g., *Sprinkle salt over the meat* vs. *Sprinkle the meat with salt*). The alternation is generally less common in Japanese; in the case of verbs of seasoning, different verbs must be used, depending on whether the process or the result is in focus (e.g., *shio o furikakeru* 'sprinkle salt' vs. *shio de ajituke suru* 'season (something) with salt').

The behavior of verbs of seasoning can now be discussed in light of the process- vs. result-orientation. First, consider the English examples given below.

(44) Process-oriented:
  a. Sprinkle salt and pepper over the meat.
  b. Put salt and pepper on the meat.

(45) Result-oriented:
  a. Sprinkle the meat with salt and pepper.
  b. Season the meat with salt and pepper.
  c. Salt and pepper the meat.

In the process-oriented descriptions in (44), more focus is on the caused motion of the seasoning. Accordingly, the seasoning (*salt* and *pepper*) is realized as the direct object of the verb (*sprinkle, put*). In contrast, in the result-oriented descriptions in (45), the goal participant (*meat*) is foregrounded, highlighting the result. As a result, the goal participant is realized as the direct object of the verb. Interestingly, the terms of seasoning, *salt* and *pepper*, are commonly used as denominal verbs, as in (45c). That is, they occur in the result-oriented construction, in parallel with *sprinkle* (45a) and *season* (45b).

Turning next to Japanese, the following examples show that Japanese has verbs of seasoning which display the same case-marking patterns as the English process- and result-oriented descriptions.

(46) Process-oriented:
  Niku ni shio, koshō o furu.
  meat DAT salt pepper ACC sprinkle
  'Sprinkle salt and paper over the meat.'

(47) Result-oriented:
  a. Niku o shio, koshō de aji-tsuke-suru.
  meat ACC salt pepper INST flavor-attach-do
  'Season the meat with salt and pepper.'
  b. Niku o shio-koshō-suru.
  meat ACC salt-pepper-do
  'Salt and pepper the meat.'

(48) In-between:
  a. Niku ni shio, koshō de aji-tsuke-suru.
  meat DAT salt pepper INST flavor-attach-do
  '(synonymous with) Season the meat with salt and pepper.'
  b. Niku ni shio-koshō-suru
  meat DAT salt-pepper-do
  '(synonymous with) Salt and pepper the meat.'

In (46), in the process-oriented description with the verb *furu* 'sprinkle', the term for seasoning (*shio* 'salt', *koshō* 'pepper') is realized with the accusative case *o*, while the goal participant *niku* 'meat' is marked by *ni* (goal particle). Meanwhile, in (47a), in the result-oriented description with the verb *aji-tsuke-suru* 'season', the goal participant *niku* 'meat' is marked by the accusative case *o*, while the term for seasoning (*shio* 'salt', *koshō* 'pepper') is marked by *de* (*with*-equivalent). A similar pattern is observed for *shio-koshō-suru* 'to salt and pepper' in (47b), where the goal participant *niku* 'meat' is marked by the accusative case *o*.

Japanese has a third pattern, which I call the "in-between" pattern, one that matches neither the process- nor the result-oriented descriptions, lying somewhere between the two. This is observed with *aji-tsuke-suru* 'season' ((47a) vs. (48a)) and *shio-koshō-suru* [(lit.) salt-pepper-do] ((47b) vs. (48b)). To use the latter as an example, the verb displays two case marking patterns: the goal participant *niku* 'meat' can be marked by the accusative particle *o*, as in (47b) (the result-oriented pattern) or by the goal particle *ni*, as shown in (48b) (the in-between pattern). Interestingly, the latter turns out to be much more frequent than the former. The question is why.

I offer two possible explanations. The first is that the predicate can be considered to have derived from [(NP *ni*) *shio-koshō o suru*] (cf. Section 4.2), making it possible for the goal participant to receive the original case particle *ni*, even though the actual predicate is no longer the same. The second explanation points to the process-oriented character of Japanese. This encourages speakers to avoid using the case-marking in the result-oriented description where the goal participant *niku* 'meat' receives the accusative case *o*; instead, it is marked by *ni* (goal particle) (see Table 9 for a summary).

Table 9. Uses of *shio-koshō-suru* and *aji-tsuke-suru*

	English	Japanese
process-oriented	*Put salt and pepper on the meat.* (=44b) *Sprinkle salt and pepper over the meat.* (=44a)	*Niku ni shio, koshō o furu.* 'Sprinkle salt and pepper over the meat.' (=46)
in-between	–	*Niku ni shio, koshō de aji-tsuke-suru.* (=48a) 'Season the meat with salt and pepper' *Niku ni shio-koshō suru.* (=48b) 'Salt and pepper the meat.'
result-oriented	*Sprinkle the meat with salt and pepper.* (=45a) *Season the meat with salt and pepper.* (=45b) *Salt and pepper the meat.* (=45c)	*Niku o shio, koshō de aji-tsuke-suru.* (=47a) 'Season the meat with salt and pepper.' *Niku o shio-koshō suru.* (=47b) 'Salt and pepper the meat.'

The examples given in this section suggest that the uses of verbs of seasoning in Japanese should be approached both from morphological complexity and the viewpoint of fashions of speaking.

6. Conclusion

This chapter has identified the types of predicates that can constitute Japanese verbs of seasoning found in the BCCWJ, dividing them into two types: those taking seasoning as direct object (e.g., *shio o furikakeru* 'sprinkle salt') and those marking seasoning with the instrumental case (e.g., *shio de aji-tuke-suru* 'season (something) with salt'). When they are compared to their English counterparts, we find that Japanese verbs of seasoning behave differently with respect to locative alternation. English has a variety of alternating verbs, including some verbs of seasoning (e.g., *Sprinkle salt over the meat* vs. *Sprinkle the meat with salt*). In general, it is much less common for Japanese verbs to alternate in this way, and in the realm of seasoning in particular, different verbs must be used depending on whether the process or the result is in focus. This chapter suggests that the differences between English and Japanese can be analyzed with respect to fashions of speaking (i.e., the tendency of Japanese verbs to be less result-oriented than their English counterparts) and also with respect to morphological complexity.

The chapter contributes to a better understanding of the characteristics of the grammar of the language of recipes, shedding new light on the use of the verbs of seasoning by showing how the meaning of seasoning (the elements that move) is manifested sometimes as a noun, i.e., expressed as an argument for general verbs of adding (e.g., *kuwaeru* 'add'), and sometimes as part of a complex predicate with *suru* 'do' (e.g., *aji-tsuke-suru* 'season' where the term of seasoning is incorporated into the base of the verb *suru*). My usage-based analysis of Japanese verbs of seasoning has unearthed a pattern hitherto unnoticed for the Japanese language: culinary terms are not merely a fraction of a register of the language but have substantial relevance to grammar. It is left for future research to examine to what extent the Japanese verbs of seasoning constitute a unique typological pattern or how this relates to the characterization of "motion events" (Talmy, 1985, 2000), a much-discussed topic in Cognitive Linguistics.

References

Anderson, S. R. (1971). On the role of deep structure in semantic interpretation. *Foundations of language, 7*, 387–396.

Aoyama, F. (1987). Ryōri no bunshō ni okeru teidai-ka no yakuwari [The role of topicalization in culinary texts]. In Mizutani Shizuo kyoju kanreki kinenkai (Ed.), *Keiryō kokugo-gaku to nihongo shori: Riron to ōyō* [Mathematical Linguistics and Language Processing for Japanese: Theory and Practice] (pp. 285–303). Tokyo: Akiyama Shoten.

Brown, G., & Yule, G. (1983). *Discourse analysis*. Cambridge: Cambridge University Press. https://doi.org/10.1017/CBO9780511805226

Chujo, K., & Uchiyama, M. (2004). Tōkei-teki shihyō o riyō-shita tokuchōgo chūshutsu ni kansuru kenkyū. [Using statistical measures to extract specialized vocabulary from a corpus]. *Kanto-Kōshin-Etsu Eigo Kyōiku Gakkai Kiyō* [The bulletin of the Kanto-koshin-etsu English Language Education Society] *18*, 99–108.

Fukui, N., Miyagawa, S., & Tenny, C. (1985). Verb classes in English and Japanese: A case study in the interaction of syntax, morphology and semantics. *Lexicon Project Working Papers 3, Center for cognitive science*. MIT, Cambridge, MA.

Harada, S. I. (2000[1973]). Counter Equi NP deletion. In N. Fukui. (Ed.), *Shintakusu to imi: Harada Shin-ichi gengogaku ronbun senshu* [Syntax and meaning: S. I. Harada collected works in linguistics], (pp.181–215). Tokyo: Taishukan.

Haspelmath, M. (1993). More on the typology of inchoative/causative verb alternations. In B. Comrie & M. Polinsky (Eds.), *Causatives and transitivity* (pp. 87–120). Amsterdam: John Benjamins. https://doi.org/10.1075/slcs.23.05has

Hunston, S. (2002). *Corpora in applied linguistics*. Cambridge: Cambridge University Press. https://doi.org/10.1017/CBO9781139524773

Ichikawa, S. (Ed.). (1995). *Shinpen-eiwa-katsuyō-daijiten* [The Kenkyusha dictionary of English collocations]. Tokyo: Kenkyusha.

Ikarashi, K., Fukutome, N., & Tsuyukubo, M. (2016). Kyōshoku katei no chōri-jisshu ni okeru daigakusei no ishiki-chōsa: "Kiru koto" o oshieru negate ishiki nit suite. [A report on university students' attitudes toward the practical cooking component of home economics teacher training: General lack of confidence in ability to teach cutting process]. *Bunka Gakuen Daigaku Kiyō* [The Bulletin of Bunka Gakuen University], *47*, 153–163.

Ikegami, Y. (1981). *"Suru" to "naru" no gengogaku* [The linguistics of "do" and "become"]. Tokyo: Taishukan.

Ikegami, Y. (1985). 'Activity'-'accomplishment'-'achievement': A language that can't say 'I burned it, but it didn't burn' and one that can. In A. Makkai (Ed.)., *Linguistics and philosophy: Essays in honor of Rulon S. Wells* (pp. 265–304). Amsterdam: John Benjamins. https://doi.org/10.1075/cilt.42.21ike

Ikegami, Y. (2000). 'Bounded' vs. 'unbounded' to 'cross-category harmony' (17). ['Bounded' vs. 'unbounded' and 'cross-category harmony' (17)] *Eigo Seinen* [The Rising Generation], *146*(5), 316–319.

Ikegami, Y. (2008). Subjective construal as a 'fashion of speaking' in Japanese. In María de los Ángeles Gómez González, J. Lachlan Mackenzie, and Elsa M. González Álvarez (Eds.), *Current trends in contrastive linguistics: Functional and cognitive perspectives* (pp. 227–250). Amsterdam: John Benjamins. https://doi.org/10.1075/sfsl.60.14ike

Ishikawa, S. (2008a). *Eigo Kōpasu to gengo kyōiku: dēta to shite no tekusuto* [English corpora and language teaching: Texts as data]. Tokyo: Taishukan.

Ishikawa, S. (2008b). Korokēshon no Kyōdo o dō hakaru ka: daisu-keisū, t-sukoa, sōgo-jōhōryō o chūshin toshite. [How to calculate the strength of collocations: The case of Dice coefficient, t-score and MI-score]. *Gengo-shori gakkai dai14-kai nenji taikai chūtoriaru shiryō* [Proceedings of the Tutorial Program of the 14th Annual Meeting of the Association for Natural Language Processing], 40–50.

Ishikawa, S. (2012). *Bēshikku kōpasu gengo-gaku* [A basic guide to corpus linguistics]. Tokyo: Hitsuji Shoboo.

Iwata, S. (2008). *Locative alternation: A lexical-constructional approach.* Amsterdam: John Benjamins. https://doi.org/10.1075/cal.6

Kageyama, T. (1980). The Role of thematic relations in the spray paint hypallage. *Papers in Japanese Linguistics, 7*, 35–64. https://doi.org/10.1515/jjl-1980-1-205

Kageyama, T. (1996). *Dōshi imiron* [Verb semantics]. Tokyo: Kuroshio.

Kishimoto, H. (2001). Locative alternation in Japanese: A case study in the interaction between syntax and lexical semantics. *Journal of Japanese linguistics, 17*, 59–81. https://doi.org/10.1515/jjl-2001-0106

Kunihiro, T. (1981). Goi no kōzō no hikaku [The comparison of lexical structures]. In T. Kunihiro (Ed.), *Imi to goi* [Meaning and Lexicon] (pp. 15–52). Tokyo: Taishukan.

Kunihiro, T. (1997). Risō no kokugo jiten. [A proposal for the improvement of Japanese dictionaries]. Tokyo: Taishukan.

Langacker, R. W. (2000). A dynamic usage-based model. In M. Barlow & S. Kemmer (Eds.), *Usage-based models of language*, (pp. 1–63). Stanford: CSLI Publications.

Lehrer, A. (1974). *Semantic fields and lexical structure.* Amsterdam: North-Holland Publishing Company.

Levin, B. (1993). *English verb classes and alternations: A preliminary investigation.* Chicago: University of Chicago Press.

Maruta, T., & Suga, K. (Eds.) (2000). *Nichi-Eigo no jita no kōtai.* [Causative alternation in Japanese and English]. Tokyo: Hitsuji Shobō.

Matsumoto, Y. (1997). Kūkan idō no gengo hyōgen to sono kakuchō [Expressions for motion event and their extension]. In M. Nakau (Ed.), *Kūkan to idō no hyōgen* [Expressions for space and motion] (pp.125–230). Tokyo: Kenkyuusha.

Matsumoto, Y. (1999). Kōbirudo kōpasu to eiwa jiten ni okeru spray/load kōtai [The spray/load alternation in the COBUILD corpus and English-Japanese dictionaries. *Meiji gakuin daigaku kyōiku kenkyūjo kiyō* [The Bulletin of Meiji Gakuin Research Center for Foreign Language Education], *9*, 23–35.

Mikami, A. (1969). *Zō wa hana ga nagai: Nihon bunpō nyūmon* [Elephants have a long trunk: An introduction to Japanese grammar]. Tokyo: Kuroshio.

National Institute for Japanese Language and Linguistics. The Balanced Corpus of Contemporary Written Japanese (Chunagon). Retrieved from https://chunagon.ninjal.ac.jp/search

Nishimura, Y., & Hasegawa, S. (2016). Goi, bunpo, konomareru īmawashi: Ninchi-bunpō no shiten [Lexicon, grammar and fashions of speaking: from the viewpoint of Cognitive Grammar]. In K. Fujita and Y. Nishimura (Eds.), *Nichi-ei taishō goi to bunpō heno tōgō teki apurōchi* [Integrated approaches to lexicon and grammar: Contrastive analyses of Japanese and English] (pp. 282–307). Tokyo: Kaitakusha.

Nonaka, D. (2016, July). How to cook with the locative alternation. Paper presented at the 6th UK Cognitive Linguistics Conference, Bangor University.

Nonaka, D. (2017a). Chōmiryō o kakeru koto o arawasu nihongo no dōshi to bashokaku kōtai: Gendai nihongo kaki-kotoba kinkō kōpasu o mochī-te [Verbs of seasoning in Japanese and the locative alternation: An analysis based on the Balanced Corpus of Contemporary Written Japanese]. *Tōkyō Daigaku Gengo-gaku Ronshū* [Tokyo University Linguistics Papers], *38*, 177–195.

Nonaka, D. (2017b). *Hi-kōtai-dōshi ga kōtai-suru toki: Ruisui to bunmyaku kara miru kōbun no seisansei* [When non-alternating verbs alternate: Constructional productivity, analogy and context]. *Human Linguistics Review*, *2*, 47–63.

Okutsu, K. (1980). Dōshi bunkei no hikaku. In T. Kunihiro (Ed.), *Bunpō* [Grammar] (pp. 63–100). Tokyo: Taishukan.

Okutsu, K. (1981). Idō henka dōshi bun: Iwayuru spray paint hypallage ni tsuite [The constructions for motion and change: On the so-called spray paint hypallage]. *Kokugo-gaku* [Japanese Linguistics], *127*, 21–33.

Pinker, S. (1989). *Learnability and cognition: The acquisition of argument structure*. Cambridge, MA: MIT Press.

Shibatani, M. (1990). *The Languages of Japan*. Cambridge: Cambridge University Press.

Sinclair, J. M. (1991). *Corpus, Concordance, Collocation*. Oxford: Oxford University Press.

Stubbs, M. (2002). *Words and phrases: Corpus studies of lexical semantics*. Oxford: Blackwell.

Takano, T., & Ueshima, S. (2003). Cooking scenario: Reshipi no shinario-ka to sono ōyō [Cooking scenario: Cooking support system with cooking scenario], *Denshi Jōhō Tsūshin Gakkai Gijutsu Kenkyū Hōkoku* [Technical Report of the Institute of Electronics, Information and Communication Engineers], *103*(190), 19–24.

Talmy, L. (1985). Lexicalization patterns: Semantic structure in lexical forms. In T. Shopen (Ed.), *Language typology and syntactic description, Vol. 3: Grammatical categories and the lexicon* (pp. 57–149). Cambridge: Cambridge University Press.

Talmy, L. (2000). *Toward a cognitive semantics, Vol. II: Typology and process in concept structuring*. Cambridge, MA: MIT Press.

Taylor, J. R. (2006). Polysemy and the lexicon. In G. Kristiansen, M. Achard, R. Dirven & F. J. R. D. Mendoza Ibáñez (Eds.), *Cognitive linguistics: Current applications and future perspectives* (pp. 51–80). Berlin: Mouton de Gruyter.

Taylor, J. R. (2012). *The mental corpus: How language is represented in the mind*. Oxford: Oxford University Press. https://doi.org/10.1093/acprof:oso/9780199290802.001.0001

Washio, R. (1997). Resultatives, compositionality and language variation. *Journal of East Asian Linguistics*, *6*, 1–49. https://doi.org/10.1023/A:1008257704110

Whorf, B. L. (1956). *Language, thought, and reality*. Cambridge, MA: MIT Press.

Yoshikawa, C. (1995). *Nichi-ei hikaku dōshi no bunpō* [A contrastive analysis of Japanese and English verbs]. Tokyo: Kuroshio.

Yumoto, Y. (2010). Variation in N-V compound verbs in Japanese. *Lingua*, *120*, 2388–2404. https://doi.org/10.1016/j.lingua.2010.04.004

Yumoto, Y. (2015). Nihongo no dōshi renyōkei o shuyōbu to suru dōmeishi ni tsuite. [On the nouns containing V-infinitive as a head] *Gengo bunka kyōdō kenkyū purojekuto* [Joint project on language and culture], 89–98.

CHAPTER 10

Motion expressions in Japanese wine-tasting descriptions

Yuko Yoshinari
Gifu University

This chapter analyzes motion expressions for wine aromas and flavors found in a corpus of wine-tasting notes, applying a typological theory of motion expressions (Talmy, 2000). Japanese wine-tasting descriptions are typically metaphoric, attempting to convey the motion of an entity, particularly aroma and flavor, around the sensory organs, similar to the case of English (Caballero, 2007). However, the following distinct features are observed in the Japanese wine-tasting context: (i) path-of-motion verbs are more predominantly used than manner-of-motion verbs to describe wine; (ii) a combination of a deictic verb and another verb (e.g., *de-te-kuru* [exit-CONJ-come] 'come out') is more frequently used than a single deictic verb. These characteristics mirror the patterns observed in Japanese descriptions of motion events in space.

Keywords: deixis, manner-of-motion verbs, metaphorical motion, motion events, path-of-motion verbs, wine-tasting notes

1. Introduction

Wine-tasting notes contain abundant metaphorical expressions (cf. Caballero, 2007). For instance, an English wine-tasting notes reads: "Exotic red berry aromas … *sneak up* on you rather than hit you over the head" (Lehrer, 2009, p. 40). Here, the verb phrase *sneak up* is used metaphorically, as if an aroma can be seen in motion. Furthermore, Caballero (2007) observes that English wine-tasting notes frequently contain manner-of-motion verbs such as *power* (1a) and *glide* (1b).

(1) a. Classy Chablis that stands as a monument to the 2000 vintage. So elegant and refined, *powering its way across* the palate with a fireball of intensely concentrated lime, kiwi, pineapple, dried herbs, freshly cut grass and spices.

b. Bright and focused, offering delicious blueberry, plum and spice flavors that *glide* smoothly *through* the silky finish. (Caballero, 2007, p. 2102)

https://doi.org/10.1075/celcr.25.10yos

In (1a), *power* expresses the vigorous "motion" of the wine's aroma and flavor, whereas in (1b), *glide* expresses its non-overpowering "motion." Notably, when wine-tasting notes contain manner-of-motion verbs as in (1), "'manner' is not concerned with actual motion but rather, with organoleptic perception, particularly perception via nose and mouth" (Caballero, 2007, p. 2102). Moreover, the trajectories of the aroma and flavor's motions are described by using prepositions such as *across* in (1a) and *through* in (1b).

Caballero (2007, 2017) argues that the use of motion verbs in English wine-tasting notes is consistent with how motion events in physical space are ordinarily described (e.g., *John walked into the room.*), following the typological pattern identified by Talmy (1985, 1991, 2000). According to Talmy, the basic motion event includes several semantic components: a moving entity (Figure); the reference entity with respect to which the Figure is moving or on which it is located (Ground); the trajectory of the Figure's motion (Path); and the way the Figure moves (Manner). Based on how the language encodes the Path component, Talmy classifies languages into two groups: "verb-framed languages" expressing Path in the verb, and "satellite-framed languages" expressing Path outside the verb. For example, English is categorized as a satellite-framed language, which expresses Path by a preposition (or "satellite") such as *into* in (2a), and Manner by the main verb. Meanwhile, Japanese, a verb-framed language, encodes Path in the main verb *hairu* 'enter' as in (2b).

(2) a. John ran into the room.
    b. John ga hashit-te heya ni hait-ta.
       John NOM run-CONJ room DAT enter-PST
       '(lit.) John entered the room running.'

This typological feature of Japanese, combined with the findings of Caballero (2007, 2017), leads to questions: How do Japanese wine tasters/critics describe their sensory experiences upon tasting wine? Do their descriptions follow a typological pattern of motion events similar to those of English wine-descriptions? To explore these questions, this chapter analyzes wine-tasting texts in Japanese, with a focus on motion expressions, especially the perceived "motion" of taste, smell, and mouthfeel. It examines the preferred verb types in Japanese wine-descriptions by analyzing the corpus compiled for this study (see Section 3, for more on the method). To be more specific, the chapter asks the following questions:

(3) a. What kinds of verbs are used in Japanese wine-descriptions?
    b. Do the Japanese texts contain motion expressions? If so, do they correspond to the patterns of verb-framed languages?
    c. What are the specific features of Japanese wine-descriptions?

The chapter shows that Japanese wine-descriptions use the same types of verbs as the descriptions of literal motion in space, particularly manner-of-motion verbs and path-of-motion verbs, following the patterns of verb-framed languages ((3a) and (3b)). It also finds that Japanese utilizes items from different lexical categories to express Manner, arguably as a trade-off for the paucity of manner-of-motion verbs in Japanese ((3c)).

The chapter proceeds as follows: Section 2 reviews the literature; Section 3 describes the method; Section 4 presents results with a discussion; and Section 5 offers a conclusion, elaborating on the typological implications of the present study.

2. Review of literature

2.1 Studies of wine-tasting notes

Studies on the characteristics of wine-tasting descriptions use different methods and take various perspectives. One study includes wine-experts as participants to produce a hierarchically structured vocabulary of mouthfeel characteristics of red wine (Gawel, Iland, & Francis, 2001). Another includes both experts and novices and examines the differences in their wine-tasting performances (Hughson & Boaks, 2001, 2002). Lehrer (2009) comprehensively explores wine descriptions by providing old and new wine descriptors and examining the wine descriptions of ordinary wine drinkers (non-experts) using several experiment paradigms. One such paradigm is to allow these wine drinkers to note down their own descriptions. Another is to discuss descriptions with a group.

A common way to study wine descriptions is to compile a data corpus by collecting wine-tasting notes. The data can then be used to examine the style of tasting notes (López-Arroyo & Roberts, 2014) or their vocabulary and grammar (Brochet & Dubourdieu, 2001; Caballero, 2007; Caballero & Suárez-Toste, 2010; Paradis & Eeg-Olofsson, 2013; Suárez-Toste, 2007). For instance, Brochet and Dubourdieu (2001) analyze the tasting notes of four expert wine tasters and find they all use expressions considered "prototypical" by combining descriptive terms to express their visual (e.g., *brown, purple*), olfactory (e.g., *apricot, pear*), gustatory (e.g., *acidic, sweet*), trigeminal (e.g., *tannic, hot*), hedonistic (e.g., *great, good*), and idealistic (e.g., *honestic, personality*) experience (Brochet & Dubourdieu, 2001, p. 190). Several studies compare the characteristics of Spanish and English wine-descriptions (Breit, 2014; Caballero & Ibarretxe-Antuñano, 2015). Breit (2014) reports a strong contrast between the free and literary manner of English and the concise style of Spanish tasting notes after comparing 110 notes on six red wines in English and Spanish taken from the internet.

Very few attempts have been made to study Japanese wine descriptions. Fukushima and Tanaka (2016) analyze wine and Japanese *sake* tasting notes from a corpus, focusing on the use of mimetic words (or, in their terms, "sound-symbolic words"), such as *honnori* 'slightly' and *tappuri* 'fully', which co-occur with the expressions of taste and smell. They find sound-symbolic words are frequently used to express an abstract taste (e.g., characterization of flavor, complexity), not to refer to a particular substance such as *remon* 'lemon' (cf. Fukushima, this volume).[1]

The work most relevant to this chapter is a series of studies conducted by Caballero independently and by Caballero together with her co-authors. Based on the analysis of her own wine corpus consisting of 12,000 tasting notes, the studies discuss such aspects as winespeak imagery (Caballero & Suárez-Toste, 2010), use of metaphors (Caballero & Suárez-Toste, 2008), typological differences between English and Spanish (Caballero & Ibarretxe-Antuñano, 2015), and verbs of motion (Caballero, 2007). As the studies show, analyzing wine-tasting notes can yield meaningful insight into gustatory and olfactory sensory expressions, including preferred expressions, motivations for using metaphorical expressions, and the use of diversity and universality to express organoleptic experiences.

2.2 Motion expressions in wine-tasting notes

One of Caballero's studies (2007) is especially important for this chapter in terms of analyzing motion verbs from a typological point of view. She argues manner-of-motion verbs showing the way movements occur (i.e., *run, jump, dance*) are frequently used in English wine descriptions, and the use of metaphorical motion expressions seems to be related to the typological theory of motion expressions. For example, in the English wine description "earthy flavors **run though** this firm-textured red," the manner-of-motion verb **run** is combined with the path preposition **through,** following the typical pattern of satellite-framed languages. This also means flavor is recognized as the agent of the motion. Caballero points out that motion verbs in wine-tasting descriptions may evoke an animate view of wine, as they require agents whose bodies can move (p. 2109). An example of this appears in the following description: "It strikes the right balance of weight and tang. It's a refreshing wine with the legs to run the race" (p. 2109). Here, the wine is conceptualized as an animate being with the legs to run, arguably an instantiation of a metaphor, "Wines are animate beings" (p. 2111).

1. Fukushima and Tanaka (2016) use the term "sound symbolic" in a broad sense, covering not only phonomimes but also phenomimes.

There are a number of studies on Japanese motion event descriptions of physical space (Matsumoto, 2017; Koga, Koloskova, Mizuno, & Aoki, 2008; Yoshinari, Eguchi, Mano, & Matsumoto, 2016). However, only a few studies have analyzed how motion events are described in wine-tasting notes in Japanese. While Fukushima and Tanaka (2016) offer an insightful report on Japanese wine-tasting descriptions, to the best of my knowledge, no Japanese work has applied Talmy's two-way typology to examine motion expressions related to gustatory and olfactory senses in wine-tasting descriptions. This chapter undertakes this task.

3. Method

3.1 Japanese data on wine-tasting notes

A Japanese wine-tasting corpus was created by gathering wine-tasting notes from issues of the *Real Wine Guide*, a magazine featuring introductory articles on wine. This magazine aims to give readers information on wine, especially fine wines at reasonable prices. It includes such information as the transformation of grapes into wine and the history of the wine industry. More importantly for the present purposes, it contains reviews, consisting of basic information about wines (e.g., brand name, producing district, year, price), wine-tasting scores, and tasting notes, written by the tasters, including the editors of the magazine, liquor traders, and private wine lovers. The comments are short texts (150 to 300 characters) with a focus on the wines' features that characterize tasters' olfactory, gustatory, and tactile sensations. Example (4) is a wine-tasting note from these data.

(4) Aruzasu 5 hinshu no burendo. Kaori ga totemo hanayakade, raichi, shiroi bara, shirokoshō nado no supaisukō ga arimasu. Tororitoshita shitazawaride, san ga yutaka. Yoin mo yaya nagame desu. Nihonjin no madamu ga "osushi ni au wain" o mezashite tsukurareta sōde, sassoku tameshite-mimashita. Shiromi, kairui, kani, akami, uni, tamago towa subarashī chōwa. Sumeshi, wasabi, shōyu ni au noga fushigi desu.
'This wine is a blend of five varieties of grapes in Alsace. The aroma is very gorgeous, resulting from the combination of the fragrances of lychee, white rose, and spicy flavor like white pepper. It has a thick, tactile, and rich acidity, and gives a slightly long reverberation. I heard that a Japanese madam made it to suit *sushi* perfectly, and I tested it straightaway. It was amazingly matched with white fish, shellfish, shrimp, crab, red fish, sea urchin eggs, and chicken eggs. It's interesting to note that it also goes well with vinegar rice, wasabi, soy sauce and sliced ginger.' (*Real Wine Guide* vol. 29, 2010, p. 120)

The comment begins with information on the grape's distribution, aroma, and flavor. After introducing the background information on how the wine was produced, the writer suggests that the wine complements the taste of sushi. As in this example, wine-tasting notes typically include information about a wine, an explanation of the wine's aroma and taste, and the writer's feelings or recommendations on what to drink it with.

For this study, I randomly collected about 1,800 comments from magazine issues of the past several years to analyze how wine tastes are described. I focused on verbs that convey the taster's olfactory, gustatory, and tactile sensations.[2]

3.2 Target forms for investigation

3.2.1 *Verbs and predicates*

First, I selected verbs and predicates used to express either sensory experiences, like flavor, aroma, and mouthfeel, or components, such as mineral, tannin, and acid. Examples of the former are shown in (5) and the latter in (6).

(5) Kaori wa toji-teiru. Shikashi, metarikkuna tōn o tomonai,
smell TOP close-PROG. but, metallic tone ACC accompany
taryōno mineraru ga sonzaishi-teiru.
abundant mineral NOM exit-PROG
'(lit.) The smell of the wine is closing. But considerable minerals accompany with metallic tone.'

(6) Ekitai wa yori namerakani nari, ume-tekina sanmo
liquid TOP more smoothly become apricot-like acidity also
de-te-kuru kara tamarimasen.
exit-CONJ-come because feel.overjoyed
'The liquid becomes smoother and the acidity like Japanese apricot aftertaste comes out and I feel overjoyed.'

These examples contain several different verbs: *tojiru* 'close', *tomonau* 'accompany', and *sonzaisuru* 'exist' in (5), and *naru* 'become', *deru* 'exit', and *tamaranai* 'be overjoyed' in (6).[3]

The abovementioned verbs express different concepts, where some express a motion. In wine-tasting notes, this typically is the movement of a component,

2. The wine-tasting comments come from the following issues: the *Real Wine Guide* vol. 8, 10 (2005), 21 (2008), 29 (2010), 36 (2012), 60 (2018), 64 (2019).

3. Some verbs have a context-specific meaning. For example, *tojiru* in (5) elsewhere means 'close', but here it means that a wine is not very aromatic, suggesting that the verb can obtain a new meaning when used in the context of a wine-tasting description.

aroma, or flavor of wine – a "conceptualized" movement of an entity that moves in or out of the wine, as described in *umeteki-na san mo dete-kuru* 'acidity like Japanese apricot comes out' in (6). Or they can express other concepts, such as 'existence' (*sonzaisuru* 'exist') in (5), 'change-of-state' (*naru* 'become') in (6), or a feeling (*tamaranai* 'feeling of being overjoyed') in (6).

A detailed analysis of semantic classes of verbs is given in Section 4. To more easily understand the semantic classes, it seems wise to clarify the usage of the term "motion verbs," as I do here, following Matsumoto (2017). According to Matsumoto, there are three types of Japanese motion verbs.

(7) Motion verbs:
  a. path-of-motion verbs: e.g., *deru* 'exit', *hirogaru* 'spread'
  b. manner-of-motion verbs: e.g., *tadayou* 'float', *hashiru* 'run'
  c. deictic verbs: e.g., *iku* 'go', *kuru* 'come'

An important point about this classification is that deictic verbs represent an independent class, accompanying the more commonly discussed path-of-motion verbs and manner-of-motion verbs. For Talmy (2000), the deictic component is part of Path. In contrast, Matsumoto (2017) suggests dividing the Path component into two: a deictic path, i.e., "Deixis," which indicates the direction of the Figure's movement toward the speaker or away from the speaker, and a non-deictic path, i.e., "Path," which solely indicates the direction of the Figure's movement like UP and DOWN.

A deictic verb can be used as an independent verb (e.g., *iku/kuru* 'go/come') or as a complex predicate (e.g., V-*te-iku*/V-*te-kuru* 'go V-ing/come V-ing), wherein the deictic verb takes a special slot – that is, the latter part of the predicate (e.g., *de-te-iku* [exit-CONJ-go] 'go out', *hait-te-kuru* [enter-CONJ-come] 'come inside'). Further, a deictic verb can be combined with the other types of motion verbs: in (8), a path-of-motion verb, *hairu* 'enter', is combined with *kuru* 'come', while in (9), it is combined with a manner-of-motion verb, *hashiru* 'run'.

(8) John wa heya ni hait-te-ki-ta.
  John TOP room DAT enter-CONJ-come-PST
  'John came into the room.'

(9) John wa heya no naka ni hashit-te-ki-ta.
  John TOP room GEN inside DAT run-CONJ-come-PST
  'John ran into the room.'

Frequent use of deictic verbs as complex predicates by Japanese speakers for spatial motion expressions has been reported in various studies (Koga et al., 2008; Yoshinari, 2014, 2015, 2016). The question of interest here is how this tendency is realized in wine descriptions – a question re-examined in Section 4.

To analyze the verbs and predicates in the wine-tasting corpus, I categorized them based on the type of verb stem (i.e., the base verbs). In other words, I did not take into consideration the information on the non-base parts, such as tense (e.g., past: *de-ta* 'exited'), aspect (e.g., progressive: *de-teiru* 'be exiting'), and polarity (e.g., negative: *de-nai* 'do not exit'), or the information expressed by the auxiliary verbs following the stem, such as *-tekureru* (showing beneficiary on act) or *-teshimau* (showing regret). Instead, I grouped the verbs and predicates with the same stem together under the same infinitive form of the verbs, such as *de-ru* 'exit'.[4] I also examined the token and type frequency of the base verbs (see Table 1).

3.2.2 *Nouns and noun phrases*

In my next step, I examined the types of nouns and noun phrases co-occurring with the verbs and predicates and classified them into those expressing Figure and Ground, as exemplified in (10).

(10) Figure:
 a. aroma and flavor: e.g., *kaori* 'scent', *ajiwai* 'flavor'
 b. components of wine: e.g., *mineraru* 'mineral', *san* 'acidity'

(11) Ground:
 a. a region in oral cavity:
  e.g., *kuchi no naka* 'inside the mouth', *shita* 'tongue'
 b. a region in nasal cavity: e.g., *hana* 'nose', *bikō* 'nasal passage'

These identifications are helpful, as an examination of the combination of Figure and verbs allows us to explore how wine aromas and flavors are described in Japanese wine-tasting notes. The inspection of the type of nouns and noun phrases expressing Ground permits us to explore the typological patterns of motion expressions – that is, how the Path components are expressed – whether inside or outside the verbs. We can thereby determine whether Japanese wine-descriptions tend to be satellite- or verb-framed.

4. Results and discussion

4.1 Verb types and usage ratio

The corpus contains 1,848 comments about the tastes of the wine. My analysis included determining the token frequency of 7,485 verbs, with 874 types of base verbs. From the data, I selected 103 types of verbs based on the frequency of use

4. An exception to this generalization is a verb of existence; I treated this as two predicates: *aru* 'exist' and *nai* 'not exist'.

(more than 10 times); this accounted for 77.4% of all verbs (token frequency). As summarized in Table 1, I categorized the verb types into four major semantic groups: Act, State, Motion, and Opinion (see the left-most column). Each group was further categorized into subtypes (see the middle column). Finally, I listed the verbs according to token frequency (the far-right column shown in parentheses). The table also indicates the percentage of usage for each group and verb type.

As Caballero (2007) notes in her discussion of the verbs in English wine-tasting notes, not all verbs used are motion verbs. Similarly, the verbs used in Japanese wine-tasting notes are not limited to motion verbs. I considered non-motion verbs as well, as it allows me to compare the proportion of the use of motion verbs to other verbs. While my classification is original, it draws on previous studies (Levin, 1993; Teramura, 1982).

Table 1. Classification of verbs in wine descriptions

Group	Verb type	Verb (frequency)
Act (13.0%)	Action (10.5%)	*suru* 'do' (339), *miseru* 'show' (40), *tsukuru* 'make' (31), *karamu* 'entangle' (30), *hyōgensuru* 'express' (30), *tsuzuku* 'continue' (29), *tatsu* 'stand' (21), *dekiru* 'can do' (18), *sonaeru* 'prepare' (17), *ajiwau* 'taste' (16), *hikaru* 'shine' (14), *sadamaru* 'be fixed' (12), *hakkisuru* 'demonstrate/show one's ability' (12)
	Effect (2.5%)	*ataeru* 'give' (39), *iyasu* 'heal' (21), *sasaeru* 'support' (16), *rensōsaseru* 'associate' (15), *shiageru* 'complete' (12), *umidasu* 'create' (11), *shimeru* 'tighten' (11), *nokosu* 'leave' (11), *kuwaeru* 'add' (11), *osaeru* 'restrain' (10)
State (51.9%)	Existence (25.9%)	*aru* 'exist' (1142), *nai* 'not exist' (303), *sonzaisuru* 'exist' (42), *dōkyosuru* 'live together' (13)
	Condition (7.5%)	*motsu* 'have' (158), *nokoru* 'stay' (41), *najimu* 'adapt oneself' (37), *baransu o toru* 'keep balance' (30), *ochitsuku* 'settle in' (29), *hukumu* 'include/have' (27), *sumu* 'be clear' (23), *medatsu* 'stand out' (22), *kiwadatsu* 'be conspicuous' (21), *obiru* 'bear/have' (13), *tamotsu* 'keep' (12), *himeru* 'keep something to oneself' (12), *kakeru* 'be short of' (10)
	Change-of-state (18.5%)	*naru* 'become' (167), *kaoru* 'perfume' (104), *kiku* 'be effective' (86), *jukusu* 'ripen' (73), *jūjitsusuru* 'enrich' (66), *tojiru* 'close' (56), *matomaru* 'be united' (53), *gyōshukusuru* 'condense' (51), *shiagaru* 'be completed' (49), *masu* 'increase' (47), *tsuku* 'stick' (45), *kuwawaru* 'be added' (42), *hiraku* 'open' (39), *jukuseisuru* 'ripen' (31), *michiru* 'be filled' (30), *hikishimeru* 'tighten' (22), *chijikomaru* 'curl oneself' (21), *chōwasuru* 'harmonize' (20), *kawaru* 'change' (19), *majiru* 'be mixed' (19), *shimaru* 'be tightened' (12), *kanjukusuru* 'fully ripen' (11), *hikishimaru* 'be tightened' (11)

(*continued*)

Table 1. (*continued*)

Group	Verb type	Verb (frequency)
Motion (20.0%)	Manner (3.9%)	*tadayou* 'float' (78), *noru* 'ride' (69), *hajikeru* 'burst' (17), *hisomu* 'be concealed' (17), *tomonau* 'accompany' (45)
	Path (14.0%)	*deru* 'appear/exit' (197), *tsumaru* 'be packed' (143), *hirogaru* 'spread' (102), *afureru* 'overflow' (92), *nobiru* 'stretch' (50), *shūchūsuru* 'converge' (41), *hairu* 'enter' (33), *tachiagaru* 'stand up' (29), *tokekomu* 'melt into' (25), *kao o dasu* 'make an appearance' (21), *arawareru* 'emerge' (18), *koeru* 'exceed' (16), *kieru* 'disappear' (15), *agaru* 'go up' (12), *wakiagaru* 'arise' (10), *appusuru* 'improve' (10)
	Deixis (0.3%)	*kuru* 'come' (15)
	Path-causative (1.3%)	*hanatsu* 'put out/emit' (15), *dasu* 'take out' (13), *toru* 'take off' (13), *ōu* 'spread over' (12), *hikidasu* 'bring out' (12), *tsutsumikomu* 'enclose' (11)
	Simple movement (0.5%)	*tsutawaru* 'be conveyed' (27)
Opinion (15.1%)	Feelings (13.6%)	*kanjiru* 'feel' (464), *omou* 'think' (95), *tanoshimu* 'enjoy' (82), *wakaru* 'find out' (41), *odoroku* 'be surprised' (35), *tamaranai* 'be overjoyed' (22), *kininaru* 'be concerned' (13), *oboeru* 'feel' (12), *kanshinsuru* 'admire' (10)
	Judgement (1.5%)	*yoku dekiru* 'be done well' (71), *sugureru* 'be superior to' (16)

There are four major semantic categories: "Act" refers to the entity's (i.e., aroma, flavor, tannin, acid etc.) dynamic action; "State" refers to the entity's situation/status; "Motion" refers to the entity's movement; and "Opinion" refers to the writer's comment. Each category has subtypes. Act has two subtypes: <Action>, expressing the entity's behavior with intransitive verbs, and <Effect>, expressing the action's influence on something else using transitive verbs. Example (12) shows examples including each verb, respectively.[5]

(12) Act

a. <Action>

Soko ni tsuyome no tarukō ga **karamu.**

there DAT strong GEN oaky.aroma NOM **entangle**

'Strong oaky aroma is entangled in there.'

5. The symbol, "< >," is used for showing the verb types. Verbs are shown in bold.

b. <Effect>
(Mineraru ga) wain zentai ni yori kihin to tsuya
mineral NOM wine whole DAT more elegance and luster
o **atae**, …
ACC **give**
'(Mineral) gives elegance and luster to the whole wine, …'

State has three subtypes: <Existence>, expressing the entity's existence; <Condition>, expressing how to exist; and <Change-of-state>, expressing how to change its state. (13) gives an example of each subtype.

(13) State
a. <Existence>
Kokochiyoi minerarukan to fukuzatsusei no **aru** kaori.
comfortable mineral.feeling and complexity GEN **exist** aroma
'Aromas with pleasant sense of mineral and complexity.'
b. <Condition>
Ekitai wa chūyo no nōdo o **mochi**, ….
liquid TOP medium GEN density ACC **have**
'Liquid has medium body, … '
c. <Change-of-state>
Mineraru-ga totemo yoku **kaoru**.
mineral NOM very well **be.fragrant**
'Mineral is well scented.'

Motion is divided into five subtypes. The first three are verbs expressing the entity's self-motion, namely manner-of-motion verbs (<Manner>), path-of-motion verbs (<Path>), and deictic verbs (<Deixis>) in (14a–c). The fourth is <Path-causative>, covering causative verbs of path-of-motion as in (14d). The fifth is <Simple movement>, expressing a movement like *tsutawaru* 'be conveyed' in (14e), where information on the wine's elegance is transmitted to the drinker.

(14) Motion
a. <Manner>
Kono wain kara wa kinoko to daichi no miwakutekina
this wine from TOP mushroom and earth GEN fascinating
kaori ga **tadayou**.
fragrance NOM **float**
'Fascinating fragrance of mushroom and earth {float/exude} from this wine.'

b. <Path>
Kajitsukan wa shikari **de-teiru.**
fruitiness TOP definitely **exit-PROG**
'Fruitiness is {coming out/oozing} definitely.'

c. <Deixis>
Mineraru no horonigasa ga **ki-te,** …
mineral GEN bittersweet NOM **come-CONJ**
'Bittersweet taste of mineral came, …'

d. <Path-causative>
Kuroi fūmi ga zentai o **ōu.**
black flavor SUB whole OBJ **cover**
'Flavors of black cover the whole drink.'

e. <Simple movement>
Hin no yosa ga bashibashi **tsutawat-te-kuru.**
quality GEN goodness NOM vigorously **spread-CONJ-come**
'Elegance is conveyed vigorously.'

Opinion has two subtypes: <Feelings>, expressing how the writer feels personally, and <Judgement>, expressing how the writer values the wine. One example of each subtype is shown in (15).

(15) Opinion

a. <Feelings>
Eregansu mo **kanjiru** ii kaori da.
elegance also **feel** good aroma is
'(It is) a good aroma making you feel elegance.'

b. <Judgement>
Totemo **yoku dekita** wain da.
very **well done** wine is
'(I conclude that this is) an excellent wine.'

When we turn to the characteristics of the distribution of these verbs in Table 1, we see the verbs of the State group are used most frequently to describe wine. The usage rates of <Existence> (25.9%) and <Change-of-state> (18.5%) are higher than other types of verbs. The higher rate of usage suggests information on what constitutes or 'exists in' the taste and flavor of wine is one of the most important characteristics to be conveyed when wine tasters experience wine. An examination of co-occurrence patterns for the verbs and the semantic arguments shows that *aru* 'there is …' and *nai* 'there is not …' frequently co-occur, not only with wine components (i.e., tannin, mineral, acid), but also with taste terms (i.e., sweetness, fruit flavor) and texture terms (i.e., thickness). As for verbs of <Change-of-state>, changes in a wine's taste and smell are often expressed, as in *oishiku-naru* 'become delicious' and *kaoru* 'be fragrant'.

Verbs of motion are the most frequently used after state verbs. However, the usage rate is not equal among the motion subtypes. <Path> verbs are the most frequently used. The following section provides more detailed observations.

4.2 Usage of motion verbs

4.2.1 *Patterns of motion expressions in Japanese wine-descriptions*

As Table 1 shows, in the motion group, path-of-motion verbs are more frequently used than manner-of-motion verbs in Japanese wine-descriptions (<Path>: 14.0%, <Manner>: 3.9%). This seems consistent with the pattern of a verb-framed language, wherein Path is expressed in the main verb. For example, in Japanese, only path-of-motion verbs are frequently used to express the movement of a wine's aroma and flavor, as in (16), while manner-of-motion verbs are also frequently used in English (Caballero, 2007). Verbs of <Path> are combined with the components of wine, such as *kaori* 'aroma', *ajiwai* 'flavor', and *san* 'acidity'. These combinations include *kaori-ga tachiagaru* [aroma-NOM rise] 'the smell rises' and *san-ga nobiru* [acidity-NOM stretch] 'acidity stretches'.

(16) Hanayakana kaori ga kuchi ippaini **hirogaru.**
gorgeous aroma NOM mouth fully **spread**
'The gorgeous aroma spreads throughout the whole mouth.'

Japanese compound verbs combining manner- and path-of-motion verbs, such as *toke-komu* [melt-enter] 'melt into', *waki-agaru* [spout-rise] 'arise', *hashiri-mawaru* [run-circle] 'run around', *shimi-wataru* [soak-cross] 'penetrate through', are also used. These verbs are counted as <Path>, because a Path component is placed in the head position of a compound verb (the last verb).

Path is also expressed in the main verb by using causative path verbs. Verbs categorized in <Path-causative> are used with the subject, such as the winemaker in (17a) and the wine itself in (17b).

(17) a. Ryōhinshu no iitokoro o umaku **hikidashi-teiru.**
both.varieties GEN good.point ACC successfully **draw-PROG**
'(The wine maker) draws out the distinctive qualities of both varieties of grapes.'

b. Chikayoriyasui kaori o **hanatsu** '03 desu ga, …
easily.recognized aroma ACC **emit** 2003 is but
'The 2003 vintage wine which emits familiar aroma …'

Path components are mostly encoded in the main verb for both self-motion and caused motion expressions. The results clearly show Japanese metaphorical motion expressions are consistent with the Japanese typological patterns of motion expressions, wherein Path is encoded in the main verb, thus showing a verb-framed language pattern.

4.2.2 *Compensation for manner-of-motion verbs*

The result shows that manner-of-motion verbs are rarely used in the Japanese wine-descriptions. It remains the issue how the Japanese realizes precise expressions of wine aromas and flavors without using them. That is because manner-of-motion verbs play a significant role in describing wine properties in the English wine-descriptions.

Caballero (2007) notes that manner-of-motion verbs help wine critics describe the most salient properties of wine, including organoleptic perceptions of the wine's taste and smell, commonly using a scalar expression, namely the degree of intensity and persistence of aromas and flavors. The former (intensity) has two scales: '+/−force' which correspond to the semantic components of "lower/higher energy," and '+/−speed,' the more general notion, which subsumes "rate" and "smooth motion." She adjusts manner-of-motion verbs to the specific context of wine tasting to articulate the assessment of a wine's aroma and flavors. For instance, verbs such as *burst* or *explode* are placed on the positive extreme of the intensity cline '+force,' while verbs such as *glide* or *float* are placed in both '−force' and '−speed.'

This characteristic raises the question: How does Japanese compensate for the paucity of manner-of-motion verbs in wine descriptions? Recall that the rate of manner-of-motion verbs was only 3.9% in Table 1. That is, how does the Japanese language express the characteristics mentioned by Caballero (2007), when the number of manner-of-motion verbs is so limited?

One possible answer is that other parts of speech such as adjectives, adverbs, and other types of verbs are adopted to express wine's intensity or the persistence of its aromas and flavors; this, in fact, can be predicted based on the observations of Japanese descriptions of actual motion events given below.

In the first place, Japanese has fewer manner-of-motion verbs than English (Matsumoto, 2017) and other verb-framed languages such as French and Spanish (Wienold & Schwarze, 2002). Slobin's series of studies (1996, 2000, 2004, 2006) reveal that Manner components are expressed well in the descriptions of motion events in satellite-framed languages, but are omitted in verb-framed languages. Yoshinari et al. (2016) note that Manner tends to be ignored in the Japanese description of motion events, depending on the type of motion event, and adverbs are used instead of verbs to express Manner, such as *kakeashide* 'at a run' instead of a verb meaning 'run'. Moreover, in a linguistic experiment, Akita, Matsumoto and Ohara (2009) demonstrate that Japanese speakers basically express Manner in the same way as English speakers, using mimetic words as in (18). The mimetic *gan* expresses a loud clanking sound, used here adverbially with a quotative particle *to*.

(18) Bōru ga gan.to teppan no ue ni ochi.ta.
ball NOM clankingly plate GEN avobe DAT fell.PST
'A ball clanged onto a plate on the ground' (Akita et al., 2009, p. 7)

These studies show that other parts of speech are adopted to express Manner in Japanese; in the case of wine, classes such as adverbs, nouns, and adjectives are used instead of manner-of-motion verbs to express wine's salient properties, such as intensity and the persistence of the aroma and flavor.

Let us now turn to the elements (part of speech class) co-occurring with verbs to express wine's properties. First, verbs of <Existence>, the most frequently used type in the wine-tasting corpus, are used to express higher/lower intensity of wine aroma and flavor. These verbs, such as *aru/nai* 'exist/not exist', are commonly used in combination with various subjects to express the existence of aroma and flavor e.g., *kaori-ga aru* 'aromas exist' or *sanmi-ga nai* 'sour flavor does not exist'. How they exist can be expressed using adjectives indicating the intensity of an entity, such as *koi/usui aji* 'strong/weak taste' or *tsuyoi/yowai kaori* 'strong/weak aroma', as illustrated in (19).

(19) Yutakana kajitsumi to chikarazuyoi kaori, san mo
rich fruity.flavor and powerful aroma acid also
tekidoni **ari**, ...
moderately **exist**
'(The wine) has a rich fruity flavor, strong aroma and moderate acidity, ...'

This sentence shows the higher intensity of the flavor and aroma through such adjectives as *yutakana* 'rich' and *chikarazuyoi* 'strong', and the middle intensity of acidity through the adverb *tekidoni* 'moderately'. In the data, the adverbs expressing degree of intensity, such as *shikkari* 'sufficiently', *jūbunni* 'enough', *kichinto* 'properly', *sukoshi* 'a little', *hodohodoni* 'modestly', and *mattaku (nai)* 'absolutely none', are used with *aru/nai*.

The intensity of the wine's aroma and flavor is also described by a combination of verbs of <Existence> and specific nouns, including the meaning of power or quantity, as in (20).

(20) Hodoyoi jūryōkan ga **aru.**
appropriate heavy.weight NOM **exist**
'(This wine) is massive appropriately.'

The basic meaning of *jūryōkan* is 'heavy weight', and this sentence means the wine is thick and heavy, i.e., "full-bodied." The combination of this kind of noun with a verb of <Existence> as in (20) expresses the intensity of the olfactory and gustatory sensations created by the wine. This pattern is frequently used in the data; to give an example, (21a) shows higher intensity, and (21b) shows lower intensity.

(21) a. *atsumi-ga aru* 'have thickness', *chikara-ga aru* 'have power', *gyōshukukan-ga aru* 'be condensed', *koku-ga aru* 'rich flavor', *nōdo-ga aru* 'high density', *nomigotae-ga aru* 'substantial drink', *ikioi-ga aru* 'tremendous boost', *suki-ga nai* 'full'

b. *karoyakasa-ga aru* 'light', *suki-ga aru* 'flimsy', *omosa-ga nai* 'lightweight', *nōkōsa-ga nai* 'not thick', *mitsudo-ga nai* 'no density'

Second, the combination of *suru* 'do' from <Action> and adverbs of manner to indicate the degree of intensity, as illustrated in (22) and (23), is also used often.

(22) San ga ikiikito **shi-teiru.**
acid NOM actively **do-PROG**
'(The wine) has strong acidity.'

(23) Mineraru ya tannin ga shikkarito **shi-ta** wain.
mineral and tannin NOM sufficiently **do-PST** wine
'(It is) the wine with sufficient minerals and tannin (tannoids).'

The modification of acid by using *ikiikito suru* 'do actively/vivid' to describe wine represents the strong acidity referred to in (22). The phrase *shikkarito shita* 'massive/robust' expresses plenty of minerals and tannin in (23). The verb *suru*, which belongs to <Action> expressing the entity's behavior, can also depict the current status in the form of *shiteiru* and *shita*. Hence, it is useful to express the wine properties by using a combination of adverbs and the verb *suru*.

The adverbs can be used with other verbs as well, as in (24) and (25).

(24) Orenji, kokutō, supaisu ga honnori **kaoru.**
orange blown.sugar spice NOM slightly **be.fragrant**
'(The wine has) light aromas of orange, brown sugar and spice.'

(25) Honokani **kanjiru** umami.
faintly **feel** umami (savoury)
'It is faintly savoury.'

The combination of the adverb and the verb expresses '–force' intensity of wine aroma in (24) and '–force' intensity of wine taste in (25).

Another salient property of wine, the persistence of aroma and flavor, is also expressed by adjectives, as in (26), and adverbs, as in (27). The combination of a specific noun and verb is the key to expressing persistence.

(26) Yoin wa totemo nagai.
aftertaste TOP very long
'It leaves a long aftertaste.'

(27) Kaori ga zutto **tsuzuku.**
aroma NOM forever **continue**
'The aroma exists for a long time.'

The noun *yoin*, which includes the meaning of the time of tasting, can express durability or persistence through the addition of the adjectives *nagai/mijikai* 'long/short', as in (26). The combination of the verb *tsuzuku* 'continue' with aroma and flavor can express persistence. The addition of adverbs such as *nagaku/zutto* 'for a long time' suggests longer persistence. The use of a negative form like *tsuzuka-nai* 'not continue' represents shorter persistence.

It should be noted that the adverbs used to express wine's properties in some examples include mimetic expressions like *shikkarito* 'firmly' in (23); and *honnori* 'slightly' in (24). This usage corroborates with Fukushima and Tanaka's (2016) observation that sound-symbolic expressions are often used in Japanese wine-descriptions. My data show a similar tendency. Various mimetic expressions are frequently used, helping wine tasters express the salient properties of wine that would be expressed by manner-of-motion verbs in English wine-descriptions.

As the preceding examples illustrate, in Japanese, specific nouns, adjectives, and adverbs are utilized to make up for the paucity of manner-of-motion verbs in wine descriptions. According to Caballero (2007), the salient properties of wine, such as the intensity and persistence (durability) of aroma and flavor, are expressed by manner-of-motion verbs in English. In contrast, in Japanese, these properties are expressed by different means, namely, by verbs combined with a specific type of noun or a variety of adjectives and adverbs. To be more specific, to render a higher/lower intensity, verbs of <Existence> (*aru/nai* 'exist/not exist') are used with adjectives (e.g., *yutakana kaori* 'rich aroma') or a specific type of noun, such as a noun referring to a flavor, *koku* 'richness' in (21), while the verb *suru* 'do' is used with adverbs (e.g., *ikiiki-to suru* 'do vividly'). To render a longer/shorter durability, specific types of nouns and predicates related to persistence are used with adjectives and adverbs (see (26),(27)).

4.2.3 *The role of path-of-motion verbs*

Finally, I would like to emphasize that path-of-motion verbs play an important role in wine-tasting descriptions. These verbs are effectively combined with adverbs to elaborate on the details of wine properties. For instance, the path-of-motion verb *hirogaru* 'spread' expressing the trajectory of aroma or flavor movement in various directions is frequently used. Examples (28) and (29) show how the intensity and persistence of wine's properties are expressed using the path-of-motion verb *hirogaru* 'spread' and an adverb, respectively.

(28) Kajitsumi ga kuchi ippaini **hirogat-ta.**
fruity.flavor NOM mouth full **spread-PST**
'A fruity flavor spreads throughout the mouth.'

(29) Kaori ga jinwari **hirogaru.**
aroma NOM gradually **spread**
'An aroma spreads slowly and gradually.'

In (28), the intensity of flavor traveling across the taster's oral cavity is expressed by the adverbial *kuchi ippaini* 'mouth full of', together with the verb *hirogaru* 'spread'. By indicating the Ground *kuchi* 'palate' and status of flavor *ippaini* 'full', the sentence expresses the effect of the flavor. Interestingly, the combination of *hirogaru* and Ground expresses an additional meaning of intensity. Most of the Ground for the verb *hirogaru* is *kōchū/kuchi no naka* 'inside the mouth', expressing the place (mouth) where something (aroma and flavor) spreads. It implies 'mouth full of' – using the adverb *ippaini* 'full'; in other words, it expresses the '+force' intensity.

In (29), the slow speed but long persistence of aroma is expressed by the mimetic adverb, *jinwari* 'gradually', in combination with the verb *hirogaru* 'spread'. Basically, these adverbials (*ippaini, jinwari*) express how wine's flavor and aroma spread. They also represent the property of taste.

The degree of persistence of a wine's aroma and flavor is expressed by using path-of-motion verbs like (30).

(30) Kaori ga suguni **kieru.**
aroma NOM immediately **disappear**
'The aroma of the wine disappears immediately.'

In (30), the path-of-motion verb *kieru* 'disappear' is combined with the adverb *suguni* to express a shorter durability or persistence of aroma. An example in the data expressing short persistence/lingering is *patto kieru* 'instantly disappear', and one expressing longer persistence/lingering is *nakanaka kienai* 'hardly disappear'.

4.3 Semantic arguments of verbs

This section reiterates the types of semantic arguments of different verbs and predicates. Following are some examples.

(31) Sugusama kajitsu to daichi no hukuzatsuna aji ga
immediately fruit and earthy GEN complicated taste NOM
kōchū o **ōu.**
inside.the.mouth ACC **cover**
'A complicated combination of fruity and earthy flavor immediately spreads throughout the mouth.'

(32) (San ga) ekitai ni eregansu o atae, rinkaku o **keiseishi**,
acidity NOM liquid DAT elegance ACC give outline ACC **form**
rittaitekina aji o **tsukuru**.
three.dimensional taste ACC **make**
'(Acidity) gives elegance to wine, forms its outline, and adds dimensions to the taste.'

Example (31) shows a description of motion events, where *aji* 'taste' (Figure) spreads throughout (Path) the mouth (Ground). Example (32) shows a description of caused motion events, where *san* 'acidity' (Causer) brings about changes of wine through giving, forming, and making. Interestingly, both descriptions take an inanimate semantic argument as "subject" – something commonly observed in wine descriptions.

The discovery that Japanese wine-descriptions employ transitive sentences with an inanimate subject is somewhat unexpected (see Abe, this volume, for a similar discussion). It is frequently noted that Japanese does not tend to use an inanimate subject in a transitive construction, as in (33).

(33) a. *Kaze ga mado o wat-ta.
wind NOM window ACC break(transitive)-PST
'The wind broke the window.'
b. Kaze de mado ga ware-ta.
wind by window NOM break(intransitive)-PST
'The window broke because of the wind.'

This difference in grammaticality between the two sentences in (33) sharply contrasts with the case of wine-tasting notes in (31) and (32), where the inanimate agent, such as wine elements (aroma, flavor, tannin, etc.), can be the semantic arguments of transitive verbs.

In sum, the examination of the verb types and their usage frequency in wine descriptions indicates that Japanese wine-tasting notes often use verbs of <Existence>, <Change-of-state>, and <Path>. Furthermore, the typical semantic arguments of these verbs are the wine's aroma, flavor, and components. These results suggest a construction with an inanimate subject is frequently used in wine-tasting notes (see Abe, this volume, for a similar observation). As Caballero (2007) and Suárez-Toste (2007) note, metaphorical techniques such as personification help to express the properties of wine and are frequently used in English wine-tasting notes. It is reserved for future work to detail the types of metaphors used in Japanese wine descriptions.

4.4 Specific feature of motion expressions in Japanese: Deixis

Some studies claim that Japanese speakers tend to give deictic information, Deixis, when they describe motion events (literal) by using a deictic verb in a complex predicate (Koga et. al., 2008; Yoshinari, 2016). The complex predicate consists of the base verb and a deictic verb such as *arui-te-iku* [walk-CONJ-go] 'go walking' or *hait-te-kuru* [enter-CONJ-come] 'come entering'. In these forms, the deictic verbs *iku/kuru* 'go/come' add deictic information with reference to the speaker: V-*te-iku* indicates 'away from the speaker', and V-*te-kuru* indicates 'towards the speaker'. In my corpus, out of the 7,485 verbs, V-*te-iku* is used 81 times (1.1%) and V-*te-kuru,* 350 times (4.7%). The usage of complex predicates is not that frequent, but when they appear, they tend to be combined with a particular verb because in the corpus the deictic verbs appear much less frequently as independent verbs: *iku* (2 times), *kuru* (24 times).

Let us now analyze the use of complex predicates. Firstly, many combinations appear with verbs of <Change-of-state>, as in *oishiku-nat-te-iku* 'become delicious', *toke-te-iku* 'melt gradually', and *najin-de-kuru* 'gradually become fit'. In these instances, the predicates do not mean the direction toward the speaker but the change of state, referring to the passing of time. For example, *tokeru* 'melt' and *toke-te-iku* [melt-CONJ-go] both indicate that the state of something changes, but the latter expresses the continuation of change, as in (34).

(34) Katamarijō no ekisu ga yukkurito shita no ue de
clumpy GEN extract NOM slowly tongue GEN above LOC
toke-te-iki...
melt-CONJ-go
'A clump of extract has been melting on the tongue slowly'

As (34) shows, to emphasize this sense, the pattern occasionally co-occurs with adverbs of manner, such as *yukkurito* 'slowly', *jinwari* 'gradually', *suguni* 'immediately', and so on.

Secondly, the deictic verbs frequently combine with verbs of <Path>, as in *de-te-kuru* [exit-CONJ-come] and *hirogat-te-iku* [spread-CONJ-go]. The deictic verb *iku* 'go' is seldom used; it means a continuous movement when used with an adverb of manner, as in (35). The sentence expresses that it takes time for the wine to spread in the mouth, much like the combination of verbs in <Change-of-state>.

(35) Ekitai ga yukkurito kuchi no naka ni **hirogat-te-iku.**
liquid NOM slowly mouth GEN inside DAT **spread-CONJ-go**
'The wine has been spreading slowly throughout the mouth.'

Most of the time, the deictic verb *kuru* is combined with path-of-motion verbs, yielding two types of meaning: a continuation of moving as in (36) and a direction toward the speaker as in (37).

(36) Jikan totomoni meruro rashisa ga **de-te-kuru**.
time along.with Merlot identity NOM **exit-CONJ-come**
'The essence of Merlot comes out with time.'

(37) Wain kara iso no kaori ga **de-te-kuru** to, supagettī ga
wine from ocean GEN flavor NOM **exit-CONJ-come** when spaghetti NOM
tabe-taku-naru.
eat-want-become
'When the flavor of ocean exudes from wine, it makes me crave to eat spaghetti.'

Example (36) expresses the change in the wine's taste, where the characteristic taste of Merlot is developed with time. In (37), the flavor does not literally move to the speaker. However, there is a difference in meaning between the phrases of *kaori-ga deru* [aroma-NOM exit] and *kaori-ga de-te-kuru* [aroma-NOM exit-CONJ-come]. Both show the appearance of aromas. In addition, the predicate *de-te-kuru* expresses the aroma's movement toward the speaker (taster). The movement does not target the direction of the speaker; rather, it is a spreading movement in the area where the speaker is located. Furthermore, what is conveyed here by the predicate *de-te-kuru* is the appearance of flavor and its intensity. The verb *deru* 'exit/come out' connotes the meaning 'appear'. When it is combined with the deictic verb, the complex predicate *de-te-kuru* evokes a vivid image, conveying that the flavor has appeared and directly approached the drinker's taste buds. In other words, path-of-motion verbs can serve as a useful means to describe wine's properties more adequately when paired with the deictic verb *kuru*. Stated differently, the combination of a path-of-motion verb and the deictic verb *kuru* allows tasters to vividly express their organoleptic perceptions in Japanese.

An important finding is that when the verbs are combined with a deictic verb, be it a <Path> or a <Change-of-state> verb, the complex predicates express a change in the tastes and smells of wine over time; they also show the perceived (but non-veridical) movement of tastes and smells toward the taster to elaborate on the wine's properties. Whether this characteristic is specific to Japanese or common among languages that combine complex predicates with deictic verbs, such as Korean, is left for future investigation.

5. Conclusion

This chapter has investigated how Japanese writers convey the characteristics of the wine they taste, drawing on data from Japanese wine-tasting notes in wine magazines. It has considered how wine connoisseurs describe the properties of wine. My analysis shows the verbs used in wine-tasting notes can be classed into four main semantic categories: Act, State, Motion, and Opinion. Importantly, each category consists of distinct sub-types, and the identification of the verbs belonging to these subtypes sheds critical light on the typological characteristics of Japanese, especially the distinction of path-of-motion vis-à-vis manner-of-motion verbs (see Table 1). Future studies will confirm whether these categories can be used to analyze wine tasting notes in other languages.

One major finding of this chapter is that path-of-motion verbs are more commonly used than manner-of-motion verbs in Japanese to describe wine's properties, such as intensity or persistence of aroma and flavor. This use is in line with the general typological pattern of verb-framed languages in the physical spatial domain, where path-of-motion verbs are employed to express the notion of Path, a trajectory of motion (Talmy, 1985, 2000).

This stands in stark contrast to the pattern of satellite-framed languages such as English, specifically their use of a satellite element (e.g., preposition) to express the notion of Path, with verbs reserved to express Manner and Motion (Talmy, 1985, 2000). Needless to say, this pattern is also observed in the description of wine's properties, as argued in Caballero (2007). However, it should be highlighted that the languages express wine's salient properties in a different way following their own typological patterns of motion expressions.

To reiterate, to express the persistence of wine's aroma, English uses a manner-of-motion verb (e.g., *sail*) and a path preposition (e.g., *on*), as in "the aroma sails on and on," whereas Japanese uses a path-of-motion verb (e.g., *hirogaru* 'spread') in combination with a deictic verb (e.g., V-*te-kuru*) and an adverbial element, such as a mimetic word (e.g., *jinwari* 'gradually'), as in *kaori-ga jinwari hirogat-te-iku* 'aroma gradually/slowly spreads in time'. Despite the apparent differences in the form-meaning mapping patterns in the two languages, the purpose of using motion expressions seems the same – that is, to elaborate on and vividly render the characteristics of wine.

A careful reader may argue that the scope of study is insufficient to make a generalization about the typology of motion events (Talmy, 1985, 2000), as Japanese is not a typical verb-framed language, as claimed by scholars like Matsumoto (2017). Specifically, Japanese can adopt a complex predicate consisting of Manner, Path, and Deixis (without yielding any semantic incongruity among these elements), whereas other verb-framed languages such as Spanish predominantly use a single verb, expressing one semantic component, namely Path, as a main predicate.

To arrive at a generalization, it is necessary to compare a satellite-framed language to a more typical verb-framed language, such as a Romance language. This possibility calls for more studies investigating to what extent the typological theory of motion events can be extended to cover metaphorical motion expressions.

References

Akita, K., Matsumoto, Y., & Ohara, K. (2009). Deictic path expressions and manner lexicon in the typology of motion expressions, *Lexicon Forum*, *5*, 1–25. Tokyo: Hituzi Shobo Publishing.

Breit, W. B. (2014). Appraisal theory applied to the wine tasting sheet in English and Spanish, *Iberica*, *27*, 97–120.

Brochet, F., & Dubourdieu, D. (2001). Wine descriptive language supports cognitive specificity of chemical senses. *Brain and Language*, *77*, 187–196. https://doi.org/10.1006/brln.2000.2428

Caballero, R. (2007). Manner-of-motion verbs in wine description, *Journal of Pragmatics*, *39*, 2095–2114. https://doi.org/10.1016/j.pragma.2007.07.005

Caballero, R. (2017). Metaphorical motion constructions across specialized genres: Cognitive foundations of language structure and use. In I. Ibarretxe-Antuñano (Ed.), *Motion and space across languages: Theory and applications* (pp. 229–254). Amsterdam/Philadelphia: John Benjamins. https://doi.org/10.1075/hcp.59.10cab

Caballero, R., & Ibarretxe-Antuñano, I. (2015). From physical to metaphorical motion: A cross-genre approach, *Proceedings of the Net Words Final Conference*, 155–157. Retrieved from http://ceur-ws.org/Vol-1347/paper35.pdf

Caballero, R., & Suárez-Toste, E. (2008). Translating the senses. Teaching the metaphors in winespeak. In F. Boers & S. Lindstromberg (Eds.), *Cognitive linguistic approaches to teaching vocabulary and phraseology* (pp. 241–259). Berlin: Mouton.

Caballero, R., & Suárez-Toste, E. (2010). A genre approach to imagery in winespeak. In G. Low, Z. Todd, A. Deignan, & L. Cameron (Eds.), *Researching and applying metaphor in the real world* (pp.265–287). Amsterdam/Philadelphia: John Benjamins. https://doi.org/10.1075/hcp.26.15cab

Fukushima, H., & Tanaka, S. (2016). Mikakuhyōgen-niokeru onshōchōgo-no shiyōgenri [The roles of sound symbolisms in the tasting descriptions]. *Journal of the Japanese Society for Artificial Intelligence*, *31*(6), 1–8.

Gawel, R., Iland, P. G., & Francis, I. L. (2001). Characterizing the astringency of red wine: A case study. *Food Quality and Preference*, *12*(1), 83–94. https://doi.org/10.1016/S0950-3293(00)00033-1

Hughson, A., & Boakes, R. (2001). Perceptional and cognitive aspects of wine tasting expertise. *Australian Journal of Psychology*, *53*, 103–108. https://doi.org/10.1080/00049530108255130

Hughson, A., & Boakes, R. (2002). The knowing nose: The role of knowledge in wine expertise. *Food Quality and Preference*, *13*, 463–472. https://doi.org/10.1016/S0950-3293(02)00051-4

Koga, H., Koloskova, Y., Mizuno, M., & Aoki, Y. (2008). Expressions of spatial motion events in English, German, and Russian: With special reference to Japanese. In C. Lamarre, T. Ohori, & T. Morita (Eds.), *Typological studies of the linguistic expression of Motion events, Volume II. A contrastive study of Japanese, French, English, Russian, German and Chinese: Norwegian Wood* (pp.13–44). 21st Century COE Program Center for Evolutionary Cognitive Sciences at the University of Tokyo.

Lehrer, A. (2009). *Wine and conversation.* Oxford University Press: New York. https://doi.org/10.1093/acprof:oso/9780195307931.001.0001

Levin, B. (1993). *English verb class and alternations: A preliminary investigation.* Chicago: University of Chicago Press.

López-Arroyo, B., & Roberts, R. (2014). English and Spanish descriptors in wine tasting terminology. *Terminology, 20*(1), 25–49. https://doi.org/10.1075/term.20.1.02lop

Matsumoto, Y. (2017). *Idōhyōgen-no ruikeiron* [Typology of motion expressions]. Tokyo: Kurosio Publisher.

Paradis, C., & Eeg-Olofsson, M. (2013). Describing sensory experience: The genre of wine reviews. *Metaphor and Symbol, 28*(1), 22–40. https://doi.org/10.1080/10926488.2013.742838

Real Wine Guide, 8, 10 (2005), *21* (2008), *29* (2010), *36* (2012), *60* (2018), *64* (2019). Tokyo: Real Wine Guide.

Slobin, D. I. (1996). From 'thought and language' to 'thinking of speaking'. In J. Gumperz & S. Levinson (Eds.), *Rethinking linguistic relativity* (pp.70–96). Cambridge: Cambridge University Press.

Slobin, D. I. (2000). Verbalized events: A dynamic approach to linguistic relativity and determinism. In S. Niemeier & R. Dirven (Eds.), *Evidence for linguistic relativity* (pp.107–138). Amsterdam/Philadelphia: John Benjamins. https://doi.org/10.1075/cilt.198.10slo

Slobin, D. I. (2004). The many ways to search for a frog: Linguistic typology and the expression of motion events. In S. Strömqvist & L. Verhoeven (Eds.), *Relating events in narrative, vol.2: Typological and contextual perspectives* (pp.219–257). Mahwah, NJ: Lawrence Erlbaum.

Slobin, D. I. (2006). What makes manner of motion salient? Explorations in linguistic typology, discourse, and cognition. In M. Hickmann & S. Robert (Eds.), *Space in languages: Linguistic systems and cognitive categories* (pp.59–81). Amsterdam/Philadelphia: John Benjamins. https://doi.org/10.1075/tsl.66.05slo

Suárez-Toste, E. (2007). Metaphor inside the wine cellar: On the ubiquity of personification schemas in winespeak. *Metaphorik, 12*(1), 53–64.

Talmy, L. (1985). Lexicalization patterns: Semantic structure in lexical forms. In T. Shopen (Ed.), *Language typology and syntactic description, 3* (pp.57–149). Cambridge University Press.

Talmy, L. (1991). Path to realization. *Proceedings of the Seventeenth Annual Meeting of the Berkeley Linguistics Society, 17*, 480–519. https://doi.org/10.3765/bls.v17i0.1620

Talmy, L. (2000). *Toward a cognitive semantics, Vol. II: Typology and process in concept structuring.* Cambridge, MA: MIT Press.

Teramura, H. (1982). *Nihongo no shintakkusu to imi* [Syntax and semantics of Japanese language], Vol. I. Tokyo: Kurosio Publisher.

Wienold, G., & Schwarze, C. (2002). The lexicalization of movement concepts in French, Italian, Japanese and Korean: Towards a realistic typology. *Arbeitspaper, 112*, 1–32.

Yoshinari, Y. (2014). Nihongo rashii hyōgen o kenshōsuru hōhō no teian: nihongo bogo washa to gakushūsha no idōjishōkijutsu no hikaku yori [What is a suitable Japanese expression for describing motion events?: A comparison between Japanese native speakers and intermediate Japanese learners]. *Journal CAJLE, 15*, 21–40.

Yoshinari, Y. (2015). Describing motion events in Japanese L2 acquisition: How to express deictic information. In I. Ibarretxe-Antuñano & A. Hijazo Gascón (Eds.), *New horizons in the study of motion: Bringing together applied and theoretical perspectives* (pp. 32–63). Cambridge Scholars Publishing, Cambridge.

Yoshinari, Y. (2016). Influence of L1 English on the descriptions of motion events in L2 Japanese with focus on deictic expressions. In K. Kabata & K. Toratani (Eds.), *Cognitive-functional approaches to the study of Japanese as a second language* (pp. 275–300). Boston/Berlin: De Gruyter Mouton. https://doi.org/10.1515/9781614515029-013

Yoshinari, Y., Eguchi, K., Mano, M., & Matsumoto, Y. (2016). Dainigengo ni okeru idōjishō no gengoka: nihongowasha ga mochiiru eego to hangarīgo no kenkyū. [A study of motion events by Japanese learners of English and Hungarian] *Studies in Language Sciences, 15*, 142–174.

CHAPTER 11

Applying force dynamics to analyze taste descriptions in Japanese online columns

Sayaka Abe
Middlebury College

This chapter analyzes taste descriptions, applying force dynamics (Talmy, 1988), which uses a schematic structure to characterize force relations. I extracted 90 descriptions from online food columns to examine causal interactions in which Food acts upon Taster or on another Food, to find that they can be classified into four basic force relations. The influenced entity can: undergo a change (CAUSED); overcome a blockage (OVERCOMING); be prevented from changing (BLOCKED); or remain unchanged despite a force acting against it/her (PERSEVERING). The classification reveals that the CAUSED pattern is predominant, indicating that Food or Taster tends to be conceptualized as a malleable entity that "gives in" to (another) Food.

Keywords: causation, change, nonliteral motion, gastronomy, force relation, sensory quality

1. Introduction

People's food experiences have become widely accessible through media as our culinary culture has diversified and internet-based communication has thrived, as seen in online travel columns, personal blogs, restaurant review sites, and so forth. Comments on food may involve varying degrees of creativity, ranging, for example, from "it's delicious" to "the creamy sauce harmonizes with the solid texture of the vegetables." Food writers and copywriters often craft expressions that evoke certain imageries and sensations in order to attract a specific clientele. For example, in a gourmet magazine, a sticky rice tamale may be depicted as being "punched up with shiitake and chorizo" (Rothman, 2018, p. 83). In another example, dishes of an upscale restaurant may be framed in terms of seduction, as in "succulent pork belly paired with seductively seared *foie gras*" (Jurafsky, 2014, p. 101). These examples vividly describe physical and psychological impacts of food on other entities (i.e., *shiitake* and *chorizo* on the tamale, and *foie gras* on customers,

https://doi.org/10.1075/celcr.25.11abe

respectively). In the Cognitive Linguistics literature, tastes have been analyzed in terms of motion. Caballero (2007, 2017) identifies an underlying metaphor in the usage of manner-of-motion verbs in a corpus of reviews of wine. For example, the expression "creep[ing] up sideways" (Caballero, 2007, p. 2106) can be analyzed as involving a metaphor whereby the wine is conceptualized as an ANIMATED BEING (cf. Yoshinari, this volume).

Although studies of figurative motions have made substantial advancements in revealing conceptualization patterns that underlie depictions of taste, not all food/taste descriptions are expressed in terms of motion. Consider Example (1).

(1) chōmiryō ni make-nai kaori no tsuyoi dashi
seasoning by be.defeated-NEG aroma GEN strong broth
'*dashi* with strong aroma that is not overpowered by seasonings'

(1) describes the condition of *dashi* 'broth' used in a dish called *oyakodon* 'chicken and egg (rice) bowl'. With the use of …*ni makenai* '(will) not give in to …', the writer conceptualizes *dashi* 'broth' as resisting the seasoning. There is a force relation in this event, but not due to the *dashi*'s overt action or motion, for example, of permeating into another food (element). As illustrated through this example, what makes food descriptions expressive is often associated with the interactions or oppositions among event participants – not necessarily the end result (i.e., an occurrence or non-occurrence of action/change).

Examples like (1) raise the following two questions.

Question 1. What types of force relations are present in taste descriptions?
Question 2. How are the force relations linguistically encoded?

To answer these questions, I analyze food descriptions extracted from Japanese online columns (Section 3.1). For Question 1, I draw upon force dynamics (FD) (Talmy, 1976, 1988, 2000) as a model that accounts for various force interactions involving human and non-human participants (see Section 3.2). FD is a schematic system that consists of a focal entity, the "agonist" or the affectee or causee, and another entity with which it interacts, the "antagonist" or the causer.[1] This two-part system captures multiple causal relations. As my focus is on entities that appear in taste descriptions, I posit that event participants are of two types: Food (presented hereafter with an uppercase F to refer to food or drink or their ingredients, elements or tastes) and Taster (hereafter with an uppercase T to refer to the person who consumes the food or the drink). I hypothesize that Food (or Taster) as an agonist undergoes four basic force relations identified in Talmy (1988). The

1. I designate both "affectee" and "causee," which are distinct (cf. Bohnemeyer, Enfield, Essegbey & Kita, 2010), as the agonist, unless the difference becomes relevant.

influenced entity can: (i) undergo a forced change; (ii) overcome a blockage; (iii) be prevented from changing; and (iv) remain unchanged despite a force acting against it (Hypothesis 1). For ease of reference, I assign the following labels to the four patterns: (i) CAUSED, (ii) OVERCOMING; (iii) BLOCKED; and (iv) PERSEVERING.

To address Question 2, I focus on the forms of the predicates expressing a force relation, such as *makeru* 'lose/be defeated' in (1). Given that a force relation requires at least two event participants, I assume that the predicates co-occur with the two event participants presumably within the same clause. For instance, a verb can be transitive (e.g., *hikidasu* 'draw; pull') or intransitive with a *ni*-marked phrase as in (1). It is also likely that verbs can be marked by the causative morpheme *-(s)ase* to express a force relation (e.g., *odorokaseru* 'surprise', whereby the intransitive verb *odoroku* 'be surprised' is combined with the morpheme to mean 'surprise [someone]').

There is another pivotal aspect of Japanese that is relevant to the present discussion: Japanese is classified as a "become" language, whereas English is classified as a "do" language (Ikegami, 1981; Kageyama, 1996).[2] This contrast can be seen by comparing different morphosyntactic patterns that describe the same scene: i.e., Japanese typically uses intransitive verbs ("become"-type verbs), whereas English typically uses transitive verbs ("do"-type verbs). The difference is associated with the language's preference with regard to having animacy as the subject of a transitive verb or a predicate in a causative form. English can take an inanimate subject of a transitive or causative predicate, whereas Japanese has a tendency to avoid this combination (Nishimura, 1998). This difference is shown in (2a) and (2b), from Nabeshima (2011), as well as another alternative sentence in (2c).

(2) a. The introduction of the new technology increased the output.

b. atarashī gijutsu o dōnyū-shita node, sanshutsuryō
new technology ACC introduce-do.PST since output
ga fue-ta.
NOM increase-PST (Nabeshima, 2011, p. 185)

c. atarashii gijutsu no dōnyū de, sanshutsuryō
new technology GEN introduction by output
ga fue-ta.
NOM increase-PST
'Due to the introduction of the new technology, the output increased.'

The English example in (2a) is mono-clausal and uses the transitive verb *increase*. It co-occurs with an inanimate subject that expresses the cause (*the introduction of the new technology*) and the object (*the output*). By contrast, the Japanese counterpart in (2b) has the intransitive verb *fue-ta* 'increased' whose subject is *sanshutsuryō*

2. The shorthand "do" and "become" are adopted based on Ikegami's (1981) terms, *suru* and *naru*, which literally mean 'do' and 'become', respectively.

'the output', and the cause is expressed by the subordinate clause marked by *node* 'because'. It literally translates as: 'Since (they) implemented the new technology, the output increased'. These examples show that English displays the *do*-language pattern taking an inanimate entity as the subject of the transitive verb (2a), and Japanese exhibits the *become*-language pattern by avoiding an inanimate subject with the transitive verb (2b). It should be noted that this *become*-language pattern shows that an event participant in a force relation does not necessarily appear in a single argument (noun phrase), but can be part of an event, which may be expressed by a clause as in (2b). Furthermore, considering that the *node*-marked clause can be replaced by a *de*-marked phrase, as seen in (2c) (*atarashii gijutsu no doonyuu de* 'due to the introduction of the new technology'), it seems possible to see a variety of means to indicate a causal relation using an intransitive verb.

This *become*-language pattern may suggest that all verbs used in taste descriptions are intransitive. However, my initial observation indicates that taste descriptions can include transitive or causative predicates when a scene involving two non-human event participants is portrayed figuratively (see Yoshinari, this volume, for an analogous point). This suggests that there is more formal variability present in food descriptions than assumed based on the *become*-language characteristics. Reflecting on these points, I hypothesize as follows: The predicates that express a force relation in the data can be intransitive or transitive, which may be further marked by a causative morpheme *-(s)ase* (Hypothesis 2). To reiterate, I expect to see a variety of formal means to express the force dynamic patterns, some of which may conform to the *become*-language pattern, whereas others may not.

To put this discussion in a larger context, this chapter aims toward a better understanding of how humans conceptualize, embody and describe basic, but often culturally-bound, activities of tasting and appreciating food. Because FD as a schematic system that characterizes the causation of events uniquely identifies the intrinsic proclivities of participants, such as their inclination toward motion or rest, it can offer new insights into the linguistic encoding of sensory experiences (cf. Winter, 2019). It is further notable that taste descriptions involving force relations cannot be conveyed by a single sensory adjective, such as *amai* 'sweet' or *nigai* 'bitter', but use predicates that express dynamic events, such as *hikidasu* 'draw out' and *makeru* 'lose/be defeated' (as in (1)). This suggests that these force dynamic expressions are originally used in the concrete domain but are extended to an imaginative use mediated by the schematic structure proposed by Talmy (1988), a point that conforms with embodied cognition (e.g., Johnson, 1987).[3]

3. FD, in fact, allows for domain-neutral characterizations of force relations, including physical, sensational and psychological motion or a lack thereof (cf. Kövecses, 2000a, 2000b on metaphors of emotion, Abe, 2007, 2016, on the polysemy of grammaticalized forms).

The remainder of the chapter is organized as follows. Section 2 introduces the patterns of FD using examples from food descriptions. Section 3 describes the data and methodology. Section 4 presents the results with examples, and Section 5 discusses whether Hypothesis 1 and Hypothesis 2 can be maintained. Section 6 concludes the chapter.

2. Force dynamic patterns in food descriptions

Force dynamics (Talmy, 1976, 1988, 2000) has been adopted by several cognitive-functional linguists and psycholinguists to characterize various grammatical constructions, such as transitivity and modality (Croft, 1991; Sweetser, 1990, respectively), metaphor and causation (Kövecses, 2000a, 2000b; Lakoff, 1990), and the psychological processing of causation and language (Wolff, 2007; Wolff & Thorstad, 2017). One of the many advantages of FD (Copley, 2019) is that it differentiates between various causal relations that have the same end result, that is, the occurrence or nonoccurrence of a motion or action.

FD schemata consist of two conflicting force elements, Agonist (AGO), the participant in focal attention, and Antagonist (ANT), an entity that has some kind of effect on the AGO. They can create four basic patterns of force relations, mentioned in Section 1, repeated below.

- CAUSED: The AGO undergoes a move caused by another entity (Figure 1)
- OVERCOMING: The AGO overcomes a blockage and moves (Figure 2)
- BLOCKED: The AGO is prevented from moving (Figure 3)
- PERSEVERING: The AGO remains in place despite a force against it (Figure 4)

These four patterns, referred to as "basic steady-state force-dynamic patterns," make up a subset of the FD system proposed by Talmy.[4] Presented below in Figures 1–4 are illustrations of the four patterns. For ease of exposition, I simplify Talmy's

4. Some of the other patterns that are commonly observed in descriptions of food in Japanese, including the present data, are what Talmy identifies as "shifting force-dynamic patterns," which have the same results as the basic four, except that the relative strength of AGO and ANT shifts during the force interaction. The four shifting FD patterns (with the respective shorthand in square brackets) that parallel the basic steady-state patterns are as follows: (a) *placement* of ANT that causes AGO to move [ONSET CAUSATION]; (b) the *removal* of ANT to let AGO move [LETTING GO >> BLOCKAGE REMOVAL]; (c) the *placement* of blockage (ANT) to prevent AGO from moving [ONSET BLOCKAGE]; (d) *removal* of ANT letting AGO stay [LETTING STAY]. The examples, respectively, are as follows: (a) *The ball's hitting it made the lamp topple from the table*; (b) *The plug's coming loose let the water flow from the tank*; (c) *The water's dripping on it made the fire die down*; (d) *The stirring rod's breaking let the particles settle.*

visual representations and use examples of taste descriptions instead of citing the original examples.

Figure 1 illustrates the first pattern, "CAUSED," which depicts a physical force interaction represented by the sentence: *The salt pulls out the umami of the meat.*[5]

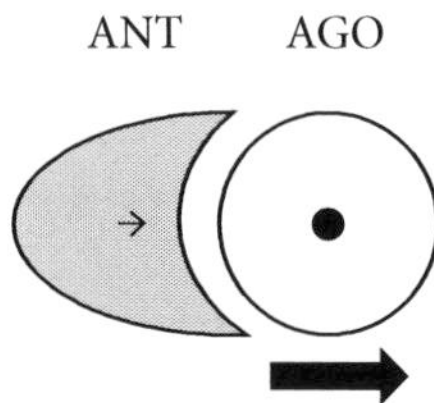

Figure 1. The salt pulls out the umami of the meat

The two force elements, AGO and ANT, are represented by a circle and a concave figure, respectively.[6] The FD pattern is determined by the force tendency of each element (action or rest, notated by a small arrow "→" or a dot placed within a force element, respectively) and the relative strength of the two elements (indicated by the presence and absence of the shading). The resulting state of the AGO, either "motion" (occurrence or realization of an event) or "rest" (nonoccurrence or nonrealization of an event), is indicated by a large arrow or a large dot, respectively, below the AGO element. The force of the salt (ANT), in this case, the action of pulling, is stronger than the tendency of the *umami*'s (AGO) to rest; thus, the resulting state is the motion of the *umami* (represented by the arrow below the agonist), as if it "gives in" to the power of salt.[7]

Let us look at the three other possibilities of ANT-AGO relationships.[8] Figure 2 illustrates the pattern of "OVERCOMING," which has the same end result as the previous example, but involves a different cause. Consider the example *The umami*

5. *Umami* refers to savoriness or the "fifth taste" – with the other four being sweetness, sourness, bitterness and saltiness; here the word will be used in its untranslated form.

6. The figures used to represent FD relations, such as Figure 1, are modified from Talmy's (1988) original figures, but they retain all the essential force components of the originals.

7. Although this diagram may look counterintuitive for the representation of the action of pulling (as opposed to pushing), this is the proper representation for ANT pulls AGO. The difference between pulling and pushing is spatial in nature, discussed by Talmy as one of the "further distinctions" as a parameter of the FD system (2000, pp. 462–464).

8. The physical examples introduced by Talmy (2000) are as follows: *The ball kept rolling because the wind was blowing on it* (Figure 1); *The ball kept rolling despite the wind blowing against it* (Figure 2); *The wind prevented the ball from rolling down the hill* (Figure 3); and *The ball did not move despite the wind* (Figure 4).

overflows from the meat, a pattern with the same AGO element (*umami*), which is created to compare with the previous example.

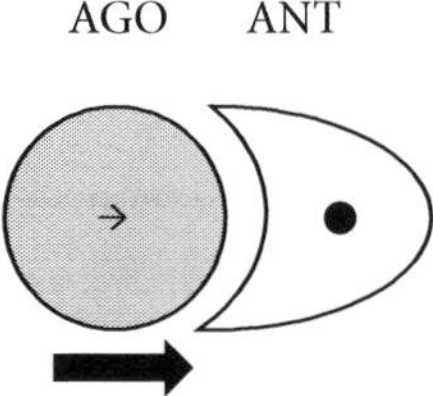

Figure 2. The umami overflows from the meat

Here, the result is the motion of the *umami*, but unlike the motion in the previous example, this motion occurs because the *umami*'s tendency to move is stronger than the tendency of the meat (or more precisely, the meat's outer surface) to block it.

Similarly, the causality for a resulting non-action is represented by the combination of two opposing force tendencies, representing the pattern "BLOCKED," as in Figure 3, which represents the expression *The sweetness supports the umami of the fish.*

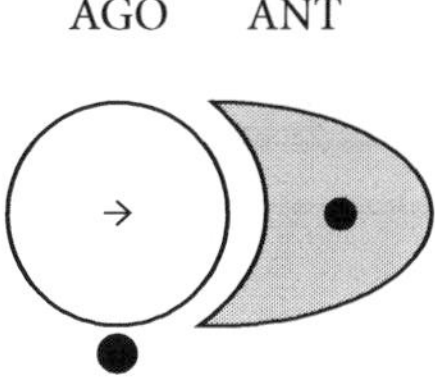

Figure 3. The sweetness supports the umami of the fish

In this case, the *umami* (AGO) is conceptualized as something that would not hold on its own and is supported by the sweetness (of another food item) (ANT), thereby resulting in rest.

Figure 4 illustrates the last of the four patterns, "PERSEVERING," in which the AGO remains "in place" despite a force acting against it. The example *The umami would not give in to the power of other ingredients* represents this pattern.

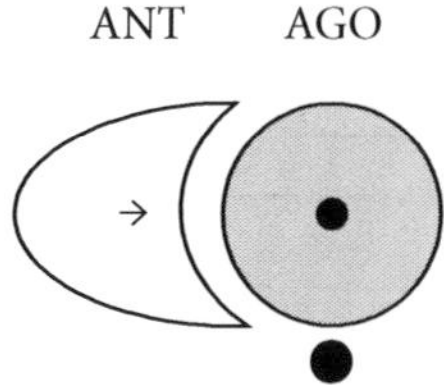

Figure 4. The umami would not give in to the power of other ingredients

Here, the end result of the rest is caused by the *umami*'s tendency to rest being stronger than the other ingredients' ability to push it.

3. Data and methodology

3.1 Data

An online Japanese food column series, *Shunmi e no izanai* 'An invitation to taste in season', was used for this analysis.[9] In this series, online columns are added monthly or by seasonal theme. Each column post consists of multiple subtexts with headings centered on a special ingredient as the theme (e.g., salmon), while featuring a certain restaurant. These columns typically discuss food preparation processes, the chefs' professional attitudes, and so forth, along with their recommended dishes. The entire dataset used for this analysis, which contains 66 posts with over 120,000 characters in total (thus, an average of over 1,800 characters per column), was retrieved during the years 2017 and 2018. The analyzed texts include main bodies and comments on photos, which are in full sentences, but do not include column or section titles. The 66 columns were imported into qualitative analysis software for manual coding of tokens, to be described in Section 3.2.

3.2 Methodology

After loading the text sets into qualitative analysis software,[10] I manually searched for descriptions expressing causal relations in which Food acts upon (another) Food or Taster. That is, I judged if each description expresses a causal relation by examining the meaning of the predicate in the matrix clause (e.g., *hikidasu* 'draw out' as in *umami o hikidasu* 'draw out umami'). When applicable, I checked for relevant linguistic contexts, such as a preceding clause or sentence, because the two force participants are not necessarily available within a single clause.[11]

In total, there were 90 descriptions, all of which were found to belong to one of the four patterns introduced in Section 2. I further separated each pattern into

9. The website can be accessed at https://hitosara.com/dish/.

10. MAXQDA, software for qualitative data analysis, 1989-2017, VERBI

11. I included sentences that end with a copula and those that do not. The latter are commonly found in a rhetorical style called *taigen dome* (nominal ending) with which a noun phrase ends a sentence.

two types according to the type of focal entity that Food acts upon: another Food or Taster. Thus, in total there are two sets of the four basic patterns, which I call Food-on-Food, presented in (3), and Food-on-Taster, presented in (4).

(3) F-on-F patterns
   a. CAUSED: Food is "moved" or changed by another Food (ANT)
      e.g., 'The salt (ANT) draws out the *umami* (AGO).'
   b. OVERCOMING: Food "moves" or changes despite an obstacle, another Food (ANT)
      e.g., 'The juice (AGO) overflows from the meat (ANT).'
   c. BLOCKED: The attempted "movement" or change of Food is blocked by another Food (ANT)
      e.g., 'The sweetness (ANT) supports the *umami* of the fish (AGO).'
   d. PERSEVERING: Food maintains its state despite another Food (ANT) "moving" against it
      e.g., 'The *umami* (AGO) would not give in to the power of other ingredients (ANT).'

(4) F-on-T patterns
   a. CAUSED: Taster is psychologically "moved" or changed by Food (ANT)
      e.g., 'The chocolate (ANT) seduces me (AGO).'
   b. OVERCOMING: Taster psychologically "moves" or changes despite an obstacle, Food (ANT)
      e.g., 'I managed to eat the burger.'
   c. BLOCKED: The psychological "movement" or change of Taster is blocked by Food (ANT)
      e.g., 'I can't get out of drinking.'
   d. PERSEVERING: Taster maintains her state despite Food (ANT) psychologically "moving" against her
      e.g., 'I patiently wait for the dish.'

For the former set, Food-on-Food patterns (F-on-F) means the two event participants are both Food elements, whereas for the latter, Food-on-Taster patterns (F-on-T) means that one participant is Food and the other is Taster.

As shown through the labels CAUSED, OVERCOMING, BLOCKED, and PERSEVERING in (3) and (4) (see Section 4 for examples), the two sets share the same general patterns represented by the labels. To distinguish between the two types of the same pattern (e.g., CAUSED for F-on-F and F-on-T), I further used different labels based on their meanings. For instance, the CAUSED pattern is characterized as ENHANCED for F-on-F, and AFFECTED for F-on-T (see Table 1 in Section 4.1)

4. Results

4.1 Overview

As noted in Section 3, there are 90 tokens that display FD patterns. They consist of 33 tokens of the F-on-F patterns and 57 tokens of the F-on-T patterns. Table 1 summarizes the distribution of the data. For each of the four F-on-F and four F-on-T patterns, in each of the eight cells, the number of tokens and a semantic descriptive label (e.g., "ENHANCED" for CAUSED) are presented in parentheses and in double quotes, respectively.

Table 1. Token frequency for the FD patterns with semantic labels

		Results: motion	Results: rest	Total
F-on-F	Stronger ANT	CAUSED (19) → "ENHANCED" (Section 4.2.1)	BLOCKED (7) → "CONFINED" or "SUPPORTED" (Section 4.2.3)	33
	Stronger AGO	OVERCOMING (2) → "OVERFLOWING" (Section 4.2.2)	PERSEVERING (5) → "ROBUST" (Section 4.2.4)	
F-on-T	Stronger ANT	CAUSED (49) → "AFFECTED" (Section 4.3.1)	BLOCKED (4) → "TRAPPED" (Section 4.3.3)	57
	Stronger AGO	OVERCOMING (3) → "MANAGING" (Section 4.3.2)	PERSEVERING (1) → "PATIENT" (Section 4.3.4)	
Total		73	17	**90**

Table 1 indicates that the F-on-T pattern (57/90, about 63%) occurred more frequently than the F-on-F pattern (33/90, about 37%). Sections 4.2 and 4.3 detail how the four patterns of F-on-F and the four patterns of F-on-T surface as lexical forms and grammatical constructions.

4.2 FOOD-ON-FOOD PATTERNS: FOOD AS AN AGONIST

4.2.1 *"ENHANCED" (CAUSED)*

There are 19 tokens of this pattern. Food, as the AGO of force interaction, most frequently undergoes an enhancement of its inherent quality, as schematized in Figure 5. This corresponds to the pattern presented in Figure 1.[12]

12. Each of Figures 1–4 has 2 corresponding figures, one as an F-on-F patterns (Section 4.2) and one as an F-on-T pattern (Section 4.3). Figures 1 corresponds to Figures 5 and 9; Figure 2 to Figures 6 and 10; Figure 3 to Figures 7 and 11; and Figure 4 to Figures 8 and 12.

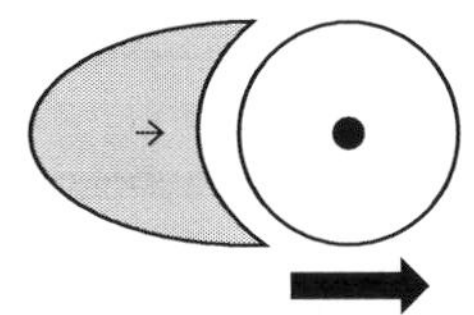

Figure 5. Food (ANT) ENHANCES Food (AGO)

Force interactions of this pattern commonly arise between elements within the same dish or item. AGO contains, or is, some kind of sensory quality, such as *aji* 'taste', *umami, fūmi* 'flavor', *nigami* 'bitterness', and so forth. ANT, on the other hand, tends to be a tangible entity, such as, fish skin, salt, sauce, egg and so forth, though it can also be a sensory quality, such as *amami* 'sweetness'. In addition, there are a few instances in which two menu items interact. This occurs in the description of the pairing of a dish with a drink, e.g., *rizotto* 'risotto' (AGO) enhanced by *wain* 'wine' (ANT); the pairing of a dish with another dish, e.g., mackerel (AGO) enhanced by rice and miso (ANT); and the pairing of food's taste with drink. In another type of AGO-ANT combination, which I refer to as self-enhancement, AGO and ANT belong to a single food element, for example, the texture of rice (AGO) is enhanced by being slightly browned (ANT), or the tenderness and flavor of meat (AGO) is enhanced by its rareness or rawness (ANT).

The most frequent types of predicates denote the actions of raising and/or pulling (*hikitateru* 'pull-stand' or *hikiageru* 'pull-raise' [5], *hikitat-aseru* 'make pull-up' [2], *kiwadat-aseru* 'make stand' [1], *hikidasu* 'draw out' [3]). There were a few instances of predicates denoting the creation of a new quality within a food item (*umidasu* 'produce/create' [2]; *tsukuru* 'make' [1]); absorbing (*tataeru* 'absorb' [1], *suu* 'inhale' [1]); modification or adjustment (*fukami ga kuwawaru* 'deepen; intensify', '[lit.] depth-NOM add.itself' [1]; *yawarageru* 'soften'; and *osu* 'push'). All examples but one (see (7)) have transitive or causative predicates.

In (5), a column about a barbecue describes how two types of salt enhance the way the meat tastes by drawing upon an inherent element, *umami*.

(5) dochira mo niku no umami o saidaigenni hiki-dasu
both also meat GEN umami ACC maximally pull-out
tateyakusha da
leading.actor COP
'Both [kinds of salt] are leading actors for maximally drawing out the *umami* of the meat.' (#1 *Yakiniku* 'barbecue')

This comment was made after an explanation of two types of salt, *sakishio* '(lit.) before salt' and *atoshio* '(lit.) after salt', which are applied during and after the cooking process, respectively. The event in question is described using a noun-modifying clause with the verbal compound *hiki-dasu* '(lit.) pull-take out', modifying the head noun *tateyakusha* 'leading actors', followed by the copula *da*. Here, the actor (both types of salt) is ANT, and the undergoer (the *umami* of the meat) is AGO.

In (6), *dochiramo* 'both' refers to the 'miso' and 'rice' that appear in the prior sentence. The matrix predicate in (6) is transitive, with *yawarageru* 'soften' conveying that the subtle sweetness of rice and miso (AGO) helps to soften (or 'enhance') the saltiness of mackerel (ANT).

(6) dochira mo honnorito amami ga ari,[13] saba no shioke o
either.one also subtly sweetness NOM exist mackerel GEN salt ACC
yawarage-te...
soften-CONJ
'both [miso and rice] have subtle sweetness and softens the saltiness of mackerel'
(#65 *Saba* 'mackerel')

The example in (7), the only intransitive example of the ENHANCED pattern, illustrates a common construction for expressing a caused event in Japanese:

(7) kakiage no abura mo awasaru koto de, fukami mo kuwawari, ...
kakiage GEN oil also combine NMLZ by depth also add
'by *kakiage*'s oil joining, depth is added...'
(#13 *Sakuraebi kakiage tempura soba* 'shrimp tempura buckwheat noodle')[14]

As noted in Section 1 (cf. (2b) and (2c)), Japanese favors the use of an intransitive verb and an adverbial clause to express a causal relationship with the latter expressing the causer. The example in (7) manifests this pattern: the predicate is an intransitive verb *kuwawaru* 'add', and the phrase marked by *koto de* 'by -ing' expresses the means by which a depth of taste was added to the shrimp.

One of the characteristics in terms of the event participants is that the ANT entity, which is often an ingredient, is itself already a composite or is an ingredient that has been processed/cooked in a certain way. This is represented linguistically as an embedded construction. In (8), for example, the egg as the ANT entity is expressed through a noun-modifying clause, describing an egg that has been beaten with perfect balance.

13. *Ari* is the stem of the verb, which roughly adds the meaning of 'and' as in 'exist and'. For the remainder of this chapter, verbs that end in this form (a verbal form ending in /i/, or /e/ at the clause boundary) are glossed with the meaning of the verb for ease of exposition.

14. *Kakiage* is a type of tempura, traditionally fried together with mixed vegetable strips. Here the original word *kakiage* is used for convenience.

(8) zetsumyōna kagen de tok-are-ta tamago ga migotoni dashi
perfect balance with beat-PASS-PST egg NOM amazingly broth
o sui…
ACC absorb
'an egg that was beaten with perfect balance absorbs the broth to my amazement, and…' (#9 *Oyako-don* 'chicken and egg bowl')

Conceptually, the causer (ANT) is itself affected by the very act it performs on the AGO as the "affectee" (the participant undergoing the state change that makes the final link in the causal chain), namely, by taking the AGO's quality into itself.

4.2.2 *"Overflowing" (overcoming)*

Two examples correspond to this type; they depict the outward motion of a food element. This pattern is schematized in Figure 6.

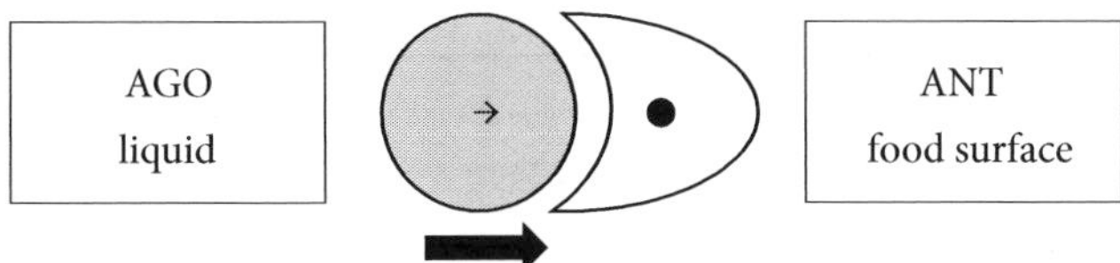

Figure 6. Food (AGO) OVERFLOWS FROM Food (ANT)

The two instances use the verb *afureru* 'overflow' and another variation of *afure-dasu* 'overflow-come.out'. Both are intransitive verbs. The example in (9) illustrates one of them.

(9) pukkurito fukuranda hanbāgu kara afureru niku-jiru
plumply swollen hamburger.patty from overflowing meat-juice
'meat juice that overflows from the plump, swollen hamburger steak'
(#6 *Hanbāgu* 'hamburger steak')

In this example, the intransitive verb *afureru* 'overflow' is used with *hanbāgu kara* 'from hamburger steak', evoking the imagery of juice bursting out of the surface of the steak, conceptualized as having intrinsic energy.

4.2.3 *"Confined" and "supported" (blocked)*

This pattern is characterized in terms of Food's tendency to "move" being blocked by another Food, as schematized in Figure 7.

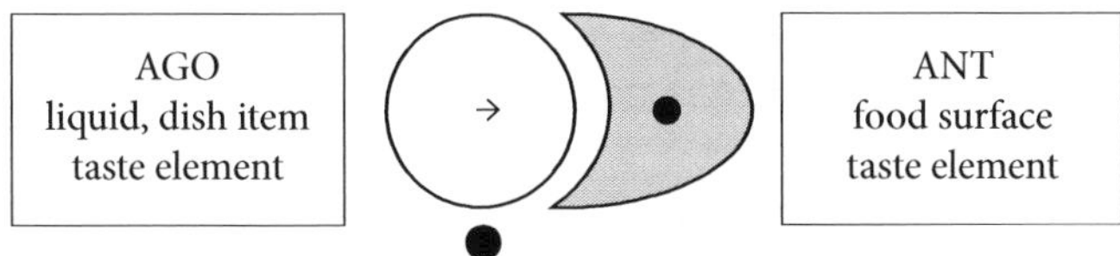

Figure 7. Food (AGO) IS BLOCKED BY Food (ANT)

There are seven instances of this type. The blocked object can be a physical object like juice (of meat, for example) or an intangible substance, such as *umami*. The predicates found in the data, which are mostly in passive form, are: *tojikome-rareru* 'be locked in', as in *fukami to koku-ga tojikome-rare* 'depth and richness (of the taste) are locked in, and…' and *umami-ga tojikome-rare* '*umami* is locked in, and…'; and *sueru* 'fix/place' as in *mein ni suerare-nagara mo* 'while being fixed or placed by the main dish.'

The example in (10), uses the transitive verb *himeru* 'confine [a secret]' or 'secretly contains', which typically implies a sense of secrecy or mysteriousness.

(10) kōbashī abura no kaori to afuredasu nikujiru o hime, …
aromatic oil GEN aroma and overflow meat ACC confine
'confining the aroma of sweet-smelling oil and overflowing juice, …'
(#33 *Oshare niku* 'fashionable meat')

This phrase is part of a description of a steak that contains juice (AGO) that is about to overflow.

The present FD pattern also surfaces as an expression of support; there are three instances of this type, expressed using two types of verbs, *sasaeru* 'support' and *uketomeru* 'receive and hold', one of which is illustrated in (11).

(11) ringo no yōna umami ya mitsu no yōna amasa ga saba no
apple GEN like umami and syrup GEN like sweetness NOM mackerel GEN
umami o sasaemasu
umami ACC support.POL
'Apple-like *umami* and syrup-like sweetness support the *umami* of mackerel.'
(#65 *Saba* 'mackerel')

This sentence is preceded by the statement 'a certain type of wine to be combined with mackerel'. The *umami* of the mackerel is a focal entity (i.e., AGO), and it is to be supported by the apple-like *umami* and syrup-like sweetness of the wine (ANT).

4.2.4 *"ROBUST" (PERSEVERING)*

This pattern is characterized in terms of Food that has a tendency to "rest" and remains unaffected by another Food, as schematized in Figure 8.

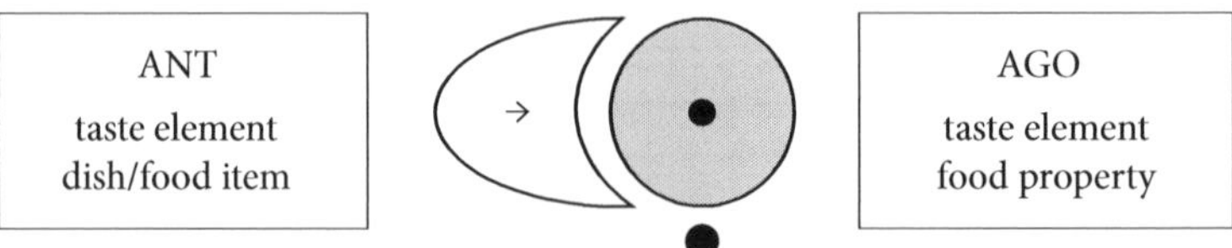

Figure 8. Food (AGO) RESISTS Food (ANT)

There are five instances of this type, including …*ni makenai* 'not be beaten by …' and *ni hike o toranai* 'not be overpowered by …'. Here is an example of the former.

(12) mein shokuzai ni makezu, shikkarito kome ga kosei o
main ingredients DAT be.lost.NEG firmly rice NOM individuality ACC
hakki-shi-teiru
exert-do-PROG
'without being overshadowed by main ingredients, the rice surely exerts its unique character' (#35 *Kome* 'rice')

This example demonstrates the rice's state of being unique without being overpowered by other main dishes. Other AGO elements of this pattern include the presence (of oyster) (*sonzaikan*) or the soy bean paste (*miso*) of a bowl dish.

4.3 FOOD-ON-TASTER: TASTER AS AN AGONIST

4.3.1 *"AFFECTED" (CAUSED)*

This category has the largest number of occurrences of all eight FD types. Based on the 49 attested tokens, the antagonistic Food found in this pattern is likely to represent an entire dish or ingredient, or its overall taste or quality. Taster represents potential customers, e.g., *otozureru-mono* 'visitors', or metonymically, parts that belong to them (e.g., *kibun* 'heart', *shokuyoku* 'appetite', etc.). Both types are labeled as "Taster" in Figures 9–12. Taster as the AGO is conceptualized as experiencing a change of affective state caused by Food. This pattern is schematized in Figure 9.

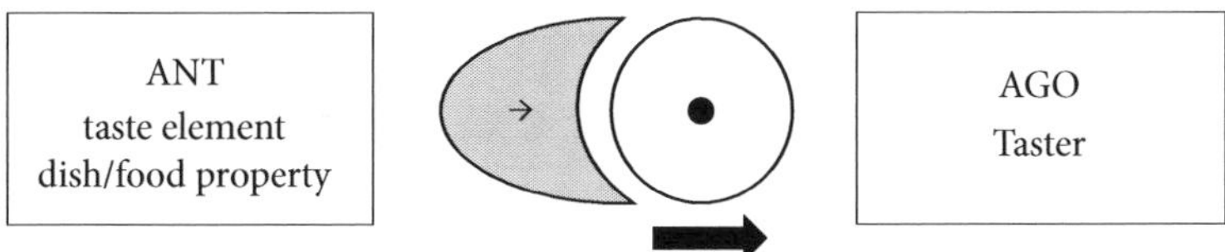

Figure 9. Taster (AGO) IS (PSYCHOLOGICALLY)

Examples of this pattern fall into one of three semantic subcategories: EMOTIONAL IMPACT (22 tokens), SENSORY IMPACT (19 tokens) or the BEHAVIORAL IMPACT (i.e., triggering of certain behaviors or actions; eight tokens). As mentioned in Section 1, Japanese tends to avoid transitive verbs (referred to as the "do"-type) with an inanimate subject, in favor of an intransitive verb (the "become"-type) with a subordinate clause expressing a reason. To demonstrate the extent to which this tendency applies, the collected examples are classified into these two structural types and organized into the aforementioned semantic categories in Table 2.

Table 2. Semantic and formal types of F-on-T, CAUSE

	"do"	"become"	Total
EMOTIONAL IMPACT	transitive (6) causative (1)	intransitive (12) passive (3)	22
SENSORY IMPACT	transitive (6) causative (5)	intransitive (5) passive (1) potential (2)	19
BEHAVIORAL IMPACT	causative (1)	intransitive (6) potential (1)	8
Total	**19**	**30**	**49**

The composition of each predicate type is as follows: under the "do"-type, I have included transitive verbs and causative-marked predicates; under the "become"-type, I have included intransitive verbs, passivized forms (e.g., *osow-areru* [attack-PASS] 'be attacked') and potential forms (e.g., *kanji-rareru* [feel-POT] 'it feels; I can feel').

Overall, unlike the CAUSED pattern in the F-on-F set (i.e., ENHANCED), causative/transitive constructions in the present set, in which Food acts on Taster as the object, are relatively infrequent.

First, in 22 tokens of the AFFECTED pattern (22/49, about 45%), Food has an EMOTIONAL IMPACT on Taster. Seven of these have a predicate that belongs to the "do"-type. See the example in (13).

(13) mata, hābutī wa iro o nagameru dake demo, rirakkusu kōka
also herbal.tea TOP color ACC gaze only with.also relax effect
o motarashi-te-kureru
ACC bring-CONJ-give.me
'Also, as for herbal tea, even gazing at its color brings a relaxation-effect [for me/us"].' (#2 *Hābutī* 'herbal tea')

In this case, 'herbal tea' appears as the topic of the sentence, acting as the agent of having a 'relaxation effect' on people who consume it. Two of the five transitive instances, including (13), occur with a benefactive auxiliary *-te-kureru* 'for me' (or 'give'), which expresses the writer's (Taster's) appreciation of the effect. EMOTIONAL IMPACT is expressed more commonly by "become"-type predicates (15/22, about 68%), as illustrated in (14).

(14) kapperīni ni karami-tsui-ta nōkōna tomato no ajiwai ni omowa-zu
capellini DAT tangle-attach-PST thick tomato GEN flavor to think-NEG
kao ga hokorobu
face NOM loosen
'to the thick texture/taste of tomato blends with capellini, (I) cannot help but smile.' (#18 *Kapperīni* 'capellini')

In this example, the idiomatic phrase *kao ga hokorobu* 'smile (spontaneously)' describes a facial expression of happiness in response to the food's taste. The noun phrase marked by the particle *ni* 'to the thick texture/taste of tomato blends' expresses the stimulus (ANT). Similar examples include emotive predicates: *emi ga koboreru* (smile NOM overflow) 'smile overflows', and *torokeru* 'melts (from pleasure)'. Other "become"-type expressions include those in which the cause of an emotion is expressed through a subordinate clause, such as a hypothetical (or *-to* 'if/when') clause (one token) and a topic phrase (one token). In addition, there were two instances in which a cause (or the ANT) was mentioned in a preceding sentence.

As for the second semantic category, SENSORY IMPACT (19/49, about 39%), one in which Taster senses something by Food as a stimulus, the construction types are split between "do"-type and "become"-type predicates (11 and 8 tokens, respectively). The transitive predicates include *shokuyoku o sosoru* 'induce appetite', which appears twice, *shokuyoku o shigeki-suru* 'stimulate appetite' and *shigeki o ataeru* 'give stimulation'.[15] As for causative constructions, all five occurrences use the verb *kanjiru* 'feel', as *kanji-saseru* 'make (me/us) feel'. The "become"-type examples include expressions of causes through a subordinate clause ending in a stem form, which appear four times, one stating a reason marked by *kara*, a noun phrase + *ni*, time expressions (e.g., *uchini* 'while'), a topic phrase and a preceding sentence.

The last semantic category of the AFFECTED pattern, BEHAVIORAL IMPACT, forms the smallest group (8/49, about 16%). The only "do"-type verb attested for this type is an idiomatic adjective, *ōjōgiwa-ga warui* 'not knowing when to stop', appearing in its causative form, as in (15).

(15) … kono wazukana yoin ga, dojō o ip-piki, sake o mō
this subtle after.taste NOM loach ACC one-CL sake ACC another
ip-pai to, ōjōgiwa o waruku-sase-te-iru yōni mo
one-CL QUOT stopping.point ACC bad-CAUS-CONJ-PROG like also
omo-e-te-kuru
think-POT-CONJ-come
'(it) also looks to me like…this subtle aftertaste makes it difficult (for me) to stop, as (I) go, one more loach, one more sake, and so on.' (#32 *Dojō* 'loach')

This sentence follows a description of the taste of loach, a type of fish, and expresses how addictive it is, making it hard for the Taster to stop the cycle of eating it and following it up with *sake*. The rest of the BEHAVIORAL IMPACT examples have "become"-type verbs, typically intransitive verbs, collocated with various constructions

15. *Ataeru* 'give' in the last example (*shigeki o ataeru*) is an elliptical element in the sentence in the data, because *shigeki o* 'stimulation ACC' shares the same predicate as another object in the sentence.

that encode the cause of the behavioral influence brought about by Food. The example in (16) uses *susumu* 'proceed.'

(16) ryōri no oishisa ni wain ga susumu
dish GEN tastiness to wine NOM proceed
'(in response) to the tastiness of the dish, one can keep drinking wine' ('[lit.] wine proceeds'). (#33 *Oshare niku* 'fashionable meat')

Here, the temptation (caused by a tasty dish) is conceptualized as a psychological shift from 'being able to resist' to 'not being able to resist'. The verb *susumu* 'proceed' follows the nominative-marked *wain* 'wine'. The cause of "keep drinking" is expressed through the phrase *ryōri no oishisa ni* 'to the tastiness of the dish.'

4.3.2 *"Managing" (overcoming)*

Unlike the other three patterns (presented in Sections 4.3.1, 4.3.3 and 4.3.4), examples of emotional OVERCOMING do not appear in the data. However, there are three instances of idiomatic expressions that convey a sense of pressure or resistance at a physical level. For example, the noun, *hagotae* 'a texture that challenges the teeth' or 'a texture that feels substantial', is used in the phrase *hagotae ga aru* 'there is a solid texture (that offers a pleasant resistance)'. Taster experiences a certain physical difficulty – a positive experience, as in meat with a substantial, solid texture, as opposed to tough meat, which has a negative connotation. This pattern is represented in Figure 10.

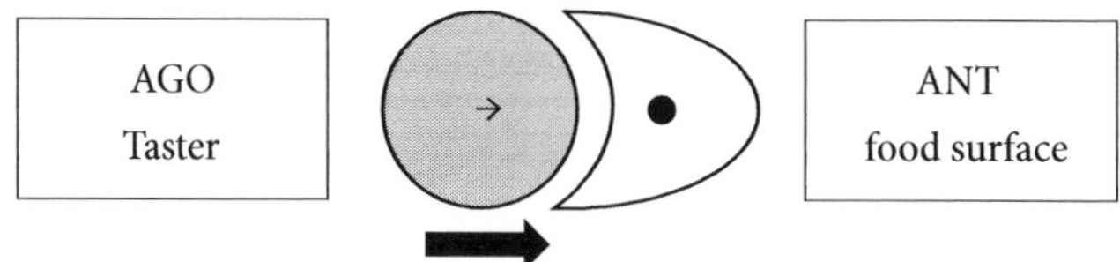

Figure 10. Taster (AGO) MANAGES (eating) Food (ANT)

4.3.3 *"Trapped" (blocked)*

Four examples of this pattern surface as the metaphorical confinement of Taster's feeling. Taster is depicted as someone who is "locked" or "trapped" in Food, as schematized in Figure 11.

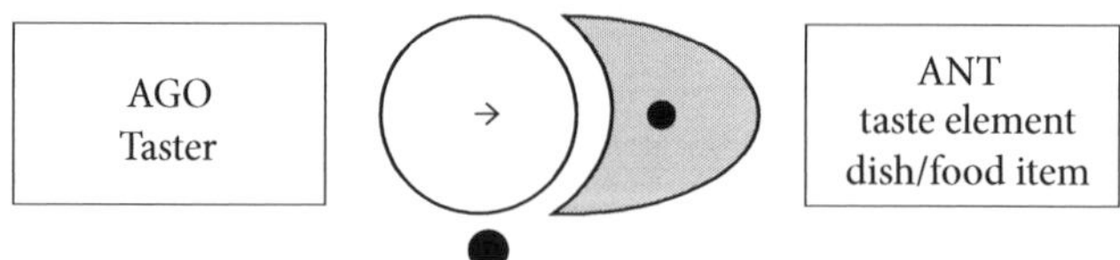

Figure 11. Taster (AGO) IS TRAPPED IN Food (ANT)

In one type of scenario, the writer describes a dish or an aspect of a dish (ANT) as grabbing Taster (AGO), or more precisely, his/her heart or mind. This concept is analogous to the one conveyed by the English expression *hooked*, as in "I am hooked," which is uttered when a food or some sort of entertainment media is addictive. In (17), the AGO is conceptualized as someone who falls into the trap of seductive food and cannot get out.

(17) kono miwaku no kumiawase, ichido hamaru-to nukedas-e-sōni
this seductive GEN combination once get.trapped-if get.out-POT-seem
arimasen
exist.NEG.POL
'This seductive combination [= sake and chocolate], once you are trapped in it, you can't get out of it.' (#38 *Suītsu to osake* 'sweets and alcohol')

This phrase is from a post about the pairing of sweets (in particular, chocolates) with alcohol. The sentence starts with *kono miwaku-no kumiawase* 'this seductive combination', followed by *ichido kuchi ni suru-to* 'once you take a bite'. Food (ANT) in this case, a particular combination of chocolate and *sake*, is conceptualized as a seductive trap, and Taster (AGO) is conceptualized as an agent with an intrinsic capacity for motion against the blockage.

This scenario situationally resembles some of the scenarios from the caused pattern. Both patterns can represent tasters' addiction or inability to stop eating, but the difference lies in the construal – namely, framing Food (AGO) as an action booster (resulting in the mobility of the AGO), as in (16), or as a trap (resulting in the immobility of the AGO), as in (17). In both examples, a sense of Taster's inability to control food is expressed.

Other examples of the present type, include the idiomatic expressions with *naru* 'become', such as *yamitsukini naru* '(lit.) to become severely ill (=hooked)' and the transitive *toriko ni suru* 'captivate Taster' ('[lit.] to make Taster a prisoner').

Another type of the TRAPPED pattern is shown in the single occurrence of an expression of confinement, that is, *himeru* 'secretly contain'. In (18), Food confines Taster's sense of safety.

(18) ama-karai aji-tsuke ga himeru anshin-kan
sweet-spicy flavor-apply NOM confine relief-sense
'sense of relief that is enclosed within sweet-spicy flavoring' (#37 *Sukiyaki*)

Although there is no explicit mention of to whom *anshin-kan* 'sense of relief' belongs, the context implies that it is the one who tastes the food.

4.3.4 "PATIENT" (PERSEVERANCE)

One instance in the data fits this category. Based on this specific case, this pattern manifests as Taster's patience in response to potential seduction by Food, as illustrated in Figure 12.

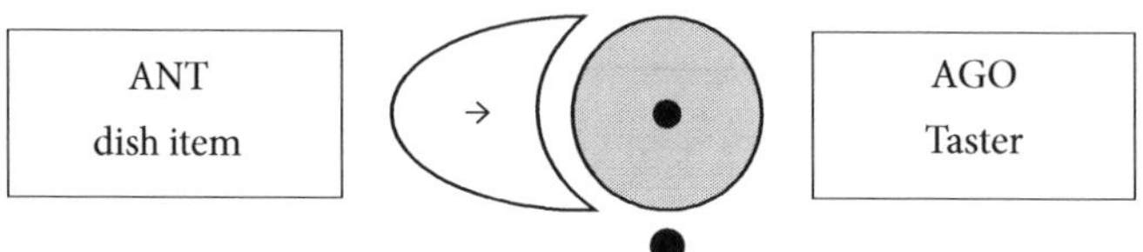

Figure 12. Taster (AGO) IS PATIENT TOWARD Food

Let us look at the example in (19).

(19) futsufustu-to kaoru nioi o tanoshimi-nagara nijup-pun
simmering-QUOT smell aroma ACC enjoy-while 20-minute
hodo shinbō
about patience
'patiently waiting for twenty minutes while enjoying the smell [of the porcini rice] being cooked' (#35 *Kome* 'rice')

Here the AGO is Taster, who is exercising patience despite an urge to try the food.[16] The aroma of food is indirectly framed as the source of this urge, or as the inclination for the action of eating.

5. Discussion

5.1 Response to Question 1

Concerning the question of what FD patterns are present (Question 1), the results suggest that for each of the two sets of data (F-on-F and F-on-T), the collected examples are all classified into Talmy's basic four patterns, thereby confirming Hypothesis 1. They also reveal a great asymmetry among the patterns in terms of their token frequencies, featuring the predominant CAUSED pattern (i.e., ENHANCED for F-on-F and AFFECTED for F-on-T).

To discuss these results further and to address the predominance of the CAUSED pattern, in what follows, I highlight the analytical characteristics of FD, focusing on

16. The noun *shinbō* occurs as a nominal ending. (See Footnote 11.) The light verb *-suru* of the full form *shinbō-suru*, which is an intransitive verb meaning 'be patient', is omitted.

comparing and contrasting among the four basic patterns, CAUSED, OVERCOMING, BLOCKED and PERSEVERING.

Let us first revisit the three criteria that generate the four basic FD patterns, listed in (20).

(20) a. Result: (i) AGO results in motion, or (ii) AGO results in rest
b. Force tendency: (i) AGO has tendency to rest, or (ii) AGO has tendency to move
c. Relative strength: (i) AGO is weaker, or (ii) AGO is stronger

As shown in (20a), FD recognizes "resting" entities (i.e., no motion or change), which we saw earlier with BLOCKED and PERSEVERING patterns, as well as the salient results of food-involved events, i.e., motion or change. The BLOCKED pattern translates as Food being CONFINED (or SUPPORTED) by another Food, or as Taster being TRAPPED by Food. Likewise, the PERSEVERING pattern manifests as Food as being ROBUST and Taster as being PATIENT. The criterion of end result (i.e., motion vs. rest) not only illuminates similarities and differences among different FD patterns, but also serves as a foundation for recognizing different processes through which the end results are realized, as addressed next.

FD further distinguishes among the different processes that lead up to an identical result, such as the force tendency of AGO and ANT, as in (20b). Thus, the resulting motion of Food that is inherently passive but ends up undergoing a change, for example, *umami* being pulled out (ENHANCED) (e.g., (5)) and that of liquid that pours out of meat on its own (OVERFLOWING) (e.g., (9)), involve AGOs of a different nature, that is, tending to rest and tending to move, respectively. The criterion of tendency also allows us to see connections between two patterns that involve similar situations. For example, one can understand intuitively through visualization that a situation in which meat juices overcome a blockage (meat surface) (OVERFLOWING) and one in which meat juices are blocked (CONFINED) have similar imageries (Figures 6 and 7), while their end results are in opposition. There is a connection between these situations: juice that pours out can be blocked, and vice versa, juice that is blocked can burst and pour out. The other two patterns, ENHANCED and ROBUST (Figures 5 and 8) also share the same schematic image. In the former, the sweetness of shrimp, for example, is drawn out by the salt, while in the latter, the same quality remains in place and is unaffected by another competing taste element or quality. Moreover, the shared schematic image between the two patterns illuminates the asymmetry between them with respect to their frequencies, that is, the overwhelming dominance of ENHANCED over ROBUST, which leads us to the next point.

The third criterion in (20c), relative strength, is also useful for interpreting the results, in which patterns with a weaker AGO are prevalent, in particular, the

CAUSED pattern. For F-on-F patterns, this means that AGO Foods are more likely to be depicted as something malleable, having passive motion, than to be depicted as having strong energy or personality. The same idea may manifest as writers' preference toward depicting Taster (i.e., F-on-T), with whom they align their own perspectives, as an entity that gives in to or is psychologically influenced by (the power of) Food (as an ANT) in some way.

In sum, we saw above how multiple criteria that constitute various force relations allow for a deeper understanding of how food and tastes are conceptualized and described. Overall, the results of the present study seem to reflect a preference toward referencing non-robust or passive characteristics of Food or Taster, influenced by, or in awe of, (another) Food. It is possible that elements like *umami* are frequently referenced precisely because they otherwise remain unrecognized (for non-experts as potential readers). More extensive research that includes additional variables (e.g., cuisine type), is needed to confirm the source of the tendency that surfaced in the data.

5.2 Response to Question 2

With regard to the linguistic encoding of the basic patterns (Question 2), the results mostly support Hypothesis 2. The data, however, include forms that Hypothesis 2 does not predict, namely, passive and potential forms, both of which reduce the valency of transitive verbs. Otherwise the predicates that express force relations in the data are either intransitive or transitive, some of which are marked by the causative morpheme. As expected, there are a wide range of forms available to express force dynamic patterns. Some of them conform to the *become*-language pattern. Others conform to the *do*-language pattern.

Let us first examine the forms of the F-on-F set. A substantial number of examples use transitive verbs and causative forms in the F-on-F set. Weaker AGOs are expressed as the object of a transitive verb (e.g., *hikidasu* 'draw; pull out'; *sasaeru* 'support') and as the object of an intransitive verb in causative form (e.g., *hikitataseru* 'make [it] stand out'), or as the subject of a passive clause (e.g., *tojikome-rareru* confine-PASS 'be confined'). In contrast, stronger AGOs tend to be expressed as the subject of an intransitive verb, occurring with a *ni*-marked phrase (e.g., …*ni makeru* 'lose/be defeated' in negative) or without accompanying any phrase indicating ANT (e.g., *afureru* 'overflow').

Turning next to F-on-T, this set exhibits a mix of transitive and intransitive verbs. The correspondence between AGO (Taster) and the form type varies greatly. For example, in the AFFECTED type, AGO can be expressed as an unstated recipient of an action expressed by a transitive verb (e.g., *motarasu* 'bringing' in (13)); an unstated subject of a transitive verb in potential form (e.g., *kanji-rareru* feel-POT 'can feel'); or metonymically as the subject of an intransitive verb used with a *ni*-marked phrase within the same clause as the verb (e.g., *amami ni odoroku* [sweetness DAT be.surprised] 'surprise at sweetness'). Moreover, the use of idiomatic expressions (e.g., *kao ga hokorobu* 'smile [spontaneously]' in (14); *emi ga koboreru* 'one cannot help but smile', '[lit.] one's smile spills over') is common. These expressions also accompany a *ni*-marked phrase expressing the stimulus that produces a psychological effect (e.g., *oishisa ni* 'to the sweetness', whereby *ni* roughly means 'responding to'). Examples of intransitive verbs corresponding to the "become"-type also include those that "outsource" an expression of cause to another clause, for example, to a subordinate clause (cf. (2)). This avoidance of the use of transitive verbs is consistent with Kawachi, Bellingham and Bohnemeyer (2018), who note that the use of morpho-syntactically looser constructions (e.g., conditionals) correlate with certain types of affectees, such as animate entities, as opposed to inanimate ones.[17]

6. Conclusion

This chapter characterizes how food is conceptualized as a dynamic entity in Japanese online food columns. It employs force dynamics (FD) (Talmy, 1976, 1988, 2000) as a systematic way of organizing the various causation patterns that underlie the construal of gastronomic experiences, ranging from the sensory level to the psychological level. The analysis shows that experiences with food – whether dynamic or static in actuality – are often construed in terms of interactions among dishes/food elements or with tasters, the same types of interactions we experience in our physical environment. Given the creative nature of the genre, linguistic manifestations of each pattern are numerous. FD, as an image-schematic system, is suitable for classifying such diverse expressions into finite patterns. Actual usage in texts per the classification system allows us to systematically see how conceptualization patterns of food can be associated with how language surfaces, as well as external factors, such as consumers' attitudes toward food and aspects of taste that writers choose to highlight in a limited amount of text.

The examination of the Japanese media of gastronomy in question reveals how writers, who take the perspective of tasters, conceive of the force that food has on (tasters) people, and how they might resist it, be overwhelmed by it, and so forth.

17. Also, these constructions are associated with a low degree of transitivity based on subject-object relationships (Hopper & Thomson, 1980), and thus, less direct expressions of causation are to be expected.

If extended to cross-linguistic analyses, such research can also suggest some commonalities that Japanese shares with other languages, such as the use of metaphors, as well as features that are relatively language-specific, for example, if tastes tend to be described as being pulled or pushed, or as moving on their own. In this regard, I hope that this chapter can help linguists to further advance ongoing discussions in areas of language and cognition, in particular, causation and embodiment, as well as on the gastronomic descriptions in general.

Acknowledgments

This paper is based on my presentation at the Conference on the Language of Japanese Food (York University, 2018). I would like to thank the participants for their valuable feedback. I would also like to thank the volume editor Kiyoko Toratani and the anonymous reviewers for their helpful suggestions on the earlier versions of this paper.

References

Abe, S. (2007). Space, time, subjectivity and beyond: The cognitive semantic development of the Japanese marker te-shimau (Unpublished doctoral dissertation). University at Buffalo, Buffalo, NY.

Abe, S. (2016). An L2 corpus study of the Japanese grammatical marker *-te-simau*: An application of force dynamics. In K. Kabata & K. Toratani (Eds.), *Cognitive-functional approaches to the study of Japanese as a second language* (pp. 203–236). Boston, Berlin: De Gruyter Mouton. https://doi.org/10.1515/9781614515029-011

Bohnemeyer, J., Enfield, N., Essegbey, J., & Kita, S. (2010). The macro-event property. In J. Bohnemeyer, & E. Pederson (Eds.), *Event representation in language and cognition* (pp. 43–67). Cambridge: Cambridge University Press. https://doi.org/10.1017/CBO9780511782039.003

Caballero, R. (2007). Manner-of-motion verbs in wine description. *Journal of Pragmatics, 39*(12), 2095–2114. https://doi.org/10.1016/j.pragma.2007.07.005

Caballero, R. (2017). From the glass through the nose and the mouth: Motion in the description of sensory data about wine in English and Spanish. *Terminology, 23*(1), 66–88. https://doi.org/10.1075/term.23.1.03cab

Copley, B. (2019). Force dynamics. In R. Truswell (Ed.), *Oxford handbook of event structure* (pp. 137–170). Oxford: Oxford University Press.

Croft, W. (1991). *Syntactic categories and grammatical relations: The cognitive organization of information*. Chicago: University of Chicago Press.

Hopper, P. J., & Thompson, S. A. (1980). Transitivity in grammar and discourse. *Language, 56*, 251–299. https://doi.org/10.1353/lan.1980.0017

Ikegami, Y. (1981). *Suru to naru no gengogaku* [Linguistics of "do" and "become"]. Tokyo: Taishukan.

Johnson, M. (1987). *The body in the mind: The bodily basis of meaning, imagination, and reason*. Chicago: University of Chicago Press. https://doi.org/10.7208/chicago/9780226177847.001.0001

Jurafsky, D. (2014). *The language of food: A linguist reads the menu*. New York: W.W. Norton & Company.

Kageyama, T. (1996). *Dōshi imiron: Gengo to ninchi no setten* [Semantics of verbs: The interface between language and cognition]. Tokyo: Kurosio Publishers.

Kawachi, K., Bellingham, E., & Bohnemeyer, J. (2018). Different types of causality and clause linkage in English, Japanese, Sidaama, and Yucatec Maya. *Papers from the 18th National Conference of the Japanese Cognitive Linguistics Association*.

Kövecses, Z. (2000a). *Metaphor and emotion: Language, culture and body in human feeling*. Cambridge: Cambridge University Press.

Kövecses, Z. (2000b). Force and emotion. In L. Albertazzi (Ed.), *Meaning and cognition: A multidisciplinary approach* (pp. 145–168). Amsterdam: John Benjamins. https://doi.org/10.1075/celcr.2.08kov

Lakoff, G. (1990). The Invariance Hypothesis. In *Cognitive Linguistics*, *1*(1): 39–74. https://doi.org/10.1515/cogl.1990.1.1.39

Nabeshima, K. (2011). *Nihongo no metafā*. [Metaphors in Japanese]. Tokyo: Kurosio Publishers.

Nishimura, Y. (1998). Kōisha to shieki kōbun [Actors and causative constructions]. In M. Nakau & Y. Nishimura (Eds.), *Kōbun to jishōkōzō* [Constructions and event structure] (pp. 107–203). Tokyo: Kenkyusha.

Rodman, J. (2018). The 2018 restaurants of the year. *Food and Wine*, *41*(5), 63–89.

Sweetser, E. (1990). *From etymology to pragmatics: Metaphorical and cultural aspects of semantic structure*. Cambridge: Cambridge University Press. https://doi.org/10.1017/CBO9780511620904

Talmy, L. (1976). Semantics causative types. In M. Shibatani (Ed.), *Syntax and semantics: The grammar of causative constructions*, *6*, (pp. 43–116). New York, NY: Academic Press.

Talmy, L. (1988). Force dynamics in language and cognition. *Cognitive Science*, *12*, 49–100. https://doi.org/10.1207/s15516709cog1201_2

Talmy, L. (2000). *Toward a cognitive semantics, Volume I: Concept structuring systems*. Cambridge, MA: MIT Press.

Winter, B. (2019). *Sensory linguistics: Language, perception and metaphor*. Amsterdam: John Benjamins. https://doi.org/10.1075/celcr.20

Wolff, P. (2007). Representing causation. *Journal of Experimental Psychology: General*, *136*, 82–111. https://doi.org/10.1037/0096-3445.136.1.82

Wolff, P., & Thorstad, R. (2017). Force dynamics. In M. R. Waldmann (Ed.), *Oxford handbook of causal reasoning* (pp. 147–167). Oxford: Oxford University Press.

Index